THE OFFICIAL GUIDE TO

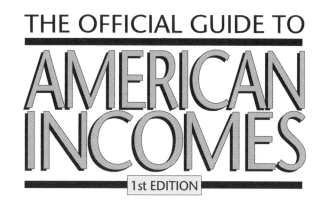

AMERICAN INCOMES

1st EDITION

THE OFFICIAL GUIDE TO

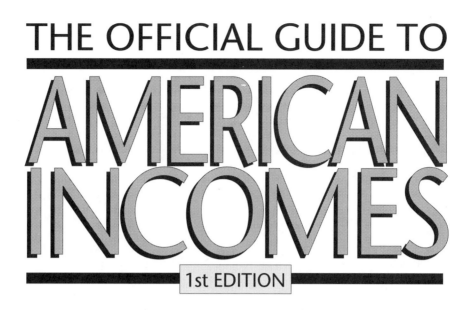

AMERICAN INCOMES

1st EDITION

A comprehensive look at how much
Americans have to spend,
with a special section
on discretionary income.

by CHERYL RUSSELL and MARGARET AMBRY

New Strategist
Publications & Consulting
P.O. Box 242, Ithaca, New York 14851
607 / 273-0913

New Strategist Publications & Consulting
P.O. Box 242, Ithaca, NY 14851
607 / 273-0913

Russell, Cheryl, 1953—
Ambry, Margaret, 1947—
The Official Guide to American Incomes.

ISBN 0-9628092-2-5

For Julien and Schuyler.

Contents

Chapter 3. Personal Income

Chapter 4. Discretionary Income

Chapter 5. Household Income Projections

Chapter 6. Spending and Wealth

Chapter 7. Poverty Trends

Chapter 8. Income and Geography Trends

Tables

Chapter 1. Income Trends

Chapter 2. Household Income

Chapter 3. Personal Income

Chapter 4. Discretionary Income

Chapter 5. Household Income Projections

Chapter 6. Spending and Wealth

Chapter 7. Poverty Trends

Chapter 8. Income and Geography Trends

Introduction

The economic fortunes and misfortunes of Americans are in the news every day. The rich are getting richer and the poor are getting poorer. The middle-class is disappearing, and America's standard of living is falling. The economic picture seems bleak—but only to the uninformed.

The real story behind Americans' incomes is complex and not easily explained. In fact there's more than one story, and some of the stories are not as bad as the headlines have people believing. The recession of the early 1990s hit Americans hard, cutting household incomes across the board. But those incomes were at record highs. Since the late 1980s, incomes have fallen, but only by a few percentage points. Once the recovery is fully underway, Americans are likely to achieve new levels of affluence.

At the same time, Americans' incomes are becoming more diverse. Many workers are stuck in low-paying jobs with little hope of advancement. Meanwhile, those with the right skills are capturing an ever-growing share of the nation's income. The well-educated are reaping enormous rewards for their investment in schooling. The pay gap between the most and least skilled workers is widening.

Americans responded to the recession of the early 1990s by cutting their spending, paying off their debts, and becoming much more cautious consumers. But even before the recession, Americans' economic prospects were changing. The incomes of some were falling while those of others were soaring. Just as our families have become more diverse over the past few decades, so have our incomes.

These are a few of the stories contained in this book:

■ Just before the recession of the early 1990s, a record proportion of households had achieved affluence. While the recession reduced this share, incomes should rise again once recovery is fully underway.

■ Households headed by middle-aged, college-educated, married couples are the most affluent in the country. As the well-educated baby-boom generation enters its peak earning years in the 1990s, the number of affluent households should soar.

■ Until the recession, women's incomes were growing rapidly, up by 30 percent during the 1990s. Men's incomes, in contrast, were growing slowly. Consequently, the 59-cent dollar (the ratio of women's incomes to men's) has become a 70-cent dollar.

■ Despite the recession, most households have discretionary spending money. Consumer cautiousness over the past few years may have more to do with a change in attitudes about spending than with a lack of spending money.

■ If household incomes continue to grow at about the same rate as they did in the 1980s, the number of households with incomes of $50,000 or more will grow by 29 percent between now and 2005.

■ Americans reduced their spending and their debts in response to the recession. Consequently, they are likely to be on a firmer financial footing during the remainder of the 1990s.

■ A shifting economy has boosted the proportion of full-time workers with low wages. This means poverty rates are likely to remain stubbornly high through the 1990s.

■ The bicoastal economy of the 1980s turned into a bicoastal recession in the 1990s. The Northeast and West were hit hardest by the economic downturn. Nevertheless, they remain the most affluent regions.

How To Use This Book

The Official Guide to American Incomes is meant to be easy to use. It is organized into the following chapters:

Income Trends Here you will find historical statistics as well as the most current income figures so that you can trace the ups and downs of Americans' economic fortunes.

Household Income The latest statistics on household and family incomes by a variety of household characteristics.

Personal Income The latest statistics on the incomes and earnings of men and women by a variety of characteristics.

Discretionary Income Calculations of the spending money available to households specially produced for *American Incomes*.

Household Income Projections A look at the incomes of households in 1995, 2000, and 2005 by age of householder.

Spending and Wealth The latest spending figures from the Bureau of Labor Statistics, as well as a review of Americans' debts and net worth.

Poverty Trends A look at the poverty population and how it has changed over the past several decades.

Income and Geography Trends The incomes of households and families by region, state, and metropolitan residence.

Most of the current income statistics in this book are from the Census Bureau's 1992 Current Population Survey, which collected income statistics for 1991. Each chapter of the book begins with a short introduction, highlighting the major points of the tables in the chapter. If you want to get a quick feel for income trends, scan the chapter introductions. If you're looking for a particular piece of information, start with the table of contents or the detailed index at the end of the book. If a term confuses you, find out what it means in the glossary.

Most of the sources for this book are the latest publicly available information from the Census Bureau, the Bureau of Labor Statistics, and the Federal Reserve Board. The federal government continues to be the best source of information about the economic well-being of Americans. The statistics in two of the chapters (Household Income Projections and Discretionary Income) were produced by TGE Demographics, Inc., specifically for *The Official Guide to American Incomes*. In combination, these income statistics should convince you that Americans' economic fortunes are far more complex than the headlines would have you believe.

Cheryl Russell
Margaret Ambry

1

Income Trends

Household and personal incomes grew much more diverse over the past decade. The proportion of households with affluent incomes reached a record high in the late 1980s. Yet the proportion of full-time workers with low earnings also increased. The incomes of women rose dramatically, but those of men stagnated. Depending on the statistics at hand, America's standard of living is either rising or falling.

Income Trends: Highlights

■   Median household income grew by just 2.8 percent between 1980 and 1991, after adjusting for inflation. But average income per household member posted much higher growth, rising by 58 percent as household size shrank.

■   The proportion of households with incomes above $50,000 reached a record high of 28 percent in 1989, then fell slightly because of the recession of the early 1990s. As well-educated baby boomers age into their peak earning years, affluence should set new records in the last half of the 1990s.

■   During the 1980s and early 1990s, women's incomes grew much faster (or fell much less) than men's. As a result, among full-time workers, the ratio of women's earnings to men's rose from 60 percent in 1980 to 70 percent in 1991.

The share of households with incomes of $50,000 or more climbed to a record high during the 1980s before dropping off during the recession.

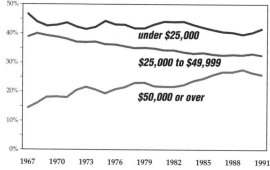

Distribution of Households by Income, 1967 to 1991

Though the proportion of households with incomes above $50,000 fell slightly in the early 1990s, it remains far above the level of the 1960s and 1970s.

(distribution of households by income; income in 1991 dollars; households as of the following year; numbers in thousands)

	number	total households	under $5,000	$5,000 to $9,999	$10,000 to $14,999	$15,000 to $24,999	$25,000 to $34,999	$35,000 to $49,999	$50,000 to $74,999	$75,000 to $99,999	$100,000 or over	median income
						percent distribution						
1991	95,669	100.0%	4.8%	10.1%	9.4%	17.4%	15.2%	17.3%	15.4%	6.0%	4.4%	$30,126
1990	94,312	100.0	4.7	9.5	9.2	17.0	15.6	17.5	15.7	6.0	4.8	31,203
1989	93,347	100.0	4.3	9.7	8.9	16.8	15.0	17.7	16.2	6.3	5.1	31,750
1988	92,830	100.0	4.6	10.1	9.0	16.7	15.1	17.7	16.0	6.0	4.8	31,344
1987	91,124	100.0	4.7	10.2	8.9	16.8	14.7	17.9	16.3	6.0	4.5	31,246
1986	89,479	100.0	4.9	10.3	8.9	17.2	15.0	17.9	15.9	5.6	4.3	30,940
1985	88,458	100.0	4.8	10.5	9.2	17.6	15.7	17.7	15.3	5.4	3.8	29,896
1984	86,789	100.0	4.6	10.8	9.5	18.1	15.6	17.6	15.1	5.1	3.5	29,383
1983	85,290	100.0	5.1	10.8	9.6	18.6	16.0	17.6	14.4	4.7	3.2	28,741
1982	83,918	100.0	5.0	11.2	9.6	18.2	16.3	18.0	14.2	4.5	3.0	28,737
1981	83,527	100.0	5.0	10.8	9.5	18.8	15.9	18.4	14.4	4.7	2.6	28,833
1980	82,368	100.0	4.8	10.6	9.4	18.3	16.1	18.8	14.7	4.6	2.6	29,309
1979	80,776	100.0	4.6	10.2	9.3	17.7	15.6	19.5	15.3	4.8	3.0	30,297
1978	77,330	100.0	4.2	10.3	9.6	17.7	15.8	19.2	15.6	4.4	3.0	30,396
1977	76,030	100.0	4.5	10.7	9.8	18.0	16.5	19.1	14.7	4.2	2.6	29,249
1976	74,142	100.0	4.3	10.9	9.9	18.0	16.6	19.6	14.5	3.9	2.4	29,088
1975	72,867	100.0	4.5	11.2	10.1	18.5	16.7	19.6	13.7	3.5	2.2	28,597
1974	71,163	100.0	4.3	10.5	9.5	17.9	17.9	19.3	14.3	4.0	2.4	29,384
1973	69,859	100.0	4.8	10.0	9.5	17.2	17.2	19.8	14.8	4.1	2.7	30,333
1972	68,251	100.0	5.3	10.3	8.9	17.8	17.1	20.0	14.0	4.0	2.5	29,746
1971	66,676	100.0	6.0	10.3	8.9	18.5	18.5	19.6	12.7	3.4	1.9	28,529
1970	64,778	100.0	6.3	9.9	8.7	18.0	19.0	19.8	12.8	3.4	2.0	28,803
1969	63,401	100.0	6.4	9.4	8.9	17.9	19.3	20.0	13.0	3.2	1.9	29,000
1968	62,214	100.0	6.7	9.4	9.3	18.6	19.8	20.2	11.7	2.7	1.6	27,973
1967	60,813	100.0	7.6	10.1	8.8	20.3	20.0	18.8	9.9	2.7	1.7	26,801

Percent change in median income

1980-91	2.8%
1967-91	12.4

Source: Bureau of the Census, Current Population Reports, Money Income of Households, Families, and Persons in the United States: 1991, *Series P-60, No. 180, 1992*

Distribution of White Households by Income, 1967 to 1991

The proportion of white households with incomes in the middle of the income distribution fell from 41 percent in 1967 to 33 percent in 1991, while the proportion of households with incomes above $50,000 grew.

(distribution of white households by income; income in 1991 dollars; households as of the following year; numbers in thousands)

	total households	total	under $5,000	$5,000 to $9,999	$10,000 to $14,999	$15,000 to $24,999	$25,000 to $34,999	$35,000 to $49,999	$50,000 to $74,999	$75,000 to $99,999	$100,000 or over	median income
							percent distribution					
1991	81,675	100.0%	3.7%	9.1%	9.1%	17.3%	15.4%	17.9%	16.3%	6.4%	4.8%	$31,569
1990	80,968	100.0	3.6	8.6	8.9	16.9	15.9	18.0	16.5	6.3	5.2	32,545
1989	80,163	100.0	3.4	8.8	8.5	16.6	15.2	18.4	17.0	6.7	5.5	33,398
1988	79,734	100.0	3.7	8.9	8.5	16.6	15.4	18.5	16.9	6.5	5.2	33,136
1987	78,519	100.0	3.6	9.1	8.5	16.6	15.0	18.6	17.3	6.3	4.9	32,921
1986	77,284	100.0	3.9	9.4	8.5	16.9	15.2	18.6	16.8	6.0	4.7	32,528
1985	76,576	100.0	4.0	9.6	8.7	17.3	16.0	18.4	16.1	5.8	4.1	31,529
1984	75,328	100.0	3.8	9.7	9.0	17.9	16.0	18.4	15.9	5.5	3.8	30,998
1983	74,170	100.0	4.1	9.7	9.2	18.4	16.5	18.4	15.1	5.0	3.5	30,132
1982	73,182	100.0	4.1	10.2	9.1	18.1	16.6	18.6	15.1	4.8	3.3	30,085
1981	72,845	100.0	4.1	9.8	9.0	18.5	16.3	19.2	15.2	5.1	2.9	30,464
1980	71,872	100.0	3.9	9.7	9.0	18.1	16.3	19.6	15.6	5.0	2.9	30,921
1979	70,766	100.0	3.8	9.3	8.8	17.4	15.9	20.2	16.1	5.2	3.3	31,766
1978	68,028	100.0	3.6	9.4	9.2	17.4	16.0	20.0	16.4	4.7	3.3	31,598
1977	66,934	100.0	3.8	9.8	9.2	17.6	16.8	19.9	15.6	4.5	2.8	30,757
1976	65,353	100.0	3.8	9.9	9.4	17.7	16.8	20.4	15.3	4.1	2.6	30,471
1975	64,392	100.0	3.9	10.2	9.7	18.2	17.0	20.3	14.6	3.8	2.4	29,906
1974	62,984	100.0	3.7	9.6	9.0	17.4	18.2	20.1	15.1	4.3	2.6	30,730
1973	61,965	100.0	4.1	9.2	8.9	16.6	17.5	20.6	15.8	4.4	2.9	31,791
1972	60,618	100.0	4.7	9.3	8.4	17.2	17.5	20.9	14.9	4.4	2.7	31,206
1971	59,463	100.0	5.4	9.5	8.4	18.0	19.0	20.4	13.5	3.7	2.1	29,841
1970	57,575	100.0	5.7	9.2	8.2	17.5	19.4	20.7	13.5	3.6	2.2	30,000
1969	56,248	100.0	5.7	8.8	8.3	17.2	19.7	21.0	13.9	3.4	2.1	30,265
1968	55,394	100.0	6.1	8.7	8.7	18.1	20.4	21.2	12.4	2.9	1.7	29,126
1967	54,188	100.0	6.9	9.3	8.2	19.8	20.7	19.8	10.6	2.9	1.8	27,949

Percent change in median income

1980-91	2.1%
1967-91	13.0

Source: Bureau of the Census, Current Population Reports, Money Income of Households, Families, and Persons in the United States: 1991, *Series P-60, No. 180, 1992*

Distribution of Black Households by Income, 1967 to 1991

The black middle class, defined as households with incomes between $25,000 and $50,000, grew from 23 to 27 percent of all black households between 1967 and 1991. The share of black households with incomes above $50,000 grew from 5 to 12 percent.

(distribution of black households by income; income in 1991 dollars; households as of the following year; numbers in thousands)

	total households	total	under $5,000	$5,000 to $9,999	$10,000 to $14,999	$15,000 to $24,999	$25,000 to $34,999	$35,000 to $49,999	$50,000 to $74,999	$75,000 to $99,999	$100,000 or over	median income
						percent distribution						
1991	11,083	100.0%	12.6%	18.2%	11.6%	18.2%	13.8%	13.4%	8.4%	2.5%	1.2%	$18,807
1990	10,671	100.0	12.8	16.9	11.6	18.3	13.8	13.3	8.8	3.1	1.3	19,462
1989	10,486	100.0	11.8	17.1	11.8	18.8	13.5	13.2	9.5	2.9	1.4	19,862
1988	10,561	100.0	11.3	19.0	12.7	18.0	13.1	12.2	9.7	2.4	1.7	18,890
1987	10,192	100.0	12.0	18.6	12.0	19.1	13.4	12.2	8.4	2.7	1.5	18,790
1986	9,922	100.0	12.6	17.5	12.3	19.0	13.2	13.1	8.4	2.6	1.1	18,740
1985	9,797	100.0	11.0	18.7	12.7	20.2	13.1	12.8	8.5	2.0	.9	18,758
1984	9,480	100.0	11.1	19.5	13.6	20.6	12.9	11.4	8.1	2.2	.7	17,659
1983	9,243	100.0	12.4	19.7	12.8	20.8	12.7	11.8	7.6	1.9	.4	17,056
1982	8,916	100.0	12.3	19.4	13.5	19.9	13.8	12.8	6.6	1.3	.5	17,051
1981	8,961	100.0	12.0	19.5	13.3	20.7	13.1	12.1	7.5	1.5	.3	17,095
1980	8,847	100.0	11.9	18.8	13.4	20.2	14.0	12.1	7.6	1.6	.5	17,814
1979	8,586	100.0	10.6	18.2	13.6	20.4	13.1	13.5	8.2	1.8	.5	18,650
1978	8,066	100.0	9.7	18.9	12.8	20.3	14.6	12.6	8.9	1.7	.6	18,989
1977	7,977	100.0	9.8	17.9	15.0	21.6	14.2	12.5	7.1	1.4	.5	18,150
1976	7,776	100.0	8.9	19.6	14.3	20.3	15.1	13.1	6.9	1.3	.4	18,119
1975	7,489	100.0	9.8	20.3	14.0	20.6	14.3	13.3	6.2	1.1	.4	17,953
1974	7,263	100.0	9.7	18.3	13.7	22.7	15.1	12.0	7.0	1.1	.3	18,275
1973	7,040	100.0	9.9	17.6	14.5	21.7	15.0	13.1	6.3	1.4	.6	18,713
1972	6,809	100.0	10.6	18.5	13.3	22.4	14.2	12.8	6.6	1.2	.6	18,215
1971	6,578	100.0	11.7	18.2	13.5	23.0	14.9	11.7	6.0	.8	.3	17,627
1970	6,180	100.0	12.2	16.6	13.5	22.4	15.8	12.0	6.3	1.0	.3	18,260
1969	6,053	100.0	12.6	15.3	14.7	23.8	15.5	11.6	5.5	.8	.2	18,294
1968	5,870	100.0	12.6	16.4	15.4	23.2	15.2	11.2	5.1	.7	.2	17,175
1967	5,728	100.0	14.3	18.2	14.2	24.9	13.5	9.8	3.6	1.1	.5	16,228

Percent change in median income

1980-91	5.6%
1967-91	15.9

Source: Bureau of the Census, Current Population Reports, Money Income of Households, Families, and Persons in the United States: 1991, *Series P-60, No. 180, 1992*

Distribution of Hispanic Households by Income, 1972 to 1991

The proportion of Hispanic households at both the bottom and the top of the income distribution grew between 1972 and 1991. Some Hispanics achieved affluence, while immigrants with low earnings inflated the low-income share.

(distribution of Hispanic households by income; income in 1991 dollars; households as of the following year; numbers in thousands)

	total households						percent distribution						median income
		total	under $5,000	$5,000 to $9,999	$10,000 to $14,999	$15,000 to $24,999	$25,000 to $34,999	$35,000 to $49,999	$50,000 to $74,999	$75,000 to $99,999	$100,000 or over	
1991	6,379	100.0%	6.8%	13.9%	12.1%	21.6%	15.8%	14.8%	10.0%	2.9%	2.1%	$22,691
1990	6,220	100.0	6.7	13.3	13.1	20.0	16.7	15.5	9.5	3.2	1.9	23,270
1989	5,933	100.0	6.9	12.8	11.5	20.5	15.6	15.6	11.6	3.2	2.3	24,078
1988	5,910	100.0	8.0	13.0	12.0	20.0	16.3	15.2	10.3	3.0	2.3	23,440
1987	5,642	100.0	7.0	14.5	12.1	20.3	15.4	14.9	10.6	3.0	2.1	23,183
1986	5,418	100.0	7.2	14.0	13.0	20.3	15.6	14.8	10.7	3.1	1.5	22,806
1985	5,213	100.0	6.7	14.9	13.5	20.2	16.2	14.6	10.0	2.8	1.1	22,107
1984	4,883	100.0	7.6	14.6	12.2	20.3	16.4	15.1	10.0	2.5	1.3	22,274
1983	4,666	100.0	7.0	16.1	12.5	22.2	16.2	14.0	8.7	2.4	.9	21,598
1982	4,085	100.0	7.2	15.4	13.1	21.6	15.9	14.4	9.6	1.5	1.3	21,624
1981	3,980	100.0	6.1	13.4	12.0	22.2	17.8	15.2	10.1	2.2	1.0	23,128
1980	3,906	100.0	6.7	13.2	13.0	22.7	16.4	15.2	9.6	2.2	1.0	22,591
1979	3,684	100.0	5.5	12.2	12.1	22.1	17.5	16.4	10.2	2.5	1.3	24,004
1978	3,291	100.0	5.3	12.6	12.0	23.3	17.3	16.9	9.5	2.1	.9	23,816
1977	3,304	100.0	5.3	13.2	12.4	24.3	18.1	15.9	8.2	1.9	.8	22,945
1976	3,081	100.0	5.9	14.8	13.8	22.4	17.1	15.8	7.8	1.8	.6	21,941
1975	2,948	100.0	6.7	13.7	13.8	24.3	17.2	15.6	6.8	1.3	.7	21,484
1974	2,897	100.0	4.9	12.3	13.7	22.7	19.5	16.4	7.9	1.7	.8	23,372
1973	2,722	100.0	4.6	11.6	13.0	24.4	18.9	15.9	9.2	1.7	.7	23,500
1972	2,655	100.0	4.4	12.3	13.4	24.9	20.1	15.3	7.3	1.4	.8	23,550

Percent change in median income

1980-91	0.4%
1972-91	-3.6

Note: Hispanics may be of any race.

Source: Bureau of the Census, Current Population Reports, Money Income of Households, Families, and Persons in the United States: 1991, *Series P-60, No. 180, 1992*

All Households: Share of Aggregate Income Accruing to Each Fifth and Top 5 Percent, 1967 to 1991

The richest households received a higher share of national income in 1991 than they did in the 1960s and 1970s. The poorest households received a smaller share.

(distribution of aggregate income by household income quintiles; households as of the following year; numbers in thousands))

| | total households | | percent distribution of aggregate income | | | | | |
		total	bottom fifth	second fifth	third fifth	fourth fifth	top fifth	top 5 percent
1991	95,669	100.0%	3.8%	9.6%	15.9%	24.2%	46.5%	18.1%
1990	94,312	100.0	3.9	9.6	15.9	24.0	46.6	18.6
1989	93,347	100.0	3.8	9.5	15.8	24.0	46.8	18.9
1988	92,830	100.0	3.8	9.6	16.0	24.3	46.3	18.3
1987	91,124	100.0	3.8	9.6	16.1	24.3	46.2	18.2
1986	89,479	100.0	3.8	9.7	16.2	24.3	46.1	18.0
1985	88,458	100.0	3.9	9.8	16.2	24.4	45.6	17.6
1984	86,789	100.0	4.0	9.9	16.3	24.6	45.2	17.1
1983	85,290	100.0	4.0	9.9	16.4	24.6	45.1	17.1
1982	83,918	100.0	4.0	10.0	16.5	24.5	45.0	17.0
1981	83,527	100.0	4.1	10.1	16.7	24.8	44.4	16.5
1980	82,368	100.0	4.2	10.2	16.8	24.8	44.1	16.5
1979	80,776	100.0	4.1	10.2	16.8	24.7	44.2	16.9
1978	77,330	100.0	4.2	10.2	16.9	24.7	44.1	16.8
1977	76,030	100.0	4.2	10.2	16.9	24.7	44.0	16.8
1976	74,142	100.0	4.3	10.3	17.0	24.7	43.7	16.6
1975	72,867	100.0	4.3	10.4	17.0	24.7	43.6	16.6
1974	71,163	100.0	4.3	10.6	17.0	24.6	43.5	16.5
1973	69,859	100.0	4.2	10.5	17.1	24.6	43.6	16.6
1972	68,251	100.0	4.1	10.5	17.1	24.5	43.9	17.0
1971	66,676	100.0	4.1	10.6	17.3	24.5	43.5	16.7
1970	64,778	100.0	4.1	10.8	17.4	24.5	43.3	16.6
1969	63,401	100.0	4.1	10.9	17.5	24.5	43.0	16.6
1968	62,214	100.0	4.2	11.1	17.5	24.4	42.8	16.6
1967	60,813	100.0	4.0	10.8	17.3	24.2	43.8	17.5

Source: Bureau of the Census, Current Population Reports, Money Income of Households, Families, and Persons in the United States: 1991, *Series P-60, No. 180, 1992*

White Households: Share of Aggregate Income Accruing to Each Fifth and Top 5 Percent, 1967 to 1991

White households with incomes at the bottom of the income distribution maintained their share of national income between 1967 and 1991. Those in the middle of the distribution lost ground.

(distribution of aggregate income by white household income quintiles; households as of the following year; numbers in thousands)

	total households	percent distribution of aggregate income						
		total	bottom fifth	second fifth	third fifth	fourth fifth	top fifth	top 5 percent
1991	81,675	100.0%	4.1%	9.9%	16.0%	24.1%	45.8%	17.9%
1990	80,968	100.0	4.2	10.0	16.0	23.9	46.0	18.3
1989	80,163	100.0	4.1	9.8	16.0	23.8	46.3	18.7
1988	79,734	100.0	4.1	10.0	16.2	24.1	45.6	18.0
1987	78,519	100.0	4.1	10.0	16.3	24.2	45.5	17.9
1986	77,284	100.0	4.1	10.0	16.3	24.2	45.4	17.8
1985	76,576	100.0	4.1	10.1	16.4	24.3	45.1	17.4
1984	75,328	100.0	4.3	10.2	16.5	24.4	44.6	16.8
1983	74,170	100.0	4.3	10.3	16.5	24.4	44.5	16.8
1982	73,182	100.0	4.2	10.3	16.6	24.4	44.4	16.7
1981	72,845	100.0	4.4	10.4	16.8	24.7	43.8	16.3
1980	71,872	100.0	4.4	10.5	17.0	24.6	43.5	16.3
1979	70,766	100.0	4.4	10.5	17.0	24.5	43.7	16.7
1978	68,028	100.0	4.4	10.5	17.0	24.5	43.6	16.6
1977	66,934	100.0	4.4	10.5	17.0	24.6	43.5	16.7
1976	65,353	100.0	4.5	10.6	17.2	24.5	43.2	16.5
1975	64,392	100.0	4.5	10.7	17.1	24.6	43.2	16.4
1974	62,984	100.0	4.5	10.9	17.1	24.4	43.0	16.4
1973	61,965	100.0	4.4	10.8	17.3	24.5	43.1	16.4
1972	60,618	100.0	4.3	10.8	17.2	24.3	43.4	16.8
1971	59,463	100.0	4.3	11.0	17.4	24.4	43.0	16.5
1970	57,575	100.0	4.2	11.1	17.5	24.3	42.9	16.5
1969	56,248	100.0	4.3	11.3	17.6	24.3	42.5	16.4
1968	55,394	100.0	4.4	11.4	17.6	24.3	42.3	16.5
1967	54,188	100.0	4.1	11.2	17.4	24.0	43.3	17.3

Source: Bureau of the Census, Current Population Reports, Money Income of Households, Families, and Persons in the United States: 1991, *Series P-60, No. 180, 1992*

Black Households: Share of Aggregate Income Accruing to Each Fifth and Top 5 Percent, 1967 to 1991

The poorest black households have been losing their share of aggregate income since the mid-1970s. The richest black households were barely touched by the recession of the early 1990s.

(distribution of aggregate income by black household income quintiles; households as of the following year; numbers in thousands)

	total households		percent distribution of aggregate income					
		total	bottom fifth	second fifth	third fifth	fourth fifth	top fifth	top 5 percent
1991	11,083	100.0%	3.1%	7.8%	15.0%	25.2%	48.9%	18.3%
1990	10,671	100.0	3.1	7.9	15.0	25.1	49.0	18.5
1989	10,486	100.0	3.2	8.0	15.0	24.9	48.9	18.2
1988	10,561	100.0	3.3	7.7	14.6	24.7	49.7	18.7
1987	10,192	100.0	3.3	7.9	14.8	24.4	49.7	19.3
1986	9,922	100.0	3.1	8.0	14.9	25.0	49.0	18.6
1985	9,797	100.0	3.5	8.3	15.2	25.0	48.0	17.6
1984	9,480	100.0	3.6	8.4	15.0	24.7	48.4	17.6
1983	9,243	100.0	3.5	8.3	15.1	25.1	47.9	17.1
1982	8,916	100.0	3.6	8.6	15.3	25.5	47.1	17.1
1981	8,961	100.0	3.7	8.5	15.2	25.3	47.3	16.6
1980	8,847	100.0	3.7	8.7	15.3	25.2	47.1	16.9
1979	8,586	100.0	3.8	8.8	15.5	25.3	46.6	16.5
1978	8,066	100.0	3.9	8.7	15.6	25.3	46.5	16.5
1977	7,977	100.0	4.2	9.2	15.5	24.9	46.3	16.8
1976	7,776	100.0	4.2	9.1	15.7	25.4	45.6	16.3
1975	7,489	100.0	4.1	9.0	16.0	25.5	45.4	16.0
1974	7,263	100.0	4.2	9.4	16.1	25.2	45.1	15.8
1973	7,040	100.0	4.1	9.4	16.0	25.1	45.5	16.6
1972	6,809	100.0	3.9	9.2	15.8	24.9	46.2	16.9
1971	6,578	100.0	4.0	9.4	16.1	25.1	45.4	16.4
1970	6,180	100.0	3.7	9.3	16.3	25.2	45.5	16.4
1969	6,053	100.0	3.9	9.7	16.5	25.1	44.7	15.9
1968	5,870	100.0	4.0	10.0	16.3	25.1	44.9	15.9
1967	5,728	100.0	3.8	9.3	15.9	24.3	46.7	18.2

Source: Bureau of the Census, Current Population Reports, Money Income of Households, Families, and Persons in the United States: 1991, *Series P-60, No. 180, 1992*

Hispanic Households: Share of Aggregate Income Accruing to Each Fifth and Top 5 Percent, 1972 to 1991

The share of aggregate income accruing to the poorest three-fifths of Hispanic households fell between 1972 and 1991 as immigrants with low incomes became a larger share of these households.

(distribution of aggregate income by Hispanic household income quintiles; households as of the following year; numbers in thousands)

	total households		**percent distribution of aggregate income**					
		total	bottom fifth	second fifth	third fifth	fourth fifth	top fifth	top 5 percent
1991	6,379	100.0%	4.0%	9.4%	15.8%	24.3%	46.5%	17.7%
1990	6,220	100.0	4.0	9.5	15.9	24.3	46.3	17.9
1989	5,933	100.0	3.8	9.5	15.7	24.4	46.6	18.1
1988	5,910	100.0	3.7	9.3	15.6	24.2	47.2	19.0
1987	5,642	100.0	3.7	9.1	15.5	24.1	47.6	19.2
1986	5,418	100.0	3.9	9.5	15.8	24.8	46.1	16.9
1985	5,213	100.0	4.1	9.4	16.1	24.8	45.6	16.6
1984	4,883	100.0	3.9	9.5	16.2	24.9	45.5	16.9
1983	4,666	100.0	4.1	9.6	16.3	24.8	45.2	16.4
1982	4,085	100.0	4.2	9.6	16.1	24.6	45.5	17.0
1981	3,980	100.0	4.4	10.3	16.6	24.7	44.0	15.9
1980	3,906	100.0	4.3	10.1	16.4	24.8	44.5	16.5
1979	3,684	100.0	4.5	10.5	16.6	24.5	44.0	16.3
1978	3,291	100.0	4.7	10.7	16.9	24.9	42.8	15.5
1977	3,304	100.0	4.9	10.7	16.9	24.6	42.9	15.6
1976	3,081	100.0	4.7	10.4	16.8	25.1	43.0	15.4
1975	2,948	100.0	4.7	10.6	16.8	24.8	43.1	16.1
1974	2,897	100.0	5.1	10.9	17.1	24.7	42.3	15.4
1973	2,722	100.0	5.1	11.1	17.1	24.7	42.0	15.0
1972	2,655	100.0	5.3	11.2	17.2	24.0	42.3	16.2

Note: Hispanics may be of any race.
Source: Bureau of the Census, Current Population Reports, Money Income of Households, Families, and Persons in the United States: 1991, Series P-60, No. 180, 1992

All Households: Average Income of Each Fifth and Top 5 Percent, 1967 to 1991

As Americans became more affluent over the past few decades, the average income of each fifth of households, from the poorest to the richest, has grown after adjusting for inflation.

(average income for household income quintiles; income in 1991 dollars; households as of the following year; numbers in thousands)

	total households	average income						average income
		bottom fifth	second fifth	third fifth	fourth fifth	top fifth	top 5 percent	
1991	95,669	$7,263	$18,149	$30,147	$45,957	$88,130	$137,532	$37,922
1990	94,312	7,498	18,789	31,034	46,790	90,804	144,595	38,977
1989	93,347	7,682	19,113	31,771	48,058	93,944	151,781	40,113
1988	92,830	7,443	18,786	31,420	47,496	90,676	143,010	39,164
1987	91,124	7,352	18,684	31,238	47,218	89,797	141,475	38,858
1986	89,479	7,175	18,458	30,887	46,530	88,071	137,970	38,224
1985	88,458	7,106	18,009	29,892	44,964	83,990	129,560	36,792
1984	86,789	7,126	17,749	29,413	44,287	81,433	122,926	36,002
1983	85,290	6,910	17,357	28,698	43,064	79,066	119,461	35,020
1982	83,918	6,824	17,269	28,585	42,513	77,972	117,817	34,633
1981	83,527	6,957	17,330	28,708	42,793	76,441	113,592	34,446
1980	82,368	7,133	17,752	29,294	43,157	76,949	114,991	34,858
1979	80,776	7,373	18,339	30,236	44,372	79,631	121,446	35,990
1978	77,330	7,436	18,261	30,152	44,169	78,857	120,030	35,775
1977	76,030	7,187	17,691	29,264	42,877	76,462	116,970	34,697
1976	74,142	7,227	17,695	29,100	42,259	74,793	113,959	34,215
1975	72,867	7,050	17,318	28,413	41,287	72,894	110,618	33,393
1974	71,163	7,303	18,152	29,253	42,248	74,852	113,776	34,362
1973	69,859	7,335	18,370	30,016	43,151	76,529	116,627	35,080
1972	68,251	7,003	18,093	29,525	42,385	76,094	117,939	34,621
1971	66,676	6,611	17,472	28,330	40,275	71,364	109,456	32,811
1970	64,778	6,569	17,792	28,651	40,388	71,510	109,761	32,982
1969	63,401	6,675	18,031	28,813	40,355	70,935	109,188	32,992
1968	62,214	6,525	17,493	27,742	38,703	67,782	104,943	31,648
1967	60,813	6,003	16,633	26,557	37,157	67,335	107,328	29,975
Percent change								
1967-91	-	21.0%	9.1%	13.5%	23.7%	30.9%	28.1%	26.5%

Source: Bureau of the Census, Current Population Reports, Money Income of Households, Families, and Persons in the United States: 1991, Series P-60, No. 180, 1992

White Households: Average Income of Each Fifth and Top 5 Percent , 1967 to 1991

The average incomes of white households in all income quintiles grew between 1967 and the late 1980s, after adjusting for inflation. Average incomes then fell slightly across the board as the recession of the early 1990s took its toll.

(average income for white household income quintiles; income in 1991 dollars; households as of the following year; numbers in thousands)

	total households	bottom fifth	second fifth	third fifth	fourth fifth	top fifth	top 5 percent	average income
				average income				
1991	81,675	$8,188	$19,553	$31,706	$47,664	$90,542	$141,155	$39,523
1990	80,968	8,423	20,192	32,486	48,414	93,263	148,756	40,549
1989	80,163	8,632	20,567	33,367	49,722	96,664	156,464	41,784
1988	79,734	8,414	20,359	33,138	49,164	93,142	147,071	40,835
1987	78,519	8,323	20,241	32,990	48,948	92,134	145,281	40,518
1986	77,284	8,015	19,899	32,518	48,202	90,445	141,785	39,816
1985	76,576	7,834	19,350	31,403	46,532	86,390	133,363	38,302
1984	75,328	7,890	19,141	30,963	45,840	83,601	126,216	37,487
1983	74,170	7,708	18,732	30,179	44,574	81,221	122,766	36,483
1982	73,182	7,522	18,594	30,014	44,014	80,127	120,820	36,060
1981	72,845	7,693	18,655	30,251	44,287	48,565	116,762	35,890
1980	71,872	7,861	19,113	30,790	44,620	78,933	117,916	36,264
1979	70,766	8,082	19,675	31,729	45,800	81,764	124,778	37,409
1978	68,028	8,079	19,494	31,564	45,515	80,856	123,438	37,101
1977	66,934	7,754	18,984	30,744	44,306	78,466	120,287	36,052
1976	65,353	7,817	18,924	30,498	43,614	76,802	117,279	35,531
1975	64,392	7,607	18,486	29,707	42,554	74,786	113,780	34,627
1974	62,984	7,883	19,412	30,570	43,563	76,755	116,746	35,635
1973	61,965	7,912	19,709	31,453	44,571	78,529	119,870	36,436
1972	60,618	7,568	19,448	30,961	43,704	78,162	121,193	35,967
1971	59,463	7,126	18,679	29,591	41,460	73,144	112,370	33,999
1970	57,575	7,087	18,982	29,842	41,549	73,225	112,710	34,136
1969	56,248	7,225	19,351	30,130	41,600	72,812	112,503	34,216
1968	55,394	7,041	18,739	28,913	39,791	69,440	108,010	32,786
1967	54,188	6,461	17,867	27,702	38,249	68,907	110,029	31,071
Percent change								
1967-91	-	26.7%	9.4%	14.5%	24.6%	31.4%	28.3%	27.2%

Source: Bureau of the Census, Current Population Reports, Money Income of Households, Families, and Persons in the United States: 1991, *Series P-60, No. 180, 1992*

Black Households: Average Income of Each Fifth and Top 5 Percent, 1967 to 1991

Between 1967 and 1991, the average income of the poorest black households barely grew, after adjusting for inflation. In contrast, the incomes of the middle and upper classes have grown substantially.

(average income for black household income quintiles; income in 1991 dollars; households as of the following year; numbers in thousands)

	total households	average income						average income
		bottom fifth	second fifth	third fifth	fourth fifth	top fifth	top 5 percent	
1991	11,083	$3,866	$9,823	$18,819	$31,518	$61,213	$91,891	$25,043
1990	10,671	4,004	10,169	19,435	38,653	63,301	95,768	25,858
1989	10,486	4,166	10,540	19,813	32,821	64,448	95,864	26,356
1988	10,561	4,269	10,020	18,865	31,952	64,357	96,928	25,878
1987	10,192	4,117	9,967	18,762	30,929	63,081	97,661	25,371
1986	9,922	3,887	10,026	18,762	31,404	61,631	93,657	25,142
1985	9,797	4,277	10,204	18,559	30,534	58,798	86,188	24,474
1984	9,480	4,201	9,894	17,618	29,096	56,947	82,729	23,551
1983	9,243	3,997	9,444	17,186	28,542	54,427	77,713	22,719
1982	8,916	4,003	9,605	17,175	28,576	52,815	76,877	22,435
1981	8,961	4,122	9,587	17,083	28,393	53,098	74,706	22,457
1980	8,847	4,260	10,007	17,729	29,165	54,437	78,071	23,119
1979	8,586	4,522	10,533	18,532	30,330	55,739	79,110	23,931
1978	8,066	4,746	10,583	18,949	30,682	56,385	80,203	24,268
1977	7,977	4,817	10,646	18,006	28,919	53,890	78,046	23,255
1976	7,776	4,762	10,550	18,194	29,416	52,824	75,717	23,149
1975	7,489	4,624	10,135	17,900	28,539	50,857	71,692	22,410
1974	7,263	4,729	10,694	18,333	28,584	51,307	71,892	22,729
1973	7,040	4,750	10,916	18,551	29,130	52,844	77,141	23,238
1972	6,809	4,512	10,546	18,163	28,666	53,167	77,539	23,010
1971	6,578	4,320	10,210	17,630	27,417	49,639	71,582	21,843
1970	6,180	4,116	10,418	18,122	28,084	50,737	73,179	22,297
1969	6,053	4,238	10,550	17,917	27,233	48,368	68,975	21,778
1968	5,870	4,140	10,224	17,023	26,279	46,915	66,626	20,918
1967	5,728	3,816	9,399	16,111	24,625	47,306	73,638	19,499
Percent change								
1967-91	–	1.3%	4.5%	16.8%	28.0%	29.4%	24.8%	28.4%

Source: Bureau of the Census, Current Population Reports, Money Income of Households, Families, and Persons in the United States: 1991, *Series P-60, No. 180, 1992*

Hispanic Households: Average Income of Each Fifth and Top 5 Percent, 1972 to 1991

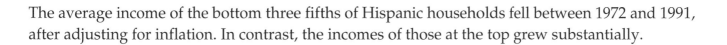

The average income of the bottom three fifths of Hispanic households fell between 1972 and 1991, after adjusting for inflation. In contrast, the incomes of those at the top grew substantially.

(average income for Hispanic household income quintiles; income in 1991 dollars; households as of the following year; numbers in thousands)

	total households	average income						average income
		bottom fifth	second fifth	third fifth	fourth fifth	top fifth	top 5 percent	
1991	6,379	$5,753	$13,622	$22,774	$35,056	$67,180	$102,435	$28,872
1990	6,220	5,880	13,799	23,217	35,349	67,524	104,433	29,149
1989	5,933	5,796	14,674	24,213	37,523	71,608	111,607	30,746
1988	5,910	5,492	13,968	23,380	36,151	70,667	113,546	29,926
1987	5,642	5,522	13,584	22,960	35,751	70,799	114,202	29,717
1986	5,418	5,576	13,620	22,779	35,663	66,347	97,164	28,797
1985	5,213	5,668	13,045	22,173	34,183	63,048	91,731	27,624
1984	4,883	5,365	13,169	22,402	34,497	63,054	93,628	27,697
1983	4,666	5,448	12,758	21,549	32,767	59,750	86,523	26,455
1982	4,085	5,516	12,824	21,514	32,859	60,722	90,553	26,687
1981	3,980	6,060	14,238	23,122	34,336	61,112	88,590	27,774
1980	3,906	5,867	13,999	22,568	34,164	61,373	90,877	27,594
1979	3,684	6,484	15,230	24,058	35,602	63,847	94,622	29,044
1978	3,291	6,560	15,061	23,727	35,055	60,261	87,186	28,132
1977	3,304	6,573	14,545	22,831	33,343	58,107	84,420	27,078
1976	3,081	6,081	13,519	21,820	32,537	55,686	79,987	25,928
1975	2,948	5,930	13,540	21,436	31,653	54,967	82,321	25,505
1974	2,897	6,873	14,709	23,188	33,394	57,209	83,588	27,075
1973	2,722	6,974	15,366	23,570	34,085	57,862	82,785	27,303
1972	2,655	7,043	14,994	23,093	32,231	56,750	86,729	27,068

Percent change

1972-1991	-	-18.3%	-9.2%	-1.4%	8.8%	18.4%	18.1%	6.7%

Note: Hispanics may be of any race.
Source: Bureau of the Census, Current Population Reports, Money Income of Households, Families, and Persons in the United States 1991, *Series P-60, No. 180, 1992*

Median Income of Households by Age of Householder, 1967 to 1991

The incomes of householders aged 65 or older grew by 64 percent between 1967 and 1991, after adjusting for inflation. The incomes of householders under age 25 fell by 13 percent.

(median income of households by age of householder; income in 1991 dollars)

	15 to 24	25 to 34	35 to 44	45 to 54	55 to 64	65 or older
1991	$18,313	$30,842	$39,349	$43,751	$33,304	$16,975
1990	18,760	31,637	40,184	43,686	33,727	17,564
1989	20,499	32,757	41,338	45,608	33,851	17,323
1988	19,618	32,706	42,085	43,995	33,276	17,181
1987	19,719	32,331	42,185	44,607	33,043	17,316
1986	19,026	32,183	40,744	44,315	33,275	17,205
1985	19,049	31,753	39,323	42,054	32,350	16,777
1984	18,389	31,114	39,043	41,314	31,584	16,778
1983	18,291	29,712	37,890	41,481	31,434	16,371
1982	19,683	30,319	37,569	39,870	31,450	15,730
1981	20,017	31,009	38,372	40,881	31,807	14,970
1980	21,036	32,001	39,101	41,573	32,349	14,532
1979	21,926	33,503	40,669	42,421	33,012	14,502
1978	22,224	33,297	40,210	42,739	32,341	14,288
1977	20,626	32,488	38,955	43,759	30,841	13,678
1976	20,320	32,090	38,340	40,502	30,753	13,670
1975	19,722	31,813	37,666	39,556	30,257	13,535
1974	21,288	32,730	39,094	40,514	30,100	13,888
1973	21,630	34,148	40,292	40,632	31,387	13,225
1972	21,660	33,366	38,921	40,262	30,780	12,789
1971	20,797	31,844	36,708	37,972	29,528	12,049
1970	21,993	31,956	36,708	37,638	29,370	11,536
1969	21,986	32,239	37,099	37,808	28,578	11,508
1968	21,778	31,041	35,499	35,304	27,562	11,488
1967	21,068	30,062	33,754	34,136	26,103	10,356
Percent change						
1967-91	-13.1%	2.6%	16.6%	28.2%	27.6%	63.9%

Source: Bureau of the Census, Current Population Reports, Money Income of Households, Families, and Persons in the United States: 1991, *Series P-60, No. 180, 1992*

Median Income of Households by Type of Household, 1980 to 1991

The incomes of married couples and nonfamily households grew significantly between 1980 and 1991, while the incomes of families headed by women or men with no spouse present barely changed.

(median income of households by household type; income in 1991 dollars)

		family households			
	total families	married-couple	female householder, no spouse present	male householder, no spouse present	nonfamily households
1991	$36,404	$41,075	$17,961	$31,010	$17,774
1990	37,210	41,679	18,829	32,880	18,434
1989	38,040	42,468	19,093	33,321	18,799
1988	37,407	41,949	18,480	32,976	18,591
1987	37,463	41,907	18,560	32,018	17,803
1986	36,962	40,855	17,817	32,685	17,583
1985	35,470	39,444	18,121	30,827	17,465
1984	34,936	38,915	17,661	32,183	17,024
1983	33,890	37,372	16,736	31,290	16,423
1982	33,643	37,137	16,930	30,226	16,270
1981	34,091	37,952	17,295	31,052	15,699
1980	35,021	38,361	17,923	31,071	15,649
Percent change					
1980-91	3.9%	7.1%	0.2%	-0.2%	13.6%

Source: Bureau of the Census, Current Population Reports, Money Income of Households, Families, and Persons in the United States: 1991, *Series P-60, No. 180, 1992*

Median Income of Households by Education of Householder, 1967 to 1991

The median income of college-educated householders grew by 18 percent between 1967 and 1990, after adjusting for inflation. In contrast, the median income of households headed by high school drop-outs fell by nearly 28 percent.

(median income of households by educational attainment of householders aged 25 or older; income in 1991 dollars)

	total households	less than 9th	9th to 12th	high school graduate	some college	bachelor's or more	bachelor's degree	master's degree	professional degree	doctoral degree
						grade or degree completed				
1991	$31,032	$13,221	$17,535	$28,487	$35,150	$52,270	$48,705	$55,173	$77,949	$70,317

	total households	high school			college				
		8 or less	1 to 3 years	4 years	total	1 to 3	4 or more	4 years	5+ years
1990	$31,987	$14,064	$18,919	$29,894	$44,836	$37,153	$52,571	$48,966	$56,821
1989	32,791	13,940	19,508	30,810	46,284	38,521	54,000	50,304	59,258
1988	32,373	14,230	19,105	31,087	45,898	37,676	53,273	48,429	59,113
1987	30,923	14,197	19,905	30,833	45,621	37,919	52,303	48,758	57,398
1986	31,954	14,476	20,055	31,280	45,490	37,355	52,745	49,450	57,023
1985	31,051	14,365	20,040	30,540	43,892	36,316	51,198	47,716	56,636
1984	30,460	14,327	20,376	30,564	42,572	35,272	49,704	46,920	53,889
1983	28,732	14,369	18,881	28,637	41,195	33,851	47,733	45,332	52,526
1982	29,583	14,495	19,991	30,023	41,855	35,001	47,755	44,704	51,646
1981	29,944	14,630	20,615	31,075	41,698	35,688	47,125	43,860	51,004
1980	30,424	14,688	21,868	32,501	42,300	35,980	47,796	45,246	50,782
1979	30,305	15,212	21,932	32,105	41,194	35,332	47,437	45,883	52,472
1978	31,313	15,416	23,413	33,442	42,945	36,935	48,565	45,744	51,875
1977	30,450	15,152	23,059	32,991	42,544	36,236	47,880	45,378	50,834
1976	30,254	15,446	23,948	32,799	42,210	36,433	47,898	45,239	51,093
1975	29,793	15,335	23,217	32,119	42,201	36,648	47,784	45,090	51,200
1974	30,541	16,172	22,732	33,485	43,102	37,161	49,158	46,581	51,989
1973	31,527	-	26,707	34,730	-	38,612	51,302	-	-
1972	30,855	-	26,713	34,239	-	38,163	50,794	-	-
1971	29,527	-	26,411	32,889	-	36,609	47,830	-	-
1970	29,540	-	26,757	33,188	-	37,201	47,623	-	-
1969	29,779	-	27,376	33,325	-	37,460	47,554	-	-
1968	28,608	-	26,884	32,033	-	35,989	45,838	-	-
1967	27,517	-	26,110	31,007	-	34,909	44,517	-	-
Percent change									
1980-90	5.1%	-4.2%	-13.5%	-8.0%	6.0%	3.3%	10.0%	8.2%	11.9%
1967-90	16.2	-	-27.5	-3.6	-	6.4	18.1	-	-

Note: Beginning in 1991, the Census Bureau changed its educational attainment categories, making 1991 statistics incompatible with those of earlier years.
Source: U.S. Bureau of the Census, various income reports

Percent of Households Receiving Government Benefits and Paying Taxes, 1980 to 1991

The average amount of federal tax American households pay fell between 1980 and 1991, but the decline has been more than made up by additional Social Security and state income taxes households now pay.

(percent of households receiving specified benefits or paying specified taxes and average amounts received or paid by these households, in 1991 dollars)

	1991	1990	1989	1988	1987	1986	1985	1984	1983	1982	1981	1980
Federal income taxes												
% paying	74.5%	75.6%	75.3%	75.0%	75.9%	77.8%	77.7%	78.0%	76.6%	76.1%	75.9%	75.6%
Aver. amount	$5,801	$5,972	$6,444	$6,215	$6,286	$6,442	$5,859	$5,620	$5,586	$6,006	$6,471	$6,545
Social Security payroll taxes												
% paying	74.7%	75.2%	75.4%	75.5%	75.2%	74.7%	74.7%	74.5%	74.2%	74.4%	74.8%	75.3%
Aver. amount	$2,807	$2,805	$2,811	$2,759	$2,579	$2,546	$2,397	$2,227	$2,132	$2,097	$2,071	$1,844
State income taxes												
% paying	65.1%	65.6%	67.5%	66.8%	66.3%	65.0%	64.5%	64.2%	63.1%	63.0%	63.0%	63.8%
Aver. amount	$1,761	$1,782	$2,102	$1,991	$1,929	$1,792	$1,684	$1,565	$1,482	$1,378	$1,338	$1,422
Government cash transfers												
% receiving	44.6%	43.5%	41.5%	41.2%	42.1%	41.7%	41.9%	42.3%	44.5%	45.9%	44.2%	44.1%
Aver. amount	$7,137	$7,097	$7,315	$7,302	$7,237	$7,286	$7,123	$7,038	$7,016	$6,925	$6,753	$6,760
Nonmeans-tested government cash transfers												
% receiving	39.6%	38.7%	37.2%	36.7%	37.5%	37.0%	37.2%	37.6%	39.9%	41.5%	39.7%	39.6%
Aver. amount	$7,128	$7,090	$7,290	$7,294	$7,206	$7,358	$7,159	$7,071	$7,007	$6,915	$6,706	$6,676
Medicare												
% receiving	22.6%	22.6%	22.6%	22.3%	22.3%	22.2%	22.0%	22.1%	21.8%	22.2%	21.9%	21.2%
Aver. amount	$3,625	$3,584	$3,475	$3,361	$3,304	$3,291	$2,690	$2,522	$2,481	$2,540	$2,292	$2,128
Regular-price school lunches												
% receiving	13.7%	14.0%	14.1%	14.0%	14.0%	13.5%	13.5%	13.0%	12.8%	12.5%	13.8%	14.9%
Aver. amount	$89	$86	$88	$104	$112	$117	$115	$121	$123	$121	$142	$170
Means-tested government cash transfers												
% receiving	9.1%	8.6%	8.1%	8.2%	8.3%	7.7%	7.8%	7.9%	7.8%	7.6%	8.0%	8.2%
Aver. amount	$4,036	$3,954	$3,995	$4,061	$4,120	$4,106	$4,096	$4,034	$4,122	$4,076	$4,023	$4,106
Medicaid												
% receiving	8.0%	7.3%	6.7%	6.0%	5.8%	5.9%	6.0%	6.1%	6.1%	6.4%	7.1%	7.1%
Aver. amount	$2,249	$2,247	$2,033	$1,986	$2,038	$1,945	$2,070	$1,935	$1,883	$1,805	$1,873	$1,855
Other means-tested government noncash transfers												
% receiving	14.1%	13.2%	12.5%	12.3%	12.5%	13.1%	13.2%	13.6%	13.8%	13.9%	13.5%	13.5%
Aver. amount	$1,898	$1,871	$1,757	$1,826	$1,866	$1,821	$1,768	$1,732	$1,719	$1,688	$1,620	$1,693

Source: Bureau of the Census, Current Population Reports, Measuring the Effects of Benefits and Taxes on Income and Poverty: 1979 to 1991, *Series P-60, No. 182-RD, 1992*

Distribution of Families by Income, 1967 to 1991

The share of families with incomes in the middle of the distribution fell sharply between 1967 and 1991, after adjusting for inflation. At the same time, the share with incomes at the top grew substantially.

(distribution of families by income; income in 1991 dollars; families as of the following year; numbers in thousands)

	total families	total	under $5,000	$5,000 to $9,999	$10,000 to $14,999	$15,000 to $24,999	$25,000 to $34,999	$35,000 to $49,999	$50,000 to $74,999	$75,000 to $99,999	$100,000 or over	median income
						percent distribution						
1991	67,173	100.0%	3.6%	6.1%	7.2%	16.0%	15.6%	19.5%	18.8%	7.5%	5.6%	$35,939
1990	66,322	100.0	3.4	5.5	7.2	15.5	15.8	19.9	19.0	7.6	6.1	36,841
1989	66,090	100.0	3.2	5.6	7.2	15.2	15.1	19.9	19.6	7.8	6.4	37,579
1988	65,837	100.0	3.3	5.7	7.3	15.5	15.5	19.9	19.4	7.6	5.9	37,062
1987	65,204	100.0	3.3	5.9	6.9	15.7	15.1	20.3	19.7	7.4	5.7	37,131
1986	64,491	100.0	3.4	5.9	7.3	15.9	15.6	20.3	19.3	7.0	5.4	36,607
1985	63,558	100.0	3.4	6.3	7.5	16.5	16.3	20.1	18.5	6.7	4.7	35,107
1984	62,706	100.0	3.5	6.3	7.9	16.7	16.3	20.3	18.4	6.3	4.4	34,650
1983	62,015	100.0	3.8	6.6	7.9	17.2	16.9	20.4	17.4	5.8	3.9	33,741
1982	61,393	100.0	3.5	6.7	8.1	17.3	17.2	20.7	17.3	5.5	3.8	33,385
1981	61,019	100.0	3.0	6.2	7.9	17.8	17.0	21.3	17.7	5.9	3.2	33,843
1980	60,309	100.0	2.8	6.1	7.7	17.3	17.1	21.9	18.2	5.8	3.3	34,791
1979	59,550	100.0	3.5	5.6	7.4	16.8	16.3	22.7	18.9	6.0	3.8	36,051
1978	57,804	100.0	2.5	5.6	7.7	16.7	16.8	22.5	19.1	5.5	3.7	35,594
1977	57,215	100.0	2.5	5.8	8.2	17.0	17.6	22.4	18.1	5.2	3.2	34,500
1976	56,710	100.0	2.2	6.1	8.3	17.2	18.0	22.9	17.7	4.7	2.9	34,298
1975	56,245	100.0	2.4	6.3	8.6	18.0	18.3	23.0	16.6	4.4	2.6	33,248
1974	55,698	100.0	2.3	5.6	8.1	17.3	19.2	22.6	17.2	4.8	2.8	33,858
1973	55,053	100.0	2.2	5.8	7.8	16.8	18.6	22.9	17.7	5.0	3.1	34,774
1972	54,373	100.0	2.4	6.0	7.6	17.5	18.7	23.1	16.8	4.8	2.9	34,099
1971	53,296	100.0	2.7	6.5	7.8	18.5	20.3	22.8	15.1	4.0	2.2	32,502
1970	52,227	100.0	2.9	6.3	7.6	18.0	21.0	22.9	15.1	4.0	2.3	32,540
1969	51,586	100.0	2.8	6.2	7.7	17.7	21.4	23.2	15.2	3.7	2.2	32,608
1968	50,823	100.0	3.0	6.2	8.4	18.9	21.9	23.2	13.6	3.1	1.8	31,185
1967	50,111	100.0	3.3	7.4	8.0	20.7	22.4	21.7	11.5	3.1	1.8	29,765

Percent change in median income

1980-91	3.3%
1967-91	20.7

Source: Bureau of the Census, Current Population Reports, Money Income of Households, Families, and Persons in the United States: 1991, *Series P-60, No. 180, 1992*

Distribution of White Families by Income, 1967 to 1991

White families have become more affluent since the late 1960s. The share with incomes of $50,000 or more nearly doubled from 18 to 34 percent. The share with incomes below $25,000 fell from 37 to 30 percent.

(distribution of white families by income; income in 1991 dollars; families as of the following year; numbers in thousands)

	total families	total	under $5,000	$5,000 to $9,999	$10,000 to $14,999	$15,000 to $24,999	$25,000 to $34,999	$35,000 to $49,999	$50,000 to $74,999	$75,000 to $99,999	$100,000 or over	median income
						percent distribution						
1991	57,224	100.0%	2.5%	4.8%	6.7%	15.7%	15.9%	20.3%	20.0%	8.0%	6.1%	$37,783
1990	56,803	100.0	2.3	4.4	6.7	15.2	16.1	20.6	20.1	8.0	6.6	38,468
1989	56,590	100.0	2.3	4.5	6.5	14.8	15.4	20.7	20.6	8.4	7.0	39,514
1988	56,492	100.0	2.5	4.5	6.5	15.1	15.8	20.7	20.5	8.1	6.3	39,047
1987	56,086	100.0	2.3	4.8	6.2	15.3	15.4	21.1	20.9	7.8	6.1	38,828
1986	55,676	100.0	2.6	4.9	6.6	15.4	15.8	21.0	20.3	7.4	5.9	38,286
1985	54,991	100.0	2.6	5.2	6.8	16.0	16.6	20.8	19.5	7.2	5.2	36,901
1984	54,400	100.0	2.6	5.1	7.2	16.2	16.7	21.2	19.4	6.7	4.8	36,293
1983	53,890	100.0	2.9	5.3	7.3	16.9	17.3	21.3	18.4	6.2	4.3	35,331
1982	53,407	100.0	2.8	5.3	7.4	17.0	17.6	21.5	18.3	5.9	4.1	35,052
1981	53,269	100.0	2.4	5.0	7.2	17.4	17.3	22.2	18.6	6.4	3.5	35,550
1980	52,710	100.0	2.1	5.0	6.9	16.8	17.3	22.8	19.2	6.2	3.6	36,249
1979	52,243	100.0	1.9	4.4	6.7	16.2	16.7	23.6	19.9	6.4	4.2	37,619
1978	50,910	100.0	2.0	4.4	7.2	16.2	16.9	23.4	20.0	5.8	4.1	37,063
1977	50,530	100.0	2.0	4.7	7.4	16.5	18.0	23.3	19.1	5.6	3.5	36,076
1976	50,083	100.0	1.8	4.9	7.6	16.8	18.1	23.8	18.7	5.1	3.2	35,625
1975	49,873	100.0	1.9	5.2	7.9	17.5	18.6	23.8	17.5	4.7	2.9	34,578
1974	49,440	100.0	1.9	4.5	7.3	16.7	19.6	23.5	18.1	5.2	3.1	35,186
1973	48,919	100.0	1.8	4.8	7.0	16.1	18.9	23.9	18.9	5.3	3.4	36,344
1972	48,477	100.0	2.0	5.0	6.9	16.8	19.1	24.1	17.8	5.2	3.2	35,427
1971	47,641	100.0	2.3	5.4	7.2	17.8	20.8	23.8	15.9	4.3	2.4	33,725
1970	46,535	100.0	2.4	5.5	7.0	17.3	21.4	23.9	15.9	4.2	2.5	33,756
1969	46,022	100.0	2.3	5.5	6.9	16.9	21.8	24.2	16.1	4.0	2.4	33,856
1968	45,437	100.0	2.5	5.4	7.6	18.2	22.5	24.3	14.4	3.3	1.9	32,287
1967	44,814	100.0	2.8	6.4	7.3	20.1	23.1	22.8	12.2	3.3	2.0	30,895

Percent change in median income

1980-91	4.2%
1967-91	22.3

Source: Bureau of the Census, Current Population Reports, Money Income of Households, Families, and Persons in the United States: 1991, *Series P-60, No. 180, 1992*

Distribution of Black Families by Income, 1967 to 1991

The share of black families with incomes of $50,000-plus more than doubled between 1967 and 1991, climbing from 6 to 15 percent. At the other extreme, the share with incomes below $5,000 also rose, from 8 to 11 percent.

(distribution of black families by income; income in 1991 dollars; families as of the following year; numbers in thousands)

	total families	total	under $5,000	$5,000 to $9,999	$10,000 to $14,999	$15,000 to $24,999	$25,000 to $34,999	$35,000 to $49,999	$50,000 to $74,999	$75,000 to $99,999	$100,000 or over	median income
						percent distribution						
1991	7,716	100.0%	11.4%	15.0%	11.1%	18.4%	14.5%	14.8%	10.3%	3.1%	1.4%	$21,548
1990	7,471	100.0	10.9	13.8	11.2	18.8	14.2	15.1	10.7	3.9	1.5	22,325
1989	7,470	100.0	9.7	13.7	12.6	18.9	13.7	14.6	11.5	3.7	1.6	22,197
1988	7,409	100.0	9.7	14.4	12.9	18.1	13.6	14.0	12.1	3.2	2.1	22,254
1987	7,202	100.0	9.9	14.8	11.7	19.4	14.0	14.3	10.6	3.4	1.8	22,068
1986	7,096	100.0	10.0	14.1	12.2	19.0	14.2	15.2	10.6	3.3	1.4	21,877
1985	6,921	100.0	9.2	15.2	12.1	21.2	13.8	14.9	10.1	2.5	1.1	21,248
1984	6,778	100.0	9.9	15.5	13.7	20.8	13.9	13.0	9.6	2.7	0.9	20,228
1983	6,681	100.0	10.3	16.4	12.8	20.3	14.4	14.1	8.9	2.3	0.5	19,912
1982	6,530	100.0	9.4	17.4	13.6	19.6	14.7	15.1	8.0	1.7	0.5	19,373
1981	6,413	100.0	8.4	16.2	13.5	21.1	14.6	14.6	9.4	1.9	0.3	20,054
1980	6,317	100.0	7.9	15.1	13.9	20.9	15.1	14.5	9.8	2.1	0.6	20,974
1979	6,184	100.0	7.1	15.1	13.8	21.5	14.0	15.4	10.3	2.3	0.6	21,302
1978	5,906	100.0	6.7	15.5	12.3	21.1	15.9	14.9	10.7	2.1	0.6	21,951
1977	5,806	100.0	6.8	14.8	15.1	22.4	15.0	14.6	9.0	1.7	0.6	20,609
1976	5,804	100.0	5.3	16.3	14.4	21.1	16.6	15.5	8.6	1.6	0.5	21,191
1975	5,586	100.0	5.8	16.0	14.6	22.1	16.2	15.8	7.8	1.4	0.4	21,276
1974	5,491	100.0	5.8	15.4	14.3	23.2	16.3	14.7	8.6	1.3	0.4	21,010
1973	5,440	100.0	6.1	14.9	15.2	22.9	16.4	14.5	7.7	1.7	0.6	20,975
1972	5,265	100.0	6.2	15.5	14.0	23.2	15.7	15.1	8.1	1.5	0.6	21,056
1971	5,157	100.0	6.0	16.2	13.7	25.2	16.6	13.6	7.3	1.0	0.4	20,351
1970	4,928	100.0	7.3	14.6	13.5	24.2	17.7	13.8	7.4	1.2	0.3	20,707
1969	4,774	100.0	7.3	13.1	15.1	25.6	17.6	13.4	6.6	0.9	0.2	20,738
1968	4,646	100.0	7.1	14.6	16.3	25.0	16.9	13.0	6.0	0.8	0.3	19,364
1967	4,589	100.0	8.4	17.1	15.1	26.9	15.8	10.8	4.3	1.1	0.5	18,291

Percent change in median income

1980-91	2.7%
1967-91	17.8

Source: Bureau of the Census, Current Population Reports, Money Income of Households, Families, and Persons in the United States: 1991, *Series P-60, No. 180, 1992*

Distribution of Hispanic Families by Income, 1972 to 1991

The share of Hispanic families with incomes at both the top and bottom of the income scale grew substantially between 1972 and 1991, while the share with incomes in the middle fell.

(distribution of Hispanic families by income; income in 1991 dollars; families as of the following year; numbers in thousands)

	total families	total	under $5,000	$5,000 to $9,999	$10,000 to $14,999	$15,000 to $24,999	$25,000 to $34,999	$35,000 to $49,999	$50,000 to $74,999	$75,000 to $99,999	$100,000 or over	median income
						percent distribution						
1991	5,177	100.0%	6.4%	12.4%	11.9%	21.5%	16.5%	15.0%	10.7%	3.2%	2.3%	$23,895
1990	4,981	100.0	5.8	11.6	13.0	20.6	16.7	16.5	10.3	3.6	2.1	24,417
1989	4,840	100.0	5.8	11.0	11.4	20.6	16.2	16.9	12.3	3.5	2.3	25,753
1988	4,823	100.0	7.2	10.6	11.7	20.5	16.8	15.9	11.8	3.4	2.2	25,063
1987	4,576	100.0	6.1	12.5	12.0	21.1	15.8	15.5	11.9	3.1	2.1	24,339
1986	4,403	100.0	6.0	11.8	13.1	20.2	16.5	15.8	11.5	3.5	1.6	24,848
1985	4,206	100.0	5.3	12.6	13.6	20.3	17.1	15.6	11.1	3.1	1.3	24,084
1984	3,939	100.0	6.4	11.8	12.0	20.6	17.4	16.5	11.0	2.8	1.5	24,686
1983	3,788	100.0	6.3	13.0	12.5	22.8	17.7	14.5	9.5	2.6	1.0	23,151
1982	3,369	100.0	5.6	13.2	13.5	21.9	16.8	15.3	10.6	1.7	1.4	23,118
1981	3,305	100.0	4.7	11.6	11.3	22.7	18.8	16.1	11.3	2.4	1.1	24,793
1980	3,235	100.0	4.7	11.1	13.1	23.1	17.5	16.5	10.4	2.2	1.2	24,354
1979	3,029	100.0	4.1	10.3	11.5	22.4	18.2	17.8	11.5	2.7	1.6	26,079
1978	2,741	100.0	3.6	10.9	11.6	23.8	18.1	18.3	10.3	2.3	1.0	25,355
1977	2,764	100.0	3.7	10.7	12.3	24.5	19.5	17.5	8.8	2.2	0.8	24,613
1976	2,583	100.0	3.8	12.0	13.9	23.9	18.0	17.0	8.6	2.2	0.6	23,523
1975	2,499	100.0	4.8	12.0	13.6	24.6	18.6	17.0	7.4	1.4	0.8	23,147
1974	2,475	100.0	3.4	10.4	13.1	23.2	21.0	17.8	8.6	1.8	0.9	25,036
1973	2,365	100.0	3.0	9.3	12.6	24.9	20.8	17.1	9.8	1.9	0.6	25,148
1972	2,312	100.0	3.3	10.1	12.8	25.1	21.9	16.6	7.8	1.5	0.9	25,102

Percent change in median income

1980-91	-1.9%
1972-91	-4.8

Note: Hispanics may be of any race.
Source: Bureau of the Census, Current Population Reports, Money Income of Households, Families, and Persons in the United States: 1991, *Series P-60, No. 180, 1992*

All Families: Share of Aggregate Income Accruing to Each Fifth and Top 5 Percent, 1967 to 1991

The richest fifth of American families received 44 percent of national income in 1991, up from 41 percent in 1967. The bottom fifth of families received less in 1991 than they did in 1967.

(distribution of aggregate income by family income quintiles; families as of the following year; numbers in thousands)

	total families	total	lowest fifth	second fifth	third fifth	fourth fifth	highest fifth	top 5 percent
							percent distribution of aggregate income	
1991	67,173	100.0%	4.5%	10.7%	16.6%	24.1%	44.2%	17.1%
1990	66,322	100.0	4.6	10.8	16.6	23.8	44.3	17.4
1989	66,090	100.0	4.6	10.6	16.5	23.7	44.6	17.9
1988	65,837	100.0	4.6	10.7	16.7	24.0	44.0	17.2
1987	65,204	100.0	4.6	10.8	16.8	24.0	43.8	17.2
1986	64,491	100.0	4.6	10.8	16.8	24.0	43.7	17.0
1985	63,558	100.0	4.7	10.9	16.8	24.1	43.5	16.7
1984	62,706	100.0	4.7	11.0	17.0	24.3	42.9	16.0
1983	62,015	100.0	4.7	11.1	17.1	24.3	42.8	15.9
1982	61,393	100.0	4.8	11.2	17.1	24.2	42.7	15.9
1981	61,019	100.0	5.1	11.3	17.4	24.4	41.8	15.3
1980	60,309	100.0	5.2	11.5	17.5	24.3	41.5	15.3
1979	59,550	100.0	5.3	11.6	17.5	24.0	41.7	15.8
1978	57,804	100.0	5.3	11.6	17.5	24.1	41.5	15.6
1977	57,215	100.0	5.3	11.6	17.5	24.2	41.4	15.7
1976	56,710	100.0	5.5	11.8	17.6	24.1	41.1	15.6
1975	56,245	100.0	5.5	11.8	17.6	24.1	41.1	15.5
1974	55,698	100.0	5.6	12.0	17.5	24.0	41.0	15.4
1973	55,053	100.0	5.5	11.9	17.5	24.0	41.1	15.5
1972	54,373	100.0	5.5	11.9	17.5	23.9	41.4	15.9
1971	53,296	100.0	5.5	12.0	17.6	23.8	41.0	15.6
1970	52,227	100.0	5.5	12.2	17.6	23.8	40.9	15.6
1969	51,586	100.0	5.6	12.4	17.7	23.7	40.6	15.6
1968	50,823	100.0	5.7	12.4	17.7	23.7	40.5	15.6
1967	50,111	100.0	5.4	12.2	17.5	23.5	41.4	16.4

Source: Bureau of the Census, Current Population Reports, Money Income of Households, Families, and Persons in the United States: 1991, *Series P-60, No. 180, 1992*

White Families: Share of Aggregate Income Accruing to Each Fifth and Top 5 Percent, 1967 to 1991

The richest fifth of white families received 43 percent of all income accruing to white families in 1991, up slightly from 41 percent in 1967. The poorest fifth received just 5 percent.

(distribution of aggregate income by white family income quintiles; families as of the following year; numbers in thousands)

	total families	percent distribution of aggregate income						
		total	bottom fifth	second fifth	third fifth	fourth fifth	top fifth	top 5 percent
1991	57,224	100.0%	5.0%	11.0%	16.7%	23.8%	43.4%	16.8%
1990	56,803	100.0	5.1	11.1	16.6	23.6	43.6	17.1
1989	56,590	100.0	5.0	11.0	16.6	23.4	44.0	17.7
1988	56,492	100.0	5.1	11.1	16.8	23.7	43.3	17.0
1987	56,086	100.0	5.1	11.2	16.9	23.8	43.1	16.9
1986	55,676	100.0	5.1	11.2	16.9	23.8	43.1	16.8
1985	54,991	100.0	5.1	11.2	16.9	23.9	42.9	16.5
1984	54,400	100.0	5.2	11.4	17.1	24.1	42.2	15.7
1983	53,890	100.0	5.2	11.5	17.2	24.1	42.1	15.7
1982	53,407	100.0	5.3	11.5	17.2	24.0	42.0	15.7
1981	53,269	100.0	5.5	11.7	17.4	24.2	41.2	15.1
1980	52,710	100.0	5.6	11.9	17.6	24.0	40.9	15.1
1979	52,243	100.0	5.7	11.9	17.5	23.8	41.1	15.6
1978	50,910	100.0	5.7	12.0	17.6	23.9	40.9	15.5
1977	50,530	100.0	5.7	12.0	17.6	23.9	40.8	15.5
1976	50,083	100.0	5.8	12.1	17.7	23.8	40.6	15.4
1975	49,873	100.0	5.8	12.1	17.6	23.9	40.6	15.4
1974	49,440	100.0	5.9	12.3	17.5	23.7	40.5	15.3
1973	48,919	100.0	5.9	12.3	17.6	23.7	40.5	15.3
1972	48,477	100.0	5.8	12.2	17.5	23.6	40.9	15.7
1971	47,641	100.0	5.8	12.4	17.6	23.6	40.6	15.5
1970	46,535	100.0	5.8	12.5	17.7	23.6	40.5	15.4
1969	46,022	100.0	5.9	12.7	17.7	23.5	40.2	15.5
1968	45,437	100.0	6.0	12.7	17.7	23.5	40.1	15.5
1967	44,814	100.0	5.8	12.5	17.5	23.3	40.9	16.2

Source: Bureau of the Census, Current Population Reports, Money Income of Households, Families, and Persons in the United States: 1991, *Series P-60, No. 180, 1992*

Black Families: Share of Aggregate Income Accruing to Each Fifth and Top 5 Percent, 1967 to 1991

The richest fifth of black families received 47 percent of all income accruing to black families in 1991, up slightly from 45 percent in 1967. The poorest fifth received just 3 percent.

(distribution of aggregate income by black family income quintiles; families as of the following year; numbers in thousands)

	total families	percent distribution of aggregate income						
		total	bottom fifth	second fifth	third fifth	fourth fifth	top fifth	top 5 percent
1991	7,716	100.0%	3.2%	8.4%	15.7%	25.4%	47.4%	17.3%
1990	7,471	100.0	3.3	8.6	15.6	25.3	47.3	17.3
1989	7,470	100.0	3.4	8.8	15.4	25.2	47.3	17.1
1988	7,409	100.0	3.3	8.5	15.2	25.1	47.9	17.7
1987	7,202	100.0	3.3	8.6	15.5	24.9	47.7	17.9
1986	7,096	100.0	3.4	8.8	15.5	25.2	47.1	17.6
1985	6,921	100.0	3.7	9.1	15.7	25.2	46.3	16.8
1984	6,778	100.0	3.7	8.9	15.5	24.9	46.9	16.7
1983	6,681	100.0	3.7	9.0	15.9	25.6	45.9	16.1
1982	6,530	100.0	3.9	9.1	15.9	25.8	45.4	16.1
1981	6,413	100.0	4.1	9.4	16.0	25.7	44.9	15.4
1980	6,317	100.0	4.2	9.6	16.0	25.4	44.8	15.6
1979	6,184	100.0	4.3	9.6	15.9	25.4	44.7	15.6
1978	5,906	100.0	4.3	9.7	16.3	25.3	44.4	15.5
1977	5,806	100.0	4.6	9.8	16.0	25.0	44.6	15.8
1976	5,804	100.0	4.8	9.9	16.4	25.4	43.5	15.3
1975	5,586	100.0	4.9	10.2	16.8	25.3	42.9	14.8
1974	5,491	100.0	4.8	10.2	16.6	25.2	43.2	14.8
1973	5,440	100.0	4.8	10.2	16.4	24.9	43.7	15.7
1972	5,265	100.0	4.6	10.1	16.3	25.0	44.0	15.7
1971	5,157	100.0	4.9	10.6	16.7	24.8	43.1	15.2
1970	4,928	100.0	4.6	10.6	16.8	24.9	43.1	15.2
1969	4,774	100.0	4.9	10.9	17.0	24.8	42.4	14.9
1968	4,646	100.0	5.0	10.8	16.6	24.8	42.7	15.0
1967	4,589	100.0	4.7	10.3	16.4	24.0	44.6	17.3

Source: Bureau of the Census, Current Population Reports, Money Income of Households, Families, and Persons in the United States: 1991, Series P-60, No. 180, 1992

Hispanic Families: Share of Aggregate Income Accruing to Each Fifth and Top 5 Percent, 1972 to 1991

The richest fifth of Hispanic families received 46 percent of all income accruing to Hispanic families in 1991, up sharply from 41 percent in 1967. The poorest fifth received just 4 percent.

(distribution of aggregate income by Hispanic family income quintiles; families as of the following year; numbers in thousands)

	total families	total	bottom fifth	second fifth	third fifth	fourth fifth	top fifth	top 5 percent
		percent distribution of aggregate income						
1991	5,177	100.0%	4.1%	9.7%	15.9%	24.1%	46.2%	17.6%
1990	4,981	100.0	4.3	9.8	16.0	24.2	45.7	17.5
1989	4,840	100.0	4.1	10.0	16.1	24.5	45.4	17.6
1988	4,823	100.0	4.0	9.8	15.9	24.2	46.1	18.4
1987	4,576	100.0	4.0	9.5	15.6	24.1	46.7	18.7
1986	4,403	100.0	4.2	9.9	16.2	24.7	45.1	16.4
1985	4,206	100.0	4.4	9.9	16.3	24.6	44.7	16.2
1984	3,939	100.0	4.2	10.1	16.6	24.7	44.4	16.4
1983	3,788	100.0	4.4	10.3	16.6	24.5	44.2	15.9
1982	3,369	100.0	4.6	10.1	16.5	24.5	44.4	16.4
1981	3,305	100.0	4.8	10.8	16.9	24.6	43.0	15.4
1980	3,235	100.0	4.9	10.7	16.7	24.6	43.2	16.0
1979	3,029	100.0	5.0	11.0	16.8	24.4	42.9	15.9
1978	2,741	100.0	5.3	11.2	17.1	24.7	41.7	15.0
1977	2,764	100.0	5.5	11.3	17.1	24.5	41.6	14.9
1976	2,583	100.0	5.4	11.1	17.0	24.8	41.8	15.0
1975	2,499	100.0	5.2	11.1	17.1	24.7	41.9	15.6
1974	2,475	100.0	5.7	11.5	17.5	24.4	41.0	14.9
1973	2,365	100.0	5.8	11.8	17.4	24.4	40.6	14.4
1972	2,312	100.0	5.8	11.8	17.5	23.8	41.2	15.7

Note: Hispanics may be of any race.
Source: Bureau of the Census, Current Population Reports, Money Income of Households, Families, and Persons in the United States: 1991, *Series P-60, No. 180, 1992*

All Families: Average Income of Each Fifth and Top 5 Percent, 1967 to 1991

The average income of families at all income levels rose between 1967 and 1991, after adjusting for inflation. The biggest gains went to families in the top two-fifths of the income distribution.

(average income for family income quintiles; income in 1991 dollars; families as of the following year; numbers in thousands)

	total families	average income						average income
		bottom fifth	second fifth	third fifth	fourth fifth	top fifth	top 5 percent	
1991	67,173	$9,734	$23,105	$35,851	$51,997	$95,530	$147,817	$43,237
1990	66,322	10,247	23,900	26,808	52,935	98,377	154,357	44,447
1989	66,090	10,359	24,184	37,571	54,055	101,780	163,042	45,590
1988	65,837	10,197	23,848	37,111	53,298	97,792	152,797	44,450
1987	65,204	10,157	23,872	37,069	53,053	96,956	151,779	44,222
1986	64,491	9,990	23,501	36,471	52,115	94,926	147,598	43,400
1985	63,558	9,675	22,711	35,132	50,356	90,627	139,104	41,700
1984	62,706	9,547	22,413	34,658	49,563	87,341	130,249	40,705
1983	62,015	9,236	21,823	33,648	47,964	84,381	125,729	39,410
1982	61,393	9,256	21,785	33,370	47,332	83,371	124,500	39,024
1981	61,019	9,782	22,126	33,958	47,682	81,741	119,935	39,058
1980	60,309	10,199	22,904	34,695	48,140	82,433	121,726	39,675
1979	59,550	10,765	23,750	35,870	49,395	85,589	129,585	41,074
1978	57,804	10,599	23,588	35,499	48,911	84,099	126,852	40,539
1977	57,215	10,282	22,865	34,483	47,588	81,584	123,614	39,360
1976	56,710	10,444	22,780	34,068	46,549	79,567	120,429	38,682
1975	56,245	10,205	22,226	33,119	45,351	77,481	117,113	37,676
1974	55,698	10,584	23,104	33,811	46,321	49,216	119,368	38,606
1973	55,053	10,746	23,451	34,457	47,090	80,794	121,931	39,308
1972	54,373	10,454	23,031	33,829	46,198	80,122	122,832	38,728
1971	53,296	9,999	22,020	32,217	43,631	75,150	114,585	36,603
1970	52,227	9,963	22,343	32,305	43,577	74,936	114,108	36,626
1969	51,586	10,149	22,635	32,391	43,390	74,312	114,138	36,563
1968	50,823	9,837	21,676	30,968	41,416	70,770	109,094	34,935
1967	50,111	9,106	20,606	29,619	39,723	70,141	110,975	33,022
Percent change								
1967-91	–	6.9%	12.1%	21.0%	30.9%	36.2%	33.2%	30.9%

Source: Bureau of the Census, Current Population Reports, Money Income of Households, Families, and Persons in the United States: 1991, *Series P-60. No. 180, 1992*

White Families: Average Income of Each Fifth and Top 5 Percent, 1967 to 1991

The average income of the poorest fifth of white families grew by 14 percent between 1967 and 1991, versus a 37 percent gain for white families in the top fifth.

(average income for white family income quintiles; income in 1991 dollars; families as of the following year; numbers in thousands)

	total families	average income						average income
		bottom fifth	second fifth	third fifth	fourth fifth	top fifth	top 5 percent	
1991	57,224	$11,407	$24,997	$37,773	$53,913	$98,313	$152,297	$45,274
1990	56,803	11,834	25,778	38,568	54,723	101,161	159,082	46,406
1989	56,590	11,975	26,222	39,479	55,887	104,844	168,279	47,673
1988	56,492	11,814	25,853	38,979	55,049	100,399	157,377	46,412
1987	56,086	11,794	25,864	38,958	54,864	99,534	156,196	46,194
1986	55,676	11,381	25,341	38,235	53,818	97,497	151,746	45,254
1985	54,991	10,930	24,450	36,830	52,070	93,281	143,357	43,512
1984	54,400	10,913	24,280	36,404	51,192	89,718	133,898	42,501
1983	53,890	10,549	23,564	35,290	49,534	86,643	129,011	41,116
1982	53,407	10,544	23,527	34,972	49,013	85,698	127,769	40,750
1981	53,269	11,012	23,836	35,542	49,218	83,968	123,209	40,715
1980	52,710	11,455	24,615	36,234	49,593	84,459	124,763	41,272
1979	52,243	12,125	25,526	37,462	50,827	87,855	133,119	42,759
1978	50,910	11,798	25,202	36,992	50,265	86,195	130,336	42,091
1977	50,530	11,452	24,585	36,018	48,982	83,666	126,985	40,940
1976	50,083	11,566	24,319	35,485	47,908	81,633	123,832	40,184
1975	49,873	11,170	23,624	34,397	46,621	79,413	120,399	39,045
1974	49,440	11,683	24,595	35,131	47,568	81,151	122,320	40,025
1973	48,919	11,906	25,113	35,963	48,527	82,831	125,324	40,869
1972	48,477	11,571	24,599	35,167	47,498	82,183	126,157	40,204
1971	47,641	10,931	23,448	33,424	44,788	76,958	117,631	37,912
1970	46,535	10,909	23,721	33,476	44,712	76,724	117,172	37,908
1969	46,022	11,121	24,063	33,628	44,586	76,148	117,467	37,863
1968	45,437	10,788	22,977	32,074	42,435	72,403	112,172	36,135
1967	44,814	9,999	21,942	30,703	40,766	71,702	113,601	34,204
Percent change								
1967-91	-	14.1%	13.9%	23.0%	32.2%	37.1%	34.1%	32.4%

Source: Bureau of the Census, Current Population Reports, Money Income of Households, Families, and Persons in the United States: 1991, *Series P-60, No. 180, 1992*

Black Families: Average Income of Each Fifth and Top 5 Percent, 1967 to 1991

The average income of the poorest black families fell between 1967 and 1991, after adjusting for inflation. In contrast, the average income of the black middle and upper classes grew substantially.

(average income of black family income quintiles; income in 1991 dollars; families as of the following year; numbers in thousands)

	total families	average income						average income
		bottom fifth	second fifth	third fifth	fourth fifth	top fifth	top 5 percent	
1991	7,716	$4,369	$11,594	$21,585	$35,022	$65,286	$95,201	$27,571
1990	7,471	4,721	12,325	22,394	36,295	67,860	99,563	28,714
1989	7,470	4,911	12,703	22,351	36,511	68,603	98,953	29,014
1988	7,409	4,841	12,336	22,220	36,628	69,813	103,161	29,147
1987	7,202	4,760	12,293	22,026	35,472	67,957	101,937	28,501
1986	7,096	4,782	12,457	22,000	35,670	66,620	99,402	28,306
1985	6,921	5,018	12,283	21,238	34,025	62,614	90,697	27,036
1984	6,778	4,785	11,595	20,138	32,318	60,801	86,497	25,927
1983	6,681	4,673	11,256	19,942	32,174	57,743	81,001	25,157
1982	6,530	4,771	11,225	19,501	31,685	55,758	79,334	24,589
1981	6,413	5,123	11,876	20,172	32,395	56,628	77,793	25,239
1980	6,317	5,519	12,546	20,966	33,193	58,564	81,510	26,158
1979	6,184	5,746	12,845	21,269	33,912	59,737	83,461	26,703
1978	5,906	5,821	13,081	22,066	34,201	60,112	83,879	27,056
1977	5,806	5,896	12,676	20,587	32,255	57,480	81,420	25,779
1976	5,804	6,131	12,850	21,155	32,890	56,255	79,221	25,855
1975	5,586	6,148	12,801	21,179	31,852	54,053	74,471	25,207
1974	5,491	6,101	12,956	20,997	31,906	54,619	75,144	25,316
1973	5,440	6,057	12,968	20,817	31,655	55,562	79,533	25,413
1972	5,265	5,939	12,859	20,810	32,028	56,367	80,551	25,602
1971	5,157	5,925	12,836	20,281	30,128	52,416	73,880	24,317
1970	4,928	5,619	12,990	20,641	30,604	52,867	74,580	24,542
1969	4,774	5,877	13,081	20,471	29,781	50,978	71,657	24,098
1968	4,646	5,730	12,475	19,216	28,681	49,350	69,065	23,093
1967	4,589	5,249	11,433	18,171	26,621	49,509	76,734	21,372
Percent change								
1967-91	–	-16.8%	1.4%	18.8%	31.6%	31.9%	24.1%	29.0%

Source: Bureau of the Census, Current Population Reports, Money Income of Households, Families, and Persons in the United States: 1991, *Series P-60, No. 180, 1992*

Hispanic Families: Average Income of Each Fifth and Top 5 Percent, 1972 to 1991

The average income of the poorest two-fifths of Hispanic families plunged between 1972 and 1991 as low-earning immigrants pulled down the numbers.

(average income of Hispanic family income quintiles; income in 1991 dollars; families as of the following year; numbers in thousands)

	total families	average income						average income
		bottom fifth	second fifth	third fifth	fourth fifth	top fifth	top 5 percent	
1991	5,177	$6,125	$14,502	$23,887	$36,148	$69,358	$105,813	$29,998
1990	4,981	6,569	14,924	24,432	36,999	69,830	107,087	30,544
1989	4,840	6,601	16,049	25,767	39,249	72,770	112,833	32,070
1988	4,823	6,209	15,382	25,063	38,104	72,587	115,503	31,461
1987	4,576	6,232	14,781	24,227	37,365	72,391	116,063	30,993
1986	4,403	6,392	14,960	24,543	37,446	68,509	99,906	30,370
1985	4,206	6,488	14,502	23,920	36,078	65,539	94,936	29,306
1984	3,939	6,193	14,936	24,540	36,604	65,647	97,186	29,584
1983	3,788	6,174	14,379	23,233	34,168	61,677	88,961	27,926
1982	3,369	6,391	14,200	23,157	34,433	62,414	92,226	28,119
1981	3,305	6,988	15,770	24,703	35,996	62,950	89,960	29,281
1980	3,235	7,035	15,569	24,324	35,836	62,995	93,405	29,151
1979	3,029	7,620	16,902	26,003	37,613	66,217	98,040	30,871
1978	2,741	7,744	16,550	25,315	36,554	61,706	89,002	29,575
1977	2,764	7,780	16,228	24,533	35,050	59,639	85,634	28,647
1976	2,583	7,422	15,386	23,475	34,243	57,743	82,958	27,653
1975	2,499	6,958	14,941	23,018	33,178	56,358	84,124	26,891
1974	2,475	8,075	16,305	24,873	34,717	58,432	85,000	28,481
1973	2,365	8,412	17,135	25,217	35,351	58,846	83,749	28,637
1972	2,312	8,206	16,599	24,620	33,575	58,081	88,548	28,215
Percent change								
1972-91	-	-25.4%	-12.6%	-3.0%	7.7%	19.4%	19.5%	6.3%

Note: Hispanics may be of any race.
Source: Bureau of the Census, Current Population Reports, Money Income of Households, Families, and Persons in the United States: 1991, *Series P-60, No. 180, 1992*

Median Income of Families by Age of Householder, 1947 to 1991

Between 1947 and 1991, the median incomes of families headed by 45-to-54-year-olds increased the most, up by 156 percent after adjusting for inflation.

(median income of families by age of householder; income in 1991 dollars)

	15 to 24	25 to 34	35 to 44	45 to 54	55 to 64	65 or older
1991	$16,848	$31,539	$41,859	$49,606	$40,014	$24,805
1990	16,902	32,822	42,789	49,149	40,678	26,103
1989	18,743	33,911	44,157	50,637	41,347	25,354
1988	19,344	33,999	44,717	48,576	40,495	24,989
1987	19,796	33,889	44,305	49,652	39,672	25,155
1986	18,572	33,421	43,485	48,293	39,559	24,769
1985	19,100	32,940	41,352	46,395	38,740	24,255
1984	18,078	32,978	40,839	45,202	38,413	23,878
1983	18,879	31,111	39,596	44,558	37,657	23,466
1982	20,325	31,751	39,150	43,776	35,777	22,963
1981	21,157	32,488	40,024	44,178	38,045	21,670
1980	22,826	33,780	40,829	45,108	38,944	21,319
1979	23,947	35,537	42,174	46,566	40,335	20,839
1978	24,084	35,057	41,322	45,632	39,004	20,462
1977	22,361	34,110	40,649	44,894	37,112	19,633
1976	21,643	33,912	39,872	43,650	36,957	19,997
1975	21,210	33,102	28,584	42,578	36,035	19,526
1974	22,689	33,974	40,254	43,450	35,740	19,695
1973	23,125	35,222	41,284	43,927	36,881	18,543
1972	22,844	34,237	40,243	43,118	35,814	18,307
1971	21,833	32,454	37,548	40,753	34,726	17,232
1970	23,207	32,493	37,628	39,973	34,235	16,664
1969	23,040	32,837	37,894	40,086	33,352	16,603
1968	22,486	31,507	36,272	37,692	31,843	16,590
1967	21,927	30,373	34,665	36,305	30,174	14,738
1966	21,711	29,155	33,234	34,286	29,353	14,104
1965	21,501	28,040	31,330	32,807	27,419	13,779
1964	19,383	26,581	30,360	31,330	27,062	13,644
1963	17,166	25,866	28,962	30,328	26,504	13,710
1962	17,756	24,508	28,349	29,233	25,824	13,304
1961	17,731	24,403	27,345	28,128	24,386	12,681
1960	16,978	24,068	27,155	27,401	23,611	12,254
1959	16,659	23,809	26,468	26,451	23,443	12,202
1958	16,409	22,586	24,742	24,889	22,352	11,564

(continued)

(continued from previous page)

(median income of families by age of householder; income in 1991 dollars)

	15 to 24	25 to 34	35 to 44	45 to 54	55 to 64	65 or older
1957	$17,371	$23,087	$24,811	$24,887	$21,314	$11,119
1956	17,435	22,685	24,663	24,898	21,019	11,733
1955	15,534	21,038	23,014	23,814	20,477	10,887
1954	14,628	19,847	21,722	22,440	18,900	10,700
1953	14,841	20,491	21,604	22,877	19,448	10,497
1952	14,514	19,059	20,520	20,596	17,994	10,764
1951	14,847	18,438	19,583	19,569	17,586	9,414
1950	13,584	17,493	18,943	19,151	16,937	9,893
1949	12,432	16,812	17,506	18,227	16,554	9,902
1948	13,584	16,396	17,904	18,746	16,900	9,913
1947	13,198	16,496	18,533	19,361	18,021	10,288
Percent change						
1947-91	27.7%	91.2%	125.9%	156.2%	122.0%	141.1%

Source: Bureau of the Census, Current Population Reports, Money Income of Households, Families, and Persons in the United States: 1991, *Series P-60, No. 180, 1992*

Median Income of Families by Family Type and Presence of Children, 1974 to 1991

Since 1974, the median income of all families with children has fallen because of the meager incomes of the growing share of families headed by single parents.

(median income of families by family type; income in 1991 dollars)

	all families		married-couple families		female householder, no spouse present		male householder, no spouse present	
	no children	one or more	no children	one or more	no children	one or more	no children	one or more
1991	$36,943	$34,990	$39,083	$42,514	$26,111	$13,012	$32,323	$24,171
1990	38,077	35,670	39,864	42,996	28,157	13,643	35,265	26,272
1989	38,479	36,750	40,468	43,930	28,321	14,256	35,168	27,192
1988	37,897	36,433	39,978	43,556	27,861	13,671	35,176	26,330
1987	37,312	36,974	39,232	43,674	27,222	13,626	32,368	27,813
1986	36,788	36,415	39,047	42,671	25,242	12,627	-	-
1985	35,145	35,069	37,294	40,947	25,213	12,754	-	-
1984	34,850	34,480	37,069	40,298	24,273	12,805	-	-
1983	33,969	33,262	36,026	38,515	22,630	12,516	-	-
1982	33,217	33,553	35,160	38,672	22,949	12,752	-	-
1981	33,330	34,352	35,392	39,636	22,270	13,922	-	-
1980	34,088	35,357	35,884	40,225	23,915	14,007	-	-
1979	34,622	37,177	36,432	41,627	24,514	15,087	-	-
1978	34,213	36,703	35,933	41,183	24,153	14,195	33,198	29,508
1977	33,016	35,744	34,582	40,183	23,365	14,012	32,496	29,494
1976	32,427	35,607	34,266	39,493	21,829	13,625	29,171	30,053
1975	31,537	34,513	32,848	38,112	22,456	13,293	33,485	28,520
1974	31,672	35,441	32,893	39,120	23,642	13,691	32,158	28,061
Percent change								
1974-91	16.6%	-1.3%	18.8%	8.7%	10.4%	-5.0%	0.5%	-13.9%

Source: Bureau of the Census, Current Population Reports, Money Income of Households, Families, and Persons in the United States: 1991, Series P-60, No. 180, 1992

Median Income of Families by Type of Family and Work Experience, 1947 to 1991

Between 1949 and 1991, the median income of married couples with working wives rose by over 137 percent, after adjusting for inflation. The incomes of those with nonworking wives rose just 87 percent.

(median income of families by family type and work experience; income in 1991 dollars)

	married-couple families			male householder, no spouse present	female householder, no spouse present
	total	wife in paid labor force	wife not in paid labor force		
1991	$40,995	$48,169	$30,075	$28,351	$16,692
1990	41,574	48,745	31,539	30,268	17,645
1989	42,340	49,720	31,575	30,587	18,060
1988	41,895	49,171	31,339	30,886	17,668
1987	41,818	48,858	31,940	30,223	17,604
1986	40,767	47,653	32,065	31,020	16,959
1985	39,366	46,114	31,083	28,635	17,291
1984	38,818	45,445	30,913	30,576	16,783
1983	37,439	43,964	30,155	29,982	16,184
1982	37,069	43,228	30,344	28,693	16,361
1981	37,890	44,211	30,724	30,065	16,568
1980	38,297	44,483	31,397	28,993	17,224
1979	39,441	45,758	32,589	30,936	18,185
1978	39,024	44,611	32,599	32,216	17,226
1977	37,964	43,679	32,462	31,287	16,734
1976	37,152	42,949	31,943	29,487	16,534
1975	36,030	41,774	30,904	31,493	16,586
1974	36,538	42,568	32,098	30,594	17,026
1973	37,594	43,968	32,948	30,997	16,728
1972	36,513	42,630	32,381	31,611	16,387
1971	34,729	40,617	30,792	27,562	16,161
1970	34,680	40,484	30,683	29,720	16,796
1969	34,572	40,200	30,693	28,830	16,669
1968	33,035	38,606	29,679	26,449	16,174
1967	31,671	37,356	28,557	25,567	16,111
1966	30,328	35,776	27,580	24,887	15,516
1965	28,933	34,237	26,252	24,484	14,066
1964	28,016	33,019	25,615	23,409	13,976
1963	26,966	31,858	24,700	23,354	13,133
1962	26,007	30,981	23,935	23,715	13,001
1961	25,300	30,123	34,435	21,285	12,543
1960	24,842	29,186	23,349	20,557	12,554

(continued)

(continued from previous page)

(median income of families by family type and work experience; income in 1991 dollars)

	married-couple families			male householder, no spouse present	female householder, no spouse present
	total	wife in paid labor force	wife not in paid labor force		
1959	$24,404	$28,899	$22,917	$19,883	$11,913
1958	23,054	26,954	21,614	18,478	11,889
1957	23,029	27,423	21,582	20,457	12,338
1956	22,883	27,410	21,373	19,174	12,672
1955	21,525	26,313	20,247	19,611	11,565
1954	20,211	24,889	18,895	18,723	10,700
1953	20,529	25,385	19,336	19,317	11,530
1952	19,205	23,173	18,028	17,096	10,570
1951	17,466	22,288	17,489	16,614	10,684
1950	17,914	20,809	17,233	16,193	9,991
1949	16,802	20,283	16,081	14,835	11,059
1948	17,009	-	-	17,129	10,730
1947	17,498	-	-	16,524	12,224
Percent change					
1949-91	144.0%	137.5%	87.0%	91.1%	50.9%

Source: Bureau of the Census, Current Population Reports, Money Income of Households, Families, and Persons in the United States: 1991, *Series P-60, No. 180, 1992*

Median Income of Married Couples by Work Experience, 1987 to 1991

Two-income couples in which both husband and wife work full-time, year-round had a median income of more than $57,000 in 1991. Even these couples suffered a drop in income since the late 1980s because of the recession.

(median income of married couples by work experience; income in 1991 dollars)

	1991	*1990*	*1989*	*1988*	*1987*
Married-couple families	$40,995	$41,574	$42,340	$41,895	$41,818
Husband worked	45,995	46,212	47,023	46,893	46,762
Wife worked	49,178	49,326	50,248	50,110	50,075
Wife worked full-time, year-round	54,391	54,857	55,980	56,068	55,492
Wife did not work	36,240	37,017	38,664	37,670	38,464
Husband worked full-time, year-round	50,092	49,578	50,657	50,417	50,574
Wife worked	52,707	52,406	53,395	53,486	53,393
Wife worked full-time, year-round	57,092	57,385	58,207	58,590	58,615
Wife did not work	40,518	40,728	42,288	41,614	42,630
Husband did not work	23,084	23,262	22,449	22,981	23,051
Wife worked	28,556	28,939	28,862	30,438	30,758
Wife worked full-time, year-round	34,278	34,014	33,346	36,029	36,900
Wife did not work	21,616	21,683	20,840	20,763	20,711

Source: Bureau of the Census, Current Population Reports, Money Income of Households, Families, and Persons in the United States: 1991, *Series P-60, No. 180, 1992*

Per Capita Income by Race and Hispanic Origin, 1967 to 1991

Per capita income grew by more than $5,000 between 1967 and 1991, after adjusting for inflation. Since 1980, it has grown by nearly $2,000 dollars.

(per capita income by race and Hispanic origin; income in 1991 dollars)

	all races	white	black	Hispanic
1991	$14,617	$15,510	$9,170	$8,662
1990	14,992	15,907	9,396	8,778
1989	15,439	16,362	9,608	9,215
1988	15,109	15,999	9,522	9,160
1987	14,856	15,758	9,166	9,176
1986	14,502	15,350	8,956	8,699
1985	13,940	14,773	8,658	8,371
1984	13,539	14,340	8,228	8,391
1983	13,057	13,846	7,870	8,002
1982	12,794	13,573	7,636	7,762
1981	12,813	13,573	7,753	8,086
1980	12,887	13,625	7,950	8,051
1979	13,193	13,940	8,179	8,157
1978	13,025	13,715	8,140	7,992
1977	12,467	13,146	7,702	7,625
1976	12,086	12,740	7,535	7,289
1975	11,676	12,292	7,203	6,900
1974	11,665	12,274	7,133	7,177
1973	11,949	12,584	7,275	7,081
1972	11,562	12,172	7,055	-
1971	10,798	11,364	6,516	-
1970	10,477	11,061	6,164	-
1969	10,395	10,972	6,091	-
1968	9,866	10,419	5,708	-
1967	9,245	9,770	5,260	-
Percent change				
1967-91	58.1%	58.8%	74.3%	-

Note: Hispanics may be of any race.
Source: Bureau of the Census, Current Population Reports, Money Income of Households, Families, and Persons in the United States: 1991, Series P-60, No. 180, 1992

All Men: Distribution by Income, 1967 to 1991

The proportion of men with incomes of $50,000 or more almost doubled between 1967 and 1991, while the share with incomes between $25,000 and $50,000 fell from 32 to 29 percent.

(distribution of men by income for those with income; income in 1991 dollars; men as of the following year; numbers in thousands)

| | total men | number with income | percent distribution | | | | | | | median income |
			under $5,000	$5,000 to $9,999	$10,000 to $14,999	$15,000 to $24,999	$25,000 to $49,999	$50,000 to $74,999	$75,000 or over	
1991	93,760	88,653	12.1%	13.0%	12.6%	21.1%	29.3%	7.6%	4.3%	$20,469
1990	92,840	88,220	11.7	12.6	12.4	21.0	29.9	8.1	4.3	21,147
1989	91,955	87,454	11.7	12.4	11.8	20.8	30.4	8.1	4.8	21,850
1988	91,034	86,584	12.2	12.2	11.9	20.4	30.8	8.2	4.4	21,769
1987	90,256	85,713	12.7	12.2	12.3	20.1	30.3	8.3	4.1	21,324
1986	89,368	84,471	13.1	12.5	11.8	20.3	30.1	8.0	4.1	21,268
1985	88,478	83,631	13.4	12.6	11.8	20.5	30.1	7.9	3.8	20,646
1984	87,304	82,183	14.0	13.0	11.9	20.3	29.8	7.5	3.5	20,450
1983	86,014	80,795	14.8	13.0	11.6	21.2	29.2	6.9	3.2	20,048
1982	84,955	79,722	14.5	13.1	12.1	20.5	29.8	6.8	3.2	19,874
1981	83,958	79,688	14.1	12.7	11.3	21.1	31.0	6.6	3.1	20,367
1980	82,949	78,661	13.4	12.6	11.4	21.3	31.8	6.6	3.1	20,736
1979	81,947	78,129	13.1	12.2	11.2	20.1	33.0	7.1	3.4	21,680
1978	80,969	75,609	13.3	11.9	11.1	20.3	32.3	7.8	3.4	22,064
1977	79,863	74,015	13.8	12.0	10.9	20.1	32.9	7.0	3.3	21,816
1976	78,782	72,775	13.8	12.2	11.3	20.0	32.9	7.0	2.9	21,613
1975	77,560	71,234	13.7	12.4	11.3	20.8	32.7	6.4	2.7	21,455
1974	76,363	70,863	13.5	11.8	10.7	20.1	33.9	6.9	3.1	22,180
1973	75,040	69,387	13.4	11.0	10.3	19.5	35.0	7.5	3.4	23,246
1972	73,572	67,474	13.8	11.3	9.7	20.6	34.6	6.7	3.5	22,853
1971	72,469	66,486	14.6	11.8	10.0	21.1	33.9	5.7	2.8	21,814
1970	70,592	65,008	15.1	11.4	9.8	21.1	34.3	5.5	2.7	21,996
1969	69,027	63,882	15.2	11.2	9.9	21.0	34.1	6.0	2.7	22,224
1968	67,611	62,501	15.5	11.0	10.4	21.7	34.2	5.1	2.2	21,604
1967	66,519	61,444	16.3	11.5	9.3	24.5	31.8	4.1	2.4	20,835

Percent change in median income

1989-91	-6.3%
1980-89	5.4
1973-80	-10.8
1967-73	11.6

Source: Bureau of the Census, Current Population Reports, Money Income of Households, Families, and Persons in the United States: 1991, *Series P-60, No. 180, 1992*

All Women: Distribution by Income, 1967 to 1991

Between 1967 and 1991, the proportion of women with incomes below $5,000 fell from 43 to 27 percent. The proportion with incomes above $25,000 climbed from 6 to 18 percent.

(distribution of women by income for those with income; income in 1991 dollars; women as of the following year; numbers in thousands)

	total women	number with income	percent distribution							median income
			under $5,000	$5,000 to $9,999	$10,000 to $14,999	$15,000 to $24,999	$25,000 to $49,999	$50,000 to $74,999	$75,000 or over	
1991	101,483	92,569	26.5%	21.7%	14.9%	19.3%	15.0%	1.8%	0.7%	$10,476
1990	100,680	92,245	27.4	21.1	14.7	18.8	15.3	1.9	0.7	10,494
1989	99,838	91,399	27.7	21.2	14.2	19.2	15.3	1.8	0.7	10,571
1988	99,019	90,593	28.5	21.3	14.6	18.6	14.8	1.6	0.6	10,228
1987	98,225	89,661	29.5	21.6	14.2	18.7	14.0	1.5	0.5	9,945
1986	97,320	87,822	30.5	22.0	14.0	18.3	13.4	1.3	0.5	9,457
1985	96,354	86,531	31.2	21.8	14.0	18.2	13.1	1.3	0.4	9,135
1984	95,282	85,555	31.6	22.3	14.4	18.0	12.1	1.1	0.4	9,003
1983	94,269	83,781	32.8	22.2	14.0	18.6	11.1	1.0	0.4	8,759
1982	93,145	82,505	33.8	22.7	14.6	17.5	10.3	0.8	0.3	8,387
1981	92,228	82,139	34.4	22.7	14.0	18.5	9.6	0.6	0.2	8,251
1980	91,133	80,826	35.3	22.4	14.3	17.9	9.2	0.7	0.2	8,142
1979	89,914	79,921	36.0	21.6	15.0	17.5	9.2	0.6	0.3	8,010
1978	88,617	71,864	34.3	22.3	15.1	18.5	9.0	0.6	0.2	8,208
1977	87,399	65,407	32.6	23.6	15.0	18.8	9.2	0.5	0.2	8,493
1976	86,157	63,170	33.3	23.8	15.6	17.8	8.8	0.5	0.2	8,200
1975	84,982	60,807	33.7	24.2	15.4	17.9	8.2	0.4	0.1	8,204
1974	83,599	59,642	34.0	23.8	15.5	17.8	8.3	0.4	0.2	8,088
1973	82,244	57,029	34.9	22.7	15.6	17.7	8.4	0.5	0.2	8,068
1972	80,896	54,487	35.6	22.5	14.1	18.8	8.3	0.4	0.2	7,973
1971	79,565	52,603	37.4	21.8	14.5	18.0	7.7	0.4	0.2	7,610
1970	77,649	51,647	39.2	20.9	14.7	17.2	7.4	0.4	0.2	7,377
1969	76,277	50,224	39.6	19.8	15.8	17.6	6.5	0.4	0.2	7,370
1968	74,889	48,544	40.4	19.7	16.7	16.4	6.3	0.3	0.1	7,294
1967	73,584	46,843	43.1	19.2	14.4	17.5	5.0	0.6	0.3	6,757

Percent change in median income

1989-91	-0.9%
1980-89	29.8
1973-80	0.9
1967-73	19.4

Source: Bureau of the Census, Current Population Reports, Money Income of Households, Families, and Persons in the United States: 1991, *Series P-60, No. 180, 1992*

White Men: Distribution by Income, 1967 to 1991

The proportion of white men with incomes between $25,000 and $50,000 fell from 34 to 30 percent between 1967 and 1991. At the same time, the proportion with both higher and lower incomes grew.

(distribution of white men by income for those with income; income in 1991 dollars; men as of the following year; numbers in thousands)

| | total men | number with income | percent distribution | | | | | | | median income |
			under $5,000	$5,000 to $9,999	$10,000 to $14,999	$15,000 to $24,999	$25,000 to $49,999	$50,000 to $74,999	$75,000 or over	
1991	80,049	76,578	10.8%	12.3%	12.4%	21.2%	30.4%	8.2%	4.7%	$21,395
1990	79,555	76,480	10.6	11.8	12.1	21.1	31.0	8.6	4.7	22,061
1989	78,908	75,858	10.8	11.5	11.5	20.6	31.7	8.7	5.2	22,916
1988	78,230	75,247	11.2	11.2	11.6	20.6	31.9	8.7	4.7	22,979
1987	77,743	74,647	11.6	11.3	11.9	20.1	31.6	8.9	4.5	22,666
1986	77,212	73,827	12.1	11.8	11.3	20.4	31.3	8.6	4.5	22,443
1985	76,617	73,222	12.4	11.9	11.5	20.2	31.4	8.5	4.1	21,659
1984	75,487	72,162	13.0	12.2	11.6	20.2	31.2	8.1	3.8	21,586
1983	74,805	71,231	13.7	12.2	11.4	21.3	30.5	7.5	3.5	21,092
1982	74,043	70,477	13.5	12.4	11.7	20.5	31.1	7.3	3.4	21,011
1981	72,449	70,351	13.2	12.0	10.9	21.0	32.3	7.2	3.4	21,611
1980	72,449	69,420	12.2	11.9	11.1	21.1	33.2	7.2	3.3	22,057
1979	71,887	69,247	12.2	11.5	10.8	19.9	34.2	7.7	3.7	22,648
1978	71,308	67,273	12.4	11.3	10.6	20.3	33.3	8.3	3.7	23,110
1977	70,407	65,974	12.9	11.5	10.2	20.0	34.2	7.2	3.6	22,850
1976	69,555	64,946	12.9	11.5	10.9	19.7	34.2	7.6	3.2	22,785
1975	68,573	63,629	12.8	11.7	10.9	20.5	34.1	7.0	2.9	22,538
1974	67,667	63,207	12.7	11.1	10.3	19.7	35.2	7.4	3.4	23,235
1973	66,550	62,082	12.6	10.5	9.8	19.0	36.4	8.1	3.7	24,392
1972	65,385	60,565	12.9	10.8	9.2	20.1	36.0	7.2	3.8	23,970
1971	64,611	59,729	13.7	11.3	9.5	20.7	35.5	6.2	3.1	22,870
1970	63,002	58,447	14.1	11.0	9.2	20.7	35.9	6.0	3.0	23,121
1969	61,645	57,343	14.2	10.9	9.2	20.5	35.8	6.5	2.9	23,386
1968	60,498	56,219	14.4	10.6	9.7	21.4	36.0	5.5	2.4	22,641
1967	59,524	55,270	15.3	11.0	8.6	24.2	33.8	4.4	2.6	21,935

Percent change in median Income

1989-91	-6.6%
1980-89	3.9
1973-80	-9.6
1967-73	11.2

Source: Bureau of the Census, Current Population Reports, Money Income of Households, Families, and Persons in the United States: 1991, Series P-60, No. 180, 1992

White Women: Distribution by Income, 1967 to 1991

In contrast to white men, the proportion of white women with incomes between $25,000 and $50,000 tripled between 1967 and 1991, rising from 5 percent to 15 percent.

(distribution of white women by income for those with income; income in 1991 dollars; women as of the following year; numbers in thousands)

	total women	number with income	percent distribution							median income
			under $5,000	$5,000 to $9,999	$10,000 to $14,999	$15,000 to $24,999	$25,000 to $49,999	$50,000 to $74,999	$75,000 or over	
1991	85,510	78,721	26.2%	21.2%	15.1%	19.4%	15.4%	1.9%	0.7%	$10,721
1990	85,012	78,566	27.1	20.6	14.8	19.1	15.6	2.0	0.7	10,751
1989	84,508	77,933	27.4	20.8	14.3	19.5	15.5	1.8	0.7	10,777
1988	84,035	77,493	28.2	21.0	14.5	18.9	15.2	1.7	0.7	10,480
1987	83,552	76,940	29.0	21.2	14.4	18.9	14.4	1.6	0.6	10,199
1986	83,003	75,587	30.3	21.5	14.0	18.6	13.7	1.4	0.5	9,643
1985	82,345	74,640	31.0	21.4	14.1	18.3	13.3	1.4	0.5	9,312
1984	81,603	73,977	31.7	21.8	14.5	18.2	12.3	1.1	0.4	9,109
1983	80,901	72,643	32.6	21.7	14.1	18.7	11.4	1.0	0.4	8,912
1982	80,066	71,624	33.7	22.3	14.6	17.6	10.6	0.8	0.4	8,501
1981	79,591	71,566	34.3	22.4	14.0	18.6	9.9	0.7	0.2	8,343
1980	78,766	70,573	35.5	21.9	14.3	17.9	9.4	0.7	0.3	8,187
1979	77,882	69,839	36.0	21.2	15.0	17.6	9.3	0.6	0.3	8,085
1978	77,091	62,695	34.4	21.9	15.2	18.6	9.1	0.7	0.2	8,307
1977	76,194	56,813	32.5	23.2	15.0	19.1	9.4	0.6	0.3	8,622
1976	75,239	55,026	33.5	23.3	15.5	18.0	9.0	0.5	0.3	8,268
1975	74,351	52,936	33.7	23.7	15.5	18.1	8.4	0.4	0.1	8,288
1974	73,312	52,038	33.7	23.6	15.6	17.9	8.6	0.5	0.2	8,180
1973	72,248	49,741	34.7	22.4	15.3	18.0	8.8	0.5	0.2	8,146
1972	71,226	47,519	35.7	22.1	13.9	19.0	8.6	0.5	0.2	8,025
1971	70,293	45,941	37.1	21.4	14.5	18.4	7.9	0.4	0.2	7,736
1970	68,793	45,288	39.0	20.4	14.6	17.7	7.6	0.4	0.2	7,473
1969	67,680	44,025	39.2	19.4	15.7	18.2	6.9	0.4	0.2	7,543
1968	66,543	42,482	39.7	19.2	16.7	17.1	6.7	0.4	0.2	7,511
1967	66,240	41,045	42.4	18.7	14.4	18.2	5.3	0.6	0.3	6,960

Percent change in median Income

1989-91	-0.5%
1980-89	31.6
1973-80	0.5
1967-73	17.0

Source: Bureau of the Census, Current Population Reports, Money Income of Households, Families, and Persons in the United States: 1991, *Series P-60, No. 180, 1992.*

Black Men: Distribution by Income, 1967 to 1991

The proportion of black men with incomes between $25,000 and $50,000 climbed from 13 to 21 percent between 1967 and 1991.

(distribution of black men by income for those with income; income in 1991 dollars; men as of the following year; numbers in thousands)

	total men	number with income	percent distribution							median income
			under $5,000	$5,000 to $9,999	$10,000 to $14,999	$15,000 to $24,999	$25,000 to $49,999	$50,000 to $74,999	$75,000 or over	
1991	10,252	8,943	21.6%	18.7%	14.8%	20.4%	21.0%	2.5%	0.8%	$12,962
1990	10,074	8,820	19.9	19.2	14.5	20.8	21.4	3.5	0.8	13,409
1989	9,948	8,806	19.5	19.5	14.0	22.9	20.5	2.8	0.8	13,850
1988	9,809	8,610	20.2	19.5	14.0	19.9	22.3	3.0	1.1	13,866
1987	9,668	8,488	20.6	19.3	15.7	20.9	20.2	2.8	0.7	13,446
1986	9,472	8,285	21.4	18.8	15.8	20.8	19.8	2.7	0.7	13,449
1985	9,309	8,127	20.8	19.1	13.8	23.5	19.7	2.2	0.8	13,630
1984	9,141	7,851	22.4	20.9	14.8	21.3	17.9	2.3	0.5	12,385
1983	8,986	7,587	23.9	20.2	13.5	22.3	17.8	1.9	0.5	12,335
1982	8,757	7,290	23.3	19.1	16.1	20.9	18.7	1.4	0.5	12,591
1981	8,614	7,459	22.7	18.6	14.4	22.4	20.1	1.5	0.3	12,851
1980	8,448	7,387	23.5	18.4	13.3	23.2	19.5	1.6	0.4	13,254
1979	8,292	7,288	21.0	18.7	14.2	21.4	22.2	2.0	0.5	14,019
1978	8,148	6,971	21.3	17.2	15.5	20.1	23.1	2.5	0.4	13,844
1977	8,057	6,777	20.8	17.1	16.7	22.3	20.6	1.9	0.6	13,560
1976	7,914	6,651	21.6	18.0	14.6	22.4	21.2	1.8	0.3	13,719
1975	7,720	6,485	21.1	19.0	15.1	22.5	20.9	1.1	0.2	13,475
1974	7,507	6,409	20.3	18.2	14.2	23.8	21.8	1.5	0.2	14,397
1973	7,415	6,394	20.9	16.0	14.6	24.4	22.0	1.6	0.4	14,754
1972	7,200	6,043	22.1	15.7	14.0	25.0	21.3	1.3	0.5	14,519
1971	7,041	6,024	23.1	17.0	14.5	25.7	18.4	0.9	0.3	13,639
1970	6,796	5,844	23.5	15.3	15.8	25.4	18.6	0.9	0.3	13,709
1969	6,637	5,870	24.0	14.5	16.6	26.3	17.5	1.0	0.1	13,603
1968	6,456	5,715	25.2	14.6	16.5	25.8	17.1	0.7	0.2	13,432
1967	6,318	5,572	26.0	16.6	16.3	27.5	12.8	0.7	0.3	12,554

Percent change in median income

1989-91	-6.4%
1980-89	4.5
1973-80	-10.2
1967-73	17.5

Source: Bureau of the Census, Current Population Reports, Money Income of Households, Families, and Persons in the United States: 1991, *Series P-60, No. 180, 1992*

Black Women: Distribution by Income, 1967 to 1991

The proportion of black women with incomes under $5,000 fell from 49 to 28 percent between 1967 and 1991. The proportion with incomes above $25,000 rose from 3 to 14 percent.

(distribution of black women by income for those with income; income in 1991 dollars; women as of the following year; numbers in thousands)

| | total women | number with income | percent distribution | | | | | | | median income |
			under $5,000	$5,000 to $9,999	$10,000 to $14,999	$15,000 to $24,999	$25,000 to $49,999	$50,000 to $74,999	$75,000 or over	
1991	12,288	10,727	28.3%	26.4%	13.5%	18.1%	12.2%	1.0%	.4%	$8,816
1990	12,124	10,687	30.2	25.0	14.0	16.5	12.9	1.0	.3	8,678
1989	11,966	10,577	29.9	24.9	13.0	17.6	13.1	1.2	.3	8,650
1988	11,786	10,380	30.3	24.5	15.2	17.0	12.1	.8	.1	8,461
1987	11,663	10,164	31.7	25.7	13.3	17.3	11.3	.6	.1	8,331
1986	11,447	9,819	31.5	27.2	13.3	16.7	10.3	.7	.2	8,160
1985	11,263	9,611	32.4	26.3	13.0	16.9	10.8	.5	.1	7,945
1984	11,092	9,460	31.2	27.5	14.4	16.4	9.9	.6	.1	8,080
1983	10,911	9,107	33.8	26.3	13.6	17.3	8.6	.4	-	7,615
1982	10,687	8,921	34.1	26.7	14.7	16.7	7.6	.2	.1	7,498
1981	10,511	8,829	35.5	26.2	14.0	17.2	6.9	.3	-	7,412
1980	10,317	8,596	34.6	26.7	14.1	17.0	7.3	.3	.1	7,580
1979	10,108	8,533	35.9	24.7	15.4	15.7	8.0	.3	-	7,358
1978	9,902	7,959	33.9	26.2	14.7	17.5	7.6	.2	-	7,480
1977	9,684	7,562	34.3	26.4	15.0	16.4	7.6	.2	-	7,446
1976	9,484	7,188	32.6	27.7	16.0	16.5	7.1	.2	-	7,791
1975	9,269	6,969	34.1	28.3	15.2	16.4	6.0	.1	-	7,530
1974	9,047	6,779	35.2	26.4	15.7	16.6	5.9	.2	-	7,385
1973	8,839	6,513	36.4	25.4	17.0	15.3	5.7	.1	-	7,352
1972	8,616	6,274	35.9	25.8	15.4	16.8	5.8	.2	.1	7,497
1971	8,428	6,151	40.0	25.4	14.4	14.6	5.5	.1	-	6,778
1970	8,041	5,844	40.3	25.1	15.9	13.7	5.0	.1	-	6,803
1969	7,841	5,728	43.1	23.0	17.2	12.9	3.7	.1	-	6,361
1968	7,636	5,629	45.2	23.4	16.8	11.2	3.4	-	-	5,957
1967	7,461	5,397	48.5	23.0	14.1	11.5	2.2	.5	.1	5,478

Percent change in median income

1989-91	1.9%
1980-89	14.1
1973-80	3.1
1967-73	34.2

Source: Bureau of the Census, Current Population Reports, Money Income of Households, Families, and Persons in the United States: 1991, *Series P-60, No. 180, 1992*

Hispanic Men: Distribution by Income, 1972 to 1991

While the proportion of Hispanic men with incomes under $5,000 fell between 1972 and 1991, the proportion with incomes of $5,000 to $15,000 rose sharply, from 28 to 40 percent.

(distribution of Hispanic men by income for those with income; income in 1991 dollars; men as of the following year; numbers in thousands)

	total men	number with income	percent distribution							median income
			under $5,000	$5,000 to $9,999	$10,000 to $14,999	$15,000 to $24,999	$25,000 to $49,999	$50,000 to $74,999	$75,000 or over	
1991	7,738	6,939	13.5%	21.2%	18.5%	22.5%	20.2%	2.9%	1.2%	$13,818
1990	7,502	6,767	14.8	19.6	18.9	22.7	19.8	2.9	1.2	14,037
1989	7,254	6,592	14.7	18.5	18.1	24.6	19.5	2.9	1.6	14,718
1988	7,012	6,342	15.9	16.9	18.1	23.9	20.9	2.9	1.4	15,002
1987	6,768	6,102	14.9	19.2	17.4	22.8	20.8	3.6	1.4	14,663
1986	6,517	5,870	16.7	19.5	17.4	22.1	20.1	3.2	1.1	14,331
1985	6,232	5,523	16.2	18.6	16.9	22.7	21.9	2.8	1.0	14,473
1984	5,809	5,174	17.8	18.4	15.9	22.4	21.4	2.9	1.0	14,552
1983	5,633	4,236	16.6	18.5	16.0	25.2	20.4	2.4	0.8	14,825
1982	4,592	4,092	16.8	18.2	17.2	23.4	20.9	2.5	1.0	14,918
1981	4,557	4,131	16.1	15.9	16.9	24.8	22.6	2.8	0.9	15,423
1980	4,429	3,996	15.9	15.9	16.4	26.0	22.5	2.2	1.0	15,985
1979	4,196	3,852	16.0	14.7	16.0	25.5	24.1	2.4	1.2	16,327
1978	3,880	3,447	15.1	13.4	16.2	26.7	24.7	2.8	1.1	16,909
1977	3,848	3,376	15.4	14.0	14.7	28.5	23.8	2.7	0.9	16,803
1976	3,526	3,099	17.2	14.6	16.0	24.9	24.1	2.6	0.6	16,165
1975	3,415	2,945	16.6	14.6	15.3	28.9	22.0	1.8	0.7	16,424
1974	3,519	3,052	15.9	14.6	14.7	27.1	24.4	2.2	1.1	16,908
1973	3,433	2,867	15.2	12.4	14.1	28.8	26.4	2.3	0.6	17,891
1972	3,204	2,709	15.3	13.4	14.9	27.6	26.1	1.8	0.9	17,749

Percent change in median income

1980-91	-6.1%
1980-89	-7.9
1972-80	-9.9

Note: Hispanics may be of any race.
Source: Bureau of the Census, Current Population Reports, Money Income of Households, Families, and Persons in the United States: 1991, Series P-60, No. 180, 1992

Hispanic Women: Distribution by Income, 1972 to 1991

There has been little change in the income distribution of Hispanic women since 1972, except for a rise in the proportion with incomes of $25,000 or more, increasing from 4 to 10 percent.

(distribution of Hispanic women by income for those with income; income in 1991 dollars; women as of the following year; numbers in thousands)

	total women	number with income	| percent distribution							median income
			under $5,000	$5,000 to $9,999	$10,000 to $14,999	$15,000 to $24,999	$25,000 to $49,999	$50,000 to $74,999	$75,000 or over	
1991	7,806	6,084	32.9%	26.4%	15.1%	15.6%	8.8%	0.8%	0.3%	$8,013
1990	7,559	5,903	33.7	25.3	15.5	15.1	9.3	0.9	0.2	7,849
1989	7,323	5,677	33.1	24.7	14.8	16.5	9.8	1.0	0.3	8,399
1988	7,045	5,532	34.9	24.1	15.5	14.6	10.0	0.6	0.3	8,048
1987	6,835	5,357	34.1	26.5	13.9	15.6	9.0	0.7	0.3	7,949
1986	6,588	5,096	34.5	26.3	13.9	16.0	8.8	0.5	0.2	7,876
1985	6,366	4,843	34.9	26.1	14.2	16.2	8.0	0.4	0.1	7,620
1984	5,967	4,617	35.0	25.3	15.3	16.4	7.4	0.4	0.1	7,642
1983	5,790	4,098	36.1	26.5	15.1	15.4	6.4	0.4	0.2	7,345
1982	5,119	3,832	37.2	25.8	15.6	14.8	6.3	0.3	0.1	7,323
1981	4,955	3,787	37.4	24.4	15.6	16.3	6.0	0.3	0.1	7,649
1980	4,734	3,617	38.7	25.6	16.4	14.0	5.0	0.3	0.1	7,290
1979	4,501	3,495	36.8	24.4	18.3	14.5	5.7	0.4	-	7,638
1978	4,178	2,949	35.1	25.9	17.6	16.0	5.1	0.3	0.1	7,643
1977	4,212	2,780	34.9	26.1	17.8	16.2	5.0	0.1	0.1	7,907
1976	3,922	2,568	35.7	25.6	19.3	15.2	4.0	0.2	-	7,702
1975	3,777	2,380	36.3	26.3	18.9	14.5	4.0	-	-	7,760
1974	3,743	2,353	33.8	26.7	19.5	15.7	4.1	0.1	-	7,894
1973	3,752	2,154	33.8	26.9	17.9	16.2	4.8	0.3	0.1	7,653
1972	3,511	1,928	35.1	26.2	18.6	15.8	4.1	0.2	-	8,120

Percent change in median income:

1989-91	-4.6%
1980-89	15.2
1972-80	-10.2

Note: Hispanics may be of any race.
Source: Bureau of the Census, Current Population Reports, Money Income of Households, Families, and Persons in the United States: 1991, Series P-60, No. 180, 1992

Median Income of Men by Age, 1947 to 1991

Since 1947, the incomes of men aged 65 or older have increased the most, after adjusting for inflation. The incomes of men aged 25 to 34 have grown the least.

(median income of men by age; income in 1991 dollars)

	15 to 24	25 to 34	35 to 44	45 to 54	55 to 64	65 or older
1991	$6,281	$21,595	$29,301	$31,779	$25,460	$14,357
1990	6,585	22,293	31,026	32,312	25,848	14,780
1989	6,934	23,469	32,333	34,008	26,830	14,397
1988	6,727	23,927	32,864	34,053	26,074	14,358
1987	6,543	23,891	32,422	34,154	26,236	14,300
1986	6,565	23,813	32,524	34,492	26,139	14,346
1985	6,323	23,622	32,098	32,715	25,641	13,797
1984	6,173	23,718	32,203	32,233	25,597	13,699
1983	-	22,953	30,693	31,543	25,527	13,532
1982	6,307	23,388	30,843	30,692	25,399	13,090
1981	-	24,326	31,922	31,778	26,250	12,355
1980	7,608	25,784	33,160	33,055	26,336	12,150
1979	7,833	27,004	33,763	33,525	27,660	11,840
1978	7,369	27,058	33,439	33,443	27,490	12,038
1977	6,976	26,639	33,628	33,039	26,384	11,909
1976	6,812	26,866	32,849	32,317	26,421	12,136
1975	6,897	26,748	32,308	32,007	25,786	12,018
1974	7,120	27,767	33,504	32,460	26,172	12,171
1973	-	29,110	34,714	33,678	27,563	11,848
1972	-	28,277	33,851	33,041	27,307	11,491
1971	-	27,057	31,497	30,504	25,072	10,899
1970	-	27,227	31,214	30,251	25,321	10,144
1969	-	27,565	31,267	29,795	25,162	9,776
1968	-	26,485	29,913	28,190	24,267	9,581
1967	-	25,510	28,651	27,683	22,970	8,645
1966	-	25,178	28,265	26,768	22,249	8,365
1965	-	23,923	26,738	25,340	20,908	8,427
1964	-	23,170	26,270	24,552	19,969	8,233
1963	-	22,373	25,494	23,837	20,046	8,152
1962	-	21,651	24,861	23,345	19,932	7,931
1961	-	21,142	23,996	22,299	19,265	7,367
1960	-	20,743	23,387	21,910	18,142	7,182
1959	-	20,460	22,930	20,913	18,059	6,793
1958	-	19,341	21,358	19,523	17,212	6,454
1957	-	19,523	21,189	20,068	16,438	6,346

(continued)

(continued from previous page)

(median income of men by age; income in 1991 dollars)

	15 to 24	25 to 34	35 to 44	45 to 54	55 to 64	65 or older
1956	-	$19,376	$21,051	$19,836	$16,413	$6,539
1955	-	18,188	19,915	19,368	16,101	6,258
1954	-	17,090	18,895	17,776	14,903	5,914
1953	-	17,420	18,683	17,922	15,362	5,401
1952	-	16,519	17,540	16,486	14,230	5,897
1951	-	15,824	17,408	15,786	13,668	4,851
1950	-	15,393	16,916	16,068	12,965	5,126
1949	-	14,482	15,518	14,467	12,442	5,343
1948	-	14,161	15,835	14,701	12,539	5,188
1947	-	13,783	16,012	15,089	13,192	5,380
Percent change						
1947-91	-	56.7%	83.0%	110.6%	93.0%	166.9%

Source: Bureau of the Census, Current Population Reports, Money Income of Households, Families, and Persons in the United States: 1991, *Series P-60, No. 180, 1992*

Median Income of Women by Age, 1947 to 1991

Since 1947, the incomes of women aged 65 or older have increased the most, after adjusting for inflation. The incomes of women aged 55 to 64 have grown the least.

(median income of women by age; income in 1991 dollars)

	15 to 24	25 to 34	35 to 44	45 to 54	55 to 64	65 or older
1991	$5,197	$12,964	$15,125	$14,724	$9,902	$8,189
1990	5,108	13,119	15,114	14,829	9,796	8,382
1989	5,205	13,434	15,163	14,436	10,065	8,408
1988	5,164	13,315	14,444	13,839	9,645	8,178
1987	5,285	13,163	14,381	13,504	9,041	8,268
1986	5,025	12,812	13,749	12,899	9,167	7,984
1985	4,799	12,505	13,006	12,176	9,080	7,991
1984	4,731	12,312	12,533	11,671	8,962	7,891
1983	-	11,625	12,108	11,269	8,729	7,811
1982	4,776	11,358	11,185	10,688	8,416	7,643
1981	-	11,486	11,135	10,627	8,125	7,191
1980	5,170	11,540	10,699	10,596	8,152	6,994
1979	5,196	11,687	10,835	10,300	8,073	6,922
1978	5,210	11,782	11,711	11,445	9,026	6,780
1977	4,933	12,719	11,935	12,219	9,769	6,655
1976	4,604	12,318	11,827	12,224	9,296	6,457
1975	4,566	12,243	11,403	12,277	9,452	6,403
1974	4,650	11,846	11,681	12,384	9,508	6,264
1973	-	11,952	11,860	12,417	9,900	6,115
1972	-	11,672	11,847	12,476	9,844	5,825
1971	-	11,203	11,477	12,384	9,736	5,391
1970	-	10,635	11,377	12,192	9,715	5,019
1969	-	10,371	11,190	12,299	9,648	4,829
1968	-	10,408	10,997	11,788	9,306	4,736
1967	-	9,815	10,641	11,560	8,825	4,214
1966	-	9,093	10,022	10,672	8,567	4,198
1965	-	8,988	9,892	10,195	8,041	3,919
1964	-	8,229	9,130	9,740	7,719	3,848
1963	-	7,591	8,773	9,452	7,256	3,763
1962	-	7,366	8,641	9,389	6,930	3,820
1961	-	7,799	8,897	8,775	6,202	3,579
1960	-	7,423	8,603	8,891	5,985	3,473
1959	-	7,444	7,965	8,762	6,168	3,435
1958	-	7,248	7,881	8,172	5,752	3,366
1957	-	7,667	7,967	8,118	5,993	3,309

(continued)

(continued from previous page)

(median income of women by age; income in 1991 dollars)

	15 to 24	25 to 34	35 to 44	45 to 54	55 to 64	65 or older
1956	-	$7,243	$7,988	$8,052	$6,276	$3,396
1955	-	7,493	7,404	8,074	5,883	3,276
1954	-	7,384	7,379	7,612	5,574	3,237
1953	-	7,716	7,519	7,965	5,495	3,095
1952	-	7,463	7,505	7,453	5,557	3,093
1951	-	7,811	7,402	6,386	4,659	2,580
1950	-	7,044	6,800	6,457	4,772	2,760
1949	-	6,952	6,752	6,126	5,259	2,713
1948	-	7,013	6,930	6,810	4,455	3,062
1947	-	6,838	7,497	7,277	5,414	3,101

Percent change

| 1947-91 | - | 89.6% | 101.7% | 102.3% | 82.9% | 164.1% |

Source: Bureau of the Census, Current Population Reports, Money Income of Households, Families, and Persons in the United States: 1991, *Series P-60, No. 180, 1992*

Median Income of Men by Work Experience, 1967 to 1991

The incomes of men who work full-time, year-round are lower today than they were 20 years ago, after adjusting for inflation.

(median income of men by work experience; income in 1991 dollars)

	total working men	worked full-time		worked part-time	
		total	50 to 52 weeks	total	50 to 52 weeks
1991	$21,857	$25,527	$29,421	$3,979	$6,928
1990	22,428	25,886	28,843	4,107	7,157
1989	23,479	26,892	30,020	3,718	7,202
1988	23,731	26,933	30,689	3,637	7,075
1987	23,761	26,577	31,108	3,398	7,058
1986	23,340	26,804	31,386	3,468	7,009
1985	22,505	26,220	30,626	3,462	6,818
1984	22,319	26,233	30,436	3,298	6,911
1983	21,978	25,488	29,922	3,261	6,598
1982	21,902	25,110	30,028	3,489	6,907
1981	22,767	25,830	30,626	3,389	6,703
1980	23,187	26,396	30,801	3,396	6,923
1979	23,831	27,411	31,315	3,635	6,876
1978	24,482	27,418	31,740	3,299	6,645
1977	23,785	26,863	31,520	3,026	6,062
1976	23,619	26,699	30,851	3,008	5,785
1975	23,445	26,460	30,919	2,918	5,940
1974	23,936	27,033	31,132	2,997	6,193
1973	25,053	28,241	32,278	3,062	5,754
1972	24,513	27,513	31,295	3,018	5,371
1971	23,347	26,131	29,702	2,816	5,360
1970	23,586	26,112	29,568	2,843	5,425
1969	23,849	26,300	28,440	2,845	5,237
1968	23,273	25,434	27,688	3,089	4,664
1967	22,587	24,617	26,947	3,110	4,705

Source: Bureau of the Census, Current Population Reports, Money Income of Households, Families, and Persons in the United States: 1991, *Series P-60, No. 180, 1992*

Median Income of Women by Work Experience, 1967 to 1991

Since 1967, the median income of women who work full-time, year-round has grown by $5,000 after adjusting for inflation, driving up the incomes of all working women.

(median income of women by work experience; income in 1991 dollars)

	total women	worked full-time		worked part-time	
		total	50 to 52 weeks	total	50 to 52 weeks
1991	$12,884	$17,902	$20,553	$4,476	$7,340
1990	12,765	17,608	20,656	4,421	7,475
1989	12,891	17,795	20,616	4,284	7,399
1988	12,775	17,779	20,270	4,171	7,479
1987	12,733	17,636	20,275	4,186	4,535
1986	12,447	16,950	20,172	3,912	7,572
1985	11,807	16,290	19,777	3,678	7,028
1984	11,372	15,966	19,375	3,593	7,333
1983	11,254	16,008	19,028	3,769	7,190
1982	10,950	15,662	18,541	3,810	7,065
1981	10,917	15,464	18,141	3,694	7,380
1980	10,962	15,252	18,530	3,694	7,101
1979	11,001	14,973	18,683	3,565	7,125
1978	10,591	15,061	18,866	3,299	6,907
1977	10,073	14,715	18,572	3,097	6,786
1976	9,850	14,505	18,570	3,109	6,812
1975	9,580	14,185	18,186	3,088	6,783
1974	9,350	14,176	18,291	2,829	6,621
1973	9,430	14,004	18,280	2,787	5,924
1972	9,761	14,095	18,108	2,669	6,062
1971	9,436	13,772	17,674	2,585	5,546
1970	9,003	13,521	17,554	2,417	5,735
1969	8,863	13,098	17,205	2,430	5,365
1968	9,075	12,684	16,102	2,908	5,520
1967	8,821	12,367	15,571	2,803	5,268

Source: Bureau of the Census, Current Population Reports, Money Income of Households, Families, and Persons in the United States: 1991, *Series P-60, No. 180, 1992*

Median Earnings of Men Who Work Full-Time, Year-Round, by Race and Hispanic Origin, 1960 to 1991

The median earnings of men who work full-time, year-round have fallen since 1980. The drop has been particularly sharp for Hispanic men.

(median earnings of men who work full-time, year-round, by race and Hispanic origin; income in 1991 dollars)

	total men	white	black	Hispanic
1991	$29,421	$30,266	$22,075	$19,771
1990	28,843	30,096	22,002	19,941
1989	30,129	31,349	22,436	20,164
1988	30,689	31,348	23,453	20,552
1987	31,108	31,807	22,927	20,902
1986	31,386	32,219	22,790	20,896
1985	30,626	31,723	22,125	21,583
1984	30,436	31,411	21,808	22,206
1983	29,922	30,655	22,089	22,111
1982	30,028	30,776	22,087	21,915
1981	30,626	31,300	22,262	22,252
1980	30,801	31,703	22,419	22,437
1979	31,315	32,033	23,261	22,786
1978	31,740	32,274	24,907	23,679
1977	31,520	32,455	22,510	23,251
1976	30,851	31,672	23,186	23,542
1975	30,919	31,636	23,525	22,812
1974	31,132	31,801	22,878	23,317
1973	32,278	33,230	22,738	-
1972	31,295	32,495	22,396	-
1971	29,702	30,523	21,075	-
1970	29,568	30,416	21,001	-
1969	28,440	30,199	20,326	-
1968	27,688	28,432	19,198	-
1967	26,947	27,750	17,924	-
1966	26,528	-	-	-
1965	25,440	-	-	-
1964	25,070	-	-	-
1963	24,459	-	-	-
1962	23,893	-	-	-
1961	23,447	-	-	-
1960	22,706	-	-	-
Percent change				
1980-1991	-4.5%	-4.5%	-1.5%	-11.9%

Note: Hispanics may be of any race. Source: Bureau of the Census, Current Population Reports, Money Income of Households, Families, and Persons in the United States: 1991, Series P-60, No. 180, 1992

Median Earnings of Women Who Work Full-Time, Year-Round, by Race and Hispanic Origin, 1960 to 1991

Between 1980 and 1991, the median earnings of women who work full-time, year-round grew by 11 percent, after adjusting for inflation.

(median earnings of women who work full-time, year-round, by race and Hispanic origin; income in 1991 dollars)

	total women	white	black	Hispanic
1991	$20,553	$20,794	$18,720	$16,244
1990	20,656	20,892	18,799	16,331
1989	20,616	20,784	19,100	17,203
1988	20,270	20,515	19,040	17,091
1987	20,275	20,472	18,885	17,415
1986	20,172	20,408	18,310	17,194
1985	19,777	19,995	18,111	16,539
1984	19,375	19,537	17,985	16,445
1983	19,028	19,235	17,353	15,950
1982	18,541	18,749	17,284	15,831
1981	18,141	18,303	16,929	16,219
1980	18,530	18,663	17,661	16,018
1979	18,683	18,829	17,345	15,540
1978	18,866	19,018	17,799	16,294
1977	18,572	18,689	17,450	16,197
1976	18,570	18,697	17,541	16,000
1975	18,186	18,208	17,539	15,585
1974	18,291	18,422	17,223	15,549
1973	18,280	18,566	15,833	-
1972	18,108	18,399	15,789	-
1971	17,674	17,858	15,845	-
1970	17,554	17,848	14,665	-
1969	17,205	17,554	13,859	-
1968	16,102	16,546	12,598	-
1967	15,571	16,055	11,984	-
1966	15,268	-	-	-
1965	15,245	-	-	-
1964	14,828	-	-	-
1963	14,418	-	-	-
1962	14,168	-	-	-
1961	13,892	-	-	-
1960	13,777	-	-	-
Percent change				
1980-91	10.9%	11.4%	6.0%	1.4%

Note: Hispanics may be of any race. Source: Bureau of the Census, Current Population Reports, Money Income of Households, Families, and Persons in the United States: 1991, *Series P-60, No. 180, 1992*

Median Income of Men by Education, 1967 to 1991

Between 1967 and 1990, incomes rose faster than inflation only for the best-educated men. Incomes fell by nearly one-third for those who dropped out of high school.

(median income of men aged 25 or older by educational attainment; income in 1991 dollars)

	total men	less than 9th	9th to 12th	high school graduate	some college	grade or degree completed bachelor's or more	bachelor's degree	master's degree	professional degree	doctoral degree
1991	$23,686	$10,319	$14,736	$21,546	$26,591	$39,803	$36,067	$43,125	$63,741	$51,845

	total men	years of school completed							
		high school			college				
		8 or less	1 to 3 years	4 years	total	1 to 3	4 or more	4 years	5+ years
1990	$24,275	$10,712	$15,736	$22,582	$33,647	$28,273	$39,374	$36,588	$44,284
1989	25,100	11,016	15,854	23,772	35,334	28,989	41,233	38,079	45,926
1988	25,366	11,420	16,191	24,385	35,475	29,232	41,087	37,210	46,094
1987	25,253	11,593	16,828	24,112	35,881	29,378	40,636	37,373	45,050
1986	25,529	10,040	16,657	24,577	35,853	29,506	41,397	39,281	45,048
1985	24,920	9,947	16,293	24,050	34,895	28,588	40,444	37,598	44,625
1984	24,762	9,864	16,413	24,661	34,186	28,005	39,690	36,950	43,087
1983	24,044	9,819	16,621	24,081	33,724	27,913	38,637	35,888	41,955
1982	24,121	10,286	17,213	24,303	33,148	28,472	37,678	35,098	40,990
1981	25,031	10,770	18,047	25,687	34,009	29,490	38,535	35,744	41,337
1980	25,783	10,561	19,092	26,829	34,434	29,807	38,366	36,142	41,762
1979	26,803	10,827	20,153	28,473	35,500	30,956	39,478	37,050	42,678
1978	26,995	11,384	21,026	28,940	35,470	31,196	40,665	37,886	43,242
1977	26,668	11,641	21,600	28,461	35,226	30,702	39,932	37,478	43,333
1976	26,512	11,435	21,866	28,417	35,594	30,605	39,722	37,757	42,320
1975	26,357	11,303	21,383	28,674	35,817	31,644	40,420	37,942	43,406
1974	27,300	11,832	23,403	29,751	37,046	32,569	41,987	37,788	42,409
1973	28,283	12,880	24,883	31,261	38,286	33,680	42,436	40,228	46,254
1972	27,578	12,732	24,470	30,389	38,632	33,659	43,336	41,479	45,885
1971	26,045	12,270	23,921	28,718	37,310	32,557	41,478	39,731	43,734
1970	26,025	11,952	24,191	28,930	37,607	32,581	41,822	40,051	44,279
1969	26,197	11,854	24,472	29,156	37,616	32,475	42,366	41,114	43,983
1968	25,237	12,042	23,734	27,932	35,509	31,137	40,672	39,259	42,406
1967	24,260	11,218	23,101	27,179	34,969	30,598	39,602	37,858	41,974
Percent change									
1980-90		-5.9%	1.4%	-17.6%	-15.8%	-2.3%	-5.1%	2.6%	1.2%	6.0%
1967-90		0.1	-4.5	-31.9	-16.9	-3.8	-7.6	-0.6	-3.4	5.5

Note: Beginning in 1991, the Census Bureau changed its educational attainment categories, making 1991 statistics incompatible with those of earlier years.
Source: U.S. Bureau of the Census, various income reports

Median Income of Women by Education, 1967 to 1991

In contrast to men, incomes rose between 1967 and 1990, after adjusting for inflation, for women of nearly all educational levels. The biggest gains went to the most educated women.

(median income of women aged 25 or older by educational attainment; income in 1991 dollars)

	total women	less than 9th	9th to 12th	high school graduate	some college	bachelor's or more	bachelor's degree	master's degree	professional degree	doctoral degree
						grade or degree completed				
1991	$11,580	$6,268	$7,055	$10,818	$13,963	$23,627	$20,967	$29,747	$34,063	$37,242

	total women	8 or less	1 to 3 years	4 years	total	1 to 3	4 or more	4 years	5+ years
		high school			**college**				
			years of school completed						
1990	$11,723	$6,155	$7,324	$11,079	$19,074	$15,338	$23,409	$21,178	$28,088
1989	11,874	6,178	7,414	11,462	19,255	15,640	23,782	21,360	28,631
1988	11,604	5,991	7,246	11,220	19,163	15,385	23,555	21,196	27,022
1987	11,228	6,017	7,487	10,880	18,362	14,860	22,458	20,103	26,635
1986	10,667	5,831	7,248	10,399	17,987	14,386	22,455	20,045	26,848
1985	10,323	5,843	7,202	10,301	17,383	13,949	21,820	19,314	26,178
1984	10,160	5,781	7,282	10,269	16,727	13,720	20,791	17,874	25,786
1983	9,926	5,694	7,171	10,240	16,338	13,249	20,233	17,239	24,884
1982	9,449	5,512	7,025	9,925	15,461	12,231	19,215	16,697	23,876
1981	9,194	5,529	7,038	9,820	15,314	12,485	18,273	15,871	23,264
1980	9,089	5,496	7,037	9,769	15,036	12,460	18,223	15,900	23,071
1979	8,934	5,309	7,250	9,792	14,573	11,965	18,241	15,299	22,361
1978	9,355	5,467	7,469	10,536	15,169	12,520	18,713	16,326	22,935
1977	9,818	5,439	7,928	11,370	16,048	13,445	19,600	17,406	23,880
1976	9,500	5,556	7,849	11,293	15,808	12,616	19,582	17,525	24,074
1975	9,481	5,457	8,015	11,022	16,292	13,091	20,176	18,073	25,250
1974	9,234	5,594	8,210	11,029	16,159	13,039	20,239	16,996	24,094
1973	9,431	5,405	8,185	11,457	16,251	13,172	20,323	17,934	25,789
1972	9,299	5,105	8,259	11,526	15,997	12,646	21,160	18,429	26,323
1971	8,987	4,749	8,156	11,357	15,607	11,793	20,919	18,126	26,358
1970	8,558	4,620	7,872	11,213	15,567	12,275	20,365	17,684	26,018
1969	8,463	4,415	8,082	11,201	15,494	12,131	20,109	18,004	24,738
1968	8,317	4,473	7,866	11,103	14,578	11,731	19,167	16,031	24,406
1967	7,902	4,078	7,654	10,915	14,734	11,567	19,409	16,606	25,165
Percent change									
1980-90		29.0%	12.0%	4.1%	13.4%	26.9%	23.1%	28.5%	33.2%	21.7%
1967-90		48.4	50.9	-4.3	1.5	29.5	32.6	20.6	27.5	11.6

Note: Beginning in 1991, the Census Bureau changed its educational attainment categories, making 1991 statistics incompatible with those of earlier years.
Source: U.S. Bureau of the Census, various income reports

Ratio of Women's Earnings to Men's Earnings, 1960 to 1991

The 59-cent dollar is now the 70-cent dollar as women's earnings have increased relative to men's. Black women earn 85 cents for every dollar black men earn, while the ratio for whites is far less.

(ratio of the median earnings of women who work full-time, year-round to the median earnings of men who work full-time, year-round, by race and Hispanic origin)

	all races	white	black	Hispanic
1991	69.9%	68.7%	84.8%	82.2%
1990	71.6	69.4	85.4	81.9
1989	68.5	66.2	85.1	85.3
1988	66.0	65.4	81.2	83.2
1987	65.2	64.4	82.4	83.3
1986	64.3	63.3	80.3	82.3
1985	64.6	63.0	81.9	76.6
1984	63.7	62.2	82.5	74.1
1983	63.6	62.7	78.6	72.1
1982	61.7	60.9	78.2	72.2
1981	59.2	58.5	76.0	72.9
1980	60.2	58.9	78.8	71.4
1979	59.7	58.8	74.6	68.2
1978	59.4	58.9	71.5	68.8
1977	58.9	57.6	77.5	69.7
1976	60.2	59.0	75.7	68.0
1975	58.8	57.6	74.6	68.3
1974	58.6	57.9	75.3	66.7
1973	56.6	55.9	69.6	-
1972	57.9	56.6	70.5	-
1971	59.5	58.5	75.2	-
1970	59.4	58.7	69.8	-
1969	58.9	58.1	68.2	-
1968	58.2	58.2	65.6	-
1967	57.8	57.9	66.9	-
1966	57.6	-	-	-
1965	59.9	-	-	-
1964	59.1	-	-	-
1963	58.9	-	-	-
1962	59.3	-	-	-
1961	59.2	-	-	-
1960	60.7	-	-	-

Note: Hispanics may be of any race.
Source: Bureau of the Census, Current Population Reports, Money Income of Households, Families, and Persons in the United States: 1991, *Series P-60, No. 180, 1992*

All Persons: Full-Time Workers With Low Earnings, 1974 to 1989

Forty-eight percent of men under age 25 who work full-time or are looking for full-time work had low earnings in 1989, up from 31 percent in 1974.

(workers with full-time, year-round attachment to the labor force and low earnings, in percent)

	1989	1984	1979	1974
Both sexes				
Aged 18 to 64	22.7%	22.7%	18.2%	17.6%
Under age 25	50.4	49.1	36.2	36.0
Aged 25 to 34	23.0	20.3	14.6	13.5
Aged 35 to 54	16.8	17.2	14.2	13.6
Aged 55 to 64	19.6	19.4	16.6	17.5
Aged 65 or older	33.6	40.6	37.8	40.4
Men				
Aged 18 to 64	18.0	18.0	12.5	11.6
Under age 25	47.5	47.1	31.4	31.0
Aged 25 to 34	19.3	17.5	10.6	9.4
Aged 35 to 54	11.6	11.4	7.8	7.2
Aged 55 to 64	13.6	13.3	10.5	11.0
Aged 65 or older	28.5	33.1	32.8	39.3
Women				
Aged 18 to 64	30.0	30.4	28.6	30.4
Under age 25	54.2	51.7	43.0	43.3
Aged 25 to 34	28.7	25.1	22.2	23.5
Aged 35 to 54	24.8	27.0	26.5	28.1
Aged 55 to 64	30.0	30.3	28.5	31.2
Aged 65 or older	42.1	56.3	48.4	43.3
Household relationship				
In families	22.6	23.1	18.4	17.6
In married-couple families	20.3	20.8	16.9	16.2
In married-couple families with children under age 18	20.4	20.3	16.8	15.4
In female-headed families	35.8	39.0	31.0	31.3
In female-headed families with children under age 18	37.2	39.7	34.4	37.5
Years of school completed				
Less than 12 years	43.6	41.5	32.6	29.1
12 years	27.0	26.0	19.5	17.8
13 or more years	13.2	12.9	10.2	9.5

Note: A worker is considered to have low earnings if annual earnings are less than the poverty level for a four-person family. Workers who are attached to the labor force full-time, year-round are those who worked 35 hours a week or more or worked fewer hours for nonvoluntary reasons and spent at least 50 weeks during the year at work or looking for work.
Source: Bureau of the Census, Current Population Reports, Workers With Low Earnings: 1964 to 1990, Series P-60, No. 178, 1992

56 THE OFFICIAL GUIDE TO AMERICAN INCOMES

White Persons: Full-Time Workers with Low Earnings, 1974 to 1989

Seventeen percent of white men and 30 percent of white women had low earnings in 1989, despite working full-time or looking for full-time work. The share among women was about the same as in 1974, while among men the proportion increased sharply.

(white workers with full-time, year-round attachment to the labor force and low earnings, in percent)

	1989	1984	1979	1974
Both sexes				
Aged 18 to 64	21.8%	21.3%	16.8%	16.3%
Under age 25	49.7	46.9	34.7	34.3
Aged 25 to 34	21.7	18.5	13.0	12.3
Aged 35 to 54	16.1	16.1	12.9	12.4
Aged 55 to 64	18.4	18.2	15.3	16.3
Aged 65 or older	32.2	38.7	36.4	38.6
Men				
Aged 18 to 64	16.9	16.5	11.3	10.5
Under age 25	46.8	44.5	29.5	29.1
Aged 25 to 34	18.1	15.5	9.3	8.4
Aged 35 to 54	10.7	10.5	6.9	6.4
Aged 55 to 64	13.0	12.5	9.6	10.1
Aged 65 or older	27.3	32.1	31.9	37.2
Women				
Aged 18 to 64	29.5	29.5	27.4	29.3
Under age 25	53.6	50.2	42.3	42.1
Aged 25 to 34	27.7	23.8	20.4	22.6
Aged 35 to 54	24.7	26.2	25.3	27.0
Aged 55 to 64	28.3	29.0	26.9	29.4
Aged 65 or older	40.7	52.9	46.0	42.5
Household relationship				
In families	21.6	21.6	17.0	16.2
In married-couple families	19.8	20.0	16.0	15.3
In married-couple families with children under age 18	19.8	19.3	15.8	14.4
In female-headed families	34.3	35.3	26.3	26.4
In female-headed families with children under age 18	36.0	35.9	28.9	32.5
Years of school completed				
Less than 12 years	42.5	39.7	30.4	26.8
12 years	26.0	24.4	18.2	16.9
13 or more years	12.6	12.3	9.8	9.2

Note: A worker is considered to have low earnings if annual earnings are less than the poverty level for a four-person family. Workers who are attached to the labor force full-time, year-round are those who worked 35 hours a week or more or worked fewer hours for nonvoluntary reasons and spent at least 50 weeks during the year at work or looking for work.
Source: Bureau of the Census, Current Population Reports, Workers With Low Earnings: 1964 to 1990, *Series P-60, No. 178, 1992*

Black Persons: Full-Time Workers with Low Earnings, 1974 to 1989

Over half of black men under age 25 who worked full-time or were looking for full-time work had low earnings in 1989, up from 45 percent in 1974. Among black women in that age group, 59 percent of full-time workers had low earnings in 1989.

(black workers with full-time, year-round attachment to the labor force and low earnings, in percent)

	1989	1984	1979	1974
Both sexes				
Aged 18 to 64	30.6%	34.7%	29.9%	28.8%
Under age 25	56.5	66.2	49.0	48.8
Aged 25 to 34	32.5	33.9	26.4	23.2
Aged 35 to 54	22.7	25.1	25.0	23.8
Aged 55 to 64	30.5	31.9	30.4	32.7
Aged 65 or older	53.3	55.3	55.2	61.0
Men				
Aged 18 to 64	27.2	32.9	24.6	22.8
Under age 25	54.3	68.3	49.0	44.9
Aged 25 to 34	29.2	34.5	21.8	19.4
Aged 35 to 54	19.7	19.6	17.4	15.9
Aged 55 to 64	19.9	25.0	21.7	23.2
Aged 65 or older	-	40.2	-	61.2
Women				
Aged 18 to 64	34.3	36.7	36.4	37.8
Under age 25	59.0	63.3	49.1	54.6
Aged 25 to 34	36.3	33.4	31.9	28.8
Aged 35 to 54	25.7	31.1	34.3	34.8
Aged 55 to 64	43.5	39.5	41.5	49.3
Aged 65 or older	-	-	-	-
Household relationship				
In families	30.8	36.0	31.1	29.8
In married-couple families	26.6	29.4	26.2	25.3
In married-couple families with children under age 18	26.7	29.1	25.7	24.7
In female-headed families	39.4	49.3	43.9	46.3
In female-headed families with children under age 18	39.6	47.4	45.4	47.7
Years of school completed				
Less than 12 years	49.0	49.9	43.6	40.3
12 years	33.3	38.2	29.2	25.8
13 or more years	18.6	19.9	15.9	13.6

Note: A worker is considered to have low earnings if annual earnings are less than the poverty level for a four-person family. Workers who are attached to the labor force full-time, year-round are those who worked 35 hours a week or more or worked fewer hours for nonvoluntary reasons and spent at least 50 weeks during the year at work or looking for work.
Source: Bureau of the Census, Current Population Reports, Workers With Low Earnings: 1964 to 1990, Series P-60, No. 178, 1992

Hispanic Persons: Full-Time Workers with Low Earnings, 1974 to 1989

Hispanics who worked full-time or were looking for full-time work were more likely to have low earnings in 1989 than in 1974. Thirty-seven percent of full-time workers had low earnings in 1989, up from 27 percent in 1974.

(Hispanic workers with full-time, year-round attachment to the labor force and low earnings, in percent)

	1989	*1984*	*1979*	*1974*
Both sexes				
Aged 18 to 64	36.6%	34.2%	29.1%	27.0%
Under age 25	58.0	58.5	49.1	44.5
Aged 25 to 34	36.8	31.6	24.7	24.3
Aged 35 to 54	29.0	25.2	22.1	21.2
Aged 55 to 64	29.0	34.4	29.3	30.8
Aged 65 or older	-	-	-	-
Men				
Aged 18 to 64	33.3	30.2	22.5	20.6
Under age 25	55.7	61.6	46.2	41.8
Aged 25 to 34	34.2	28.6	17.7	19.9
Aged 35 to 54	23.9	18.0	14.6	13.4
Aged 55 to 64	24.3	23.6	22.4	19.4
Aged 65 or older	-	-	-	-
Women				
Aged 18 to 64	42.5	41.8	41.8	42.0
Under age 25	62.8	52.1	54.2	49.4
Aged 25 to 34	41.7	37.4	38.9	36.0
Aged 35 to 54	37.1	38.4	36.8	39.4
Aged 55 to 64	37.2	55.1	44.8	-
Aged 65 or older	-	-	-	-
Household relationship				
In families	36.1	33.2	28.1	26.9
In married-couple families	32.9	30.5	26.2	25.2
In married-couple families with children under age 18	33.5	30.6	25.5	24.6
In female-headed families	45.8	47.2	40.4	40.9
In female-headed families with children under age 18	49.6	50.1	42.6	41.6
Years of school completed				
Less than 12 years	50.2	47.5	39.1	35.8
12 years	34.1	30.0	25.6	23.7
13 or more years	18.3	17.6	14.6	11.1

Note: A worker is considered to have low earnings if annual earnings are less than the poverty level for a four-person family. Workers who are attached to the labor force full-time, year-round are those who worked 35 hours a week or more or worked fewer hours for nonvoluntary reasons and spent at least 50 weeks during the year at work or looking for work.
Source: Bureau of the Census, Current Population Reports, Workers With Low Earnings: 1964 to 1990, Series P-60, No. 178, 1992

Distribution of Persons by Relative Income, 1964 to 1989

Income inequality is on the rise. The proportion of persons with low or high incomes relative to the median stood at 37 percent in 1989, up from 29 percent in 1969.

(distribution of persons by income relative to median income; persons as of the following year; numbers in thousands)

	1989	*1984*	*1979*	*1974*	*1969*	*1964*
All persons	245,992	233,816	222,903	209,341	199,495	189,512
Relative income						
Less than .50	22.1%	21.8%	20.0%	18.7%	17.9%	19.2%
Less than .25	8.3	8.2	6.7	5.5	5.5	6.7
.25 to .49	13.7	13.7	13.3	13.2	12.4	12.6
.50 to .74	14.1	14.0	14.5	15.3	15.0	14.5
.75 to .99	13.9	14.2	15.5	15.9	16.9	16.3
1.00 to 1.24	12.7	12.4	13.8	14.9	15.0	14.3
1.25 to 1.99	22.6	23.4	24.3	24.1	24.2	23.9
2.00 and over	14.7	14.1	11.9	11.0	10.9	11.7
2.00 to 2.99	9.9	10.0	8.6	8.2	8.1	8.7
3.00 and over	4.8	4.2	3.3	2.8	2.8	3.1
Less than .50 or 2.00 and over	36.7	36.0	32.0	29.7	28.8	31.0

Note: Relative income is calculated in the following way: 1. An income is assigned to each person equal to the income of the person's family. Persons who live alone or with nonrelatives are assigned their personal incomes. 2. These incomes are then adjusted for differences in family size using equivalence factors which reduce the incomes assigned to members of large families compared to members of small families because living costs increase as family size increases. 3. The median level of equivalence-adjusted income is determined using the entire universe of persons. 4. Each person is assigned a relative income equal to the ratio of his or her equivalence-adjusted income to the median equivalence-adjusted income. Low relative income is equivalence-adjusted income that is less than one-half of the median equivalence-adjusted income. High relative income is equivalence-adjusted income at least twice that of the median equivalence-adjusted income. Median relative income for the entire universe of persons is by definition equal to 1.00. Population subgroups may have median relative incomes below or above 1.00 depending on the distribution of relative income within the population subgroups.
Source: Bureau of the Census, Current Population Reports, Trends in Relative Income: 1964 to 1989, Series P-60, No. 177, 1991

Distribution of Persons by Age and Relative Income, 1964 to 1989

Only among the elderly are incomes moving closer to the median. Among people under age 18, incomes fell sharply relative to the median since the 1960s, from 91 to 84 percent.

(distribution of persons by age and income relative to median income; persons as of the following year; numbers in thousands)

	1989	1984	1979	1974	1969	1964
UNDER AGE 18						
Total	64,144	62,447	63,375	66,113	68,997	69,588
Percent of all persons	26.1%	26.7%	28.4%	31.6%	34.6%	36.7%
Relative Income						
Less than .50	29.1	28.7	24.5	22.3	19.4	21.2
.50 to .99	30.3	31.0	33.6	35.6	38.0	36.4
1.00 to 1.99	32.2	32.6	35.3	36.2	36.6	36.2
2.00 and over	8.4	7.7	6.6	5.9	6.0	6.3
Median relative income	.84	.84	.88	.89	.91	.90
AGED 18 TO 64						
Total	152,282	144,551	135,333	122,101	111,435	102,548
Percent of all persons	61.9%	61.8%	60.7%	58.3%	55.9%	54.1%
Relative Income						
Less than .50	17.3	17.5	15.1	13.9	12.9	14.5
.50 to .99	25.7	25.8	27.0	28.2	28.4	27.1
1.00 to 1.99	38.7	39.0	42.5	43.4	44.0	42.5
2.00 and over	18.3	17.7	15.4	14.5	14.7	15.9
Median relative income	1.13	1.13	1.14	1.13	1.14	1.14
AGED 65 OR OLDER						
Total	29,566	26,818	24,194	21,127	19,063	17,376
Percent of all persons	12.0%	11.5%	10.9%	10.1%	9.6%	9.2%
Relative Income						
Less than .50	31.5	29.3	36.2	35.6	42.0	39.4
.50 to .99	34.2	34.4	36.7	35.6	30.0	29.9
1.00 to 1.99	24.9	26.4	20.7	22.0	21.3	21.5
2.00 and over	9.4	9.9	6.4	6.8	6.7	9.2
Median relative income	.73	.76	.64	.65	.59	.63

Note: Relative income is calculated in the following way: 1. An income is assigned to each person equal to the income of the person's family. Persons who live alone or with nonrelatives are assigned their personal incomes. 2. These incomes are then adjusted for differences in family size using equivalence factors which reduce the incomes assigned to members of large families compared to members of small families because living costs increase as family size increases. 3. The median level of equivalence-adjusted income is determined using the entire universe of persons. 4. Each person is assigned a relative income equal to the ratio of his or her equivalence-adjusted income to the median equivalence-adjusted income. Low relative income is equivalence-adjusted income that is less than one-half of the median equivalence-adjusted income. High relative income is equivalence-adjusted income at least twice that of the median equivalence-adjusted income. Median relative income for the entire universe of persons is by definition equal to 1.00. Population subgroups may have median relative incomes below or above 1.00 depending on the distribution of relative income within the population subgroups.
Source: Bureau of the Census, Current Population Reports, Trends in Relative Income: 1964 to 1989, Series P-60, No. 177, 1991

Distribution of Persons by Race and Hispanic Origin and Relative Income, 1964 to 1989

Slightly fewer blacks had low incomes relative to the median in 1989 than in 1969, but the share has grown among whites. For both blacks and whites, the share with relatively high incomes has grown.

(distribution of persons by race and Hispanic origin and income relative to median income; persons as of the following year; numbers in thousands)

	1989	1984	1979	1974	1969	1964
WHITE						
Total	206,853	198,941	191,742	182,361	175,193	167,098
Percent of all persons	84.1%	85.1%	86.0%	87.1%	87.8%	88.2%
Relative income						
Less than .50	18.8	18.6	16.7	15.5	14.7	15.5
.50 to .99	28.1	28.0	29.9	31.1	31.6	30.7
1.00 to 1.99	37.2	38.0	40.3	41.3	41.9	40.9
2.00 and over	16.0	15.4	13.1	12.0	11.9	12.9
Median relative income	1.06	1.06	1.06	1.05	1.05	1.06
BLACK						
Total	30,332	28,087	25,944	23,696	22,029	20,505
Percent of all persons	12.3%	12.0%	11.6%	11.3%	11.0%	10.8%
Relative income						
Less than .50	43.9	44.1	44.1	43.3	42.6	48.5
.50 to .99	27.3	29.7	30.0	32.3	34.7	31.6
1.00 to 1.99	23.8	21.6	22.7	21.5	19.5	17.6
2.00 and over	5.0	4.6	3.2	2.9	3.1	2.3
Median relative income	.60	.58	.58	.59	.58	.52
HISPANIC ORIGIN						
Total	20,746	16,916	13,371	11,200	-	-
Percent of all persons	8.4%	7.2%	6.0%	5.4%	-	-
Relative income						
Less than .50	40.1	38.4	34.2	34.1	-	-
.50 to .99	31.8	32.6	36.5	37.4	-	-
1.00 to 1.99	22.9	24.0	24.9	24.9	-	-
2.00 and over	5.2	5.0	4.3	3.6	-	-
Median relative income	.63	.66	.69	.69	-	-

Note: Hispanics may be of any race. Relative income is calculated in the following way: 1. An income is assigned to each person equal to the income of the person's family. Persons who live alone or with nonrelatives are assigned their personal incomes. 2. These incomes are then adjusted for differences in family size using equivalence factors which reduce the incomes assigned to members of large families compared to members of small families because living costs increase as family size increases. 3. The median level of equivalence-adjusted income is determined using the entire universe of persons. 4. Each person is assigned a relative income equal to the ratio of his or her equivalence-adjusted income to the median equivalence-adjusted income. Low relative income is equivalence-adjusted income that is less than one-half of the median equivalence-adjusted income. High relative income is equivalence-adjusted income at least twice that of the median equivalence-adjusted income. Median relative income for the entire universe of persons is by definition equal to 1.00. Population subgroups may have median relative incomes below or above 1.00 depending on the distribution of relative income within the population subgroups.
Source: Bureau of the Census, Current Population Reports, Trends in Relative Income: 1964 to 1989, Series P-60, No. 177, 1991

Distribution of Persons by Education and Relative Income, 1964 to 1989

Only among college graduates have incomes remained stable. Those with less education have seen their incomes fall sharply relative to the median.

(distribution of persons by education and income relative to median income; persons aged 25 to 64 as of the following year; numbers in thousands)

	1989	1984	1979	1974	1969	1964
DID NOT FINISH HIGH SCHOOL						
Total	21,862	23,550	26,562	30,056	34,204	38,361
Percent of all persons	17.2%	20.2%	25.0%	31.4%	38.4%	45.6%
Relative income						
Less than .50	38.4	34.4	29.0	25.0	21.7	22.6
.50 to .99	32.5	33.4	33.9	34.7	34.5	31.7
1.00 to 1.99	24.5	27.2	31.5	34.6	37.0	36.8
2.00 and over	4.5	5.1	5.6	5.8	6.8	9.0
Median relative income	.65	.72	.80	.85	.91	.93
COMPLETED HIGH SCHOOL, NO COLLEGE						
Total	50,402	47,100	42,130	38,203	33,897	28,799
Percent of all persons	39.7%	40.4%	39.7%	39.9%	38.1%	34.2%
Relative income						
Less than .50	15.7	14.7	11.0	9.1	7.5	7.7
.50 to .99	29.5	28.1	28.4	28.9	27.9	26.9
1.00 to 1.99	41.9	43.1	47.2	48.6	49.9	48.2
2.00 and over	12.9	14.1	13.4	13.4	14.6	17.2
Median relative income	1.08	1.11	1.17	1.17	1.20	1.23
COMPLETED 1 TO 3 YEARS OF COLLEGE						
Total	24,844	20,777	17,406	12,863	9,984	8,132
Percent of all persons	19.6%	17.8%	16.4%	13.4%	11.2%	9.7%
Relative income						
Less than .50	10.2	10.9	8.6	7.0	5.9	5.5
.50 to .99	24.0	23.4	23.7	22.2	20.3	20.1
1.00 to 1.99	45.5	44.7	48.0	49.9	50.8	48.2
2.00 and over	20.2	21.0	19.7	21.0	23.0	26.2
Median relative income	1.29	1.29	1.29	1.32	1.37	1.43

(continued)

(continued from previous page)

(distribution of persons by education and income relative to median income; persons aged 25 to 64 as of the following year; numbers in thousands)

	1989	1984	1979	1974	1969	1964
COMPLETED COLLEGE						
Total	29,863	25,278	20,117	14,659	10,874	8,916
Percent of all persons	23.5%	21.7%	18.9%	15.3%	12.2%	10.6%
Relative income						
Less than .50	4.6	5.4	5.1	3.9	3.8	5.8
.50 to .99	13.2	13.2	14.4	13.3	12.3	10.5
1.00 to 1.99	41.8	42.4	46.6	48.1	46.5	44.1
2.00 and over	40.4	38.9	33.9	34.7	37.4	39.6
Median relative income	1.75	1.71	1.61	1.67	1.70	1.72

Note: Relative income is calculated in the following way: 1. An income is assigned to each person equal to the income of the person's family. Persons who live alone or with nonrelatives are assigned their personal incomes. 2. These incomes are then adjusted for differences in family size using equivalence factors which reduce the incomes assigned to members of large families compared to members of small families because living costs increase as family size increases. 3. The median level of equivalence-adjusted income is determined using the entire universe of persons. 4. Each person is assigned a relative income equal to the ratio of his or her equivalence-adjusted income to the median equivalence-adjusted income. Low relative income is equivalence-adjusted income that is less than one-half of the median equivalence-adjusted income. High relative income is equivalence-adjusted income at least twice that of the median equivalence-adjusted income. Median relative income for the entire universe of persons is by definition equal to 1.00. Population subgroups may have median relative incomes below or above 1.00 depending on the distribution of relative income within the population subgroups.
Source: Bureau of the Census, Current Population Reports, Trends in Relative Income: 1964 to 1989, Series P-60, No. 177, 1991

2

Household Income

Behind America's growing income inequality are diversifying households and workers. At the top of the income scale are middle-aged, college-educated, married couples. At the bottom are young families headed by high school dropouts. The recession of the early 1990s lowered incomes across the board, leaving intact these income disparities.

Household Income: Highlights

■ Median household income fell by 3.5 percent between 1990 and 1991 as the recession of the early 1990s took its toll. Nearly all types of households experienced a drop in income between 1990 and 1991.

■ By age, the most affluent households are those headed by people aged 45 to 54, with a median income of $43,751 in 1991. This is the age group now filling with baby boomers.

■ By household type, the most affluent households are headed by white married couples, with a median income of $41,584 in 1991. Households with the lowest incomes are headed by black women who live alone, with a median income of just $8,492.

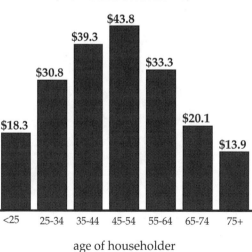

Median household income peaks among 45-to-54-year-olds at $43,800.

(1991 income in thousands)

age of householder

All Households: Median Income, 1990 and 1991

Median income declined for virtually every type of household between 1990 and 1991 because of the recession. The biggest drops were experienced by male-headed families and by households headed by 65-to-74-year-olds.

(median income of households, 1990 and 1991; income in 1991 dollars; numbers in thousands)

	total households	1991 median income	1990 median income	percent change 1990-91
Total	95,669	$30,126	$31,203	-3.5%
Type of household				
Family households	67,173	36,404	37,210	-2.2
Married-couple families	52,457	41,075	41,679	-1.4
Female householder, no spouse present	11,692	17,961	18,829	-4.6
Male householder, no spouse present	3,025	31,010	32,880	-5.7
Nonfamily households	28,496	17,774	18,434	-3.6
Female householder	16,068	14,321	14,692	-2.5
Living alone	14,361	12,834	13,076	-1.9
Male householder	12,428	23,022	23,435	-1.8
Living alone	9,613	20,259	20,804	-2.6
Age of householder				
Aged 15 to 24	4,859	18,313	18,760	-2.4
Aged 25 to 34	20,007	30,842	31,637	-2.5
Aged 35 to 44	21,774	39,349	40,184	-2.1
Aged 45 to 54	15,547	43,751	43,686	0.1
Aged 55 to 64	12,560	33,304	33,727	-1.3
Aged 65 to 74	12,043	20,063	21,146	-5.1
Aged 75 or older	8,878	13,933	13,703	1.7
Number of earners				
No earners	20,741	11,510	11,629	-1.0
One earner	31,818	24,834	25,609	-3.0
Two or more earners	43,111	46,189	46,776	-1.3
Work experience of householder				
Worked	68,876	37,333	37,778	-1.2
Worked full-time, year-round	49,471	42,286	42,515	-0.5
Did not work	26,793	14,180	14,401	-1.5

Source: Bureau of the Census, Current Population Reports, Money Income of Households, Families, and Persons in the United States: 1991, *Series P-60, No. 180, 1992*

White Households: Median Income, 1990 and 1991

Between 1990 and 1991, the median income of white male-headed families fell by nearly 8 percent, after adjusting for inflation. This was more than twice the 3 percent decline for all white households.

(median income of white households, 1990 and 1991; income in 1991 dollars; numbers in thousands)

	total households	1991 median income	1990 median income	percent change 1990-91
Total	81,675	$31,569	$32,545	-3.0%
Type of household				
Family households	57,224	38,229	38,785	-1.4
Married-couple families	47,124	41,584	42,134	-1.3
Female householder, no spouse present	7,726	21,213	21,745	-2.4
Male householder, no spouse present	2,374	31,634	34,252	-7.6
Nonfamily households	24,451	18,461	19,225	-4.0
Female householder	13,975	14,790	15,245	-3.0
Living alone	12,490	13,317	13,645	-2.4
Male householder	10,476	24,531	24,779	-1.0
Living alone	8,029	21,126	21,779	-3.0
Age of householder				
Aged 15 to 24	3,980	19,803	20,489	-3.4
Aged 25 to 34	16,677	32,315	33,200	-2.7
Aged 35 to 44	18,331	41,202	42,124	-2.2
Aged 45 to 54	13,297	46,215	45,954	0.6
Aged 55 to 64	10,760	35,550	35,690	-0.4
Aged 65 to 74	10,581	21,087	21,976	-4.0
Aged 75 or older	8,048	14,343	14,291	0.4
Number of earners				
No earners	17,500	12,771	12,917	-1.1
One earner	26,530	26,147	26,887	-2.8
Two or more earners	37,645	47,100	47,628	-1.1
Work experience of householder				
Worked	59,285	38,814	38,933	-0.3
Worked full-time, year-round	42,965	43,572	43,614	-0.1
Did not work	22,390	15,488	15,780	-1.9

Source: Bureau of the Census, Current Population Reports, Money Income of Households, Families, and Persons in the United States: 1991, *Series P-60, No. 180, 1992*

Black Households: Median Income, 1990 and 1991

The median income of black households fell by 3.4 percent between 1990 and 1991, with the largest decline experienced by the youngest households.

(median income of black households, 1990 and 1991; income in 1991 dollars; numbers in thousands)

	total households	1991 median income	1990 median income	percent change 1990-91
Total	11,083	$18,807	$19,462	-3.4%
Type of household				
Family households	7,716	22,203	22,821	-2.7
Married-couple families	3,631	33,369	35,319	-5.5
Female householder, no spouse present	3,582	12,196	13,065	-6.6
Male householder, no spouse present	504	26,428	25,060	5.5
Nonfamily households	3,367	12,202	12,285	-0.7
Female householder	1,773	9,520	9,025	5.5
Living alone	1,596	8,492	7,997	6.2
Male householder	1,594	15,223	16,101	-5.5
Living alone	1,319	13,665	13,678	-0.1
Age of householder				
Aged 15 to 24	703	8,603	10,229	-15.9
Aged 25 to 34	2,661	19,284	19,111	0.9
Aged 35 to 44	2,636	26,233	27,106	-3.2
Aged 45 to 54	1,718	27,526	28,042	-1.8
Aged 55 to 64	1,418	20,103	20,035	0.3
Aged 65 to 74	1,245	11,555	12,478	-7.4
Aged 75 or older	702	9,151	8,161	12.1
Number of earners				
No earners	2,820	6,332	6,117	3.5
One earner	4,301	17,230	17,757	-3.0
Two or more earners	3,962	37,268	37,936	-1.8
Work experience of householder				
Worked	7,328	26,424	26,849	-1.6
Worked full-time, year-round	4,928	31,866	32,320	-1.4
Did not work	3,755	7,494	7,554	-0.8

Source: Bureau of the Census, Current Population Reports, Money Income of Households, Families, and Persons in the United States: 1991, *Series P-60, No. 180, 1992*

Hispanic Households: Median Income, 1990 and 1991

The median income of Hispanic households fell less than that of white households between 1990 and 1991, after adjusting for inflation. Nevertheless, Hispanic incomes remain far below those of whites.

(median income of Hispanic households, 1990 and 1991; income in 1991 dollars; numbers in thousands)

	total households	1991 median income	1990 median income	percent change 1990-91
Total	6,379	$22,691	$23,270	-2.5%
Type of household				
Family households	5,177	24,551	25,585	-4.0
Married-couple families	3,532	28,833	29,787	-3.2
Female householder, no spouse present	1,261	13,323	13,133	1.4
Male householder, no spouse present	383	23,298	26,527	-12.2
Nonfamily households	1,202	15,733	14,875	5.8
Female householder	542	11,420	11,202	1.9
Living alone	443	9,160	9,309	-1.6
Male householder	660	19,009	18,433	3.1
Living alone	444	15,455	14,293	8.1
Age of householder				
Aged 15 to 24	556	16,554	15,352	7.8
Aged 25 to 34	1,821	22,664	22,608	0.2
Aged 35 to 44	1,641	26,254	27,717	-5.3
Aged 45 to 54	979	28,909	29,381	-1.6
Aged 55 to 64	728	24,952	25,799	-3.3
Aged 65 to 74	417	15,855	14,717	7.7
Aged 75 or older	238	11,122	10,264	8.4
Number of earners				
No earners	1,038	7,471	7,345	1.7
One earner	2,219	17,250	17,899	-3.6
Two or more earners	3,122	34,500	34,798	-0.9
Work experience of householder				
Worked	4,800	27,337	27,994	-2.3
Worked full-time, year-round	3,238	31,785	32,815	-3.1
Did not work	1,579	10,056	9,846	2.1

Note: Hispanics may be of any race.

Source: Bureau of the Census, Current Population Reports, Money Income of Households, Families, and Persons in the United States: 1991, *Series P-60, No. 180, 1992*

Distribution of Households by Income and Demographic Characteristics, 1991

The most affluent households are those headed by married couples and by people aged 45 to 54. Both types of households had a median income of more than $40,000 in 1991.

(households by selected characteristics and income in 1991; households as of 1992; numbers in thousands)

	total households	under $15,000	$15,000 to $24,999	$25,000 to $34,999	$35,000 to $49,999	$50,000 to $74,999	$75,000 to $99,999	$100,000 or over	median income
Total	95,669	23,228	16,631	14,553	16,586	14,709	5,715	4,246	$30,126
Race and Hispanic origin									
White	81,675	17,865	14,131	12,609	14,647	13,285	5,217	3,922	31,569
Black	11,083	4,703	2,018	1,533	1,483	933	279	135	18,807
Hispanic	6,379	2,090	1,377	1,007	946	640	185	134	22,691
Type of household									
Family households	67,173	10,908	10,648	10,561	13,278	12,848	5,110	3,821	36,404
Married-couple families	52,457	5,330	7,662	8,335	11,142	11,593	4,766	3,628	41,075
Female householder, no spouse present	11,692	5,026	2,378	1,668	1,513	801	188	116	17,961
Male householder, no spouse present	3,025	550	608	558	623	453	156	77	31,010
Nonfamily households	28,496	12,320	5,983	3,993	3,308	1,862	605	425	17,774
Female householder	16,068	8,332	3,352	1,907	1,462	697	194	124	14,321
Living alone	14,361	8,075	3,020	1,615	1,078	411	98	65	12,834
Male householder	12,428	3,988	2,631	2,085	1,846	1,165	411	301	23,022
Living alone	9,613	3,634	2,171	1,574	1,225	638	205	167	20,259
Age of householder									
Aged 15 to 24	4,859	1,958	1,323	816	506	198	45	13	18,313
Aged 25 to 34	20,007	4,056	3,695	3,663	4,323	2,944	876	452	30,842
Aged 35 to 44	21,774	3,057	2,927	3,426	4,752	4,646	1,778	1,189	39,349
Aged 45 to 54	15,547	2,201	1,777	2,066	2,830	3,685	1,660	1,329	43,751
Aged 55 to 64	12,560	2,668	2,004	1,861	2,246	2,027	910	844	33,304
Aged 65 to 74	12,043	4,506	2,833	1,854	1,303	899	339	311	20,063
Aged 75 or older	8,878	4,785	2,072	867	627	311	107	108	13,933

Note: Because Hispanics may be of any race, race and Hispanic origin numbers will not add to total households.
Source: Bureau of the Census, Current Population Reports, Money Income of Households, Families, and Persons in the United States: 1991, *Series P-60, No. 180, 1992*

Distribution of Households by Income and Labor Force Characteristics, 1991

The most affluent households are those with two earners, those in which the householder works full-time, and those with a college-educated householder.

(households by selected characteristics and income in 1991; households as of 1992; numbers in thousands)

	total households	under $15,000	$15,000 to $24,999	$25,000 to $34,999	$35,000 to $49,999	$50,000 to $74,999	$75,000 to $99,999	$100,000 or over	median income
Total	95,669	23,228	16,631	14,553	16,586	14,709	5,715	4,246	$30,126
Number of earners									
No earners	20,741	12,845	4,120	1,905	1,101	505	124	142	11,510
One earner	31,818	8,189	7,829	5,917	5,130	2,873	968	912	24,834
Two or more earners	43,111	2,195	4,682	6,731	10,354	11,332	4,623	3,193	46,189
Work experience of householder									
Worked	68,876	9,171	11,128	11,438	14,385	13,505	5,319	3,930	37,333
Worked full-time	60,739	6,047	9,393	10,257	13,483	12,806	5,082	3,670	39,661
50 weeks or more	49,471	3,258	6,951	8,386	11,508	11,398	4,643	3,327	42,286
27 to 49 weeks	7,518	1,336	1,642	1,383	1,447	1,104	331	275	30,279
26 weeks or less	3,750	1,454	799	489	529	303	108	68	19,614
Worked part-time	8,138	3,124	1,736	1,181	902	700	237	259	20,078
50 weeks or more	3,709	1,176	824	568	492	369	114	165	23,226
27 to 49 weeks	1,929	688	459	300	205	174	62	41	20,260
26 weeks or less	2,499	1,259	453	312	205	156	61	53	14,847
Did not work	26,793	14,058	5,503	3,115	2,201	1,204	396	317	14,180
Education of householders aged 25+									
Total	90,810	21,270	15,308	13,737	16,080	14,511	5,670	4,233	31,032
Less than 9th grade	9,357	5,222	2,033	984	692	318	59	48	13,221
9th to 12th grade	10,362	4,504	2,302	1,453	1,160	717	154	71	17,535
High school graduate	30,178	7,059	5,949	5,364	5,877	4,289	1,092	548	28,487
Some college	14,984	2,495	2,461	2,495	3,222	2,865	938	508	35,150
Associate degree	5,041	635	664	853	1,159	1,121	435	174	39,700
Bachelor's degree	13,137	991	1,407	1,758	2,623	3,383	1,629	1,346	48,705
Master's degree	5,211	279	356	629	1,031	1,311	880	724	55,173
Professional degree	1,586	59	89	126	175	288	297	553	77,949
Doctoral degree	955	28	46	75	141	218	186	262	70,316

Source: Bureau of the Census, Current Population Reports, Money Income of Households, Families, and Persons in the United States: 1991, *Series P-60, No. 180, 1992*

Distribution of Households Within Income Fifth and Top 5 Percent, 1991

Over 80 percent of households in the top income fifth are headed by married couples. In contrast, over half of households in the bottom income fifth are men or women who live alone.

(households by selected characteristics and income quintile; number of households as of 1992; numbers in thousands)

	total households	bottom fifth	second fifth	third fifth	fourth fifth	top fifth	top 5 percent
Total	95,669	19,134	19,134	19,134	19,134	19,134	4,784
Race and Hispanic origin	100.0%	100.0%	100.0%	100.0%	100.0%	100.0%	100.0%
White	85.4	75.6	84.6	86.6	89.0	91.1	92.3
Black	11.6	21.6	12.6	10.5	8.1	5.2	3.3
Hispanic	6.7	9.3	8.1	6.9	5.3	3.7	3.1
Type of household	100.0%	100.0%	100.0%	100.0%	100.0%	100.0%	100.0%
Family households	70.2	44.6	62.2	72.8	82.4	89.1	89.9
Married-couple families	54.8	19.7	43.8	57.6	70.4	82.7	85.1
Female householder, no spouse present	12.2	22.7	14.9	11.5	8.2	3.9	2.9
Male householder, no spouse present	3.2	2.3	3.5	3.7	3.7	2.6	1.9
Nonfamily households	29.8	55.4	37.8	27.2	17.6	10.9	10.1
Female householder	16.8	38.1	21.7	12.9	7.6	3.7	3.1
Living alone	15.0	37.1	19.8	10.9	5.4	1.9	1.7
Male householder	13.0	17.3	16.1	14.3	10.0	7.2	7.0
Living alone	10.0	15.9	13.5	10.9	6.2	3.8	3.8
Age of householder	100.0%	100.0%	100.0%	100.0%	100.0%	100.0%	100.0%
Aged 15 to 24	5.1	8.7	7.9	5.3	2.7	0.8	0.4
Aged 25 to 34	20.9	17.2	21.2	25.6	25.0	15.6	10.9
Aged 35 to 44	22.8	13.0	16.8	23.5	29.5	30.9	28.0
Aged 45 to 54	16.3	9.5	10.4	14.2	18.9	28.4	31.5
Aged 55 to 64	13.1	11.7	11.5	12.9	13.7	15.8	19.4
Aged 65 to 74	12.6	18.9	18.2	12.3	7.2	6.3	7.2
Aged 75 or older	9.3	21.0	14.0	6.2	3.1	2.1	2.6
Number of earners	100.0%	100.0%	100.0%	100.0%	100.0%	100.0%	100.0%
No earners	21.7	58.9	28.2	12.9	5.4	2.9	3.2
One earner	33.3	33.6	46.4	41.0	27.5	17.9	20.9
Two or more earners	45.1	7.6	25.4	46.1	67.0	79.2	75.8
Work experience of householder	100.0%	100.0%	100.0%	100.0%	100.0%	100.0%	100.0%
Worked	72.0	36.7	63.5	78.8	88.3	92.6	92.6
Worked full-time	63.5	22.8	52.8	71.0	83.0	87.9	86.9
50 weeks or more	51.7	11.2	38.2	58.3	71.4	79.4	78.5
27 to 49 weeks	7.9	5.2	9.4	9.4	8.7	6.6	6.6
26 weeks or less	3.9	6.4	5.2	3.3	2.9	1.9	1.8
Worked part-time	8.5	13.9	10.7	7.8	5.4	4.8	5.7
50 weeks or more	3.9	5.0	5.0	3.8	3.0	2.5	3.6
27 to 49 weeks	2.0	3.0	2.8	1.9	1.2	1.1	0.9
26 weeks or less	2.6	5.8	2.9	2.2	1.1	1.1	1.2
Did not work	28.0	63.3	36.5	21.2	11.7	7.4	7.4

Note: Because Hispanics may be of any race, race and Hispanic origin percentages will not total to 100. Source: Bureau of the Census, Current Population Reports, Money Income of Households, Families, and Persons in the United States: 1991, Series P-60, No. 180, 1992

Distribution of Households by Income Fifth and Top 5 Percent, 1991

Over half of married couples have incomes that place them in the top two income fifths. In contrast, nearly half of women who live alone have incomes in the bottom fifth.

(households by selected characteristics within income quintiles; households as of 1992; numbers in thousands)

	total households	total	bottom fifth	second fifth	third fifth	fourth fifth	top fifth	top 5 percent
Total	95,669	100.0%	20.0%	20.0%	20.0%	20.0%	20.0%	5.0%
Race and Hispanic origin								
White	81,675	100.0	17.7	19.8	20.3	20.8	21.4	5.4
Black	11,083	100.0	37.2	21.8	18.1	14.0	8.9	1.4
Hispanic	6,379	100.0	27.9	24.4	20.7	15.9	11.1	2.3
Type of household								
Family households	67,173	100.0	12.7	17.7	20.7	23.5	25.4	6.4
Married-couple families	52,457	100.0	7.2	16.0	21.0	25.7	30.2	7.8
Female householder, no spouse present	11,692	100.0	37.1	24.3	18.8	13.5	6.3	1.2
Male householder, no spouse present	3,025	100.0	14.4	22.1	23.7	23.7	16.2	3.0
Nonfamily households	28,496	100.0	37.2	25.4	18.3	11.8	7.3	1.7
Female householder	16,068	100.0	45.3	25.8	15.4	9.1	4.4	0.9
Living alone	14,361	100.0	49.4	26.3	14.5	7.2	2.6	0.6
Male householder	12,428	100.0	26.6	24.8	22.0	15.4	11.1	2.7
Living alone	9,613	100.0	31.7	26.8	21.7	12.3	7.5	1.9
Age of householder								
Aged 15 to 24	4,859	100.0	34.3	30.9	20.9	10.5	3.3	0.4
Aged 25 to 34	20,007	100.0	16.4	20.3	24.5	23.9	14.9	2.6
Aged 35 to 44	21,774	100.0	11.4	14.8	20.6	26.0	27.2	6.1
Aged 45 to 54	15,547	100.0	11.6	12.8	17.4	23.2	34.9	9.7
Aged 55 to 64	12,560	100.0	17.9	17.6	19.6	20.8	24.1	7.4
Aged 65 to 74	12,043	100.0	30.0	29.0	19.6	11.4	10.0	2.9
Aged 75 or older	8,878	100.0	45.2	30.1	13.4	6.7	4.6	1.4
Number of earners								
No earners	20,741	100.0	54.3	26.0	11.9	5.0	2.7	0.7
One earner	31,818	100.0	20.2	27.9	24.7	16.5	10.8	3.1
Two or more earners	43,111	100.0	3.4	11.3	20.4	29.8	35.1	8.4
Work experience of householder								
Worked	68,876	100.0	10.2	17.6	21.9	24.5	25.7	6.4
Worked full-time	60,739	100.0	7.2	16.6	22.4	26.1	27.7	6.8
50 weeks or more	49,471	100.0	4.3	14.8	22.5	27.6	30.7	7.6
27 to 49 weeks	7,518	100.0	13.2	23.9	24.0	22.0	16.8	4.2
26 weeks or less	3,750	100.0	32.4	26.5	16.7	14.8	9.6	2.3
Worked part-time	8,138	100.0	32.6	25.1	18.5	12.6	11.2	3.4
50 weeks or more	3,709	100.0	26.0	25.7	19.4	15.7	13.1	4.7
27 to 49 weeks	1,929	100.0	29.8	27.8	19.2	12.4	10.8	2.3
26 weeks or less	2,499	100.0	44.7	22.2	16.5	8.1	8.5	2.2
Did not work	26,793	100.0	45.2	26.1	15.1	8.3	5.3	1.3

Note: Because Hispanics may be of any race, race and Hispanic origin numbers will not add to total households. Source: Bureau of the Census, Current Population Reports, Money Income of Households, Families, and Persons in the United States: 1991, *Series P-60, No. 180, 1992*

All Households: Distribution by Income and Household Type, 1991

Married couples have the highest incomes, a median of $41,075 in 1991. Women who live alone have the lowest incomes, a median of just $12,834.

(households by household type and income in 1991; households as of 1992, numbers in thousands)

	total households	family households			
		total	married-couple families	female householder, no spouse present	male householder, no spouse present
Total	95,669	67,173	52,457	11,692	3,025
Under $5,000	4,576	2,246	716	1,432	97
$5,000 to $9,999	9,660	3,864	1,603	2,073	188
$10,000 to $14,999	8,992	4,798	3,011	1,521	265
$15,000 to $19,999	8,376	5,127	3,553	1,288	286
$20,000 to $24,999	8,255	5,521	4,109	1,090	321
$25,000 to $29,999	7,780	5,545	4,306	941	298
$30,000 to $34,999	6,773	5,015	4,029	727	260
$35,000 to $39,999	6,327	4,921	4,036	642	242
$40,000 to $44,999	5,620	4,578	3,834	522	223
$45,000 to $49,999	4,640	3,779	3,272	349	158
$50,000 to $54,999	4,173	3,523	3,090	286	147
$55,000 to $59,999	3,353	2,976	2,686	192	98
$60,000 to $64,999	2,944	2,610	2,375	135	100
$65,000 to $69,999	2,340	2,070	1,910	97	62
$70,000 to $74,999	1,899	1,669	1,533	90	46
$75,000 to $79,999	1,668	1,473	1,375	55	42
$80,000 to $84,999	1,341	1,205	1,135	47	23
$85,000 to $89,999	1,069	951	877	33	40
$90,000 to $94,999	875	794	738	26	31
$95,000 to $99,999	762	687	641	27	20
$100,000 or over	4,246	3,821	3,628	116	77
Median income	$30,126	$36,404	$41,075	$17,961	$31,010

(continued)

(continued from previous page)

(households by household type and income in 1991; households as of 1992; numbers in thousands)

	total households	nonfamily households				
		total	total female householder	female, living alone	total male householder	male, living alone
Total	95,669	28,496	16,068	14,361	12,428	9,613
Under $5,000	4,576	2,330	1,502	1,462	828	774
$5,000 to $9,999	9,660	5,796	4,228	4,137	1,568	1,457
$10,000 to $14,999	8,992	4,194	2,602	2,476	1,592	1,403
$15,000 to $19,999	8,376	3,248	1,905	1,746	1,344	1,106
$20,000 to $24,999	8,255	2,735	1,447	1,273	1,287	1,066
$25,000 to $29,999	7,780	2,235	1,098	958	1,137	880
$30,000 to $34,999	6,773	1,758	809	657	948	694
$35,000 to $39,999	6,327	1,406	662	514	744	529
$40,000 to $44,999	5,620	1,041	419	292	623	430
$45,000 to $49,999	4,640	860	381	271	479	266
$50,000 to $54,999	4,173	651	247	163	403	245
$55,000 to $59,999	3,353	377	149	77	227	117
$60,000 to $64,999	2,944	334	117	67	217	114
$65,000 to $69,999	2,340	270	110	58	159	85
$70,000 to $74,999	1,899	231	72	46	158	77
$75,000 to $79,999	1,668	195	59	31	137	79
$80,000 to $84,999	1,341	136	43	23	92	47
$85,000 to $89,999	1,069	118	28	13	90	41
$90,000 to $94,999	875	81	32	10	49	17
$95,000 to $99,999	762	75	31	21	44	21
$100,000 or over	4,246	425	124	65	301	167
Median income	$30,126	$17,774	$14,321	$12,834	$23,022	$20,259

Source: Bureau of the Census, Current Population Reports, Money Income of Households, Families, and Persons in the United States: 1991, *Series P-60, No. 180, 1992*

White Households: Distribution by Income and Household Type, 1991

Among white households, married couples have the highest incomes, a median of $41,584 in 1991. White women who live alone have the lowest incomes, a median of $13,317.

(white households by household type and income in 1991; households as of 1992; numbers in thousands)

	total households	family households			
		total	married-couple families	female householder, no spouse present	male householder, no spouse present
Total	81,675	57,224	47,124	7,726	2,374
Under $5,000	3,014	1,321	595	675	52
$5,000 to $9,999	7,406	2,600	1,307	1,167	126
$10,000 to $14,999	7,445	3,766	2,587	983	196
$15,000 to $19,999	7,061	4,221	3,147	839	235
$20,000 to $24,999	7,070	4,678	3,654	764	260
$25,000 to $29,999	6,743	4,795	3,845	705	244
$30,000 to $34,999	5,866	4,335	3,579	553	204
$35,000 to $39,999	5,585	4,365	3,692	493	180
$40,000 to $44,999	4,932	4,012	3,444	387	181
$45,000 to $49,999	4,129	3,351	2,956	271	124
$50,000 to $54,999	3,758	3,166	2,829	230	108
$55,000 to $59,999	3,016	2,680	2,439	159	82
$60,000 to $64,999	2,657	2,346	2,162	103	82
$65,000 to $69,999	2,123	1,876	1,741	82	54
$70,000 to $74,999	1,730	1,511	1,387	78	46
$75,000 to $79,999	1,507	1,328	1,237	52	39
$80,000 to $84,999	1,262	1,130	1,080	33	18
$85,000 to $89,999	976	873	816	27	30
$90,000 to $94,999	780	706	659	18	29
$95,000 to $99,999	692	626	584	23	18
$100,000 or over	3,922	3,537	3,386	85	66
Median income	$31,569	$38,229	$41,584	$21,213	$31,634

(continued)

(continued from previous page)

(white households by household type and income in 1991; households as of 1992; numbers in thousands)

| | total households | nonfamily households | | | | |
		total	total female householder	female, living alone	total male householder	male, living alone
Total	81,675	24,451	13,975	12,490	10,476	8,029
Under $5,000	3,014	1,693	1,156	1,133	537	503
$5,000 to $9,999	7,406	4,806	3,574	3,498	1,232	1,147
$10,000 to $14,999	7,445	3,679	2,341	2,245	1,338	1,183
$15,000 to $19,999	7,061	2,840	1,713	1,575	1,128	939
$20,000 to $24,999	7,070	2,392	1,305	1,155	1,087	901
$25,000 to $29,999	6,743	1,948	958	838	990	778
$30,000 to $34,999	5,866	1,531	702	561	828	597
$35,000 to $39,999	5,585	1,220	581	453	639	447
$40,000 to $44,999	4,932	920	369	258	551	372
$45,000 to $49,999	4,129	779	350	249	428	232
$50,000 to $54,999	3,758	592	223	146	369	224
$55,000 to $59,999	3,016	336	133	69	203	117
$60,000 to $64,999	2,657	311	110	60	201	110
$65,000 to $69,999	2,123	247	101	55	146	75
$70,000 to $74,999	1,730	219	72	46	147	70
$75,000 to $79,999	1,507	179	52	29	127	70
$80,000 to $84,999	1,262	132	43	23	88	45
$85,000 to $89,999	976	103	27	12	77	31
$90,000 to $94,999	780	74	29	7	45	16
$95,000 to $99,999	692	66	29	19	37	20
$100,000 or over	3,922	385	109	60	277	152
Median income	$31,569	$18,461	$14,790	$13,317	$24,531	$21,126

Source: Bureau of the Census, Current Population Reports, Money Income of Households, Families, and Persons in the United States: 1991, *Series P-60, No. 180, 1992*

Black Households: Distribution by Income and Household Type, 1991

Black households had a median income of just $18,807 in 1991. But black married couples had a median income nearly twice as high, at $33,369.

(black households by household type and income in 1991; households as of 1992; numbers in thousands)

	total households	family households			
		total	married-couple families	female householder, no spouse present	male householder, no spouse present
Total	11,083	7,716	3,631	3,582	504
Under $5,000	1,394	828	84	707	38
$5,000 to $9,999	2,018	1,106	208	847	51
$10,000 to $14,999	1,291	856	301	494	61
$15,000 to $19,999	1,078	752	307	404	41
$20,000 to $24,999	940	676	343	288	45
$25,000 to $29,999	843	606	350	211	45
$30,000 to $34,999	690	515	321	152	42
$35,000 to $39,999	574	435	256	127	52
$40,000 to $44,999	536	444	292	119	32
$45,000 to $49,999	373	310	215	73	22
$50,000 to $54,999	271	231	156	46	28
$55,000 to $59,999	230	200	168	23	9
$60,000 to $64,999	170	153	116	23	14
$65,000 to $69,999	149	134	116	13	5
$70,000 to $74,999	112	108	96	11	-
$75,000 to $79,999	82	71	68	2	1
$80,000 to $84,999	56	54	38	11	4
$85,000 to $89,999	52	42	33	4	4
$90,000 to $94,999	53	51	41	7	2
$95,000 to $99,999	37	28	27	-	1
$100,000 or over	135	115	95	16	4
Median income	$18,807	$22,203	$33,369	$12,196	$26,428

(continued)

(continued from previous page)

(black households by household type and income in 1991; households as of 1992; numbers in thousands)

	total households	nonfamily households				
		total	total female householder	female, living alone	total male householder	male, living alone
Total	11,083	3,367	1,773	1,596	1,594	1,319
Under $5,000	1,394	565	306	293	260	241
$5,000 to $9,999	2,018	911	612	597	299	274
$10,000 to $14,999	1,291	434	205	180	229	201
$15,000 to $19,999	1,078	236	153	135	172	132
$20,000 to $24,999	940	265	113	95	152	123
$25,000 to $29,999	843	237	116	101	120	87
$30,000 to $34,999	690	174	84	76	91	74
$35,000 to $39,999	574	139	62	45	76	65
$40,000 to $44,999	536	92	40	28	52	43
$45,000 to $49,999	373	63	26	20	37	24
$50,000 to $54,999	271	41	18	11	23	16
$55,000 to $59,999	230	30	13	8	17	-
$60,000 to $64,999	170	17	4	4	13	3
$65,000 to $69,999	149	15	6	-	8	8
$70,000 to $74,999	112	4	-	-	4	2
$75,000 to $79,999	82	11	5	-	6	5
$80,000 to $84,999	56	2	-	-	2	-
$85,000 to $89,999	52	11	1	1	9	9
$90,000 to $94,999	53	2	-	-	2	1
$95,000 to $99,999	37	8	2	2	6	-
$100,000 or over	135	20	6	2	14	11
Median income	$12,202	$9,520	$8,492	$15,223	$13,665	

Source: Bureau of the Census, Current Population Reports, Money Income of Households, Families, and Persons in the United States: 1991, *Series P-60, No. 180, 1992*

Hispanic Households: Distribution by Income and Household Type, 1991

Hispanic married couples had a median income of $28,833 in 1991, just $6,142 higher than the $22,691 median income of all Hispanic households.

(Hispanic households by household type and income in 1991; households as of 1992; numbers in thousands)

		family households			
	total households	total	married- couple families	female householder, no spouse present	male householder, no spouse present
Total	6,379	5,177	3,532	1,261	383
Under $5,000	435	291	103	175	12
$5,000 to $9,999	884	607	270	311	26
$10,000 to $14,999	771	616	365	198	53
$15,000 to $19,999	715	570	363	147	61
$20,000 to $24,999	662	551	390	109	51
$25,000 to $29,999	542	470	349	74	47
$30,000 to $34,999	465	390	310	59	22
$35,000 to $39,999	393	334	272	44	18
$40,000 to $44,999	313	266	199	40	28
$45,000 to $49,999	239	199	161	22	15
$50,000 to $54,999	197	185	154	18	13
$55,000 to $59,999	140	125	101	15	9
$60,000 to $64,999	137	121	104	11	5
$65,000 to $69,999	98	92	74	13	5
$70,000 to $74,999	69	62	54	6	2
$75,000 to $79,999	60	57	52	2	3
$80,000 to $84,999	42	38	30	7	1
$85,000 to $89,999	35	30	27	3	-
$90,000 to $94,999	24	23	18	-	5
$95,000 to $99,999	25	25	23	1	2
$100,000 or over	134	125	112	7	6
Median income	$22,691	$24,551	$28,833	$13,323	$23,298

(continued)

(continued from previous page)

(Hispanic households by household type and income in 1991; households as of 1992; numbers in thousands)

	total households	nonfamily households				
		total	total female householder	female, living alone	total male householder	male, living alone
Total	6,379	1,202	542	443	660	444
Under $5,000	435	144	81	77	63	60
$5,000 to $9,999	884	277	168	164	109	92
$10,000 to $14,999	771	158	73	60	83	63
$15,000 to $19,999	715	145	55	42	90	70
$20,000 to $24,999	662	111	35	29	76	48
$25,000 to $29,999	542	72	38	22	34	27
$30,000 to $34,999	465	74	24	17	50	33
$35,000 to $39,999	393	59	15	13	44	18
$40,000 to $44,999	313	47	15	6	32	14
$45,000 to $49,999	239	41	15	5	26	9
$50,000 to $54,999	197	12	3	2	8	2
$55,000 to $59,999	140	15	2	2	13	2
$60,000 to $64,999	137	16	5	1	11	2
$65,000 to $69,999	98	6	2	1	4	1
$70,000 to $74,999	69	7	2	-	6	1
$75,000 to $79,999	60	3	-	-	3	2
$80,000 to $84,999	42	4	1	1	2	2
$85,000 to $89,999	35	5	3	-	3	-
$90,000 to $94,999	24	1	-	-	1	-
$95,000 to $99,999	25	-	-	-	-	-
$100,000 or over	134	8	6	1	3	1
Median income	$22,691	$15,733	$11,420	$9,160	$19,009	$15,455

Note: Hispanics may be of any race.
Source: Bureau of the Census, Current Population Reports, Money Income of Households, Families, and Persons in the United States: 1991, Series P-60, No. 180, 1992

All Households: Distribution by Income and Age of Householder, 1991

Householders aged 45 to 54 had the highest median income in 1991, at $43,751. Householders aged 75 or older had the lowest median income, just $13,933.

(households by age of householder and income in 1991; households as of 1992; numbers in thousands)

	total households	under 25	25 to 34	35 to 44	45 to 54	55 to 64	65 to 74	75 or older
Total	95,669	4,859	20,007	21,774	15,547	12,560	12,043	8,878
Under $5,000	4,576	575	970	681	591	577	604	578
$5,000 to $9,999	9,660	708	1,487	1,122	748	1,129	2,015	2,452
$10,000 to $14,999	8,992	675	1,599	1,254	862	962	1,887	1,755
$15,000 to $19,999	8,376	681	1,718	1,421	885	979	1,497	1,195
$20,000 to $24,999	8,255	642	1,977	1,506	893	1,025	1,336	877
$25,000 to $29,999	7,780	466	1,897	1,737	1,050	1,002	1,079	550
$30,000 to $34,999	6,773	350	1,766	1,689	1,017	859	775	318
$35,000 to $39,999	6,327	233	1,694	1,667	991	850	573	319
$40,000 to $44,999	5,620	160	1,498	1,670	946	719	436	191
$45,000 to $49,999	4,640	113	1,131	1,415	893	676	294	117
$50,000 to $54,999	4,173	72	997	1,262	909	588	253	93
$55,000 to $59,999	3,353	40	678	1,079	841	440	200	73
$60,000 to $64,999	2,944	42	559	931	782	390	182	58
$65,000 to $69,999	2,340	16	364	801	609	319	169	51
$70,000 to $74,999	1,899	28	346	572	533	290	94	36
$75,000 to $79,999	1,668	8	284	541	456	274	77	29
$80,000 to $84,999	1,341	11	201	453	364	199	80	32
$85,000 to $89,999	1,069	3	177	330	320	159	64	16
$90,000 to $94,999	875	16	104	239	276	153	73	13
$95,000 to $99,999	762	7	109	215	244	125	45	17
$100,000 or over	4,246	13	452	1,189	1,329	844	311	108
Median income	$30,126	$18,313	$30,842	$39,349	$43,751	$33,304	$20,063	$13,933

Source: Bureau of the Census, Current Population Reports, Money Income of Households, Families, and Persons in the United States: 1991, Series P-60, No. 180, 1992

All Family Households: Distribution by Income and Age of Householder, 1991

Families headed by people aged 45 to 54 have the highest median income, just over $50,000 in 1991. Those headed by people under age 25 had the lowest income.

(families by age of householder and income in 1991; families as of 1992; numbers in thousands)

	total families	under 25	25 to 34	35 to 44	45 to 54	55 to 64	65 to 74	75 or older
Total	67,173	2,642	14,379	17,533	12,187	9,296	7,330	3,805
Under $5,000	2,246	378	730	447	260	201	144	86
$5,000 to $9,999	3,864	379	1,134	762	378	481	412	318
$10,000 to $14,999	4,798	340	1,044	866	480	505	903	660
$15,000 to $19,999	5,127	367	1,085	955	569	588	936	627
$20,000 to $24,999	5,521	329	1,267	1,076	597	732	950	570
$25,000 to $29,999	5,545	264	1,257	1,306	743	761	830	385
$30,000 to $34,999	5,015	179	1,212	1,325	735	684	651	227
$35,000 to $39,999	4,921	118	1,268	1,356	784	676	469	250
$40,000 to $44,999	4,578	90	1,132	1,432	773	611	382	158
$45,000 to $49,999	3,779	57	836	1,179	760	598	261	89
$50,000 to $54,999	3,523	45	782	1,085	801	513	226	71
$55,000 to $59,999	2,976	24	566	975	762	409	180	61
$60,000 to $64,999	2,610	23	461	842	712	364	160	49
$65,000 to $69,999	2,070	4	279	731	577	288	150	40
$70,000 to $74,999	1,669	11	260	528	494	263	84	28
$75,000 to $79,999	1,473	3	219	498	410	244	71	27
$80,000 to $84,999	1,205	4	173	411	338	183	76	21
$85,000 to $89,999	951	2	151	289	290	148	57	14
$90,000 to $94,999	794	12	88	211	255	145	71	13
$95,000 to $99,999	687	4	90	199	227	117	37	13
$100,000 or over	3,821	9	346	1,061	1,243	784	281	96
Median income	$36,404	$17,855	$32,289	$42,212	$50,085	$40,165	$26,749	$21,900

Source: Bureau of the Census, Current Population Reports, Money Income of Households, Families, and Persons in the United States: 1991, *Series P-60, No. 180, 1992*

Married-Couple Families: Distribution by Income and Age of Householder, 1991

Married couples are the most affluent household type, and those headed by 45-to-54-year-olds have the highest incomes, a median of $55,002 in 1991.

(married-couple families by age of householder and income in 1991; families as of 1992; numbers in thousands)

	total families	under 25	25 to 34	35 to 44	45 to 54	55 to 64	65 to 74	75 or older
Total	52,457	1,472	10,691	13,520	9,828	7,758	6,269	2,920
Under $5,000	716	49	158	121	95	138	103	53
$5,000 to $9,999	1,603	113	318	226	169	279	297	202
$10,000 to $14,999	3,011	193	550	415	275	374	713	492
$15,000 to $19,999	3,553	247	728	529	331	428	812	478
$20,000 to $24,999	4,109	248	907	660	399	570	848	477
$25,000 to $29,999	4,306	207	982	916	550	601	737	314
$30,000 to $34,999	4,029	129	1,032	1,008	551	577	569	162
$35,000 to $39,999	4,036	98	1,086	1,050	618	576	402	207
$40,000 to $44,999	3,834	64	1,004	1,200	604	525	317	120
$45,000 to $49,999	3,272	39	764	1,019	641	514	226	69
$50,000 to $54,999	3,090	29	700	964	680	468	197	53
$55,000 to $59,999	2,686	18	531	911	675	351	146	54
$60,000 to $64,999	2,375	15	424	772	649	337	140	36
$65,000 to $69,999	1,910	2	262	697	531	252	136	29
$70,000 to $74,999	1,533	7	241	504	453	232	76	20
$75,000 to $79,999	1,375	2	204	475	382	228	60	24
$80,000 to $84,999	1,135	3	164	381	316	180	73	18
$85,000 to $89,999	877	-	144	275	271	131	47	9
$90,000 to $94,999	738	2	83	196	238	142	64	12
$95,000 to $99,999	641	1	85	185	223	101	36	10
$100,000 or over	3,628	6	324	1,017	1,175	755	271	80
Median income	$41,075	$22,787	$37,997	$47,791	$55,002	$43,162	$27,230	$22,452

Source: Bureau of the Census, Current Population Reports, Money Income of Households, Families, and Persons in the United States: 1991, *Series P-60, No. 180, 1992*

Female-Headed Families: Distribution by Income and Age of Householder, 1991

Female-headed families with householders aged 35 to 74 had median incomes above $20,000 in 1991. Those headed by people under age 25 had a median of just $7,524.

(female-headed families with no spouse present by age of householder and income in 1991; families as of 1992; numbers in thousands)

	total families	under 25	25 to 34	35 to 44	45 to 54	55 to 64	65 to 74	75 or older
Total	11,692	909	2,966	3,230	1,836	1,203	823	725
Under $5,000	1,432	311	560	294	154	48	39	26
$5,000 to $9,999	2,073	251	769	484	191	174	100	104
$10,000 to $14,999	1,521	119	430	405	170	102	147	149
$15,000 to $19,999	1,288	77	292	355	204	148	93	119
$20,000 to $24,999	1,090	43	266	333	166	119	83	79
$25,000 to $29,999	941	34	189	316	150	128	67	57
$30,000 to $34,999	727	23	108	239	156	80	64	57
$35,000 to $39,999	642	12	123	225	127	78	47	30
$40,000 to $44,999	522	11	69	176	117	67	56	26
$45,000 to $49,999	349	7	37	121	75	60	30	19
$50,000 to $54,999	286	5	34	80	90	37	27	13
$55,000 to $59,999	192	1	17	32	62	52	24	5
$60,000 to $64,999	135	4	23	42	38	17	7	6
$65,000 to $69,999	97	2	6	22	24	25	9	9
$70,000 to $74,999	90	4	14	17	27	17	5	6
$75,000 to $79,999	55	-	4	20	16	8	6	1
$80,000 to $84,999	47	1	6	22	11	2	3	2
$85,000 to $89,999	33	-	5	3	6	10	5	4
$90,000 to $94,999	26	-	2	9	10	-	4	1
$95,000 to $99,999	27	-	2	7	1	12	1	3
$100,000 or over	116	4	11	27	41	20	5	9
Median income	$17,961	$7,524	$11,730	$20,996	$26,231	$25,385	$21,568	$18,267

Source: Bureau of the Census, Current Population Reports, Money Income of Households, Families, and Persons in the United States: 1991, *Series P-60, No. 180, 1992*

Male-Headed Families: Distribution by Income and Age of Householder, 1991

The $31,010 median income of all male-headed families was greater than the $30,126 median of all households in 1991, but the youngest and oldest male householders have far lower incomes.

(male-headed families with no spouse present by age of householder and income in 1991; families as of 1992; numbers in thousands)

	total families	under 25	25 to 34	35 to 44	45 to 54	55 to 64	65 to 74	75 or older
Total	3,025	261	723	784	523	335	239	161
Under $5,000	97	17	12	32	11	15	2	7
$5,000 to $9,999	188	16	48	52	18	27	15	12
$10,000 to $14,999	265	28	65	46	34	29	43	20
$15,000 to $19,999	286	43	65	70	34	13	31	30
$20,000 to $24,999	321	38	93	83	31	43	19	15
$25,000 to $29,999	298	23	86	74	43	32	26	14
$30,000 to $34,999	260	27	72	78	28	27	18	8
$35,000 to $39,999	242	8	59	82	39	21	20	13
$40,000 to $44,999	223	15	60	56	52	19	8	12
$45,000 to $49,999	158	10	35	39	44	24	5	1
$50,000 to $54,999	147	10	48	41	31	8	2	6
$55,000 to $59,999	98	5	18	31	25	6	10	2
$60,000 to $64,999	100	5	13	28	25	10	13	6
$65,000 to $69,999	62	-	11	11	22	11	5	2
$70,000 to $74,999	46	-	6	7	14	14	3	2
$75,000 to $79,999	42	1	10	4	12	9	5	1
$80,000 to $84,999	23	-	2	8	11	1	-	2
$85,000 to $89,999	40	2	2	10	12	8	6	-
$90,000 to $94,999	31	10	3	7	6	3	3	-
$95,000 to $99,999	20	3	3	6	2	5	-	-
$100,000 or over	77	-	12	18	27	8	5	7
Median income	$31,010	$23,301	$29,520	$32,410	$41,570	$31,111	$26,427	$22,299

Source: Bureau of the Census, Current Population Reports, Money Income of Households, Families, and Persons in the United States: 1991, *Series P-60, No. 180, 1992*

Nonfamily Households: Distribution by Income and Age of Householder, 1991

Nonfamily households headed by someone aged 25 to 44 have the highest median incomes, over $27,000 in 1991. Those headed by people aged 55 or older had the lowest incomes.

(nonfamily households by age of householder and income in 1991; households as of 1992; numbers in thousands)

	total nonfamilies	under 25	25 to 34	35 to 44	45 to 54	55 to 64	65 to 74	75 or older
Total	28,496	2,217	5,628	4,241	3,360	3,264	4,713	5,073
Under $5,000	2,330	197	241	233	330	376	460	492
$5,000 to $9,999	5,796	329	353	360	370	648	1,602	2,134
$10,000 to $14,999	4,194	335	555	388	382	457	984	1,094
$15,000 to $19,999	3,248	314	633	466	316	391	561	568
$20,000 to $24,999	2,735	313	710	430	296	292	386	307
$25,000 to $29,999	2,235	203	640	431	306	242	249	164
$30,000 to $34,999	1,758	171	553	364	281	175	124	90
$35,000 to $39,999	1,406	115	426	310	207	174	104	69
$40,000 to $44,999	1,041	70	366	238	173	109	54	33
$45,000 to $49,999	860	56	295	236	133	78	34	28
$50,000 to $54,999	651	27	215	177	107	75	27	22
$55,000 to $59,999	377	17	112	104	79	31	20	13
$60,000 to $64,999	334	18	98	89	71	26	23	9
$65,000 to $69,999	270	12	84	71	42	30	19	11
$70,000 to $74,999	231	16	86	45	39	26	10	8
$75,000 to $79,999	195	4	65	42	46	30	6	2
$80,000 to $84,999	136	8	29	42	26	16	4	11
$85,000 to $89,999	118	1	25	41	31	11	6	2
$90,000 to $94,999	81	5	17	28	21	8	3	-
$95,000 to $99,999	75	3	19	16	17	7	8	4
$100,000 or over	425	4	106	128	86	61	30	12
Median income	$17,774	$18,848	$27,126	$27,691	$24,732	$16,873	$11,318	$9,760

Source: Bureau of the Census, Current Population Reports, Money Income of Households, Families, and Persons in the United States: 1991, Series P-60, No. 180, 1992

Female-Headed Nonfamily Households: Distribution by Income and Age of Householder, 1991

For nonfamily households headed by women, income peaked for those aged 35 to 44 at over $27,000 in 1991. Those headed by women aged 75 or older had a median of less than $10,000.

(female-headed nonfamily households by age of householder and income in 1991; households as of 1992; numbers in thousands)

	total nonfamilies	under 25	25 to 34	35 to 44	45 to 54	55 to 64	65 to 74	75 or older
Total	16,068	986	2,155	1,603	1,715	2,011	3,535	4,063
Under $5,000	1,502	81	104	99	170	269	362	416
$5,000 to $9,999	4,228	193	142	134	236	443	1,238	1,843
$10,000 to $14,999	2,602	149	223	135	235	295	747	819
$15,000 to $19,999	1,905	139	246	175	187	270	447	440
$20,000 to $24,999	1,447	146	326	161	147	160	289	219
$25,000 to $29,999	1,098	56	254	165	186	139	172	125
$30,000 to $34,999	809	84	202	144	131	109	78	61
$35,000 to $39,999	662	44	181	114	98	105	72	48
$40,000 to $44,999	419	26	106	110	69	56	34	18
$45,000 to $49,999	381	19	104	102	69	43	20	24
$50,000 to $54,999	247	9	70	70	49	27	10	14
$55,000 to $59,999	149	8	37	45	30	15	8	5
$60,000 to $64,999	117	7	32	26	18	18	14	3
$65,000 to $69,999	110	7	27	28	21	6	15	6
$70,000 to $74,999	72	8	22	17	8	9	6	3
$75,000 to $79,999	59	4	16	11	15	11	-	2
$80,000 to $84,999	43	3	8	5	6	12	1	7
$85,000 to $89,999	28	-	6	8	7	-	5	2
$90,000 to $94,999	32	2	5	12	6	5	3	-
$95,000 to $99,999	31	1	9	6	9	-	4	2
$100,000 or over	124	2	35	35	19	18	11	5
Median income	$14,321	$17,265	$25,565	$27,711	$20,943	$14,974	$10,966	$9,283

Source: Bureau of the Census, Current Population Reports, Money Income of Households, Families, and Persons in the United States: 1991, *Series P-60, No. 180, 1992*

Women Living Alone: Distribution of Households by Income and Age of Householder, 1991

Over half of women who live alone are aged 65 or older. For these households, median income hovers around $10,000. In contrast, women aged 25 to 44 who live alone have a median income above $20,000.

(female-headed, single-person households by age of householder and income in 1991; households as of 1992; numbers in thousands)

	total women	under 25	25 to 34	35 to 44	45 to 54	55 to 64	65 to 74	75 or older
Total	14,361	555	1,604	1,358	1,517	1,891	3,461	3,976
Under $5,000	1,462	68	95	94	163	266	361	415
$5,000 to $9,999	4,137	147	130	120	224	442	1,238	1,835
$10,000 to $14,999	2,476	121	198	126	221	274	738	798
$15,000 to $19,999	1,746	86	221	152	174	260	434	420
$20,000 to $24,999	1,273	74	278	145	138	152	276	210
$25,000 to $29,999	958	16	210	147	172	138	165	110
$30,000 to $34,999	657	28	155	129	111	105	71	57
$35,000 to $39,999	514	10	119	100	86	86	67	46
$40,000 to $44,999	292	2	49	88	62	48	26	16
$45,000 to $49,999	271	-	54	87	49	37	20	24
$50,000 to $54,999	163	-	29	55	36	22	8	14
$55,000 to $59,999	77	-	14	29	15	9	4	5
$60,000 to $64,999	67	-	8	22	10	14	13	-
$65,000 to $69,999	58	2	10	14	10	3	15	4
$70,000 to $74,999	46	-	16	13	7	5	3	3
$75,000 to $79,999	31	-	7	2	13	7	-	2
$80,000 to $84,999	23	-	-	2	2	11	-	7
$85,000 to $89,999	13	-	2	1	5	-	4	2
$90,000 to $94,999	10	-	3	3	1	-	3	-
$95,000 to $99,999	21	-	-	6	9	-	4	2
$100,000 or over	65	-	7	23	10	11	10	5
Median income	$12,834	$12,760	$22,881	$26,345	$19,171	$14,197	$10,760	$9,170

Source: Bureau of the Census, Current Population Reports, Money Income of Households, Families, and Persons in the United States: 1991, *Series P-60, No. 180, 1992*

Male-Headed Nonfamily Households: Distribution by Income and Age of Householder, 1991

The median income of nonfamily households headed by elderly men was about $12,000 in 1991, just half the median of all male-headed nonfamily households.

(male-headed nonfamily households by age of householder and income in 1991; households as of 1992; numbers in thousands)

	total nonfamilies	under 25	25 to 34	35 to 44	45 to 54	55 to 64	65 to 74	75 or older
Total	12,428	1,231	3,473	2,638	1,645	1,252	1,178	1,010
Under $5,000	828	116	136	135	160	107	98	76
$5,000 to $9,999	1,568	136	211	226	134	206	364	292
$10,000 to $14,999	1,592	186	332	253	147	162	237	276
$15,000 to $19,999	1,344	175	387	291	128	121	114	127
$20,000 to $24,999	1,287	168	384	269	149	132	98	88
$25,000 to $29,999	1,137	146	386	266	121	103	77	39
$30,000 to $34,999	948	87	352	220	150	65	45	30
$35,000 to $39,999	744	71	246	197	109	69	32	20
$40,000 to $44,999	623	44	259	128	104	53	20	16
$45,000 to $49,999	479	37	191	135	64	35	14	4
$50,000 to $54,999	403	19	145	108	59	49	17	8
$55,000 to $59,999	227	8	75	59	50	15	12	7
$60,000 to $64,999	217	12	67	63	53	8	9	6
$65,000 to $69,999	159	5	57	42	21	24	4	5
$70,000 to $74,999	158	8	64	28	32	18	4	5
$75,000 to $79,999	137	1	49	31	30	19	5	-
$80,000 to $84,999	92	5	20	37	20	4	2	4
$85,000 to $89,999	90	1	20	33	24	11	1	-
$90,000 to $94,999	49	3	12	16	15	3	-	-
$95,000 to $99,999	44	2	10	11	8	7	4	2
$100,000 or over	301	2	71	92	68	42	19	7
Median income	$23,022	$20,061	$28,510	$27,679	$29,257	$20,888	$12,552	$12,375

Source: Bureau of the Census, Current Population Reports, Money Income of Households, Families, and Persons in the United States: 1991, *Series P-60, No. 180, 1992*

Men Living Alone: Distribution by Income and Age of Householder, 1991

Over half of men who live alone are aged 25 to 54. Their median incomes are above $24,000. Younger and older men who live alone have median incomes far below that level.

(male-headed, single-person households by age of householder and income in 1991; households as of 1992; numbers in thousands)

	total men	under 25	25 to 34	35 to 44	45 to 54	55 to 64	65 to 74	75 or older
Total	9,613	601	2,320	2,122	1,380	1,103	1,100	986
Under $5,000	774	90	124	132	155	101	96	76
$5,000 to $9,999	1,457	106	183	217	121	189	349	292
$10,000 to $14,999	1,403	129	277	225	129	151	219	273
$15,000 to $19,999	1,106	92	308	254	118	108	106	120
$20,000 to $24,999	1,066	93	305	240	132	118	96	82
$25,000 to $29,999	880	48	291	240	104	96	63	39
$30,000 to $34,999	694	15	254	182	123	53	42	26
$35,000 to $39,999	529	14	139	166	97	64	31	18
$40,000 to $44,999	430	11	152	84	97	51	19	16
$45,000 to $49,999	266	4	88	87	44	29	12	3
$50,000 to $54,999	245	-	71	66	47	41	15	7
$55,000 to $59,999	117	-	18	35	34	10	12	7
$60,000 to $64,999	114	-	24	38	33	8	5	6
$65,000 to $69,999	85	-	23	20	13	19	4	5
$70,000 to $74,999	77	-	12	16	27	14	3	5
$75,000 to $79,999	79	-	11	26	18	18	5	-
$80,000 to $84,999	47	2	6	22	12	1	-	4
$85,000 to $89,999	41	-	2	21	13	5	-	-
$90,000 to $94,999	17	-	1	6	9	1	-	-
$95,000 to $99,999	21	-	-	7	6	2	4	2
$100,000 or over	167	-	30	38	50	23	18	7
Median income	$20,259	$13,436	$24,339	$24,805	$26,651	$20,068	$12,357	$12,180

Source: Bureau of the Census, Current Population Reports, Money Income of Households, Families, and Persons in the United States: 1991, *Series P-60, No. 180, 1992*

White Households: Distribution by Income and Age of Householder, 1991

White households headed by 45-to-54-year-olds have the highest incomes, a median of $46,215 in 1991. Those headed by people aged 75 or older have the lowest incomes.

(white households by age of householder and income in 1991; households as of 1992; numbers in thousands)

	total households	under 25	25 to 34	35 to 44	45 to 54	55 to 64	65 to 74	75 or older
Total	81,675	3,980	16,677	18,331	13,297	10,760	10,581	8,048
Under $5,000	3,014	332	609	401	396	401	406	470
$5,000 to $9,999	7,406	502	1,022	775	531	834	1,600	2,142
$10,000 to $14,999	7,445	585	1,206	940	702	776	1,629	1,608
$15,000 to $19,999	7,061	593	1,380	1,137	715	806	1,350	1,080
$20,000 to $24,999	7,070	567	1,639	1,208	733	865	1,225	832
$25,000 to $29,999	6,743	414	1,623	1,460	851	884	988	524
$30,000 to $34,999	5,866	308	1,536	1,429	844	727	715	306
$35,000 to $39,999	5,585	213	1,485	1,439	846	765	540	298
$40,000 to $44,999	4,932	131	1,297	1,472	816	634	400	182
$45,000 to $49,999	4,129	108	1,027	1,250	787	578	274	104
$50,000 to $54,999	3,758	63	885	1,127	820	551	228	84
$55,000 to $59,999	3,016	36	606	948	751	408	194	73
$60,000 to $64,999	2,657	35	505	834	707	360	160	58
$65,000 to $69,999	2,123	14	329	722	568	277	163	50
$70,000 to $74,999	1,730	28	322	498	490	268	91	34
$75,000 to $79,999	1,507	6	268	467	409	260	69	29
$80,000 to $84,999	1,262	11	191	424	334	195	76	31
$85,000 to $89,999	976	2	157	304	296	139	62	16
$90,000 to $94,999	780	16	84	199	262	138	67	13
$95,000 to $99,999	692	6	104	192	223	109	42	15
$100,000 or over	3,922	11	402	1,106	1,216	787	301	99
Median income	$31,569	$19,803	$32,315	$41,202	$46,215	$35,550	$21,087	$14,343

Source: Bureau of the Census, Current Population Reports, Money Income of Households, Families, and Persons in the United States: 1991, *Series P-60, No. 180, 1992*

Black Households: Distribution by Income and Age of Householder, 1991

Black households headed by 45-to-54-year-olds have the highest incomes, a median of $27,526 in 1991. Those headed by people under age 25 have the lowest incomes.

(black households by age of householder and income in 1991; households as of 1992; numbers in thousands)

	total households	under 25	25 to 34	35 to 44	45 to 54	55 to 64	65 to 74	75 or older
Total	11,083	703	2,661	2,636	1,718	1,418	1,245	702
Under $5,000	1,394	218	341	245	171	137	184	98
$5,000 to $9,999	2,018	181	405	296	198	276	372	288
$10,000 to $14,999	1,291	74	338	259	125	162	211	122
$15,000 to $19,999	1,078	68	285	220	144	131	131	98
$20,000 to $24,999	940	54	265	236	131	134	94	26
$25,000 to $29,999	843	33	232	222	164	95	77	20
$30,000 to $34,999	690	27	176	206	129	94	50	8
$35,000 to $39,999	574	10	167	178	101	71	27	20
$40,000 to $44,999	536	17	156	160	109	63	31	1
$45,000 to $49,999	373	3	62	113	87	87	14	7
$50,000 to $54,999	271	8	71	93	58	26	13	3
$55,000 to $59,999	230	1	50	89	62	21	5	1
$60,000 to $64,999	170	5	27	57	50	20	12	-
$65,000 to $69,999	149	2	27	61	33	24	2	-
$70,000 to $74,999	112	-	16	55	20	18	2	1
$75,000 to $79,999	82	-	4	38	27	11	3	-
$80,000 to $84,999	56	-	4	18	27	3	4	-
$85,000 to $89,999	52	-	12	14	13	12	1	-
$90,000 to $94,999	53	-	6	23	12	7	4	-
$95,000 to $99,999	37	1	4	12	12	4	-	2
$100,000 or over	135	-	13	40	44	22	8	8
Median income	$18,807	$8,603	$19,284	$26,233	$27,526	$20,103	$11,555	$9,151

Source: Bureau of the Census, Current Population Reports, Money Income of Households, Families, and Persons in the United States: 1991, *Series P-60, No. 180, 1992*

Hispanic Households: Distribution by Income and Age of Householder, 1991

Hispanic households headed by 45-to-54-year-olds had a median income of $28,909 in 1991, not much higher than the $22,691 median for all Hispanic households.

(Hispanic households by age of householder and income in 1991; households as of 1992; numbers in thousands)

	total households	under 25	25 to 34	35 to 44	45 to 54	55 to 64	65 to 74	75 or older
Total	6,379	556	1,821	1,641	979	728	417	238
Under $5,000	435	65	128	80	56	48	29	28
$5,000 to $9,999	884	108	224	173	90	94	112	83
$10,000 to $14,999	771	85	233	184	102	72	55	41
$15,000 to $19,999	715	67	215	185	80	88	54	26
$20,000 to $24,999	662	80	206	161	93	63	41	19
$25,000 to $29,999	542	40	170	146	83	53	34	16
$30,000 to $34,999	465	33	130	146	79	44	22	11
$35,000 to $39,999	393	24	129	119	59	45	15	4
$40,000 to $44,999	313	21	89	102	57	31	8	5
$45,000 to $49,999	239	13	66	78	43	32	8	-
$50,000 to $54,999	197	6	66	57	37	24	5	1
$55,000 to $59,999	140	5	33	41	31	24	7	-
$60,000 to $64,999	137	6	45	27	38	14	5	2
$65,000 to $69,999	98	-	16	32	32	12	5	1
$70,000 to $74,999	69	1	13	19	21	14	2	-
$75,000 to $79,999	60	-	9	16	10	21	2	2
$80,000 to $84,999	42	1	9	15	9	8	-	-
$85,000 to $89,999	35	-	7	14	6	8	-	1
$90,000 to $94,999	24	-	4	10	3	6	1	-
$95,000 to $99,999	25	1	7	4	9	3	2	-
$100,000 or over	134	1	23	32	41	26	11	-
Median income	$22,691	$16,554	$22,664	$26,254	$28,909	$24,952	$15,855	$11,122

Note: Hispanics may be of any race.
Source: Bureau of the Census, Current Population Reports, Money Income of Households, Families, and Persons in the United States: 1991, *Series P-60, No. 180, 1992*

White Families: Distribution by Income and Age of Householder, 1991

The most affluent white families are those headed by householders aged 45 to 54, with a median income of more than $51,000 in 1991. Among white householders, those under age 25 have the lowest incomes.

(white families by age of householder and income in 1991; families as of 1992; numbers in thousands)

	total families	under 25	25 to 34	35 to 44	45 to 54	55 to 64	65 to 74	75 or older
Total	57,224	2,070	11,902	14,726	10,511	8,066	6,541	3,408
Under $5,000	1,453	240	474	254	172	149	100	65
$5,000 to $9,999	2,759	259	803	540	280	332	304	240
$10,000 to $14,999	3,808	280	808	635	382	394	742	566
$15,000 to $19,999	4,307	314	904	773	457	479	833	546
$20,000 to $24,999	4,699	277	1,033	863	481	638	868	540
$25,000 to $29,999	4,760	226	1,066	1,072	601	669	763	363
$30,000 to $34,999	4,312	153	1,033	1,113	598	586	611	218
$35,000 to $39,999	4,324	106	1,094	1,155	694	603	439	232
$40,000 to $44,999	3,992	62	957	1,270	673	532	352	146
$45,000 to $49,999	3,307	47	725	1,038	667	512	240	78
$50,000 to $54,999	3,137	34	679	951	719	487	204	62
$55,000 to $59,999	2,626	18	499	844	673	366	162	63
$60,000 to $64,999	2,312	19	398	735	634	341	137	49
$65,000 to $69,999	1,870	2	246	652	540	249	141	39
$70,000 to $74,999	1,489	8	232	458	446	237	82	26
$75,000 to $79,999	1,308	3	197	424	358	232	68	27
$80,000 to $84,999	1,123	5	163	380	302	181	72	20
$85,000 to $89,999	852	2	127	253	271	130	55	14
$90,000 to $94,999	694	8	70	174	233	131	66	13
$95,000 to $99,999	605	2	89	167	206	98	34	10
$100,000 or over	3,484	8	303	974	1,121	720	267	90
Median income	$37,783	$18,997	$33,916	$43,683	$51,615	$41,679	$27,508	$22,747

Source: Bureau of the Census, Current Population Reports, Money Income of Households, Families, and Persons in the United States: 1991, *Series P-60, No. 180, 1992*

White Married-Couple Families: Distribution by Income and Age of Householder, 1991

White couples headed by a householder aged 45 to 54 are the most affluent households in the country. In 1991, their median income exceeded $55,000.

(white married-couple families by age of householder and income in 1991; families as of 1992; numbers in thousands)

	total families	under 25	25 to 34	35 to 44	45 to 54	55 to 64	65 to 74	75 or older
Total	47,124	1,338	9,526	11,958	8,811	7,009	5,759	2,723
Under $5,000	607	43	137	96	82	115	88	46
$5,000 to $9,999	1,316	93	270	182	140	234	243	155
$10,000 to $14,999	2,604	181	476	328	240	311	619	449
$15,000 to $19,999	3,154	224	625	457	289	374	732	452
$20,000 to $24,999	3,658	229	789	551	335	508	791	454
$25,000 to $29,999	3,837	188	862	790	453	558	685	302
$30,000 to $34,999	3,593	122	926	893	460	501	538	154
$35,000 to $39,999	3,692	97	995	931	554	529	386	200
$40,000 to $44,999	3,438	53	874	1,092	542	466	297	114
$45,000 to $49,999	2,960	35	695	920	584	452	212	63
$50,000 to $54,999	2,828	29	631	863	632	450	177	46
$55,000 to $59,999	2,431	13	486	806	609	324	140	54
$60,000 to $64,999	2,162	13	382	699	591	313	127	36
$65,000 to $69,999	1,740	2	238	624	496	223	128	29
$70,000 to $74,999	1,379	7	223	433	413	212	73	18
$75,000 to $79,999	1,231	-	190	409	335	214	58	24
$80,000 to $84,999	1,086	3	157	365	296	178	70	17
$85,000 to $89,999	810	-	127	248	255	124	45	9
$90,000 to $94,999	655	2	66	167	227	124	58	12
$95,000 to $99,999	577	-	85	160	203	87	33	10
$100,000 or over	3,366	6	292	943	1,076	712	259	78
Median income	$41,506	$22,889	$38,374	$48,343	$55,687	$43,970	$27,760	$22,867

Source: Bureau of the Census, Current Population Reports, Money Income of Households, Families, and Persons in the United States: 1991, *Series P-60, No. 180, 1992*

White Female-Headed Families: Distribution by Income and Age of Householder, 1991

White families headed by women aged 45 to 54 have a median income of more than $28,000. In contrast, those headed by women under age 25 have a median income below $10,000.

(white female-headed families with no spouse present by age and income in 1991; families as of 1992; numbers in thousands)

	total families	under 25	25 to 34	35 to 44	45 to 54	55 to 64	65 to 74	75 or older
Total	7,726	520	1,819	2,140	1,273	811	600	564
Under $5,000	769	183	319	137	82	23	9	16
$5,000 to $9,999	1,272	146	493	295	129	82	55	73
$10,000 to $14,999	1,006	73	272	270	115	73	94	108
$15,000 to $19,999	890	50	203	256	140	91	76	73
$20,000 to $24,999	767	19	167	232	116	97	63	74
$25,000 to $29,999	671	18	127	229	104	86	58	48
$30,000 to $34,999	528	10	64	162	121	65	50	56
$35,000 to $39,999	460	-	64	167	106	59	37	27
$40,000 to $44,999	387	5	47	139	81	49	46	21
$45,000 to $49,999	235	7	11	83	55	42	23	15
$50,000 to $54,999	222	2	23	55	71	34	26	10
$55,000 to $59,999	134	1	5	19	45	36	20	8
$60,000 to $64,999	79	3	6	21	24	14	6	6
$65,000 to $69,999	78	-	2	18	23	17	9	9
$70,000 to $74,999	58	-	3	12	20	11	6	6
$75,000 to $79,999	41	-	1	11	12	9	6	1
$80,000 to $84,999	24	-	5	13	-	2	2	2
$85,000 to $89,999	18	-	-	-	6	4	4	4
$90,000 to $94,999	15	-	2	2	2	3	4	1
$95,000 to $99,999	12	-	1	2	1	6	1	-
$100,000 or over	61	2	5	16	18	7	5	7
Median income	$19,547	$7,260	$11,701	$22,070	$28,042	$27,287	$25,233	$21,222

Source: Bureau of the Census, Current Population Reports, Money Income of Households, Families, and Persons in the United States: 1991, *Series P-60, No. 180, 1992*

White Male-Headed Families: Distribution by Income and Age of Householder, 1991

Regardless of the age of the householder, white families headed by men had a median income of more than $20,000. Those headed by men aged 45 to 54 had a median income of more than $40,000.

	total families	under 25	25 to 34	35 to 44	45 to 54	55 to 64	65 to 74	75 or older
Total	2,374	212	557	629	427	246	182	120
Under $5,000	78	14	18	20	9	12	2	3
$5,000 to $9,999	170	20	41	64	11	16	7	12
$10,000 to $14,999	198	26	61	37	27	10	28	9
$15,000 to $19,999	263	40	76	60	28	14	25	20
$20,000 to $24,999	274	29	77	80	29	33	15	12
$25,000 to $29,999	252	20	78	53	44	25	20	12
$30,000 to $34,999	190	21	43	58	17	20	23	8
$35,000 to $39,999	173	9	36	57	35	15	16	6
$40,000 to $44,999	167	4	36	39	51	17	8	12
$45,000 to $49,999	112	6	18	36	29	18	5	1
$50,000 to $54,999	86	3	25	32	16	3	2	6
$55,000 to $59,999	61	4	8	20	20	6	2	2
$60,000 to $64,999	71	3	10	14	19	14	4	6
$65,000 to $69,999	53	-	6	10	22	9	5	1
$70,000 to $74,999	52	1	6	14	13	14	3	2
$75,000 to $79,999	36	3	7	3	10	9	3	1
$80,000 to $84,999	14	2	1	2	6	1	-	2
$85,000 to $89,999	25	2	-	5	10	2	6	-
$90,000 to $94,999	25	6	3	4	4	3	4	-
$95,000 to $99,999	16	2	3	5	1	5	-	-
$100,000 or over	58	-	7	15	27	1	3	5
Median income	$28,924	$20,933	$25,352	$30,091	$41,025	$32,335	$27,294	$27,665

(white male-headed families with no spouse present by age of householder and income in 1991; families as of 1992; numbers in thousands)

Source: Bureau of the Census, Current Population Reports, Money Income of Households, Families, and Persons in the United States: 1991, *Series P-60, No. 180, 1992*

Black Families: Distribution by Income and Age of Householder, 1991

The incomes of black families vary dramatically depending on the age of the householder. Those headed by a householder aged 45 to 54 had a median income of over $30,000, while those headed by someone under age 25 had a median income of less than $10,000.

(black families by age of householder and income in 1991; families as of 1992; numbers in thousands)

	total families	under 25	25 to 34	35 to 44	45 to 54	55 to 64	65 to 74	75 or older
Total	7,716	490	1,984	2,119	1,211	942	653	317
Under $5,000	877	188	308	191	80	43	45	21
$5,000 to $9,999	1,156	126	381	230	106	144	101	68
$10,000 to $14,999	859	41	235	207	72	87	139	77
$15,000 to $19,999	737	42	194	161	97	79	90	74
$20,000 to $24,999	679	33	164	191	110	91	73	17
$25,000 to $29,999	607	20	148	171	119	80	53	16
$30,000 to $34,999	508	14	124	162	86	69	40	13
$35,000 to $39,999	412	4	104	132	79	56	23	15
$40,000 to $44,999	433	11	119	132	84	60	27	1
$45,000 to $49,999	298	-	45	86	68	80	13	6
$50,000 to $54,999	218	2	44	84	51	25	9	3
$55,000 to $59,999	196	1	35	79	57	20	3	1
$60,000 to $64,999	151	5	19	53	44	18	12	-
$65,000 to $69,999	126	2	18	57	26	21	2	-
$70,000 to $74,999	104	-	13	55	17	16	2	1
$75,000 to $79,999	70	-	3	36	24	7	1	-
$80,000 to $84,999	52	-	4	16	25	3	4	-
$85,000 to $89,999	40	-	10	13	6	9	1	-
$90,000 to $94,999	52	-	6	21	12	7	4	2
$95,000 to $99,999	28	1	2	9	12	4	-	-
$100,000 or over	111	-	9	33	37	22	8	3
Median income	$21,548	$6,915	$16,633	$27,195	$31,252	$26,649	$17,210	$14,321

Source: Bureau of the Census, Current Population Reports, Money Income of Households, Families, and Persons in the United States: 1991, *Series P-60, No. 180, 1992*

Black Married-Couple Families: Distribution by Income and Age of Householder, 1991

Middle-aged black couples have relatively high incomes, with a median of over $40,000. Those headed by householders aged 65 or older had much lower incomes, with a median of less than $20,000.

(black married-couple families by age of householder and income in 1991; families as of 1992; numbers in thousands)

	total families	under 25	25 to 34	35 to 44	45 to 54	55 to 64	65 to 74	75 or older
Total	3,631	98	796	1,033	644	521	400	139
Under $5,000	88	5	16	22	12	12	18	4
$5,000 to $9,999	210	9	27	23	30	39	45	37
$10,000 to $14,999	300	10	59	60	20	43	75	33
$15,000 to $19,999	302	22	83	45	30	34	67	22
$20,000 to $24,999	344	17	82	71	50	58	55	12
$25,000 to $29,999	349	12	99	82	68	35	42	10
$30,000 to $34,999	323	9	78	93	64	50	24	5
$35,000 to $39,999	253	1	75	79	40	39	10	9
$40,000 to $44,999	292	9	94	89	46	41	14	-
$45,000 to $49,999	216	-	38	66	42	55	10	4
$50,000 to $54,999	162	-	41	62	30	17	9	2
$55,000 to $59,999	169	1	30	74	44	18	2	-
$60,000 to $64,999	116	2	16	42	33	16	7	-
$65,000 to $69,999	110	-	14	55	24	15	2	-
$70,000 to $74,999	96	-	13	55	14	10	2	1
$75,000 to $79,999	66	-	1	33	24	7	1	-
$80,000 to $84,999	38	-	4	11	17	3	3	-
$85,000 to $89,999	33	-	10	13	6	2	1	-
$90,000 to $94,999	41	-	6	18	6	7	4	-
$95,000 to $99,999	27	1	2	9	11	4	-	-
$100,000 or over	95	-	7	31	30	18	8	-
Median income	$33,307	$21,050	$32,268	$42,879	$40,787	$34,047	$19,661	$14,368

Source: Bureau of the Census, Current Population Reports, Money Income of Households, Families, and Persons in the United States: 1991, *Series P-60, No. 180, 1992*

Black Female-Headed Families: Distribution by Income and Age of Householder, 1991

Female-headed families headed by blacks under age 25 are the poorest families in the United States. Their median income was just above $5,000 in 1991, less than half the median for black female-headed families with a householder aged 35 or older.

(black female-headed families with no spouse present by age of householder and income in 1991; families as of 1992; numbers in thousands)

	total families	under 25	25 to 34	35 to 44	45 to 54	55 to 64	65 to 74	75 or older
Total	3,582	367	1,066	959	497	346	203	143
Under $5,000	742	177	282	154	63	25	28	13
$5,000 to $9,999	896	115	340	199	70	94	47	31
$10,000 to $14,999	492	29	156	143	52	28	49	35
$15,000 to $19,999	391	20	102	107	57	45	19	42
$20,000 to $24,999	289	14	72	100	57	26	14	6
$25,000 to $29,999	208	4	41	70	49	38	3	4
$30,000 to $34,999	143	3	33	56	22	10	15	2
$35,000 to $39,999	114	2	20	37	25	16	11	4
$40,000 to $44,999	112	-	13	35	34	17	12	1
$45,000 to $49,999	60	-	2	19	15	18	3	2
$50,000 to $54,999	36	-	-	20	11	5	-	-
$55,000 to $59,999	20	-	-	5	11	3	2	-
$60,000 to $64,999	20	1	3	6	9	2	1	-
$65,000 to $69,999	11	2	-	-	2	7	-	-
$70,000 to $74,999	8	-	-	-	2	6	-	-
$75,000 to $79,999	4	-	1	3	-	-	-	-
$80,000 to $84,999	10	-	-	3	6	-	1	-
$85,000 to $89,999	4	-	-	-	-	4	-	-
$90,000 to $94,999	9	-	-	2	6	-	-	2
$95,000 to $99,999	-	-	-	-	-	-	-	-
$100,000 or over	12	-	-	2	6	4	-	-
Median income	$11,414	$5,253	$8,209	$14,417	$20,617	$17,596	$13,019	$12,786

Note: Black male-headed families are not shown because there are too few of them for a reliable distribution.
Source: Bureau of the Census, Current Population Reports, Money Income of Households, Families, and Persons in the United States: 1991, Series P-60, No. 180, 1992

Hispanic Families: Distribution by Income and Age of Householder, 1991

The median income of Hispanic families tops $30,000 among those headed by people aged 45 to 64. In contrast, the median incomes of families headed by the youngest or oldest Hispanics have median incomes below $20,000.

(Hispanic families by age of householder and income in 1991; families as of 1992; numbers in thousands)

	total families	under 25	25 to 34	35 to 44	45 to 54	55 to 64	65 to 74	75 or older
Total	5,177	391	1,528	1,422	832	578	291	133
Under $5,000	331	63	126	67	37	24	9	5
$5,000 to $9,999	642	88	214	149	71	58	42	21
$10,000 to $14,999	618	53	211	156	79	48	40	30
$15,000 to $19,999	572	48	170	151	75	59	45	24
$20,000 to $24,999	543	52	165	140	77	53	36	19
$25,000 to $29,999	470	26	150	136	72	44	30	12
$30,000 to $34,999	383	16	110	117	67	43	22	9
$35,000 to $39,999	324	14	99	105	49	40	15	4
$40,000 to $44,999	257	13	60	90	52	31	7	4
$45,000 to $49,999	196	7	43	72	36	30	9	-
$50,000 to $54,999	173	2	55	54	34	24	4	1
$55,000 to $59,999	116	3	26	28	30	23	6	-
$60,000 to $64,999	118	5	35	27	31	14	5	1
$65,000 to $69,999	92	-	14	32	33	9	5	1
$70,000 to $74,999	57	1	10	15	17	12	2	-
$75,000 to $79,999	54	-	8	13	9	20	2	2
$80,000 to $84,999	34	-	5	14	7	8	-	-
$85,000 to $89,999	33	-	3	13	10	7	-	1
$90,000 to $94,999	21	-	3	9	1	6	1	-
$95,000 to $99,999	23	-	7	3	9	2	2	-
$100,000 or over	118	1	16	28	38	26	9	-
Median income	$23,895	$14,236	$21,404	$26,715	$30,407	$30,298	$21,037	$17,514

Note: Hispanics may be of any race.
Source: Bureau of the Census, Current Population Reports, Money Income of Households, Families, and Persons in the United States: 1991, *Series P-60, No. 180, 1992*

Hispanic Married-Couple Families: Distribution by Income and Age of Householder, 1991

Even among middle-aged Hispanic couples, median income does not rise much higher than $35,000. Most Hispanic couples have incomes below $30,000.

(Hispanic married-couple families by age of householder and income in 1991; families as of 1992; numbers in thousands)

	total families	under 25	25 to 34	35 to 44	45 to 54	55 to 64	65 to 74	75 or older
Total	3,532	222	1,052	986	557	417	213	85
Under $5,000	108	14	35	18	14	15	7	5
$5,000 to $9,999	272	50	72	51	24	30	31	15
$10,000 to $14,999	381	35	145	85	38	26	31	21
$15,000 to $19,999	366	29	122	103	44	34	22	12
$20,000 to $24,999	380	38	125	95	50	35	29	8
$25,000 to $29,999	349	18	115	99	54	28	25	9
$30,000 to $34,999	308	10	95	96	51	34	17	6
$35,000 to $39,999	268	11	89	82	37	37	10	4
$40,000 to $44,999	197	7	54	74	32	23	5	2
$45,000 to $49,999	163	4	39	63	28	22	6	-
$50,000 to $54,999	150	2	48	48	26	23	2	1
$55,000 to $59,999	101	-	24	25	25	23	5	-
$60,000 to $64,999	104	4	33	25	27	12	3	1
$65,000 to $69,999	74	-	11	29	25	5	5	-
$70,000 to $74,999	52	-	9	15	15	11	2	-
$75,000 to $79,999	50	-	7	13	7	19	2	1
$80,000 to $84,999	30	-	5	11	7	6	-	-
$85,000 to $89,999	31	-	3	13	10	5	-	1
$90,000 to $94,999	19	-	3	8	1	5	1	-
$95,000 to $99,999	22	-	7	3	8	2	2	-
$100,000 or over	107	1	12	28	34	23	9	-
Median income	$28,594	$17,329	$26,074	$31,951	$35,568	$35,661	$22,380	$16,589

Note: Hispanics may be of any race.
Source: Bureau of the Census, Current Population Reports, Money Income of Households, Families, and Persons in the United States: 1991, *Series P-60, No. 180, 1992*

Hispanic Female-Headed Families: Distribution by Income and Age of Householder, 1991

Hispanic women who head families alone have incomes almost as low as those of black female-headed families. Regardless of age, median incomes for these families do not rise above $20,000.

(Hispanic female-headed families with no spouse present by age of householder and income in 1991; families as of 1992; numbers in thousands)

	total families	under 25	25 to 34	35 to 44	24 to 54	55 to 64	65 to 74	75 or older
Total	1,261	113	357	349	215	126	63	39
Under $5,000	199	43	82	43	22	6	2	-
$5,000 to $9,999	329	33	129	85	44	23	10	4
$10,000 to $14,999	195	11	53	61	36	17	7	9
$15,000 to $19,999	143	5	28	36	26	24	16	8
$20,000 to $24,999	108	6	24	33	20	12	5	9
$25,000 to $29,999	73	3	21	23	11	10	3	2
$30,000 to $34,999	52	2	6	19	14	5	4	3
$35,000 to $39,999	40	1	7	17	8	3	5	-
$40,000 to $44,999	39	3	3	14	10	5	2	2
$45,000 to $49,999	19	2	-	5	3	6	3	-
$50,000 to $54,999	12	-	1	3	5	1	2	-
$55,000 to $59,999	9	1	1	3	3	-	1	-
$60,000 to $64,999	10	1	1	2	2	2	2	-
$65,000 to $69,999	13	-	-	2	7	4	-	1
$70,000 to $74,999	4	-	-	1	2	1	-	-
$75,000 to $79,999	2	-	-	-	1	1	-	1
$80,000 to $84,999	4	-	-	2	-	2	-	-
$85,000 to $89,999	2	-	-	-	-	2	-	-
$90,000 to $94,999	-	-	-	-	-	-	-	-
$95,000 to $99,999	-	-	-	-	-	-	-	-
$100,000 or over	7	-	2	-	1	3	1	-
Median income	$12,132	$6,932	$8,791	$12,765	$15,806	$18,747	-	-

Note: Hispanics may be of any race. Hispanic male-headed families are not shown because there are too few of them for a reliable distribution.
Source: Bureau of the Census, Current Population Reports, Money Income of Households, Families, and Persons in the United States: 1991, Series P-60, No. 180, 1992

All Households: Distribution by Income and Number of Earners, 1991

The more earners in a household, the higher the household income. The median income of households with four or more earners is nearly $70,000.

(households by number of earners and income in 1991; households as of 1992; numbers in thousands)

| | total households | no earners | one earner | two earners or more | | | | aver. no. of earners |
				total	two earners	three earners	four earners or more	
Total	95,669	20,741	31,818	43,111	33,300	7,223	2,588	1.40
Under $5,000	4,576	3,048	1,297	231	209	20	3	0.39
$5,000 to $9,999	9,660	6,070	2,956	634	581	50	4	0.45
$10,000 to $14,999	8,992	3,727	3,936	1,330	1,210	111	9	0.76
$15,000 to $19,999	8,376	2,337	4,107	1,932	1,732	172	27	1.00
$20,000 to $24,999	8,255	1,783	3,722	2,750	2,463	247	41	1.18
$25,000 to $29,999	7,780	1,190	3,270	3,321	2,859	397	64	1.37
$30,000 to $34,999	6,773	715	2,647	3,410	2,880	431	100	1.52
$35,000 to $39,999	6,327	516	2,264	3,547	2,950	474	123	1.63
$40,000 to $44,999	5,620	382	1,680	3,557	2,826	601	131	1.76
$45,000 to $49,999	4,640	204	1,186	3,250	2,544	534	172	1.89
$50,000 to $54,999	4,173	158	1,061	2,954	2,297	524	134	1.90
$55,000 to $59,999	3,353	104	605	2,644	1,898	579	167	2.08
$60,000 to $64,999	2,944	96	510	2,338	1,682	473	184	2.11
$65,000 to $69,999	2,340	89	377	1,873	1,275	436	162	2.15
$70,000 to $74,999	1,899	57	319	1,523	987	357	179	2.22
$75,000 to $79,999	1,668	38	311	1,319	871	286	162	2.20
$80,000 to $84,999	1,341	35	249	1,056	684	247	125	2.21
$85,000 to $89,999	1,069	19	146	905	565	191	148	2.37
$90,000 to $94,999	875	13	148	714	434	194	86	2.29
$95,000 to $99,999	762	19	114	630	382	139	109	2.37
$100,000 or over	4,246	142	912	3,193	1,971	763	459	2.20
Median income	$30,126	$11,510	$24,834	$46,189	$43,034	$55,409	$69,167	-

Source: Bureau of the Census, Current Population Reports, Money Income of Households, Families, and Persons in the United States: 1991, *Series P-60, No. 180, 1992*

White Households: Distribution by Income and Number of Earners, 1991

Among white households, those with four or more earners had a median income of over $69,000 in 1991. Two-earner households had a median income of $44,056.

(white households by number of earners and income in 1991; households as of 1992; numbers in thousands)

	total households	no earners	one earner	two earners or more				aver. no. of earners
				total	two earners	three earners	four earners or more	
Total	81,675	17,500	26,530	37,645	29,118	6,259	2,268	1.41
Under $5,000	3,014	1,964	871	179	163	13	3	0.42
$5,000 to $9,999	7,406	4,824	2,076	506	469	34	4	0.43
$10,000 to $14,999	7,445	3,292	3,119	1,034	939	86	9	0.72
$15,000 to $19,999	7,061	2,127	3,339	1,594	1,419	155	21	0.97
$20,000 to $24,999	7,070	1,682	3,104	2,284	2,039	207	37	1.14
$25,000 to $29,999	6,743	1,119	2,820	2,804	2,433	313	57	1.33
$30,000 to $34,999	5,866	676	2,293	2,897	2,457	351	89	1.49
$35,000 to $39,999	5,585	503	1,965	3,118	2,614	397	107	1.60
$40,000 to $44,999	4,932	368	1,490	3,073	2,462	497	114	1.73
$45,000 to $49,999	4,129	195	1,058	2,876	2,274	461	141	1.86
$50,000 to $54,999	3,758	149	958	2,651	2,063	470	118	1.89
$55,000 to $59,999	3,016	102	560	2,354	1,695	511	148	2.06
$60,000 to $64,999	2,657	94	470	2,093	1,512	418	163	2.08
$65,000 to $69,999	2,123	89	357	1,677	1,156	380	141	2.11
$70,000 to $74,999	1,730	57	293	1,380	896	327	157	2.20
$75,000 to $79,999	1,507	37	293	1,177	785	251	141	2.17
$80,000 to $84,999	1,262	35	240	987	646	226	115	2.18
$85,000 to $89,999	976	19	130	828	518	185	125	2.35
$90,000 to $94,999	780	13	132	635	383	172	80	2.30
$95,000 to $99,999	692	19	107	566	350	121	94	2.33
$100,000 or over	3,922	136	855	2,932	1,844	683	404	2.17
Median income	$31,569	$12,771	$26,147	$47,100	$44,056	$56,227	$69,305	-

Source: Bureau of the Census, Current Population Reports, Money Income of Households, Families, and Persons in the United States: 1991, Series P-60, No. 180, 1992

Black Households: Distribution by Income and Number of Earners, 1991

Black households with two earners have a median income nearly twice as high as those with only one earner, $33,991 versus $17,230 in 1991.

(black households by number of earners and income in 1991; households as of 1992; numbers in thousands)

| | total households | no earners | one earner | two earners or more | | | | aver. no. of earners |
				total	two earners	three earners	four earners or more	
Total	11,083	2,820	4,301	3,962	3,078	707	176	1.27
Under $5,000	1,394	997	362	35	31	4	-	0.32
$5,000 to $9,999	2,018	1,138	774	106	90	16	-	0.51
$10,000 to $14,999	1,291	342	708	241	224	17	-	0.98
$15,000 to $19,999	1,078	161	648	268	261	5	2	1.16
$20,000 to $24,999	940	68	514	359	330	24	4	1.40
$25,000 to $29,999	843	56	374	413	343	65	5	1.60
$30,000 to $34,999	690	31	273	386	317	62	7	1.73
$35,000 to $39,999	574	4	222	348	272	62	14	1.85
$40,000 to $44,999	536	3	148	384	282	88	15	2.04
$45,000 to $49,999	373	4	103	266	188	57	21	2.09
$50,000 to $54,999	271	7	61	204	150	45	9	2.07
$55,000 to $59,999	230	2	22	206	133	59	14	2.39
$60,000 to $64,999	170	2	19	149	106	31	12	2.37
$65,000 to $69,999	149	-	11	139	83	49	7	2.50
$70,000 to $74,999	112	-	10	102	69	21	12	2.41
$75,000 to $79,999	82	1	6	75	40	20	15	2.70
$80,000 to $84,999	56	-	5	51	26	16	8	-
$85,000 to $89,999	52	-	13	40	29	1	9	-
$90,000 to $94,999	53	-	5	47	29	17	1	-
$95,000 to $99,999	37	-	3	33	16	12	6	-
$100,000 or over	135	3	20	112	57	38	16	2.55
Median income	$18,807	$6,332	$17,230	$37,268	$33,991	$45,882	$59,256	-

Source: Bureau of the Census, Current Population Reports, Money Income of Households, Families, and Persons in the United States: 1991, *Series P-60, No. 180, 1992*

Hispanic Households: Distribution by Income and Number of Earners, 1991

Hispanic households with two earners have a median income that is 80 percent higher than those with only one earner, $31,363 versus $17,250 in 1991.

(Hispanic households by number of earners and income in 1991; households as of 1992; numbers in thousands)

	total households	no earners	one earner	two earners or more total	two earners	three earners	four earners or more	aver. no. of earners
Total	6,379	1,038	2,219	3,122	2,191	616	315	1.57
Under $5,000	435	272	134	29	22	6	1	0.46
$5,000 to $9,999	884	438	332	114	100	13	1	0.65
$10,000 to $14,999	771	149	430	192	177	13	2	1.10
$15,000 to $19,999	715	77	375	263	213	42	8	1.38
$20,000 to $24,999	662	31	256	375	299	62	13	1.68
$25,000 to $29,999	542	29	192	321	231	62	29	1.80
$30,000 to $34,999	465	23	147	294	195	74	25	1.89
$35,000 to $39,999	393	6	136	251	177	56	19	1.91
$40,000 to $44,999	313	4	67	242	159	49	33	2.24
$45,000 to $49,999	239	1	37	201	126	45	30	2.38
$50,000 to $54,999	197	1	30	165	115	31	19	2.33
$55,000 to $59,999	140	1	18	121	81	25	15	2.36
$60,000 to $64,999	137	1	10	126	85	22	20	2.50
$65,000 to $69,999	98	2	7	89	43	25	21	2.77
$70,000 to $74,999	69	-	8	61	27	17	18	-
$75,000 to $79,999	60	-	6	53	22	25	6	-
$80,000 to $84,999	42	1	5	36	27	6	3	-
$85,000 to $89,999	35	-	2	33	22	5	6	-
$90,000 to $94,999	24	-	4	20	12	3	5	-
$95,000 to $99,999	25	-	1	24	13	4	7	-
$100,000 or over	134	3	21	110	45	29	36	2.70
Median income	$22,691	$7,471	$17,250	$34,500	$31,363	$38,399	$49,479	-

Note: Hispanics may be of any race.
Source: Bureau of the Census, Current Population Reports, Money Income of Households, Families, and Persons in the United States: 1991, *Series P-60, No. 180, 1992*

All Families: Distribution by Income and Presence of Children, 1991

Families with preschoolers have the lowest incomes, while those with school-aged children have the highest incomes, $38,087 versus $31,843 in 1991.

(families by presence and age of children in the home, and income in 1991; families as of 1992; numbers in thousands)

	total families	no children	one or more children under age 18				average number of children
			total	all under 6 years	some <6, some 6 to 17 years	all 6 to 17 years	
Total	67,173	32,312	34,861	8,938	7,945	17,978	0.96
Under $5,000	2,442	551	1,891	667	509	715	1.51
$5,000 to $9,999	4,079	1,357	2,722	764	798	1,159	1.34
$10,000 to $14,999	4,844	2,415	2,429	677	648	1,104	1.00
$15,000 to $19,999	5,192	2,611	2,581	745	618	1,218	0.93
$20,000 to $24,999	5,553	3,016	2,536	679	562	1,294	0.86
$25,000 to $29,999	5,515	2,873	2,642	673	641	1,328	0.90
$30,000 to $34,999	4,987	2,355	2,632	629	659	1,344	0.99
$35,000 to $39,999	4,857	2,354	2,504	705	528	1,270	0.92
$40,000 to $44,999	4,538	2,053	2,485	593	559	1,332	1.03
$45,000 to $49,999	3,721	1,758	1,963	474	418	1,071	0.96
$50,000 to $54,999	3,477	1,700	1,777	359	363	1,055	0.93
$55,000 to $59,999	2,920	1,374	1,546	323	336	887	0.95
$60,000 to $64,999	2,569	1,270	1,299	297	259	743	0.90
$65,000 to $69,999	2,053	999	1,054	221	189	645	0.91
$70,000 to $74,999	1,642	783	859	219	166	474	0.89
$75,000 to $79,999	1,454	766	688	155	116	417	0.85
$80,000 to $84,999	1,195	590	605	129	138	338	0.88
$85,000 to $89,999	927	477	450	104	76	270	0.84
$90,000 to $94,999	785	477	308	53	49	207	0.68
$95,000 to $99,999	669	352	317	87	53	177	0.78
$100,000 or over	3,755	2,184	1,572	383	258	931	0.74
Median income	$35,939	$36,943	$34,990	$31,843	$31,283	$38,087	-

Source: Bureau of the Census, Current Population Reports, Money Income of Households, Families, and Persons in the United States: 1991, *Series P-60, No. 180, 1992*

All Married-Couple Families: Distribution by Income and Presence of Children, 1991

Married couples with school-aged children had a median income of nearly $47,000 in 1991. Those without children at home had an income of over $39,000.

(married-couple families by prsence and age of children in the home, and income in 1991; families as of 1992; numbers in thousands)

| | total families | no children | total | one or more children under age 18 | | | average number of children |
				all under 6 years	some <6, some 6 to 17 years	all 6 to 17 years	
Total	52,457	27,100	25,357	6,688	5,923	12,746	0.91
Under $5,000	733	372	360	122	97	141	0.99
$5,000 to $9,999	1,616	926	689	249	179	261	0.88
$10,000 to $14,999	3,030	1,827	1,202	392	365	446	0.84
$15,000 to $19,999	3,557	2,077	1,480	491	417	572	0.84
$20,000 to $24,999	4,116	2,464	1,652	507	434	711	0.79
$25,000 to $29,999	4,298	2,320	1,978	556	545	877	0.90
$30,000 to $34,999	4,045	1,930	2,115	547	578	989	1.02
$35,000 to $39,999	4,034	1,971	2,063	625	471	967	0.94
$40,000 to $44,999	3,824	1,698	2,126	536	511	1,079	1.09
$45,000 to $49,999	3,281	1,502	1,780	444	392	943	1.01
$50,000 to $54,999	3,096	1,479	1,618	337	347	934	0.96
$55,000 to $59,999	2,681	1,221	1,460	305	329	826	0.99
$60,000 to $64,999	2,373	1,138	1,235	282	252	702	0.93
$65,000 to $69,999	1,901	904	997	210	177	611	0.93
$70,000 to $74,999	1,523	709	814	209	165	439	0.92
$75,000 to $79,999	1,370	710	659	148	114	397	0.87
$80,000 to $84,999	1,140	560	580	125	136	319	0.90
$85,000 to $89,999	871	441	431	99	72	259	0.86
$90,000 to $94,999	734	443	291	48	46	197	0.70
$95,000 to $99,999	633	330	303	84	46	173	0.79
$100,000 or over	3,602	2,078	1,523	373	248	903	0.75
Median income	$40,995	$39,083	$42,514	$38,783	$38,644	$46,547	-

Source: Bureau of the Census, Current Population Reports, Money Income of Households, Families, and Persons in the United States: 1991, *Series P-60, No. 180, 1992*

Female-Headed Families: Distribution by Income and Presence of Children, 1991

The $13,012 median income of female-headed families with children is just half the $26,111 median of female-headed families with no children present.

(female-headed families with no spouse present by presence and age of children in the home, and income in 1991; families as of 1992; numbers in thousands)

	total families	no children	one or more children under age 18				
			total	all under 6 years	some <6, some 6 to 17 years	all 6 to 17 years	average number of children
Total	11,692	3,701	7,991	1,830	1,799	4,362	1.24
Under $5,000	1,573	148	1,425	496	394	535	1.77
$5,000 to $9,999	2,230	347	1,883	458	595	830	1.71
$10,000 to $14,999	1,540	466	1,075	217	276	581	1.34
$15,000 to $19,999	1,323	415	908	197	168	542	1.18
$20,000 to $24,999	1,102	392	711	138	103	470	1.10
$25,000 to $29,999	905	384	521	81	78	362	0.93
$30,000 to $34,999	694	297	397	48	67	282	0.92
$35,000 to $39,999	594	260	334	61	35	237	0.89
$40,000 to $44,999	510	234	276	43	28	205	0.79
$45,000 to $49,999	299	167	132	20	18	94	0.65
$50,000 to $54,999	264	165	99	13	8	77	0.65
$55,000 to $59,999	164	109	54	16	3	35	0.43
$60,000 to $64,999	106	71	35	8	2	24	0.46
$65,000 to $69,999	90	47	43	10	8	26	0.74
$70,000 to $74,999	67	43	24	6	1	17	-
$75,000 to $79,999	46	31	15	2	2	11	-
$80,000 to $84,999	34	17	18	2	2	14	-
$85,000 to $89,999	24	19	5	1	-	4	-
$90,000 to $94,999	24	17	7	3	-	4	-
$95,000 to $99,999	18	8	10	3	5	2	-
$100,000 or over	85	65	20	7	4	9	0.36
Median income	$16,692	$26,111	$13,012	$9,437	$9,210	$16,768	-

Source: Bureau of the Census, Current Population Reports, Money Income of Households, Families, and Persons in the United States: 1991, *Series P-60, No. 180, 1992*

Male-Headed Families: Distribution by Income and Presence of Children, 1991

Single-parent families headed by men with preschoolers had a median income of just $17,649 in 1991. Male-headed families without children at home had a median income nearly twice as high.

(male-headed families with no spouse present by presence and age of children in the home, and income in 1991; families as of 1992; numbers in thousands)

| | total families | no children | one or more children under age 18 | | | | average number of children |
			total	all under 6 years	some <6, some 6 to 17 years	all 6 to 17 years	
Total	3,025	1,512	1,513	420	224	869	0.78
Under $5,000	137	30	106	49	18	40	1.22
$5,000 to $9,999	233	83	150	58	24	68	0.99
$10,000 to $14,999	274	122	152	68	7	77	0.81
$15,000 to $19,999	312	119	194	57	33	104	0.96
$20,000 to $24,999	335	161	174	34	26	114	0.91
$25,000 to $29,999	312	168	144	36	18	90	0.73
$30,000 to $34,999	247	127	120	34	13	73	0.74
$35,000 to $39,999	230	123	107	19	21	67	0.72
$40,000 to $44,999	204	122	83	15	20	48	0.62
$45,000 to $49,999	141	89	51	11	8	33	0.57
$50,000 to $54,999	116	56	60	9	7	43	0.74
$55,000 to $59,999	76	44	32	2	4	26	0.78
$60,000 to $64,999	90	61	29	7	5	17	0.52
$65,000 to $69,999	62	48	14	2	4	8	-
$70,000 to $74,999	52	32	21	3	-	17	-
$75,000 to $79,999	39	25	14	5	-	8	-
$80,000 to $84,999	21	14	7	2	-	5	-
$85,000 to $89,999	31	18	14	3	4	7	-
$90,000 to $94,999	27	17	10	1	3	6	-
$95,000 to $99,999	17	13	4	-	2	2	-
$100,000 or over	69	41	28	4	6	19	-
Median income	$28,351	$32,323	$24,171	$17,649	$25,847	$26,487	-

Source: Bureau of the Census, Current Population Reports, Money Income of Households, Families, and Persons in the United States: 1991, *Series P-60, No. 180, 1992*

White Families: Distribution by Income and Presence of Children, 1991

The median income of white families with children at home is about the same as that of families without children at home, just under $38,000 in 1991.

(white families by presence and age of children in the home, and income in 1991; families as of 1992; numbers in thousands)

	total families	no children	one or more children under age 18				
			total	all under 6 years	some <6, some 6 to 17 years	all 6 to 17 years	average number of children
Total	57,224	28,856	28,368	7,376	6,146	14,846	0.91
Under $5,000	1,453	400	1,054	388	259	406	1.37
$5,000 to $9,999	2,759	1,054	1,705	541	429	735	1.18
$10,000 to $14,999	3,808	2,031	1,777	512	463	803	0.91
$15,000 to $19,999	4,307	2,293	2,014	600	464	950	0.86
$20,000 to $24,999	4,699	2,715	1,984	560	419	1,005	0.78
$25,000 to $29,999	4,760	2,548	2,212	583	525	1,104	0.87
$30,000 to $34,999	4,312	2,110	2,203	558	532	1,112	0.96
$35,000 to $39,999	4,324	2,137	2,187	628	433	1,126	0.90
$40,000 to $44,999	3,992	1,824	2,168	494	499	1,175	1.04
$45,000 to $49,999	3,307	1,575	1,732	438	368	926	0.95
$50,000 to $54,999	3,137	1,559	1,577	327	307	943	0.91
$55,000 to $59,999	2,626	1,262	1,364	288	288	788	0.93
$60,000 to $64,999	2,312	1,158	1,155	252	240	663	0.88
$65,000 to $69,999	1,870	921	949	210	164	575	0.89
$70,000 to $74,999	1,489	731	758	198	140	420	0.86
$75,000 to $79,999	1,308	711	597	135	104	358	0.82
$80,000 to $84,999	1,123	561	563	117	130	316	0.88
$85,000 to $89,999	852	444	408	97	66	244	0.83
$90,000 to $94,999	694	442	253	33	36	183	0.62
$95,000 to $99,999	605	328	277	70	45	162	0.75
$100,000 or over	3,484	2,051	1,433	345	234	853	0.72
Median income	$37,783	$37,870	$37,699	$34,445	$34,770	$40,698	-

Source: Bureau of the Census, Current Population Reports, Money Income of Households, Families, and Persons in the United States: 1991, Series P-60, No. 180, 1992

White Married-Couple Families: Distribution by Income and Presence of Children, 1991

White married couples with school-aged children are the most affluent families in the United States. In 1991 their median income was more than $47,000.

(white married-couple families by presence and age of children in the home, and income in 1991; families as of 1992; numbers in thousands)

	total families	no children	one or more children under age 18				
			total	all under 6 years	some <6, some 6 to 17 years	all 6 to 17 years	average number of children
Total	47,124	24,910	22,213	5,937	5,066	11,210	0.88
Under $5,000	607	312	295	96	83	116	1.00
$5,000 to $9,999	1,316	762	554	215	123	215	0.83
$10,000 to $14,999	2,604	1,620	984	331	293	359	0.80
$15,000 to $19,999	3,154	1,905	1,250	422	349	479	0.79
$20,000 to $24,999	3,658	2,277	1,381	452	344	585	0.73
$25,000 to $29,999	3,837	2,125	1,713	491	473	749	0.87
$30,000 to $34,999	3,593	1,759	1,834	506	483	845	1.00
$35,000 to $39,999	3,692	1,837	1,855	571	398	885	0.92
$40,000 to $44,999	3,438	1,561	1,877	453	465	959	1.08
$45,000 to $49,999	2,960	1,376	1,584	410	350	824	0.98
$50,000 to $54,999	2,828	1,380	1,448	306	295	847	0.94
$55,000 to $59,999	2,431	1,133	1,298	276	282	740	0.97
$60,000 to $64,999	2,162	1,053	1,109	241	237	630	0.91
$65,000 to $69,999	1,740	838	902	199	155	547	0.92
$70,000 to $74,999	1,379	664	715	189	139	387	0.88
$75,000 to $79,999	1,231	660	571	130	102	339	0.84
$80,000 to $84,999	1,086	539	547	113	128	306	0.89
$85,000 to $89,999	810	417	393	93	66	234	0.84
$90,000 to $94,999	655	413	242	32	33	177	0.64
$95,000 to $99,999	577	308	269	70	41	158	0.77
$100,000 or over	3,366	1,970	1,396	341	227	828	0.73
Median income	$41,506	$39,593	$43,179	$38,960	$39,831	$47,203	

Source: Bureau of the Census, Current Population Reports, Money Income of Households, Families, and Persons in the United States: 1991, *Series P-60, No. 180, 1992*

White Female-Headed Families: Distribution by Income and Presence of Children, 1991

White single-parent families headed by women with preschoolers have a median income of just $10,000. White female-headed families without children at home have a median income close to $28,000.

(white female-headed families with no spouse present by presence and age of children in the home, and income in 1991; families as of 1992; numbers in thousands)

	total families	no children	one or more children under age 18				
			total	all under 6 years	some <6, some 6 to 17 years	all 6 to 17 years	average number of children
Total	7,726	2,759	4,967	1,106	916	2,945	1.10
Under $5,000	769	71	698	265	172	261	1.69
$5,000 to $9,999	1,272	235	1,037	278	291	469	1.57
$10,000 to $14,999	1,006	328	678	130	165	383	1.22
$15,000 to $19,999	890	288	601	126	85	390	1.11
$20,000 to $24,999	767	314	453	84	49	320	0.93
$25,000 to $29,999	671	280	390	61	41	289	0.92
$30,000 to $34,999	528	251	278	30	36	211	0.82
$35,000 to $39,999	460	203	258	39	25	193	0.89
$40,000 to $44,999	387	167	220	30	15	175	0.83
$45,000 to $49,999	235	136	99	18	10	71	0.60
$50,000 to $54,999	222	138	85	11	8	65	0.64
$55,000 to $59,999	134	91	43	9	3	30	0.41
$60,000 to $64,999	79	53	26	4	2	20	0.46
$65,000 to $69,999	78	41	37	10	6	22	0.62
$70,000 to $74,999	58	36	22	6	1	15	-
$75,000 to $79,999	41	29	12	-	2	10	-
$80,000 to $84,999	24	15	9	2	2	5	-
$85,000 to $89,999	18	13	5	1	-	4	-
$90,000 to $94,999	15	14	-	-	-	-	-
$95,000 to $99,999	12	8	3	-	2	2	-
$100,000 or over	61	48	12	3	1	8	-
Median income	$19,547	$27,522	$15,513	$10,394	$9,927	$19,548	-

Source: Bureau of the Census, Current Population Reports, Money Income of Households, Families, and Persons in the United States: 1991, *Series P-60, No. 180, 1992*

White Male-Headed Families: Distribution by Income and Presence of Children, 1991

Like their female counterparts, men caring for preschoolers with no spouse present have lower incomes than other male-headed families. In 1991 their median income was $18,761.

(white male-headed families with no spouse present by presence and age of children in the home, and income in 1991; families as of 1992; numbers in thousands)

| | total families | no children | one or more children under age 18 | | | | average number of children |
			total	all under 6 years	some <6, some 6 to 17 years	all 6 to 17 years	
Total	2,374	1,187	1,187	333	163	691	0.77
Under $5,000	78	17	61	28	5	29	1.08
$5,000 to $9,999	170	56	114	48	15	51	0.99
$10,000 to $14,999	198	83	115	51	4	60	0.86
$15,000 to $19,999	263	100	163	52	29	81	0.93
$20,000 to $24,999	274	123	150	24	26	100	0.97
$25,000 to $29,999	252	143	109	32	12	65	0.67
$30,000 to $34,999	190	100	91	23	12	56	0.74
$35,000 to $39,999	173	98	75	18	9	47	0.65
$40,000 to $44,999	167	96	71	11	18	41	0.67
$45,000 to $49,999	112	62	50	11	8	31	0.68
$50,000 to $54,999	86	42	45	9	4	31	0.73
$55,000 to $59,999	61	38	23	2	4	18	-
$60,000 to $64,999	71	51	20	7	1	12	-
$65,000 to $69,999	53	42	11	2	3	6	-
$70,000 to $74,999	52	32	21	3	-	17	-
$75,000 to $79,999	36	23	14	5	-	8	-
$80,000 to $84,999	14	6	7	2	-	5	-
$85,000 to $89,999	25	15	10	3	-	6	-
$90,000 to $94,999	25	14	10	1	3	6	-
$95,000 to $99,999	16	12	4	-	2	2	-
$100,000 or over	58	34	24	1	6	17	-
Median income	$28,924	$33,058	$24,507	$18,761	$25,578	$26,378	-

Source: Bureau of the Census, Current Population Reports, Money Income of Households, Families, and Persons in the United States: 1991, *Series P-60, No. 180, 1992*

Black Families: Distribution by Income and Presence of Children, 1991

Black families without children at home have substantially higher incomes than those with children at home. Black families with preschoolers have the lowest incomes.

(black families by presence and age of children in the home, and income in 1991; families as of 1992; numbers in thousands)

| | total families | no children | one or more children under age 18 | | | | average number of children |
			total	all under 6 years	some <6, some 6 to 17 years	all 6 to 17 years	
Total	7,716	2,573	5,143	1,196	1,470	2,478	1.30
Under $5,000	877	123	755	250	239	266	1.78
$5,000 to $9,999	1,156	251	906	199	327	379	1.66
$10,000 to $14,999	859	311	548	136	156	256	1.30
$15,000 to $19,999	737	270	466	114	125	227	1.25
$20,000 to $24,999	679	237	442	96	118	228	1.28
$25,000 to $29,999	607	266	341	65	89	186	1.05
$30,000 to $34,999	508	163	344	50	113	180	1.26
$35,000 to $39,999	412	170	242	57	79	106	1.02
$40,000 to $44,999	433	173	260	75	49	136	0.98
$45,000 to $49,999	298	143	156	19	34	103	1.04
$50,000 to $54,999	218	86	132	18	22	92	1.09
$55,000 to $59,999	196	65	131	26	39	66	1.23
$60,000 to $64,999	151	79	72	18	13	40	0.89
$65,000 to $69,999	126	47	80	8	20	51	1.25
$70,000 to $74,999	104	32	72	16	20	36	1.23
$75,000 to $79,999	70	22	48	8	2	38	-
$80,000 to $84,999	52	19	33	7	5	21	-
$85,000 to $89,999	40	20	20	2	3	15	-
$90,000 to $94,999	52	22	31	10	5	15	-
$95,000 to $99,999	28	13	15	7	-	8	-
$100,000 or over	111	61	51	14	12	25	0.81
Median income	$21,548	$26,711	$18,822	$15,681	$15,534	$22,204	-

Source: Bureau of the Census, Current Population Reports, Money Income of Households, Families, and Persons in the United States: 1991, *Series P-60, No. 180, 1992*

Black Married-Couple Families: Distribution by Income and Presence of Children, 1991

Black couples with school-aged children only are the most affluent black households. In 1991, their median income topped $40,000.

(black married-couple families by presence and age of children in the home, and income in 1991; families as of 1992; numbers in thousands)

	total families	no children	one or more children under age 18				average number of children
			total	all under 6 years	some <6, some 6 to 17 years	all 6 to 17 years	
Total	3,631	1,502	2,129	460	599	1,070	1.13
Under $5,000	88	41	47	19	11	17	1.04
$5,000 to $9,999	210	122	87	21	35	31	0.88
$10,000 to $14,999	300	151	149	34	53	62	1.05
$15,000 to $19,999	302	140	162	50	43	68	1.09
$20,000 to $24,999	344	143	201	39	72	90	1.25
$25,000 to $29,999	349	156	193	42	50	100	1.12
$30,000 to $34,999	323	111	212	26	83	103	1.30
$35,000 to $39,999	253	105	148	35	57	56	1.07
$40,000 to $44,999	292	94	198	60	38	101	1.16
$45,000 to $49,999	216	90	126	17	26	82	1.21
$50,000 to $54,999	162	53	109	16	22	71	1.21
$55,000 to $59,999	169	49	120	19	39	62	1.35
$60,000 to $64,999	116	57	59	16	9	34	0.95
$65,000 to $69,999	110	35	75	8	18	48	1.27
$70,000 to $74,999	96	26	70	16	20	34	1.31
$75,000 to $79,999	66	20	46	6	2	38	-
$80,000 to $84,999	38	14	24	7	5	13	-
$85,000 to $89,999	33	16	17	2	-	15	-
$90,000 to $94,999	41	17	24	7	5	12	-
$95,000 to $99,999	27	12	15	7	-	8	-
$100,000 or over	95	48	47	14	9	24	0.86
Median income	$33,307	$29,917	$35,358	$34,843	$32,048	$40,327	-

Source: Bureau of the Census, Current Population Reports, Money Income of Households, Families, and Persons in the United States: 1991, Series P-60, No. 180, 1992

Black Female-Headed Families: Distribution by Income and Presence of Children, 1991

Single-parent families headed by black women with preschoolers are the poorest families in the nation. In 1991, their median income was just $7,827.

(black female-headed families with no spouse present by presence and age of children in the home, and income in 1991; families as of 1992; numbers in thousands)

	total families	no children	one or more children under age 18				average number of children
			total	all under 6 years	some <6, some 6 to 17 years	all 6 to 17 years	
Total	3,582	811	2,771	670	816	1,285	1.54
Under $5,000	742	68	673	218	214	241	1.89
$5,000 to $9,999	896	106	790	171	284	335	1.88
$10,000 to $14,999	492	123	369	85	100	184	1.55
$15,000 to $19,999	391	112	279	59	78	142	1.40
$20,000 to $24,999	289	67	222	49	46	128	1.44
$25,000 to $29,999	208	89	119	20	32	67	0.97
$30,000 to $34,999	143	35	108	15	30	63	1.29
$35,000 to $39,999	114	43	72	21	10	41	0.96
$40,000 to $44,999	112	60	52	13	10	29	0.65
$45,000 to $49,999	60	30	30	2	8	20	-
$50,000 to $54,999	36	22	14	2	-	12	-
$55,000 to $59,999	20	13	7	7	-	-	-
$60,000 to $64,999	20	13	7	3	-	4	-
$65,000 to $69,999	11	6	5	-	2	3	-
$70,000 to $74,999	8	6	2	-	-	2	-
$75,000 to $79,999	4	2	2	2	-	-	-
$80,000 to $84,999	10	1	9	-	-	9	-
$85,000 to $89,999	4	4	-	-	-	-	-
$90,000 to $94,999	9	2	7	3	-	4	-
$95,000 to $99,999	-	-	-	-	-	-	-
$100,000 or over	12	9	4	-	3	1	-
Median income	$11,414	$19,776	$9,413	$7,827	$8,192	$11,728	-

Note: Black male-headed families are not shown because there are too few of them for a reliable distribution.
Source: Bureau of the Census, Current Population Reports, Money Income of Households, Families, and Persons in the United States: 1991, Series P-60, No. 180, 1992

Hispanic Families: Distribution by Income and Presence of Children, 1991

Hispanic families without children at home have the highest median incomes, more than $28,000 in 1991. Those with preschoolers have the lowest incomes.

(Hispanic families by presence and age of children in the home, and income in 1991; families as of 1992; numbers in thousands)

| | total families | no children | one or more children under age 18 | | | | average number of children |
			total	all under 6 years	some <6, some 6 to 17 years	all 6 to 17 years	
Total	5,177	1,556	3,621	910	1,122	1,588	1.48
Under $5,000	331	48	283	86	97	101	1.88
$5,000 to $9,999	642	140	501	158	162	182	1.67
$10,000 to $14,999	618	163	455	124	167	165	1.66
$15,000 to $19,999	572	157	416	101	162	153	1.62
$20,000 to $24,999	543	169	374	85	105	184	1.45
$25,000 to $29,999	470	141	329	82	91	156	1.48
$30,000 to $34,999	383	118	265	45	95	125	1.51
$35,000 to $39,999	324	104	221	47	53	121	1.44
$40,000 to $44,999	257	82	175	34	40	100	1.42
$45,000 to $49,999	196	62	134	36	40	59	1.42
$50,000 to $54,999	173	67	106	26	31	48	1.16
$55,000 to $59,999	116	52	64	13	18	33	0.99
$60,000 to $64,999	118	49	68	19	18	32	1.08
$65,000 to $69,999	92	39	53	8	11	34	0.92
$70,000 to $74,999	57	25	33	6	7	20	-
$75,000 to $79,999	54	28	25	7	2	17	-
$80,000 to $84,999	34	14	20	7	3	10	-
$85,000 to $89,999	33	17	16	3	3	10	-
$90,000 to $94,999	21	13	8	1	1	7	-
$95,000 to $99,999	23	11	12	4	3	5	-
$100,000 or over	118	57	61	21	14	27	0.93
Median income	$23,895	$28,621	$22,064	$19,163	$19,053	$25,303	-

Note: Hispanics may be of any race.
Source: Bureau of the Census, Current Population Reports, Money Income of Households, Families, and Persons in the United States: 1991, *Series P-60, No. 180, 1992*

Hispanic Married-Couple Families: Distribution by Income and Presence of Children, 1991

Hispanic couples with school-aged children only and those without children at home have the highest median incomes, just over $30,000 in 1991.

(Hispanic married-couple families by presence and age of children in the home, and income in 1991; families as of 1992; numbers in thousands)

| | total families | no children | one or more children under age 18 | | | | average number of children |
			total	all under 6 years	some <6, some 6 to 17 years	all 6 to 17 years	
Total	3,532	1,087	2,445	658	778	1,009	1.50
Under $5,000	108	34	75	22	28	25	1.61
$5,000 to $9,999	272	90	183	83	51	49	1.45
$10,000 to $14,999	381	101	280	92	107	81	1.72
$15,000 to $19,999	366	85	281	74	125	82	1.79
$20,000 to $24,999	380	105	275	71	93	111	1.60
$25,000 to $29,999	349	87	262	71	79	111	1.63
$30,000 to $34,999	308	86	221	40	83	98	1.63
$35,000 to $39,999	268	81	188	40	49	98	1.52
$40,000 to $44,999	197	52	145	33	34	78	1.58
$45,000 to $49,999	163	44	119	33	31	55	1.48
$50,000 to $54,999	150	53	97	24	29	44	1.22
$55,000 to $59,999	101	42	59	12	17	30	1.07
$60,000 to $64,999	104	42	62	15	17	30	1.12
$65,000 to $69,999	74	35	39	4	8	27	-
$70,000 to $74,999	52	21	31	5	6	20	-
$75,000 to $79,999	50	26	24	7	2	15	-
$80,000 to $84,999	30	13	16	7	1	8	-
$85,000 to $89,999	31	16	15	2	3	10	-
$90,000 to $94,999	19	11	7	1	-	7	-
$95,000 to $99,999	22	10	12	4	3	5	-
$100,000 or over	107	53	54	18	13	24	0.95
Median income	$28,594	$32,087	$27,296	$24,122	$24,186	$31,880	-

Note: Hispanics may be of any race.
Source: Bureau of the Census, Current Population Reports, Money Income of Households, Families, and Persons in the United States: 1991, *Series P-60, No. 180, 1992*

Hispanic Female-Headed Families: Distribution by Income and Presence of Children, 1991

Single-parent families headed by Hispanic women with preschoolers have a median income that is less than half that of female-headed Hispanic families without children at home.

(Hispanic female-headed families with no spouse present by presence and age of children in the home, and income in 1991; families as of 1992; numbers in thousands)

	total families	no children	one or more children under age 18				
			total	all under 6 years	some <6, some 6 to 17 years	all 6 to 17 years	average number of children
Total	1,261	289	972	199	298	475	1.60
Under $5,000	199	11	187	52	62	73	2.10
$5,000 to $9,999	329	39	290	62	108	120	1.94
$10,000 to $14,999	195	42	153	25	57	71	1.73
$15,000 to $19,999	143	43	100	19	27	55	1.46
$20,000 to $24,999	108	38	70	11	8	51	1.19
$25,000 to $29,999	73	29	45	5	8	31	-
$30,000 to $34,999	52	17	35	5	7	23	-
$35,000 to $39,999	40	13	28	4	4	20	-
$40,000 to $44,999	39	17	22	-	4	18	-
$45,000 to $49,999	19	12	7	-	5	2	-
$50,000 to $54,999	12	9	3	2	1	-	-
$55,000 to $59,999	9	5	4	1	1	2	-
$60,000 to $64,999	10	5	5	3	-	2	-
$65,000 to $69,999	13	2	11	4	2	5	-
$70,000 to $74,999	4	2	2	1	1	-	-
$75,000 to $79,999	2	1	1	-	-	1	-
$80,000 to $84,999	4	-	4	-	2	2	-
$85,000 to $89,999	2	1	1	1	-	-	-
$90,000 to $94,999	-	-	-	-	-	-	-
$95,000 to $99,999	-	-	-	-	-	-	-
$100,000 or over	7	4	3	3	-	-	-
Median income	$12,132	$21,254	$10,216	$8,623	$9,139	$12,788	-

Note: Hispanics may be of any race. Hispanic male-headed families are not shown because there are too few of them for a reliable distribution.
Source: Bureau of the Census, *Current Population Reports*, Money Income of Households, Families, and Persons in the United States: 1991, *Series P-60, No. 180, 1992*

Married Couples, Husband Worked: Distribution by Income and Presence of Children, 1991

Among all married couples with a working husband, those with no children at home had the highest incomes, a median of $49,612 in 1991.

(married couples with a working husband by presence and age of children in the home, and income in 1991; married couples as of 1992; numbers in thousands)

	total married couples	no children	one or more children under age 18				average number of children
			total	all under 6 years	some <6, some 6 to 17 years	all 6 to 17 years	
Total	42,015	18,026	23,989	6,395	5,596	11,999	1.08
Under $5,000	348	126	223	62	65	95	1.31
$5,000 to $9,999	708	255	453	195	113	145	1.27
$10,000 to $14,999	1,493	527	966	354	288	323	1.35
$15,000 to $19,999	2,104	759	1,345	465	397	483	1.30
$20,000 to $24,999	2,647	1,098	1,549	489	407	653	1.17
$25,000 to $29,999	3,102	1,237	1,865	535	521	809	1.19
$30,000 to $34,999	3,240	1,210	2,029	535	562	933	1.23
$35,000 to $39,999	3,400	1,402	1,998	607	461	929	1.08
$40,000 to $44,999	3,329	1,262	2,067	521	497	1,049	1.21
$45,000 to $49,999	2,938	1,225	1,713	434	377	903	1.09
$50,000 to $54,999	2,842	1,264	1,578	331	339	908	1.03
$55,000 to $59,999	2,500	1,064	1,436	303	326	808	1.05
$60,000 to $64,999	2,225	999	1,226	280	250	696	0.99
$65,000 to $69,999	1,782	795	987	209	177	600	0.99
$70,000 to $74,999	1,441	633	807	208	164	435	0.96
$75,000 to $79,999	1,285	634	651	143	113	395	0.91
$80,000 to $84,999	1,073	501	572	122	132	318	0.94
$85,000 to $89,999	843	415	428	99	71	257	0.88
$90,000 to $94,999	699	411	287	48	46	194	0.73
$95,000 to $99,999	605	303	302	84	46	172	0.83
$100,000 or over	3,411	1,903	1,508	370	245	893	0.78
Median income	$45,995	$49,612	$43,721	$39,610	$39,826	$47,940	-

Source: Bureau of the Census, Current Population Reports, Money Income of Households, Families, and Persons in the United States: 1991, *Series P-60, No. 180, 1992*

Married Couples, Husband and Wife Worked: Distribution by Income and Presence of Children, 1991

Dual-earner married couples with children aged 6 or older had a median income of more than $50,000 in 1991. Those with preschoolers only had a median of $43,203.

(married couples in which both husband and wife worked by presence and age of children in the home, and income in 1991; married couples as of 1992; numbers in thousands)

	total married couples	no children	one or more children under age 18				
			total	all under 6 years	some <6, some 6 to 17 years	all 6 to 17 years	average number of children
Total	31,159	13,348	17,810	4,571	3,662	9,577	1.04
Under $5,000	137	54	83	16	22	44	1.23
$5,000 to $9,999	282	115	167	59	31	77	1.12
$10,000 to $14,999	710	274	436	149	116	171	1.19
$15,000 to $19,999	1,142	385	757	254	191	312	1.29
$20,000 to $24,999	1,677	691	986	326	231	429	1.16
$25,000 to $29,999	2,221	855	1,366	388	333	644	1.18
$30,000 to $34,999	2,291	834	1,457	375	371	711	1.21
$35,000 to $39,999	2,510	985	1,526	464	321	740	1.09
$40,000 to $44,999	2,589	961	1,628	411	352	865	1.20
$45,000 to $49,999	2,379	973	1,405	347	298	761	1.09
$50,000 to $54,999	2,230	965	1,265	261	243	761	1.02
$55,000 to $59,999	2,045	854	1,191	254	256	681	1.05
$60,000 to $64,999	1,876	822	1,054	234	203	616	0.98
$65,000 to $69,999	1,505	667	838	170	134	534	0.97
$70,000 to $74,999	1,237	543	694	176	136	382	0.95
$75,000 to $79,999	1,081	541	540	118	80	342	0.87
$80,000 to $84,999	860	416	444	83	90	271	0.89
$85,000 to $89,999	712	361	351	72	55	224	0.85
$90,000 to $94,999	563	325	238	37	36	164	0.74
$95,000 to $99,999	525	270	256	79	27	150	0.76
$100,000 or over	2,589	1,459	1,130	299	133	698	0.74
Median income	$49,178	$52,669	$46,629	$43,203	$43,079	$50,237	-

Source: Bureau of the Census, Current Population Reports, Money Income of Households, Families, and Persons in the United States: 1991, *Series P-60, No. 180, 1992*

Married Couples, Husband Worked, Wife Worked Full-Time, Year-Round: Distribution by Income and Presence of Children, 1991

The median income of dual-earner married couples in which the wife worked full-time exceeded $50,000 in 1991. Only those with preschoolers fell below this median.

(married couples in which the husband worked and the wife worked full-time, year-round by presence and age of children in the home, and income in 1991; married couples as of 1992; numbers in thousands)

| | total married couples | no children | | | one or more children under age 18 | | |
			total	all under 6 years	some <6, some 6 to 17 years	all 6 to 17 years	average number of children
Total	16,863	8,249	8,614	1,989	1,563	5,063	0.88
Under $5,000	41	26	15	1	4	10	-
$5,000 to $9,999	40	17	23	1	4	17	-
$10,000 to $14,999	172	93	79	24	12	43	0.77
$15,000 to $19,999	329	134	195	40	48	107	1.12
$20,000 to $24,999	625	325	300	80	76	145	0.90
$25,000 to $29,999	962	417	544	151	127	266	1.02
$30,000 to $34,999	1,084	479	605	137	143	324	1.00
$35,000 to $39,999	1,229	551	679	192	134	352	0.94
$40,000 to $44,999	1,398	597	801	208	145	448	1.02
$45,000 to $49,999	1,373	615	758	179	128	451	0.95
$50,000 to $54,999	1,339	670	669	135	117	416	0.85
$55,000 to $59,999	1,289	593	697	127	162	409	0.95
$60,000 to $64,999	1,119	536	583	116	106	361	0.89
$65,000 to $69,999	982	486	495	78	80	336	0.86
$70,000 to $74,999	785	364	421	114	56	250	0.85
$75,000 to $79,999	681	364	317	62	41	214	0.79
$80,000 to $84,999	551	282	269	42	52	175	0.83
$85,000 to $89,999	483	270	213	47	27	139	0.71
$90,000 to $94,999	385	232	153	27	23	103	0.65
$95,000 to $99,999	352	211	141	45	7	90	0.63
$100,000 or over	1,643	986	657	182	70	405	0.61
Median income	$54,391	$56,642	$52,348	$49,466	$48,059	$54,474	-

Source: Bureau of the Census, Current Population Reports, Money Income of Households, Families, and Persons in the United States: 1991, Series P-60, No. 180, 1992

Married Couples, Husband Worked, Wife Did Not Work: Distribution by Income and Presence of Children, 1991

The median income of single-earner married couples is far below that of dual-earner couples. In 1991, single-earner couples had a median of just $36,240.

(married couples in which the husband worked and the wife did not work by presence and age of children in the home, and income in 1991; married couples as of 1992; numbers in thousands)

	total married couples	no children	one or more children under age 18				
			total	all under 6 years	some <6, some 6 to 17 years	all 6 to 17 years	average number of children
Total	10,857	4,678	6,179	1,824	1,934	2,422	1.18
Under $5,000	211	71	140	46	43	51	1.36
$5,000 to $9,999	426	141	285	136	82	68	1.37
$10,000 to $14,999	783	254	529	205	172	152	1.49
$15,000 to $19,999	963	374	588	211	205	171	1.31
$20,000 to $24,999	971	408	563	163	176	224	1.20
$25,000 to $29,999	882	382	499	147	187	165	1.21
$30,000 to $34,999	949	377	573	160	190	222	1.29
$35,000 to $39,999	890	418	472	143	140	189	1.05
$40,000 to $44,999	740	301	439	110	145	184	1.28
$45,000 to $49,999	560	252	308	87	79	142	1.08
$50,000 to $54,999	612	299	313	70	96	147	1.06
$55,000 to $59,999	455	210	246	49	69	127	1.06
$60,000 to $64,999	350	177	173	46	47	80	1.02
$65,000 to $69,999	276	128	149	39	43	67	1.09
$70,000 to $74,999	204	91	113	32	28	53	1.03
$75,000 to $79,999	204	93	111	26	33	52	1.15
$80,000 to $84,999	213	85	128	40	41	47	1.10
$85,000 to $89,999	131	55	77	27	16	34	1.07
$90,000 to $94,999	136	86	50	11	9	30	0.67
$95,000 to $99,999	79	33	46	5	19	22	1.26
$100,000 or over	822	444	378	71	112	195	0.92
Median income	$36,240	$38,755	$33,961	$30,080	$31,954	$39,121	-

Source: Bureau of the Census, Current Population Reports, Money Income of Households, Families, and Persons in the United States: 1991, Series P-60, No. 180, 1992

Married Couples, Husband Worked Full-Time, Year-Round: Distribution by Income and Presence of Children, 1991

Couples with a husband who works full-time had a median income of more than $50,000 in 1991. Those with no children at home had the highest incomes.

(married couples in which the husband worked full-time, year-round by presence and age of children in the home, and income in 1991; married couples as of 1992; numbers in thousands)

| | total married couples | no children | one or more children under age 18 | | | | average number of children |
			total	all under 6 years	some <6, some 6 to 17 years	all 6 to 17 years	
Total	32,424	13,050	19,374	5,088	4,518	9,769	1.13
Under $5,000	119	41	78	19	23	36	1.43
$5,000 to $9,999	217	56	161	77	23	61	1.31
$10,000 to $14,999	729	213	516	196	151	168	1.44
$15,000 to $19,999	1,174	330	843	296	253	295	1.44
$20,000 to $24,999	1,610	548	1,062	334	274	453	1.31
$25,000 to $29,999	2,153	772	1,382	412	396	574	1.28
$30,000 to $34,999	2,398	754	1,643	442	479	723	1.37
$35,000 to $39,999	2,646	1,005	1,641	512	399	729	1.16
$40,000 to $44,999	2,649	908	1,741	466	434	841	1.29
$45,000 to $49,999	2,470	976	1,494	376	331	787	1.13
$50,000 to $54,999	2,396	1,013	1,383	294	295	794	1.08
$55,000 to $59,999	2,154	881	1,273	260	290	723	1.08
$60,000 to $64,999	1,935	844	1,091	246	233	612	1.02
$65,000 to $69,999	1,553	659	894	191	165	539	1.04
$70,000 to $74,999	1,256	538	718	173	156	389	0.99
$75,000 to $79,999	1,119	526	593	127	104	362	0.96
$80,000 to $84,999	949	424	525	107	125	293	0.99
$85,000 to $89,999	777	372	404	93	71	241	0.91
$90,000 to $94,999	617	355	262	42	43	176	0.77
$95,000 to $99,999	558	270	287	80	46	161	0.87
$100,000 or over	2,947	1,563	1,384	344	227	813	0.84
Median income	$50,092	$54,519	$46,858	$42,828	$42,819	$51,343	-

Source: Bureau of the Census, Current Population Reports, Money Income of Households, Families, and Persons in the United States: 1991, Series P-60, No. 180, 1992

THE OFFICIAL GUIDE TO AMERICAN INCOMES **127**

Married Couples, Husband Worked Full-Time, Year-Round, Wife Worked: Distribution by Income and Presence of Children, 1991

Dual-earner couples in which the husband worked full-time had a median income of more than $52,000 in 1991. Those with no children at home had the highest incomes.

(married couples in which the husband worked full-time, year-round and the wife worked by presence and age of children in the home, and income in 1991; married couples as of 1992; numbers in thousands)

	total married couples	no children	one or more children under age 18				average number of children
			total	all under 6 years	some <6, some 6 to 17 years	all 6 to 17 years	
Total	24,496	10,096	14,399	3,659	2,957	7,784	1.07
Under $5,000	77	32	45	5	15	25	1.32
$5,000 to $9,999	84	27	57	25	5	27	1.03
$10,000 to $14,999	305	109	196	69	55	73	1.21
$15,000 to $19,999	574	156	419	146	111	162	1.41
$20,000 to $24,999	980	346	634	207	141	286	1.26
$25,000 to $29,999	1,507	542	965	288	235	442	1.22
$30,000 to $34,999	1,669	538	1,131	301	305	526	1.31
$35,000 to $39,999	1,959	717	1,242	387	276	579	1.15
$40,000 to $44,999	2,041	692	1,349	363	297	689	1.26
$45,000 to $49,999	1,984	771	1,213	294	261	658	1.13
$50,000 to $54,999	1,891	794	1,097	231	206	660	1.05
$55,000 to $59,999	1,760	713	1,047	213	222	613	1.07
$60,000 to $64,999	1,646	710	935	204	186	544	1.01
$65,000 to $69,999	1,325	567	758	152	125	482	1.01
$70,000 to $74,999	1,085	472	612	147	128	337	0.96
$75,000 to $79,999	946	463	483	102	72	310	0.89
$80,000 to $84,999	761	359	402	71	84	247	0.93
$85,000 to $89,999	656	326	330	66	54	210	0.87
$90,000 to $94,999	501	286	215	32	34	150	0.78
$95,000 to $99,999	488	245	243	77	27	139	0.79
$100,000 or over	2,256	1,230	1,026	279	120	627	0.77
Median income	$52,707	$57,223	$49,771	$45,630	$45,705	$53,271	-

Source: Bureau of the Census, *Current Population Reports,* Money Income of Households, Families, and Persons in the United States: 1991, *Series P-60, No. 180, 1992*

Married Couples, Husband and Wife Worked Full-Time, Year-Round: Distribution by Income and Presence of Children, 1991

Dual-earner married couples in which both husband and wife work full-time are the most affluent households in the United States. Even those with preschoolers had a median income above $50,000.

(married couples in which the husband and wife worked full-time, year-round by presence and age of children in the home, and income in 1991; married couples as of 1992; numbers in thousands)

	total married couples	no children	one or more children under age 18				
			total	all under 6 years	some <6, some 6 to 17 years	all 6 to 17 years	average number of children
Total	13,625	6,576	7,049	1,613	1,271	4,165	0.88
Under $5,000	35	23	12	1	3	8	-
$5,000 to $9,999	17	7	10	1	1	8	-
$10,000 to $14,999	84	47	37	9	4	25	0.71
$15,000 to $19,999	148	58	90	27	16	47	1.01
$20,000 to $24,999	329	163	165	35	46	83	0.94
$25,000 to $29,999	612	274	338	98	81	159	0.98
$30,000 to $34,999	769	326	443	106	112	225	1.05
$35,000 to $39,999	953	405	548	161	117	270	0.99
$40,000 to $44,999	1,085	438	646	178	115	353	1.05
$45,000 to $49,999	1,123	480	644	150	112	382	0.98
$50,000 to $54,999	1,129	561	568	121	93	354	0.86
$55,000 to $59,999	1,113	507	607	102	140	364	0.94
$60,000 to $64,999	1,003	477	526	99	98	330	0.90
$65,000 to $69,999	868	414	454	67	76	312	0.91
$70,000 to $74,999	685	319	367	95	51	220	0.85
$75,000 to $79,999	601	321	279	58	36	185	0.79
$80,000 to $84,999	489	249	240	31	47	162	0.85
$85,000 to $89,999	457	254	203	45	27	131	0.72
$90,000 to $94,999	353	212	141	22	23	96	0.67
$95,000 to $99,999	327	193	134	43	7	84	0.65
$100,000 or over	1,445	848	596	164	65	367	0.64
Median income	$57,092	$60,001	$55,156	$51,267	$51,417	$56,902	-

Source: Bureau of the Census, Current Population Reports, Money Income of Households, Families, and Persons in the United States: 1991, Series P-60, No. 180, 1991

Married Couples, Husband Worked Full-Time, Year-Round, Wife Did Not Work: Distribution by Income and Presence of Children, 1991

Even if the husband worked full-time, the median income of single-earner couples amounted to just $40,518 in 1991. Those with preschoolers had a median income below $40,000.

(married couples in which the husband worked full-time, year-round and the wife did not work by presence and age of children in the home, and income in 1991; married couples as of 1992; numbers in thousands)

	total married couples	no children	one or more children under age 18				
			total	all under 6 years	some <6, some 6 to 17 years	all 6 to 17 years	average number of children
Total	7,928	2,953	4,975	1,430	1,560	1,985	1.30
Under $5,000	42	9	33	13	8	11	-
$5,000 to $9,999	132	28	104	52	18	34	1.48
$10,000 to $14,999	424	104	320	128	97	95	1.61
$15,000 to $19,999	599	174	425	149	142	133	1.48
$20,000 to $24,999	630	202	428	127	133	167	1.40
$25,000 to $29,999	646	229	417	124	161	132	1.41
$30,000 to $34,999	729	217	512	141	174	197	1.50
$35,000 to $39,999	687	288	399	125	123	151	1.16
$40,000 to $44,999	608	216	392	104	137	151	1.41
$45,000 to $49,999	486	205	281	82	69	129	1.14
$50,000 to $54,999	506	220	286	63	89	134	1.18
$55,000 to $59,999	394	168	226	47	69	110	1.14
$60,000 to $64,999	289	133	156	42	47	67	1.13
$65,000 to $69,999	228	92	136	39	40	57	1.20
$70,000 to $74,999	171	66	106	26	28	51	1.18
$75,000 to $79,999	173	63	110	26	33	52	1.36
$80,000 to $84,999	188	64	123	37	41	46	1.22
$85,000 to $89,999	121	46	75	27	16	32	1.15
$90,000 to $94,999	115	69	47	11	9	26	0.75
$95,000 to $99,999	69	25	44	3	19	22	-
$100,000 or over	691	334	357	65	107	186	1.05
Median income	$40,518	$45,215	$38,045	$33,891	$36,895	$41,792	-

Source: Bureau of the Census, Current Population Reports, Money Income of Households, Families, and Persons in the United States: 1991, *Series P-60, No. 180, 1991*

Married Couples, Husband Did Not Work: Distribution by Income and Presence of Children, 1991

Married couples with a nonworking husband had a median income of just $23,084 in 1991. Those with preschoolers had a median income of less than $15,000.

(married couples in which the husband did not work by presence and age of children in the home, and income in 1991; married couples as of 1992; numbers in thousands)

	total married couples	no children	one or more children under age 18				average number of children
			total	all under 6 years	some <6, some 6 to 17 years	all 6 to 17 years	
Total	10,442	9,073	1,368	293	327	748	0.25
Under $5,000	384	247	137	59	32	46	0.71
$5,000 to $9,999	908	671	237	54	66	116	0.57
$10,000 to $14,999	1,537	1,300	237	37	76	123	0.35
$15,000 to $19,999	1,453	1,317	135	26	21	89	0.17
$20,000 to $24,999	1,469	1,365	103	18	27	58	0.11
$25,000 to $29,999	1,196	1,083	113	21	24	68	0.17
$30,000 to $34,999	805	720	85	12	17	56	0.18
$35,000 to $39,999	634	568	65	18	10	38	0.15
$40,000 to $44,999	495	436	59	15	14	30	0.23
$45,000 to $49,999	343	276	67	10	15	41	0.31
$50,000 to $54,999	254	215	40	5	8	26	0.28
$55,000 to $59,999	181	157	24	2	4	18	0.17
$60,000 to $64,999	148	139	9	2	2	5	0.08
$65,000 to $69,999	120	109	11	-	-	10	0.09
$70,000 to $74,999	82	76	7	2	1	4	0.11
$75,000 to $79,999	85	76	9	5	2	2	0.22
$80,000 to $84,999	67	59	8	3	4	1	-
$85,000 to $89,999	28	25	2	-	1	1	-
$90,000 to $94,999	35	32	3	-	-	3	-
$95,000 to $99,999	29	28	1	-	-	1	-
$100,000 or over	191	175	15	3	3	10	0.15
Median income	$23,084	$23,588	$18,091	$14,178	$14,136	$20,012	-

Source: Bureau of the Census, Current Population Reports, Money Income of Households, Families, and Persons in the United States: 1991, Series P-60, No. 180, 1992

Married Couples, Husband Did Not Work, Wife Worked: Distribution by Income and Presence of Children, 1991

Single-earner couples in which the wife worked but the husband did not had a median income of $28,556 in 1991.

(married couples in which the husband did not work and the wife worked by presence and age of children in the home, and income in 1991; married couples as of 1992; numbers in thousands)

| | total married couples | no children | one or more children under age 18 | | | | average number of children |
			total	all under 6 years	some <6, some 6 to 17 years	all 6 to 17 years	
Total	2,514	1,891	623	110	128	385	0.44
Under $5,000	47	25	22	6	3	14	-
$5,000 to $9,999	147	77	70	10	20	41	1.03
$10,000 to $14,999	262	165	97	15	26	56	0.71
$15,000 to $19,999	259	207	52	7	7	37	0.37
$20,000 to $24,999	298	244	54	8	18	28	0.33
$25,000 to $29,999	320	259	60	18	5	37	0.31
$30,000 to $34,999	249	201	48	7	8	33	0.30
$35,000 to $39,999	203	159	44	10	8	26	0.32
$40,000 to $44,999	144	102	42	11	9	22	0.57
$45,000 to $49,999	133	94	38	5	10	23	0.51
$50,000 to $54,999	100	74	26	4	4	18	0.50
$55,000 to $59,999	67	48	19	1	1	17	-
$60,000 to $64,999	58	49	9	2	2	5	-
$65,000 to $69,999	40	34	7	-	-	6	-
$70,000 to $74,999	26	21	5	-	1	4	-
$75,000 to $79,999	40	33	7	3	2	2	-
$80,000 to $84,999	23	19	4	-	4	1	-
$85,000 to $89,999	11	8	2	-	1	1	-
$90,000 to $94,999	15	13	2	-	-	2	-
$95,000 to $99,999	7	7	-	-	-	-	-
$100,000 or over	64	51	13	3	2	9	-
Median income	$28,556	$29,244	$26,151	$27,485	$22,861	$26,733	-

Source: Bureau of the Census, Current Population Reports, Money Income of Households, Families, and Persons in the United States: 1991, Series P-60, No. 180, 1992

Married Couples, Husband Did Not Work, Wife Worked Full-Time, Year-Round: Distribution by Income and Presence of Children, 1991

Few married couples include a husband who does not work and a wife who works full-time. Those that do had a median income of $34,278 in 1991.

(married couples in which the husband did not work and the wife worked full-time, year-round by presence and age of children in the home, and income in 1991; married couples as of 1992; numbers in thousands)

| | total married couples | no children | one or more children under age 18 | | | | average number of children |
			total	all under 6 years	some <6, some 6 to 17 years	all 6 to 17 years	
Total	1,232	894	338	65	67	206	0.46
Under $5,000	5	3	2	-	-	2	-
$5,000 to $9,999	19	5	13	6	1	7	-
$10,000 to $14,999	82	41	41	3	8	30	0.85
$15,000 to $19,999	100	75	25	7	2	16	0.34
$20,000 to $24,999	141	114	28	1	15	11	0.40
$25,000 to $29,999	135	105	30	8	4	18	0.40
$30,000 to $34,999	154	117	37	7	4	25	0.35
$35,000 to $39,999	122	89	32	8	6	19	0.36
$40,000 to $44,999	101	68	33	9	4	19	0.58
$45,000 to $49,999	82	56	27	3	7	16	0.61
$50,000 to $54,999	63	43	21	4	4	13	-
$55,000 to $59,999	48	36	12	1	1	11	-
$60,000 to $64,999	32	25	7	2	2	4	-
$65,000 to $69,999	22	17	5	-	-	5	-
$70,000 to $74,999	21	17	4	-	1	3	-
$75,000 to $79,999	22	16	6	3	2	2	-
$80,000 to $84,999	20	17	4	-	4	-	-
$85,000 to $89,999	5	3	2	-	1	1	-
$90,000 to $94,999	6	6	-	-	-	-	-
$95,000 to $99,999	4	4	-	-	-	-	-
$100,000 or over	47	37	10	3	2	5	-
Median income	$34,278	$34,362	$33,994	-	-	$33,072	-

Source: Bureau of the Census, Current Population Reports, Money Income of Households, Families, and Persons in the United States: 1991, *Series P-60, No. 180, 1992*

Married Couples, Husband and Wife Did Not Work: Distribution by Income and Presence of Children, 1991

Most married couples with no workers are retired couples. The median income of nonworking couples with no children at home was $22,241 in 1991.

(married couples in which husband and wife do not work by presence and age of children in the home, and income in 1991; married couples as of 1992; numbers in thousands)

	total married couples	no children	one or more children under age 18				
			total	all under 6 years	some <6, some 6 to 17 years	all 6 to 17 years	average number of children
Total	7,927	7,182	745	183	199	363	0.19
Under $5,000	337	221	115	54	30	32	0.69
$5,000 to $9,999	760	594	166	45	47	75	0.47
$10,000 to $14,999	1,274	1,135	140	22	51	67	0.27
$15,000 to $19,999	1,194	1,110	83	18	14	51	0.13
$20,000 to $24,999	1,171	1,122	49	11	8	30	0.06
$25,000 to $29,999	877	824	53	3	19	31	0.12
$30,000 to $34,999	556	519	37	5	9	23	0.13
$35,000 to $39,999	431	409	21	8	2	11	0.06
$40,000 to $44,999	351	334	17	3	6	8	0.09
$45,000 to $49,999	210	182	28	5	5	18	0.18
$50,000 to $54,999	155	141	14	2	3	8	0.15
$55,000 to $59,999	114	109	5	1	3	1	0.07
$60,000 to $64,999	89	89	-	-	-	-	-
$65,000 to $69,999	79	75	4	-	-	4	0.05
$70,000 to $74,999	56	55	2	2	-	-	-
$75,000 to $79,999	45	43	2	2	-	-	-
$80,000 to $84,999	44	41	3	3	1	-	-
$85,000 to $89,999	17	17	-	-	-	-	-
$90,000 to $94,999	20	19	1	-	-	1	-
$95,000 to $99,999	22	20	1	-	-	1	-
$100,000 or over	127	124	2	-	1	1	0.07
Median income	$21,616	$22,241	$13,189	$9,480	$12,129	$15,925	-

Source: Bureau of the Census, Current Population Reports, Money Income of Households, Families, and Persons in the United States: 1991, *Series P-60, No. 180, 1992*

All Families: Distribution by Income and Source of Income, 1991

Families that receive at least some income from dividends had a median income of over $57,000 in 1991. Those who receive public assistance had a median income of just over $7,000.

(families by income and income source in 1991; families as of 1992; numbers in thousands)

	total families	under $5,000	$5,000 to $9,999	$10,000 to $14,999	$15,000 to $24,999	$25,000 to $34,999	$35,000 to $49,999	$50,000 to $74,999	$75,000 to $99,999	$100,000 or over	median income
Total	67,173	2,442	4,079	4,844	10,745	10,502	13,116	12,661	5,029	3,755	$35,939
Earnings	56,639	978	2,231	3,191	8,163	9,096	12,202	12,225	4,916	3,636	40,239
Wages and salary	54,452	816	2,078	2,978	7,754	8,764	11,881	11,958	4,762	3,460	40,602
Nonfarm self-employment	8,846	216	286	437	1,083	1,397	1,807	1,846	869	904	42,732
Farm self-employment	1,310	59	55	74	182	212	309	253	100	67	37,871
Social Security	15,462	244	1,110	1,956	4,036	2,971	2,436	1,611	631	467	26,017
SSI - Supplemental Security Income	2,053	132	532	397	457	200	162	128	29	16	14,491
Public assistance	3,887	1,112	1,457	576	439	168	95	26	12	2	7,435
Unemployment compensation	6,500	88	328	399	1,275	1,197	1,479	1,200	381	153	34,712
Property income	45,854	424	861	1,867	5,944	7,079	10,270	11,066	4,729	3,614	44,246
Interest	44,360	396	792	1,781	5,683	6,827	9,897	10,784	4,634	3,566	44,539
Dividends	15,963	42	111	230	1,173	1,800	3,141	4,601	2,468	2,396	57,008
Rents, royalties, estates and trusts	7,147	64	124	193	612	912	1,298	1,756	962	1,227	54,493
Retirement income	10,522	48	185	669	2,408	2,140	2,098	1,679	744	551	33,871
Private pensions	6,704	31	134	487	1,728	1,404	1,312	922	393	292	31,140
Military retirement	1,106	-	10	39	98	183	222	293	162	99	50,074
Federal employee pensions	1,184	11	23	44	245	237	255	250	67	52	36,649
State or local employee pensions	1,880	7	14	87	406	399	429	271	172	96	35,708
Other Income	9,979	358	698	726	1,546	1,504	1,996	1,802	810	540	36,171
Child support	3,690	209	379	395	742	620	683	411	155	94	26,554
Educational assistance	5,194	89	275	303	619	712	1,070	1,211	566	350	42,963

Source: Bureau of the Census, Current Population Reports, Money Income of Households, Families, and Persons in the United States: 1991, *Series P-60, No. 180, 1992*

White Families: Distribution by Income and Source of Income, 1991

White families that receive at least some income from dividends had a median income of more than $57,000 in 1991, versus a median of $37,783 for all white families.

(white families by income and income source in 1991; families as of 1992; numbers in thousands)

	total families	under $5,000	$5,000 to $9,999	$10,000 to $14,999	$15,000 to $24,999	$25,000 to $34,999	$35,000 to $49,999	$50,000 to $74,999	$75,000 to $99,999	$100,000 or over	median income
Total	57,224	1,453	2,759	3,808	9,006	9,073	11,624	11,434	4,584	3,484	$37,783
Earnings	48,601	650	1,508	2,438	6,652	7,738	10,751	11,017	4,475	3,373	41,761
Wages and salary	46,596	517	1,376	2,241	6,272	7,432	10,457	10,767	4,330	3,203	42,146
Nonfarm self-employment	8,152	178	243	403	982	1,279	1,678	1,723	807	859	43,259
Farm self-employment	1,277	56	48	71	180	208	305	250	93	67	38,018
Social Security	13,505	164	782	1,626	3,546	2,672	2,228	1,467	585	433	26,867
SSI - Supplemental Security Income	1,323	69	330	247	301	136	114	96	15	14	15,365
Public assistance	2,333	541	870	382	315	130	71	15	9	-	8,404
Unemployment compensation	5,603	61	255	309	1,064	1,035	1,322	1,088	330	139	35,771
Property income	41,599	344	718	1,626	5,335	6,390	9,343	10,132	4,344	3,367	44,633
Interest	40,315	320	663	1,553	5,124	6,170	9,022	9,886	4,257	3,322	44,905
Dividends	15,026	42	101	217	1,091	1,704	2,950	4,323	2,332	2,266	57,081
Rents, royalties, estates and trusts	6,558	55	102	178	558	844	1,189	1,609	891	1,132	54,555
Retirement income	9,644	36	151	602	2,205	1,975	1,925	1,538	697	516	34,032
Private pensions	6,200	24	106	439	1,607	1,318	1,218	848	366	274	31,257
Military retirement	997	-	10	36	89	154	196	263	156	93	50,970
Federal employee pensions	1,071	7	19	42	217	204	232	237	63	50	37,824
State or local employee pensions	1,694	7	11	72	352	356	397	251	161	86	36,341
Other Income	8,386	235	491	535	1,258	1,289	1,728	1,619	739	493	38,148
Child support	3,132	143	263	310	607	558	635	381	144	91	28,832
Educational assistance	4,300	56	189	215	489	571	887	1,068	515	311	45,538

Source: Bureau of the Census, Current Population Reports, Money Income of Households, Families, and Persons in the United States: 1991, *Series P-60, No. 180, 1992*

Black Families: Distribution by Income and Source of Income, 1991

Black families that received at least some income from dividends had a median income of more than $50,000 in 1991, versus a median of just $21,548 for all black families.

(black families by income and income source in 1991; families as of 1992; numbers in thousands)

	total families	under $5,000	$5,000 to $9,999	$10,000 to $14,999	$15,000 to $24,999	$25,000 to $34,999	$35,000 to $49,999	$50,000 to $74,999	$75,000 to $99,999	$100,000 or over	median income
Total	7,716	877	1,156	859	1,416	1,115	1,144	795	243	111	$21,548
Earnings	6,085	268	628	638	1,239	1,055	1,124	786	240	107	27,299
Wages and salary	6,006	251	613	627	1,225	1,044	1,119	781	240	105	27,512
Nonfarm self-employment	390	22	27	26	53	65	74	71	36	17	35,543
Farm self-employment	19	1	7	2	-	2	2	1	4	-	-
Social Security	1,585	71	294	274	422	239	159	90	17	18	18,122
SSI - Supplemental Security Income	635	62	189	135	143	50	33	19	3	1	12,041
Public assistance	1,378	544	514	156	97	34	22	10	1	-	6,116
Unemployment compensation	703	17	65	74	183	132	122	69	33	7	25,857
Property income	2,790	50	108	160	434	498	679	562	199	100	37,959
Interest	2,643	46	100	154	401	476	639	536	191	100	38,216
Dividends	525	-	8	4	52	71	125	156	66	41	50,142
Rents, royalties, estates and trusts	314	6	14	6	36	48	74	78	24	29	44,163
Retirement income	723	12	34	56	180	140	152	105	30	14	30,146
Private pensions	413	7	29	37	106	79	79	57	15	5	27,831
Military retirement	96	-	-	3	9	25	26	26	4	3	47,416
Federal employee pensions	95	4	5	1	24	26	21	9	4	1	32,059
State or local employee pensions	152	-	3	14	48	36	27	14	7	3	27,794
Other Income	1,237	103	169	156	232	161	222	131	45	17	22,622
Child support	482	62	105	76	113	51	38	28	8	-	14,869
Educational assistance	673	27	60	71	108	102	154	103	34	15	32,224

Source: Bureau of the Census, Current Population Reports, Money Income of Households, Families, and Persons in the United States: 1991, *Series P-60, No. 180, 1992*

Hispanic Families: Distribution by Income and Source of Income, 1991

Hispanic families that received at least some income from dividends had a median income of more than $55,000 in 1991, versus a median of just $23,895 for all Hispanic families.

(Hispanic families by income and income source in 1991; families as of 1992; numbers in thousands)

	total families	under $5,000	$5,000 to $9,999	$10,000 to $14,999	$15,000 to $24,999	$25,000 to $34,999	$35,000 to $49,999	$50,000 to $74,999	$75,000 to $99,999	$100,000 or over	median income
Total	5,177	331	642	618	1,115	853	777	556	165	118	$23,895
Earnings	4,400	142	372	495	1,001	800	760	548	165	116	27,047
Wages and salary	4,269	131	356	477	963	783	743	540	162	114	27,268
Nonfarm self-employment	431	19	32	33	104	58	67	64	30	25	29,471
Farm self-employment	19	2	1	1	6	-	-	7	2	-	-
Social Security	715	16	97	106	189	138	93	50	11	15	21,532
SSI - Supplemental Security Income	264	12	64	54	65	28	20	14	4	4	15,239
Public assistance	629	141	255	104	78	35	15	1	2	-	8,364
Unemployment compensation	607	9	62	62	152	125	110	67	13	7	26,141
Property income	2,039	40	59	111	365	388	438	389	143	105	36,580
Interest	1,933	37	54	107	334	373	422	367	136	103	36,832
Dividends	336	-	-	2	23	43	72	89	52	55	55,207
Rents, royalties, estates and trusts	276	5	8	12	39	40	49	70	32	22	44,618
Retirement income	321	1	9	25	77	70	65	41	16	17	31,596
Private pensions	184	1	4	18	47	39	39	20	9	7	29,478
Military retirement	26	-	1	1	2	2	9	10	-	1	-
Federal employee pensions	51	-	-	3	11	17	5	9	3	2	-
State or local employee pensions	60	-	3	3	16	14	12	5	3	4	-
Other Income	593	53	75	61	111	91	101	72	18	11	24,707
Child support	215	27	32	30	46	33	29	12	5	1	19,838
Educational assistance	313	14	27	28	55	55	62	50	13	9	30,814

Note: Hispanics may be of any race.
Source: Bureau of the Census, Current Population Reports, Money Income of Households, Families, and Persons in the United States: 1991, Series P-60, No. 180, 1992

Median Weekly Earnings of Families, 1991

Weekly earnings are highest for dual-income couples, regardless of race. Earnings are lowest for families maintained by women.

(families with earners by selected characteristics and median weekly earnings in 1991; families as of 1992; numbers in thousands)

	total families	median weekly earnings
ALL		
Total families with earners	43,530	$669
Married-couple families	33,930	754
One earner	12,177	455
Husband	8,784	532
Wife	2,636	279
Other family member	757	278
Two or more earners	21,753	911
Husband and wife	19,395	929
Husband and other family member(s)	1,637	838
Wife and other family member(s)	557	589
Other family members only	163	617
Female-headed families, no spouse present	7,441	385
One earner	5,090	306
Householder	4,045	315
Other family member	1,045	270
Two or more earners	2,351	622
Male-headed families, no spouse present	2,159	514
One earner	1,337	404
Two or more earners	822	736
WHITE		
Total families with earners	36,978	695
Married-couple families	30,069	767
One earner	10,851	474
Husband	7,953	549
Wife	2,252	280
Two or more earners	19,218	922
Husband and wife	17,163	940
Female-headed families, no spouse present	5,209	399
Male-headed families, no spouse present	1,701	529

(continued)

(families with earners by selected characteristics and median weekly earnings in 1991; families as of 1992; numbers in thousands)

	total families	median weekly earnings
BLACK		
Total families with earners	5,098	$484
Married-couple families	3,735	625
One earner	897	313
Husband	503	366
Wife	312	272
Two or more earners	1,838	776
Husband and wife	1,633	796
Female-headed families, no spouse present	2,003	339
Male-headed families, no spouse present	360	401
HISPANIC		
Total families with earners	3,636	495
Married-couple families	2,599	546
One earner	1,102	322
Husband	850	355
Wife	176	235
Two or more earners	1,497	732
Husband and wife	1,158	757
Female-headed families, no spouse present	701	343
Male-headed families, no spouse present	337	462

Note: Because Hispanics may be of any race, families by race and Hispanic origin will not add to total families. Data exclude families in which there is no wage or salary earner or in which the husband, wife, or other person maintaining the family is either self-employed or in the Armed Forces.
Source: Bureau of Labor Statistics, Employment and Earnings, *January 1992*

3

Personal Income

Typically, the income of Americans peaks in middle-age. But education is the most important factor determining economic well-being. As people invest more time in advanced schooling, their incomes rise dramatically. Because the baby-boom generation is highly educated, and because boomers are now entering their peak earning years, the share of Americans who earn relatively high incomes should grow substantially during the 1990s.

Personal Income: Highlights

■ The recession hit men and women differently. Men's median income fell by fully 3.2 percent between 1989 and 1991. In contrast, women's median income fell by just 0.2 percent during those years. But men's median income continues to far surpass women's, $20,469 versus $10,476 in 1991.

■ Among men, those with the highest incomes work full-time (median income: $30,331), are aged 45 to 54 (median income: $37,198), and have professional degrees (median income: $73,996).

■ Among women, those with the highest incomes work full-time (median income: $21,245), are aged 35 to 44 (median income: $23,385), and have professional degrees (median income: $46,742).

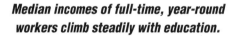

Median incomes of full-time, year-round workers climb steadily with education.

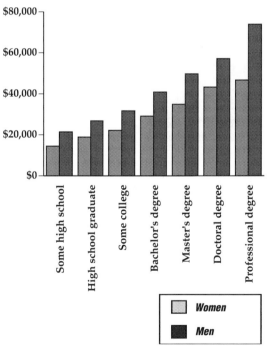

Men's Median Income, 1989 to 1991

Between 1989 and 1991, the median income of all men fell by more than 3 percent. Only men aged 75 or older saw their median income rise significantly, after adjusting for inflation.

(median income of men, 1989 to 1991; income in current dollars)

	1991	*1990*	*1989*	*percent change in real median income 1989-91*
All men	$20,469	$20,293	$19,893	-3.2%
Under age 25	6,281	6,319	6,313	-4.6
Aged 25 to 34	21,595	21,393	21,367	-3.1
Aged 35 to 44	29,301	29,773	29,437	-5.6
Aged 45 to 54	31,779	31,007	30,962	-1.6
Aged 55 to 64	25,460	24,804	24,427	-1.5
Aged 65 or older	14,357	14,183	13,107	-2.9
Aged 65 to 74	15,335	15,968	14,465	-7.8
Aged 75 or older	13,037	11,681	10,847	7.1
Education				
Total, aged 25 or older	23,686	-	-	-
Less than 9th grade	10,319	-	-	-
9th to 12th grade (no diploma)	14,736	-	-	-
High school graduate	21,546	-	-	-
Some college, no degree	26,591	-	-	-
Associate degree	29,358	-	-	-
Bachelor's degree or more	39,803	-	-	-
Bachelor's degree	36,067	-	-	-
Master's degree	43,125	-	-	-
Professional degree	63,741	-	-	-
Doctoral degree	51,845	-	-	-
Race and Hispanic origin				
White	21,395	21,170	20,863	-3.0
Black	12,962	12,868	12,609	-3.3
Hispanic	13,818	13,470	13,400	-1.6
Occupation group of longest held job (median earnings)				
Total with earnings	21,857	21,522	21,376	-2.5
Executive, administrators, and managerial	38,622	37,010	36,696	0.1
Professional specialty	37,467	36,942	35,548	-2.7
Technical and related support	28,414	28,042	27,453	-2.8
Sales	24,148	22,955	22,777	0.9
Administrative support, including clerical	21,335	20,287	19,991	0.9
Precision production, craft, and repair	22,412	22,149	22,146	-2.9

(continued)

(continued from previous page)

(median income of men, 1989 to 1991; income in current dollars)

	1991	1990	1989	*percent change in real median income 1989-91*
Machine operators, assemblers, and inspectors	$19,318	$19,389	$19,200	-4.4%
Transportation and material moving	20,853	20,053	19,474	-0.2
Handlers, equipment cleaners, helpers, and laborers	9,994	9,912	9,264	-3.2
Service workers	10,707	10,514	10,558	-2.3
Farming, forestry, and fishing	8,471	7,881	7,668	3.1

Note: Hispanics may be of any race. Current dollars are for the given year and have not been adjusted for inflation. Real dollars and real median income are adjusted for inflation.
Source: Bureau of the Census, Current Population Reports, Money Income of Households, Families, and Persons in the United States: 1991, Series P-60, No. 180, 1992

Men's Median Income: Full-Time, Year-Round Workers, 1989 to 1991

The median income of men who work full-time, year-round grew by less than 1 percent between 1989 and 1991, after adjusting for inflation. Those under age 25 or over age 64 saw their incomes fall by at least 4 percent.

(median income of men who worked full-time, year-round, 1989 to 1991; income in current dollars)

	1991	1990	1989	percent change in real median income 1989-91
All men who work full-time, year-round	$30,331	$28,979	$28,419	0.4%
Under age 25	$15,307	$15,462	$15,429	-5.0
Aged 25 to 34	26,100	25,355	24,794	-1.2
Aged 35 to 44	33,588	32,607	32,352	-1.2
Aged 45 to 54	37,198	35,732	35,390	-0.1
Aged 55 to 64	35,720	33,169	34,505	3.3
Aged 65 and older	34,473	35,520	34,105	-6.9
Aged 65 to 74	35,894	35,873	34,028	-4.0
Aged 75 or older	29,621	31,665	34,316	-10.2
Education				
Total, aged 25 or older	31,613	-	-	-
Less than 9th grade	17,623	-	-	-
9th to 12th grade (no diploma)	21,402	-	-	-
High school graduate	26,779	-	-	-
Some college, no degree	31,663	-	-	-
Associate degree	33,817	-	-	-
Bachelor's degree or more	45,138	-	-	-
Bachelor's degree	40,906	-	-	-
Master's degree	49,734	-	-	-
Professional degree	73,996	-	-	-
Doctoral degree	57,187	-	-	-
Race and Hispanic origin				
White	30,953	30,081	29,672	-1.3
Black	22,628	21,481	20,704	1.1
Hispanic	20,027	19,358	18,551	-0.7
Occupation group of longest held job (median earnings)				
Total with earnings	29,421	27,678	27,331	2.0
Executive, administrators, and managerial	41,635	40,546	40,085	-1.5
Professional specialty	42,358	41,100	39,499	-1.1
Technical and related support	32,029	30,897	31,305	-0.5
Sales	30,597	29,652	29,604	-1.0
Administrative support, including clerical	27,037	26,192	25,132	-0.9
Precision production, craft, and repair	27,508	26,506	26,490	-0.4

(continued)

(continued from previous page)

(median income of men who worked full-time, year-round, 1989 to 1991; income in current dollars)

	1991	1990	1989	percent change in real median income 1989-91
Machine operators, assemblers, and inspectors	$23,604	$22,345	$22,339	1.4%
Transportation and material moving	25,194	24,559	23,623	-1.6
Handlers, equipment cleaners, helpers, and laborers	17,508	18,426	18,061	-8.8
Service workers	19,933	18,550	18,886	3.1
Farming, forestry, and fishing	14,978	14,452	13,894	-0.5

Note: Hispanics may be of any race. Current dollars are for the given year and have not been adjusted for inflation. Real dollars and real median income are adjusted for inflation.
Source: Bureau of the Census, Current Population Reports, Money Income of Households, Families, and Persons in the United States: 1991, Series P-60, No. 180, 1992

Women's Median Income, 1989 to 1991

Women's median income fell slightly between 1989 and 1991, after adjusting for inflation. Elderly women saw their incomes fall the most.

(median income of women, 1989 to 1991; income in current dollars)

	1991	*1990*	*1989*	*percent change in real median income 1989-91*
All women	$10,476	$10,070	$9,624	-0.2%
Under age 25	5,197	4,902	4,739	1.7
Aged 25 to 34	12,964	12,589	12,231	-1.2
Aged 35 to 44	15,125	14,504	13,805	0.1
Aged 45 to 54	14,724	14,230	13,143	-0.7
Aged 55 to 64	9,902	9,400	9,163	1.1
Aged 65 or older	8,189	8,044	7,655	-2.3
Aged 65 to 74	8,135	8,190	7,948	-4.7
Aged 75 or older	8,241	7,891	7,377	0.2
Education				
Total, aged 25 or older	11,580	-	-	-
Less than 9th grade	6,268	-	-	-
9th to 12th grade (no diploma)	7,055	-	-	-
High school graduate	10,818	-	-	-
Some college, no degree	13,963	-	-	-
Associate degree	17,364	-	-	-
Bachelor's degree or more	23,627	-	-	-
Bachelor's degree	20,967	-	-	-
Master's degree	29,747	-	-	-
Professional degree	34,063	-	-	-
Doctoral degree	37,242	-	-	-
Race and Hispanic origin				
White	10,721	10,317	9,812	-0.3
Black	8,816	8,328	7,875	1.6
Hispanic	8,013	7,532	7,647	2.1
Occupation group of longest held job (median earnings)				
Total with earnings	12,884	12,250	11,736	0.9
Executive, administrators, and managerial	23,511	22,551	21,551	-
Professional specialty	24,925	23,113	22,089	3.5
Technical and related support	19,763	20,312	18,484	-6.6
Sales	7,737	7,307	6,990	1.6
Administrative support, including clerical	15,209	14,292	13,542	2.1
Precision production, craft, and repair	13,467	13,377	14,121	-3.4

(continued)

(continued from previous page)
(median income of women, 1989 to 1991; income in current dollars)

	1991	1990	1989	percent change in real median income 1989-91
Machine operators, assemblers, and inspectors	$11,294	$10,983	$10,845	-1.3%
Transportation and material moving	9,844	10,805	9,114	-12.6
Handlers, equipment cleaners, helpers, and laborers	8,599	8,270	6,654	-0.2
Service workers	6,049	5,746	5,487	1.0
Farming, forestry, and fishing	3,530	3,810	3,977	-11.1

Note: Hispanics may be of any race. Current dollars are for the given year and have not been adjusted for inflation. Real dollars and real median income are adjusted for inflation.
Source: Bureau of the Census, Current Population Reports, Money Income of Households, Families, and Persons in the United States: 1991, Series P-60, No. 180, 1992

Women's Median Income: Full-Time, Year-Round Workers, 1989 to 1991

Women who work full-time saw their incomes fall by 1 percent between 1989 and 1991, after adjusting for inflation. Working women of all ages suffered a drop in income.

(median income of women who worked full-time, year-round, 1989 to 1991; income in current dollars)

	1991	1990	1989	percent change in real median income 1989-91
All women who work full-time, year-round	$21,245	$20,591	$19,638	-1.0%
Under age 25	14,242	13,944	13,649	-2.0
Aged 25 to 34	21,022	20,184	19,700	-0.1
Aged 35 to 44	23,385	22,505	21,502	-0.3
Aged 45 to 54	22,630	21,938	20,905	-1.0
Aged 55 to 64	21,325	20,755	19,895	-1.4
Aged 65 or older	21,780	22,957	21,505	-9.0
Aged 65 to 74	21,420	22,978	21,463	-10.5
Aged 75 or older	-	22,895		
Education				
Total, aged 25 or older	22,045	-	-	-
Less than 9th grade	12,066	-	-	-
9th to 12th grade (no diploma)	14,455	-	-	-
High school graduate	18,837	-	-	-
Some college, no degree	22,143	-	-	-
Associate degree	25,002	-	-	-
Bachelor's degree or more	31,312	-	-	-
Bachelor's degree	29,087	-	-	-
Master's degree	34,939	-	-	-
Professional degree	46,742	-	-	-
Doctoral degree	43,303	-	-	-
Race and Hispanic origin				
White	21,555	20,839	19,871	-0.7
Black	19,134	18,544	17,871	-1.0
Hispanic	16,548	16,181	16,006	-1.9
Occupation group of longest held job (median earnings)				
Total with earnings	20,553	19,822	18,769	-0.5
Executive, administrators, and managerial	26,928	25,858	24,595	-0.1
Professional specialty	30,487	29,181	27,939	0.3
Technical and related support	22,497	23,992	21,750	-10.0
Sales	17,254	16,986	16,057	-2.5
Administrative support, including clerical	19,444	18,475	17,510	1.0
Precision production, craft, and repair	18,554	18,739	17,457	-5.0

(continued)

(continued from previous page)

(median income of women who worked full-time, year-round, 1989 to 1991; income in current dollars)

	1991	1990	1989	percent change in real median income 1989-91
Machine operators, assemblers, and inspectors	$14,965	$14,652	$14,463	-2.0%
Transportation and material moving	19,448	16,003	16,288	16.6
Handlers, equipment cleaners, helpers, and laborers	15,528	13,650	14,095	9.2
Service workers	12,148	12,139	11,672	-4.0
Farming, forestry, and fishing	10,205	10,007	11,305	-2.1

Note: Hispanics may be of any race. Current dollars are for the given year and have not been adjusted for inflation. Real dollars and real median income are adjusted for inflation.
Source: Bureau of the Census, Current Population Reports, Money Income of Households, Families, and Persons in the United States: 1991, Series P-60, No. 180, 1992

All Men: Distribution by Income and Selected Characteristics, 1991

Men aged 45 to 54 have the highest incomes, a median of nearly $32,000 in 1991. Those with professional degrees had a median income of nearly $64,000.

(men aged 15 or older as of 1992; numbers in thousands)

	total men	total with income	under $5,000	$5,000 to $9,999	$10,000 to $14,999	$15,000 to $24,999	$25,000 to $34,999	$35,000 to $49,999	$50,000 to $74,999	$75,000 or over	median income
						income					
Total	93,760	88,653	10,727	11,499	11,154	18,709	13,832	12,172	6,746	3,812	$20,469
Age											
Aged 15 to 24	17,181	13,516	5,893	2,906	2,059	1,954	499	172	22	12	6,281
Aged 25 to 34	21,124	20,523	1,501	2,178	2,716	5,533	4,313	2,858	1,029	395	21,595
Aged 35 to 44	19,506	19,162	1,054	1,393	1,595	3,768	3,946	3,936	2,268	1,201	29,301
Aged 45 to 54	13,114	12,891	739	899	957	2,210	2,241	2,802	1,880	1,162	31,779
Aged 55 to 64	10,036	9,845	674	1,049	1,089	2,009	1,655	1,623	1,056	690	25,460
Aged 65 to 74	8,266	8,223	536	1,876	1,607	2,120	835	586	392	270	15,335
Aged 75 or older	4,355	4,494	331	1,199	1,131	1,114	344	195	99	83	13,037
Education											
All, aged 25 or older	76,579	75,137	4,834	8,594	9,095	16,755	13,333	12,001	6,725	3,801	23,686
Less than 9th grade	7,462	7,143	1,066	2,380	1,589	1,419	424	188	54	23	10,319
9th to 12th grade (no diploma)	8,085	7,759	857	1,568	1,522	2,141	907	533	189	41	14,736
High school graduate	25,774	25,297	1,494	2,807	3,417	6,995	5,303	3,724	1,198	359	21,546
Some college, no degree	12,521	12,366	693	889	1,238	2,849	2,721	2,414	1,152	411	26,591
Associate degree	4,110	4,083	172	234	336	850	954	927	483	128	29,358
Bachelor's degree or more	18,628	18,490	553	717	993	2,501	3,023	4,215	3,648	2,839	39,803
Bachelor's degree	11,753	11,657	404	512	719	1,790	2,150	2,790	2,052	1,240	36,067
Master's degree	4,382	4,356	115	135	196	502	618	1,043	1,045	703	43,125
Professional degree	1,562	1,547	21	42	59	137	149	198	304	638	63,741
Doctoral degree	930	929	14	28	19	73	107	183	247	259	51,845
Race and Hispanic origin											
White	80,049	76,578	8,283	9,388	9,458	16,272	12,388	10,903	6,278	3,608	21,395
Black	10,252	8,943	1,932	1,675	1,326	1,828	1,035	846	228	73	12,962
Hispanic	7,738	6,939	942	1,473	1,283	1,558	850	551	200	81	13,818

Note: Because Hispanics may be of any race, the number of men by race and Hispanic origin will not add to total men.
Source: Bureau of the Census, Current Population Reports, Money Income of Households, Families, and Persons in the United States: 1991, Series P-60, No. 180, 1992

Men Who Work Full-Time, Year-Round: Distribution by Income and Selected Characteristics, 1991

Men with professional degrees who work full-time had a median income of nearly $74,000 in 1991. Those who went no further than high school had a median income of just under $27,000.

(men aged 15 or older as of 1992 who worked full-time, year-round in 1991; numbers in thousands)

	total men	total with income	under $5,000	$5,000 to $9,999	$10,000 to $14,999	$15,000 to $24,999	$25,000 to $34,999	$35,000 to $49,999	$50,000 to $74,999	$75,000 or over	median income
						income					
Total	47,897	47,892	624	1,860	4,468	10,993	10,571	10,249	5,854	3,272	$30,331
Age											
Aged 15 to 24	3,694	3,693	85	536	1,163	1,361	401	122	19	7	15,307
Aged 25 to 34	14,091	14,087	149	582	1,500	4,229	3,719	2,587	957	365	26,100
Aged 35 to 44	14,451	14,451	163	347	924	2,766	3,385	3,591	2,160	1,116	33,588
Aged 45 to 54	9,602	9,602	132	198	507	1,562	1,875	2,543	1,717	1,069	37,198
Aged 55 to 64	5,086	5,086	69	153	283	897	1,042	1,247	844	551	35,720
Aged 65 to 74	869	869	23	39	79	157	129	148	153	140	35,894
Aged 75 or older	103	103	5	5	12	21	20	12	5	23	29,621
Education											
All, aged 25 or older	44,203	44,199	539	1,324	3,306	9,632	10,170	10,128	5,836	3,265	31,613
Less than 9th grade	1,809	1,807	48	205	429	651	291	127	38	18	17,623
9th to 12th grade (no diploma)	3,083	3,083	51	223	463	1,114	645	413	141	31	21,402
High school graduate	15,027	15,025	211	546	1,492	4,244	4,055	3,156	1,034	286	26,779
Some college, no degree	8,034	8,034	86	182	433	1,755	2,155	2,099	994	330	31,663
Associate degree	2,899	2,899	30	34	111	575	771	818	447	114	33,817
Bachelor's degree or more	13,350	13,350	114	132	378	1,293	2,253	3,515	3,182	2,484	45,138
Bachelor's degree	8,456	8,456	88	104	288	993	1,694	2,388	1,849	1,052	40,906
Master's degree	3,073	3,073	18	20	68	208	399	833	884	643	49,734
Professional degree	1,147	1,147	1	4	13	58	100	157	248	566	73,996
Doctoral degree	674	674	6	4	9	34	60	137	200	223	57,187
Race and Hispanic origin											
White	42,072	42,067	539	1,501	3,676	9,285	9,391	9,151	5,437	3,087	30,953
Black	4,159	4,159	65	270	634	1,320	866	747	196	61	22,628
Hispanic	3,753	3,751	51	409	779	1,108	700	472	164	68	20,027

Note: Because Hispanics may be of any race, the number of men by race and Hispanic origin will not add to total men.
Source: Bureau of the Census, Current Population Reports, Money Income of Households, Families, and Persons in the United States: 1991, *Series P-60, No. 180, 1992*

All Women: Distribution by Income and Selected Characteristics, 1991

Women's median income was just $10,476 in 1991, but those with doctoral degrees had a median income of over $37,000.

(women aged 15 or older as of 1992; numbers in thousands)

	total women	total with income	under $5,000	$5,000 to $9,999	$10,000 to $14,999	$15,000 to $24,999	$25,000 to $34,999	$35,000 to $49,999	$50,000 to $74,999	$75,000 or over	median income
Total	101,483	92,569	24,601	20,122	13,804	17,821	8,882	4,999	1,671	669	$10,476
Age											
Aged 15 to 24	17,235	13,186	6,446	3,012	1,871	1,498	276	56	22	6	5,197
Aged 25 to 34	21,369	19,822	4,519	3,382	3,022	5,012	2,372	1,141	292	82	12,964
Aged 35 to 44	20,065	18,872	3,957	2,817	2,599	4,207	2,765	1,733	572	222	15,125
Aged 45 to 54	13,910	12,945	2,831	1,878	1,852	2,865	1,801	1,136	407	176	14,724
Aged 55 to 64	11,114	10,205	2,968	2,166	1,419	1,798	936	582	240	96	9,902
Aged 65 to 74	10,174	10,007	2,454	3,559	1,717	1,428	479	222	93	55	8,135
Aged 75 or older	7,616	7,532	1,427	3,308	1,324	1,014	254	129	44	32	8,241
Education											
All, aged 25 or older	84,248	79,383	18,156	17,110	11,933	16,323	8,606	4,943	1,648	664	11,580
Less than 9th grade	7,976	7,065	2,498	3,094	891	475	85	17	5	1	6,268
9th to 12th grade (no diploma)	9,587	8,561	2,778	2,986	1,362	1,050	275	76	19	14	7,055
High school graduate	32,088	30,149	7,332	6,699	5,485	6,904	2,474	958	190	107	10,818
Some college, no degree	13,520	13,013	2,515	2,262	2,114	3,290	1,722	800	238	72	13,963
Associate degree	5,369	5,236	845	679	730	1,426	876	524	121	35	17,364
Bachelor's degree or more	15,709	15,359	2,189	1,388	1,351	3,179	3,174	2,567	1,075	435	23,627
Bachelor's degree	11,010	10,721	1,709	1,105	1,060	2,497	2,079	1,521	556	195	20,967
Master's degree	3,793	3,745	409	227	232	565	960	866	369	118	29,747
Professional degree	564	556	38	38	55	61	92	103	78	91	34,064
Doctoral degree	342	337	34	19	5	56	43	78	72	31	37,242
Race and Hispanic origin											
White	85,510	78,721	20,620	16,707	11,905	15,276	7,733	4,399	1,504	578	10,721
Black	12,288	10,727	3,037	2,831	1,452	1,943	874	437	111	41	8,816
Hispanic	7,806	6,084	2,000	1,609	918	952	372	166	48	18	8,013

Note: Because Hispanics may be of any race, the number of women by race and Hispanic origin will not add to total women.
Source: Bureau of the Census, Current Population Reports, Money Income of Households, Families, and Persons in the United States: 1991, Series P-60, No. 180, 1992

Women Who Work Full-Time, Year-Round: Distribution by Income and Selected Characteristics, 1991

Women who work full-time had a median income of $21,245 in 1991. Those with professional or doctoral degrees had a median income of more than $40,000.

(women aged 15 or older as of 1992 who worked full-time, year-round in 1991; numbers in thousands)

	total women	total with income	income								median income
			under $5,000	$5,000 to $9,999	$10,000 to $14,999	$15,000 to $24,999	$25,000 to $34,999	$35,000 to $49,999	$50,000 to $74,999	$75,000 or over	
Total	32,491	32,476	683	2,222	5,728	11,470	6,751	3,903	1,254	464	$21,245
Age											
Aged 15 to 24	3,014	3,013	102	495	1,034	1,108	225	40	8	1	14,242
Aged 25 to 34	9,546	9,544	127	590	1,660	3,824	2,009	1,021	247	66	21,022
Aged 35 to 44	9,709	9,709	191	531	1,378	3,158	2,308	1,448	508	186	23,385
Aged 45 to 54	6,681	6,671	150	388	1,052	2,188	1,495	935	318	147	22,630
Aged 55 to 64	3,037	3,037	94	189	530	999	612	416	145	52	21,325
Aged 65 to 74	444	444	18	28	65	172	91	37	24	9	21,420
Aged 75 or older	60	60	2	1	8	20	13	7	4	5	-
Education											
All, aged 25 or older	29,477	29,463	581	1,728	4,694	10,362	6,527	3,863	1,245	464	22,045
Less than 9th grade	733	733	36	201	262	181	43	7	4	-	12,066
9th to 12th grade (no diploma)	1,822	1,819	75	326	555	606	184	53	12	8	14,455
High school graduate	10,961	10,955	250	818	2,387	4,683	1,913	716	120	67	18,837
Some college, no degree	5,631	5,630	94	207	838	2,186	1,424	680	174	26	22,144
Associate degree	2,523	2,523	35	73	257	895	691	456	88	27	25,002
Bachelor's degree or more	7,808	7,803	90	103	394	1,810	2,272	1,951	848	335	31,312
Bachelor's degree	5,265	5,261	68	89	335	1,469	1,525	1,185	454	136	29,087
Master's degree	2,024	2,024	20	8	46	285	657	636	277	96	34,939
Professional degree	312	312	1	6	12	23	57	75	61	77	46,742
Doctoral degree	206	206	2	-	1	32	33	55	56	26	43,303
Race and Hispanic origin											
White	27,318	27,307	578	1,727	4,721	9,548	5,827	3,390	1,122	393	21,555
Black	4,008	4,008	67	408	818	1,517	699	385	86	29	19,134
Hispanic	2,122	2,122	56	332	518	716	316	132	42	11	16,548

Note: Because Hispanics may be of any race, the number of women by race and Hispanic origin will not add to total women.
Source: Bureau of the Census, Current Population Reports, Money Income of Households, Families, and Persons in the United States: 1991, *Series P-60, No. 180, 1992*

All Men: Distribution by Earnings and Work Experience, 1991

Men who worked full-time, year-round had median earnings of $29,421 in 1991. In contrast, men who worked part-time had median earnings of less than $4,000.

(men aged 15 or older as of 1992, by earnings and work experience in 1991; numbers in thousands)

	total men	total who worked	worked		worked at part-time jobs	
			worked at full-time jobs			
			total	year-round	total	year-round
Total	93,760	72,064	61,685	47,897	10,379	3,867
Without earnings	21,721	24	13	9	12	10
With earnings	72,040	72,040	61,672	47,888	10,367	3,857
Under $2,500	6,071	6,071	2,137	500	3,934	502
$2,500 to $4,999	4,032	4,032	1,921	292	2,112	770
$5,000 to $7,499	4,072	4,072	2,529	802	1,543	851
$7,500 to $9,999	3,382	3,382	2,575	1,282	807	469
$10,000 to $12,499	4,706	4,706	4,042	2,583	664	425
$12,500 to $14,999	3,031	3,031	2,811	2,089	220	144
$15,000 to $17,499	4,201	4,201	3,977	3,039	224	137
$17,500 to $19,999	3,113	3,113	2,999	2,430	112	69
$20,000 to $22,499	4,593	4,593	4,430	3,661	163	115
$22,500 to $24,999	2,572	2,572	2,516	2,144	56	29
$25,000 to $29,999	6,496	6,496	6,367	5,553	129	71
$30,000 to $34,999	5,694	5,694	5,590	5,042	104	59
$35,000 to $39,999	4,692	4,692	4,648	4,233	44	24
$40,000 to $44,999	3,783	3,783	3,736	3,453	47	31
$45,000 to $49,999	2,478	2,478	2,451	2,305	26	20
$50,000 to $54,999	2,489	2,489	2,440	2,303	49	33
$55,000 to $64,999	2,248	2,248	2,217	2,109	32	22
$65,000 to $74,999	1,284	1,284	1,273	1,222	11	10
$75,000 to $84,999	1,090	1,090	1,068	1,013	22	20
$85,000 to $99,999	587	587	566	529	21	16
$100,000 or over	1,426	1,426	1,380	1,304	46	38
Median earnings	$21,857	$21,857	$25,527	$29,421	$3,979	$6,928

Source: Bureau of the Census, Current Population Reports, Money Income of Households, Families, and Persons in the United States: 1991, *Series P-60, No. 180, 1992*

White Men: Distribution by Earnings and Work Experience, 1991

PERSONS

White men who worked full-time, year-round had median earnings of $30,266 in 1991. In contrast, white men who worked only part-time had median earnings of just over $4,000.

(white men aged 15 or older as of March 1992, by earnings and work experience in 1991; numbers in thousands)

	total men	total who worked	worked at full-time jobs		worked at part-time jobs	
			total	year-round	total	year-round
Total	80,049	62,500	53,738	42,072	8,762	3,328
Without earnings	17,572	23	13	9	11	9
With earnings	62,477	62,477	53,726	42,063	8,751	3,320
Under $2,500	4,988	4,988	1,713	445	3,275	448
$2,500 to $4,999	3,258	3,258	1,539	255	1,719	608
$5,000 to $7,499	3,405	3,405	2,085	654	1,320	729
$7,500 to $9,999	2,842	2,842	2,134	1,040	709	409
$10,000 to $12,499	3,903	3,903	3,337	2,127	566	360
$12,500 to $14,999	2,515	2,515	2,327	1,714	188	124
$15,000 to $17,499	3,516	3,516	3,314	2,486	201	126
$17,500 to $19,999	2,661	2,661	2,569	2,057	92	57
$20,000 to $22,499	3,943	3,943	3,792	3,121	150	106
$22,500 to $24,999	2,251	2,251	2,200	1,872	51	27
$25,000 to $29,999	5,786	5,786	5,669	4,933	117	68
$30,000 to $34,999	5,086	5,086	4,997	4,488	90	58
$35,000 to $39,999	4,147	4,147	4,106	3,744	41	22
$40,000 to $44,999	3,400	3,400	3,360	3,103	40	30
$45,000 to $49,999	2,231	2,231	2,211	2,083	21	18
$50,000 to $54,999	2,314	2,314	2,267	2,140	47	31
$55,000 to $64,999	2,121	2,121	2,089	1,992	32	22
$65,000 to $74,999	1,183	1,183	1,176	1,129	7	5
$75,000 to $84,999	1,025	1,025	1,003	951	21	19
$85,000 to $99,999	551	551	530	495	21	16
$100,000 or over	1,353	1,353	1,308	1,233	45	37
Median earnings	$22,732	$22,732	$26,222	$30,266	$4,101	$7,074

Source: Bureau of the Census, Current Population Reports, Money Income of Households, Families, and Persons in the United States: 1991, *Series P-60, No. 180, 1992*

Black Men: Distribution by Earnings and Work Experience, 1991

Black men who worked full-time, year-round had median earnings of $22,075 in 1991. In contrast, black men who worked part-time had median earnings of just over $3,000.

(black men aged 15 or older as of 1992, by earnings and work experience in 1991; numbers in thousands)

	total men	total who worked	worked at full-time jobs		worked at part-time jobs	
			total	year-round	total	year-round
Total	10,252	6,963	5,770	4,159	1,193	367
Without earnings	3,290	-	-	-	-	-
With earnings	6,963	6,963	5,770	4,159	1,193	367
Under $2,500	848	848	332	45	516	47
$2,500 to $4,999	590	590	301	25	289	118
$5,000 to $7,499	500	500	336	118	164	84
$7,500 to $9,999	407	407	342	172	65	37
$10,000 to $12,499	616	616	548	354	68	44
$12,500 to $14,999	413	413	391	310	22	14
$15,000 to $17,499	542	542	529	446	13	3
$17,500 to $19,999	339	339	324	279	14	8
$20,000 to $22,499	470	470	465	397	5	2
$22,500 to $24,999	245	245	244	210	2	2
$25,000 to $29,999	530	530	520	467	10	3
$30,000 to $34,999	438	438	425	401	13	-
$35,000 to $39,999	381	381	381	349	-	-
$40,000 to $44,999	242	242	239	222	2	-
$45,000 to $49,999	163	163	157	143	6	2
$50,000 to $54,999	80	80	80	75	-	-
$55,000 to $64,999	60	60	60	53	-	-
$65,000 to $74,999	45	45	42	41	3	3
$75,000 to $84,999	24	24	23	23	1	1
$85,000 to $99,999	17	17	17	17	-	-
$100,000 or over	12	12	12	12	-	-
Median earnings	$15,494	$15,494	$18,313	$22,075	$3,198	$5,536

Source: Bureau of the Census, Current Population Reports, Money Income of Households, Families, and Persons in the United States: 1991, *Series P-60, No. 180, 1992*

Hispanic Men: Distribution by Earnings and Work Experience, 1991

Hispanic men who worked year-round, full-time had median earnings of $19,771 in 1991. Hispanic men who worked part-time had median earnings of $4,605.

(Hispanic men aged 15 or older as of 1992, by earnings and work experience in 1991; numbers in thousands)

	total men	total who worked	worked at full-time jobs		worked at part-time jobs	
			total	year-round	total	year-round
Total	7,738	6,075	5,243	3,753	831	329
Without earnings	1,666	3	2	2	2	2
With earnings	6,072	6,072	5,242	3,751	830	327
Under $2,500	469	469	187	24	282	26
$2,500 to $4,999	368	368	210	32	158	46
$5,000 to $7,499	553	553	412	139	141	88
$7,500 to $9,999	573	573	489	270	85	58
$10,000 to $12,499	748	748	677	491	71	44
$12,500 to $14,999	406	406	390	300	16	11
$15,000 to $17,499	480	480	465	368	14	11
$17,500 to $19,999	349	349	333	277	16	10
$20,000 to $22,499	397	397	387	321	10	8
$22,500 to $24,999	177	177	173	161	4	1
$25,000 to $29,999	462	462	456	405	6	5
$30,000 to $34,999	327	327	320	288	8	5
$35,000 to $39,999	271	271	270	234	1	1
$40,000 to $44,999	170	170	167	158	3	-
$45,000 to $49,999	86	86	81	77	5	5
$50,000 to $54,999	86	86	77	70	9	7
$55,000 to $64,999	55	55	55	54	1	1
$65,000 to $74,999	32	32	32	27	-	-
$75,000 to $84,999	26	26	26	22	-	-
$85,000 to $99,999	10	10	10	9	1	1
$100,000 or over	27	27	27	25	-	-
Median earnings	$14,500	$14,500	$16,377	$19,771	$4,605	$7,692

Note: Hispanics may be of any race.
Source: Bureau of the Census, Current Population Reports, Money Income of Households, Families, and Persons in the United States: 1991, Series P-60, No. 180, 1992

All Women: Distribution by Earnings and Work Experience, 1991

Among women who work, 52 percent work full-time, year-round. Their median earnings amounted to $20,553 in 1991. Those who worked part-time had median earnings of $4,476.

(women aged 15 or older as of 1992, by earnings and work experience in 1991; numbers in thousands)

	total women	total who worked	worked at full-time jobs		worked at part-time jobs	
			total	year-round	total	year-round
Total	101,483	61,959	42,852	32,491	19,107	8,143
Without earnings	39,687	163	64	56	99	59
With earnings	61,796	61,796	42,788	32,436	19,008	8,084
under $2,500	8,897	8,897	2,300	463	6,597	912
$2,500 to $4,999	5,446	5,446	1,769	314	3,677	1,376
$5,000 to $7,499	5,572	5,572	2,330	888	3,242	1,874
$7,500 to $9,999	4,420	4,420	2,636	1,601	1,784	1,167
$10,000 to $12,499	5,989	5,989	4,565	3,429	1,424	1,033
$12,500 to $14,999	3,735	3,735	3,221	2,627	514	347
$15,000 to $17,499	4,611	4,611	4,090	3,504	521	406
$17,500 to $19,999	3,244	3,244	3,009	2,625	235	185
$20,000 to $22,499	4,159	4,159	3,863	3,459	296	240
$22,500 to $24,999	2,361	2,361	2,242	2,013	119	80
$25,000 to $29,999	4,489	4,489	4,270	3,859	219	177
$30,000 to $34,999	3,162	3,162	3,035	2,724	127	93
$35,000 to $39,999	2,135	2,135	2,047	1,839	88	82
$40,000 to $44,999	1,204	1,204	1,146	1,034	58	43
$45,000 to $49,999	770	770	747	674	23	17
$50,000 to $54,999	504	504	482	440	21	5
$55,000 to $64,999	473	473	448	400	25	20
$65,000 to $74,999	228	228	216	199	11	11
$75,000 to $84,999	136	136	124	101	13	6
$85,000 to $99,999	86	86	86	81	-	-
$100,000 or over	175	175	163	159	13	11
Median earnings	$12,884	$12,884	$17,902	$20,553	$4,476	$7,340

Source: Bureau of the Census, Current Population Reports, Money Income of Households, Families, and Persons in the United States: 1991, Series P-60, No. 180, 1992

White Women: Distribution by Earnings and Work Experience, 1991

Among white women who work, 52 percent work full-time, year-round. Their median earnings amounted to $20,794 in 1991. Those who worked part-time had median earnings of $4,531.

(white women aged 15 or older as of 1992, by earnings and work experience in 1991; numbers in thousands)

	total women	total who worked	worked at full-time jobs		worked at part-time jobs	
			total	year-round	total	year-round
Total	85,510	52,631	35,894	27,318	16,737	7,178
Without earnings	33,033	154	58	49	97	56
With earnings	52,477	52,477	35,836	27,269	16,641	7,122
Under $2,500	7,602	7,602	1,857	396	5,745	820
$2,500 to $4,999	4,595	4,595	1,424	268	3,171	1,158
$5,000 to $7,499	4,745	4,745	1,914	724	2,831	1,646
$7,500 to $9,999	3,672	3,672	2,079	1,229	1,594	1,061
$10,000 to $12,499	5,001	5,001	3,747	2,793	1,254	905
$12,500 to $14,999	3,165	3,165	2,728	2,215	437	288
$15,000 to $17,499	3,864	3,864	3,406	2,895	458	352
$17,500 to $19,999	2,721	2,721	2,502	2,175	219	172
$20,000 to $22,499	3,572	3,572	3,300	2,957	272	225
$22,500 to $24,999	1,980	1,980	1,871	1,682	110	75
$25,000 to $29,999	3,829	3,829	3,621	3,283	208	166
$30,000 to $34,999	2,784	2,784	2,671	2,391	113	81
$35,000 to $39,999	1,814	1,814	1,737	1,550	77	71
$40,000 to $44,999	1,053	1,053	997	905	56	41
$45,000 to $49,999	691	691	669	602	22	17
$50,000 to $54,999	441	441	421	383	20	3
$55,000 to $64,999	412	412	394	353	19	13
$65,000 to $74,999	208	208	197	186	11	11
$75,000 to $84,999	112	112	100	85	13	6
$85,000 to $99,999	69	69	69	69	-	-
$100,000 or over	143	143	131	127	13	11
Median earnings	$12,992	$12,992	$18,261	$20,794	$4,531	$7,404

Source: Bureau of the Census, Current Population Reports, Money Income of Households, Families, and Persons in the United States: 1991, Series P-60, No. 180, 1992

Black Women: Distribution by Earnings and Work Experience, 1991

Among black women who work, 56 percent work full-time, year-round. Their median earnings amounted to $18,720 in 1991. Those who worked part-time had median earnings of $3,960.

(black women aged 15 or older as of 1992, by earnings and work experience in 1991; numbers in thousands)

	total women	total who worked	worked at full-time jobs		worked at part-time jobs	
			total	year-round	total	year-round
Total	12,288	7,145	5,388	4,008	1,756	703
Without earnings	5,144	-	-	-	-	-
With earnings	7,145	7,145	5,388	4,008	1,756	703
Under $2,500	994	994	340	35	654	66
$2,500 to $4,999	665	665	282	36	384	174
$5,000 to $7,499	640	640	329	136	310	178
$7,500 to $9,999	595	595	456	305	139	82
$10,000 to $12,499	767	767	655	530	112	84
$12,500 to $14,999	435	435	374	321	61	44
$15,000 to $17,499	559	559	522	463	37	30
$17,500 to $19,999	418	418	407	364	12	10
$20,000 to $22,499	448	448	434	394	14	8
$22,500 to $24,999	308	308	303	274	5	-
$25,000 to $29,999	523	523	514	449	9	9
$30,000 to $34,999	264	264	258	235	6	6
$35,000 to $39,999	248	248	242	231	6	6
$40,000 to $44,999	106	106	106	90	-	-
$45,000 to $49,999	52	52	50	46	2	-
$50,000 to $54,999	34	34	34	34	-	-
$55,000 to $64,999	47	47	40	36	7	7
$65,000 to $74,999	8	8	8	5	-	-
$75,000 to $84,999	14	14	14	6	-	-
$85,000 to $99,999	9	9	9	6	-	-
$100,000 or over	11	11	11	11	-	-
Median earnings	$12,212	$12,212	$16,237	$18,720	$3,960	$6,575

Source: Bureau of the Census, Current Population Reports, Money Income of Households, Families, and Persons in the United States: 1991, *Series P-60, No. 180, 1992*

Hispanic Women: Distribution by Earnings and Work Experience, 1991

Among Hispanic women who work, 51 percent work full-time, year-round. Their median earnings were $16,244 in 1991. Those who worked part-time had median earnings of $4,108.

(Hispanic women aged 15 or older as of 1992, by earnings and work experience in 1991; numbers in thousands)

	total women	total who worked	worked at full-time jobs		worked at part-time jobs	
			total	year-round	total	year-round
Total	7,806	4,172	3,043	2,122	1,129	437
Without earnings	3,642	8	3	3	6	3
With earnings	4,163	4,163	3,040	2,119	1,123	434
Under $2,500	622	622	214	32	408	43
$2,500 to $4,999	451	451	213	31	238	81
$5,000 to $7,499	479	479	275	112	204	118
$7,500 to $9,999	448	448	336	232	112	78
$10,000 to $12,499	503	503	421	330	81	55
$12,500 to $14,999	266	266	246	198	20	13
$15,000 to $17,499	320	320	300	252	20	14
$17,500 to $19,999	180	180	171	154	9	7
$20,000 to $22,499	233	233	225	202	9	6
$22,500 to $24,999	115	115	114	105	2	2
$25,000 to $29,999	221	221	213	192	8	7
$30,000 to $34,999	126	126	122	108	4	4
$35,000 to $39,999	74	74	69	59	5	5
$40,000 to $44,999	42	42	41	36	1	1
$45,000 to $49,999	30	30	29	29	1	-
$50,000 to $54,999	16	16	16	16	-	-
$55,000 to $64,999	20	20	20	19	-	-
$65,000 to $74,999	3	3	3	3	-	-
$75,000 to $84,999	7	7	7	4	-	-
$85,000 to $99,999	6	6	6	5	-	-
$100,000 or over	1	1	-	-	1	1
Median earnings	$10,404	$10,404	$13,124	$16,244	$4,108	$6,983

Note: Hispanics may be of any race.
Source: Bureau of the Census, Current Population Reports, Money Income of Households, Families, and Persons in the United States: 1991, Series P-60, No. 180, 1992

All Men: Distribution
by Income and Age, 1991

Among men, incomes peak in the 45-to-54 age group. In 1991, men in this age group had a median income of $31,779. Those in this age group who worked full-time had a median income of $37,198.

(men aged 15 or older as of 1992, by income and age in 1991; numbers in thousands)

	total men	15 to 24	25 to 34	35 to 44	45 to 54	55 to 64	65 to 74	75 or older
Total	93,760	17,181	21,124	19,506	13,114	10,036	8,266	4,533
Without income	5,107	3,665	601	344	223	190	44	39
With income	88,653	13,516	20,523	19,162	12,891	9,845	8,223	4,494
Under $2,500	5,824	3,682	667	500	391	305	204	75
$2,500 to $4,999	4,903	2,211	834	554	348	368	332	256
$5,000 to $7,499	6,031	1,688	1,106	727	470	543	954	542
$7,500 to $9,999	5,468	1,217	1,072	666	428	506	922	656
$10,000 to $12,499	6,365	1,254	1,538	941	573	570	885	605
$12,500 to $14,999	4,789	805	1,178	655	384	519	722	526
$15,000 to $17,499	5,521	772	1,526	979	555	551	687	451
$17,500 to $19,999	4,429	437	1,307	894	467	489	553	282
$20,000 to $22,499	5,308	545	1,621	1,178	713	590	448	213
$22,500 to $24,999	3,451	200	1,080	717	476	380	431	168
$25,000 to $29,999	7,472	387	2,363	1,992	1,107	913	520	190
$30,000 to $34,999	6,361	112	1,950	1,954	1,134	742	316	154
$35,000 to $39,999	5,162	78	1,299	1,616	1,118	700	254	97
$40,000 to $44,999	4,134	75	961	1,351	979	519	191	58
$45,000 to $49,999	2,877	18	598	970	705	405	141	40
$50,000 to $54,999	2,597	8	458	888	670	404	143	26
$55,000 to $64,999	2,610	11	362	855	764	414	158	45
$65,000 to $74,999	1,539	3	209	525	446	238	91	27
$75,000 to $84,999	1,181	4	162	404	337	190	75	9
$85,000 to $99,999	888	2	79	263	285	162	67	31
$100,000 or over	1,743	5	154	534	540	339	127	43
Median income	$20,469	$6,281	$21,595	$29,301	$31,779	$25,460	$15,335	$13,037
Full-time, year-round workers								
Number	47,881	3,690	14,086	14,450	9,602	5,080	869	103
Median income	$30,332	$15,315	$26,100	$33,585	$37,198	$35,722	$35,894	$29,621

Source: Bureau of the Census, Current Population Reports, Money Income of Households, Families, and Persons in the United States: 1991, *Series P-60, No. 180, 1992*

White Men: Distribution by Income and Age, 1991

Among white men, median income was $21,395 in 1991. For those aged 45 to 54, median income exceeded $33,000.

(white men aged 15 or older as of 1992, by income and age in 1991; numbers in thousands)

	total men	15 to 24	25 to 34	35 to 44	45 to 54	55 to 64	65 to 74	75 or older
Total	80,049	13,986	17,736	16,738	11,427	8,731	7,323	4,108
Without income	3,472	2,564	367	196	152	141	23	28
With income	76,578	11,423	17,369	16,542	11,275	8,590	7,300	4,080
Under $2,500	4,587	2,996	483	372	296	230	150	61
$2,500 to $4,999	3,695	1,816	595	374	254	247	230	179
$5,000 to $7,499	4,794	1,411	867	551	374	425	727	438
$7,500 to $9,999	4,594	1,055	861	534	353	416	795	580
$10,000 to $12,499	5,392	1,132	1,205	752	484	469	794	557
$12,500 to $14,999	4,066	694	945	551	299	429	649	499
$15,000 to $17,499	4,708	649	1,265	811	444	478	634	427
$17,500 to $19,999	3,863	381	1,096	759	396	437	520	274
$20,000 to $22,499	4,637	472	1,391	1,029	614	507	426	199
$22,500 to $24,999	3,064	183	931	623	404	351	408	163
$25,000 to $29,999	6,702	355	2,119	1,760	979	818	489	182
$30,000 to $34,999	5,686	96	1,745	1,752	1,002	643	295	154
$35,000 to $39,999	4,586	71	1,153	1,426	985	624	234	91
$40,000 to $44,999	3,714	64	858	1,181	894	480	179	58
$45,000 to $49,999	2,603	18	541	851	650	365	137	40
$50,000 to $54,999	2,407	6	421	810	618	393	133	26
$55,000 to $64,999	2,446	10	352	790	706	392	151	45
$65,000 to $74,999	1,424	3	183	470	423	228	90	27
$75,000 to $84,999	1,124	4	153	387	317	184	71	9
$85,000 to $99,999	832	2	72	242	269	154	63	31
$100,000 or over	1,651	5	133	517	512	318	126	39
Median income	$21,395	$6,595	$22,457	$30,356	$33,169	$26,541	$16,205	$13,626
Year-round, full-time workers								
Number	42,059	3,244	12,191	12,679	8,554	4,528	775	88
Median income	$30,953	$15,302	$26,659	$34,362	$38,184	$36,580	$37,925	$30,024

Source: Bureau of the Census, Current Population Reports, Money Income of Households, Families, and Persons in the United States: 1991, *Series P-60, No. 180, 1992*

Black Men: Distribution by Income and Age, 1991

Black men had a median income of just $12,962 in 1991. But full-time workers aged 45 to 54 had a median income of over $27,000.

(black men aged 15 or older as of 1992, by income and age in 1991; numbers in thousands)

	total men	15 to 24	25 to 34	35 to 44	45 to 54	55 to 64	65 to 74	75 or older
Total	10,252	2,449	2,505	2,027	1,235	978	739	319
Without income	1,309	881	194	124	63	31	14	2
With income	8,943	1,568	2,311	1,903	1,173	946	726	317
Under $2,500	951	517	151	107	77	48	43	8
$2,500 to $4,999	981	292	201	151	85	105	85	62
$5,000 to $7,499	975	216	187	139	73	100	177	84
$7,500 to $9,999	700	129	159	114	62	66	110	59
$10,000 to $12,499	760	88	258	145	80	77	71	41
$12,500 to $14,999	566	83	178	89	62	74	59	21
$15,000 to $17,499	618	93	207	124	89	54	36	16
$17,500 to $19,999	419	39	150	97	60	38	28	7
$20,000 to $22,499	495	57	175	103	66	68	19	7
$22,500 to $24,999	295	16	99	73	62	28	14	5
$25,000 to $29,999	578	24	180	181	98	70	24	2
$30,000 to $34,999	457	11	131	147	88	71	9	-
$35,000 to $39,999	395	-	88	127	100	63	16	1
$40,000 to $44,999	268	4	66	116	52	19	10	-
$45,000 to $49,999	183	-	29	83	41	28	2	-
$50,000 to $54,999	93	-	19	39	22	6	7	-
$55,000 to $64,999	77	1	4	27	25	16	4	-
$65,000 to $74,999	58	-	16	27	8	6	1	-
$75,000 to $84,999	20	-	6	2	9	-	3	-
$85,000 to $99,999	30	-	3	9	10	4	5	-
$100,000 or over	23	-	3	5	4	6	2	4
Median income	$12,962	$4,787	$15,248	$19,640	$19,922	$15,157	$8,811	$7,666
Full-time, year-round workers								
Number	4,156	354	1,387	1,240	710	395	62	8
Median income	$22,646	$15,297	$19,809	$26,891	$27,415	$26,884	-	-

Source: *Bureau of the Census, Current Population Reports,* Money Income of Households, Families, and Persons in the United States: 1991, *Series P-60, No. 180, 1992*

Hispanic Men: Distribution by Income and Age, 1991

Hispanic men who worked full-time in 1991 had a median income of just over $20,000. Those younger than age 25 had a median income of only $12,911, despite full-time work.

(Hispanic men aged 15 or older as of 1992, by income and age in 1991; numbers in thousands)

	total men	15 to 24	25 to 34	35 to 44	45 to 54	55 to 64	65 to 74	75 or older
Total	7,738	1,993	2,227	1,594	860	597	310	157
Without income	799	597	93	37	40	25	4	3
With income	6,939	1,396	2,135	1,557	820	571	305	154
Under $2,500	481	280	80	59	22	21	12	7
$2,500 to $4,999	461	183	110	51	33	35	26	22
$5,000 to $7,499	750	204	181	119	71	56	75	44
$7,500 to $9,999	723	173	247	119	63	50	45	26
$10,000 to $12,499	799	184	280	157	79	59	28	13
$12,500 to $14,999	484	102	169	105	43	33	24	7
$15,000 to $17,499	537	80	192	131	53	47	26	9
$17,500 to $19,999	388	56	122	96	59	35	9	10
$20,000 to $22,499	428	51	160	121	51	35	10	2
$22,500 to $24,999	205	16	77	59	29	10	7	6
$25,000 to $29,999	506	40	183	144	81	41	15	1
$30,000 to $34,999	344	15	115	126	55	23	5	4
$35,000 to $39,999	278	7	87	93	50	36	4	1
$40,000 to $44,999	185	2	45	61	43	30	5	-
$45,000 to $49,999	89	2	24	31	17	14	1	-
$50,000 to $54,999	87	2	21	18	29	14	3	-
$55,000 to $64,999	76	-	24	27	12	7	4	1
$65,000 to $74,999	38	-	6	11	14	6	2	-
$75,000 to $84,999	32	-	4	10	5	13	-	-
$85,000 to $99,999	17	-	3	11	1	1	1	-
$100,000 or over	32	-	4	9	12	5	3	-
Median income	$13,818	$7,943	$15,009	$18,497	$19,450	$16,666	$9,722	$7,798
Full-time, year-round workers								
Number	3,749	525	1,302	1,043	551	296	26	7
Median income	$20,036	$12,911	$19,327	$22,623	$24,412	$24,553	-	-

Note: Hispanics may be of any race.
Source: Bureau of the Census, Current Population Reports, Money Income of Households, Families, and Persons in the United States: 1991, Series P-60, No. 180, 1992

All Women: Distribution by Income and Age, 1991

Among women, income peaks at ages 35 to 44, with a median of just $15,125 in 1991. But among women who work full-time, median income rises to a peak of $23,388.

(women aged 15 or older as of 1992, by income and age in 1991; numbers in thousands)

	total women	15 to 24	25 to 34	35 to 44	45 to 54	55 to 64	65 to 74	75 or older
Total	101,483	17,235	21,369	20,065	13,910	11,114	10,174	7,616
Without income	8,914	4,049	1,547	1,193	964	910	167	84
With income	92,569	13,186	19,822	18,872	12,945	10,205	10,007	7,532
Under $2,500	13,736	4,009	2,768	2,570	1,919	1,705	502	263
$2,500 to $4,999	10,865	2,437	1,750	1,387	912	1,263	1,952	1,164
$5,000 to $7,499	11,756	1,869	1,843	1,488	1,067	1,352	2,205	1,931
$7,500 to $9,999	8,366	1,142	1,539	1,329	811	814	1,353	1,377
$10,000 to $12,499	8,208	1,204	1,779	1,521	1,056	825	1,014	808
$12,500 to $14,999	5,596	667	1,243	1,078	796	594	703	516
$15,000 to $17,499	5,821	639	1,447	1,265	909	612	563	386
$17,500 to $19,999	4,239	329	1,238	930	639	475	338	292
$20,000 to $22,499	4,621	371	1,348	1,246	744	425	297	190
$22,500 to $24,999	3,140	159	980	767	572	286	230	147
$25,000 to $29,999	5,243	173	1,405	1,561	1,041	561	347	156
$30,000 to $34,999	3,639	103	967	1,204	760	374	132	98
$35,000 to $39,999	2,458	42	613	804	525	271	133	70
$40,000 to $44,999	1,527	8	334	570	364	179	42	30
$45,000 to $49,999	1,014	6	194	360	247	132	47	29
$50,000 to $54,999	643	6	124	225	163	87	26	14
$55,000 to $64,999	669	7	108	247	160	93	41	14
$65,000 to $74,999	358	10	61	101	84	60	26	16
$75,000 to $84,999	212	5	32	71	57	28	9	11
$85,000 to $99,999	155	1	24	46	44	14	21	5
$100,000 or over	302	-	26	105	75	54	25	16
Median income	$10,476	$5,197	$12,964	$15,125	$14,724	$9,902	$8,135	$8,241
Full-time, year-round workers								
Number	32,461	3,012	9,536	9,706	6,670	3,036	442	60
Median income	$21,245	$14,238	$21,022	$23,388	$22,626	$21,332	$21,461	-

Source: Bureau of the Census, Current Population Reports, Money Income of Households, Families, and Persons in the United States: 1991, *Series P-60, No. 180, 1992*

White Women: Distribution by Income and Age, 1991

White women who work full-time had a median income of $21,556 in 1991. Full-time workers younger than age 25 had a median income of just $14,313.

(white women aged 15 or older as of 1992, by income and age in 1991; numbers in thousands)

	total women	15 to 24	25 to 34	35 to 44	45 to 54	55 to 64	65 to 74	75 or older
Total	85,510	13,926	17,581	16,757	11,830	9,549	8,992	6,874
Without income	6,789	2,950	1,230	930	809	692	110	68
With income	78,721	10,977	16,351	15,827	11,022	8,858	8,882	6,806
Under $2,500	11,857	3,360	2,412	2,254	1,687	1,508	404	234
$2,500 to $4,999	8,762	1,903	1,309	1,107	757	1,053	1,655	978
$5,000 to $7,499	9,651	1,512	1,432	1,200	859	1,122	1,861	1,665
$7,500 to $9,999	7,056	964	1,180	1,083	667	687	1,217	1,256
$10,000 to $12,499	7,054	1,050	1,416	1,279	895	702	939	773
$12,500 to $14,999	4,851	561	1,044	900	669	527	659	491
$15,000 to $17,499	4,989	551	1,202	1,035	764	538	531	367
$17,500 to $19,999	3,572	277	979	769	543	412	317	275
$20,000 to $22,499	3,998	339	1,097	1,057	655	380	386	183
$22,500 to $24,999	2,717	142	859	619	486	253	218	140
$25,000 to $29,999	4,542	156	1,214	1,304	890	502	327	149
$30,000 to $34,999	3,191	95	846	1,045	655	333	122	95
$35,000 to $39,999	2,142	37	547	660	455	253	120	69
$40,000 to $44,999	1,344	6	311	488	308	161	40	30
$45,000 to $49,999	914	6	182	305	225	122	47	27
$50,000 to $54,999	580	6	111	201	148	76	25	14
$55,000 to $64,999	596	2	90	226	141	87	36	14
$65,000 to $74,999	328	10	57	96	77	47	25	16
$75,000 to $84,999	185	-	29	62	46	28	9	11
$85,000 to $99,999	135	1	19	38	40	14	21	3
$100,000 or over	258	-	13	97	54	52	25	16
Median income	$10,721	$5,373	$13,519	$15,219	$14,913	$10,209	$8,570	$8,547
Full-time, year-round workers								
Number	27,292	2,657	7,923	8,041	5,610	2,614	390	57
Median income	$21,556	$14,313	$21,515	$23,786	$22,980	$21,859	$22,336	-

Source: Bureau of the Census, Current Population Reports, Money Income of Households, Families, and Persons in the United States: 1991, *Series P-60, No. 180, 1992*

Black Women: Distribution by Income and Age, 1991

Among all black women who work full-time, median income was below $20,000 in 1991. Only among those aged 35 to 54 did the median rise above $20,000.

(black women aged 15 or older as of 1992, by income and age in 1991; numbers in thousands)

	total women	15 to 24	25 to 34	35 to 44	45 to 54	55 to 64	65 to 74	75 or older
Total	12,288	2,647	2,918	2,435	1,552	1,188	926	623
Without income	1,562	868	212	164	119	154	38	7
With income	10,727	1,779	2,705	2,271	1,433	1,034	888	616
Under $2,500	1,272	503	213	172	156	132	70	26
$2,500 to $4,999	1,764	452	384	220	130	175	238	166
$5,000 to $7,499	1,767	285	347	231	178	195	299	232
$7,500 to $9,999	1,064	143	312	196	104	99	106	105
$10,000 to $12,499	901	128	301	186	117	95	53	21
$12,500 to $14,999	551	82	149	138	81	52	26	23
$15,000 to $17,499	626	68	190	171	98	62	26	11
$17,500 to $19,999	524	48	214	122	68	46	15	10
$20,000 to $22,499	468	19	189	146	64	36	8	6
$22,500 to $24,999	325	14	90	120	68	21	9	3
$25,000 to $29,999	556	16	144	211	123	39	17	6
$30,000 to $34,999	318	5	85	108	80	27	8	4
$35,000 to $39,999	241	5	49	114	54	10	9	-
$40,000 to $44,999	131	2	12	62	43	12	-	-
$45,000 to $49,999	64	-	9	33	14	8	-	-
$50,000 to $54,999	45	-	6	17	11	10	-	-
$55,000 to $64,999	46	4	2	13	19	5	2	-
$65,000 to $74,999	21	-	2	1	6	11	1	-
$75,000 to $84,999	13	5	-	5	4	-	-	-
$85,000 to $99,999	14	-	4	4	4	1	-	2
$100,000 or over	14	-	1	3	10	-	-	-
Median income	$8,816	$4,638	$10,801	$14,860	$13,475	$7,908	$6,140	$6,246
Full-time, year-round workers								
Number	4,007	293	1,281	1,268	801	328	33	4
Median income	$19,136	$13,553	$18,346	$21,827	$21,161	$17,167	-	-

Source: Bureau of the Census, Current Population Reports, Money Income of Households, Families, and Persons in the United States: 1991, *Series P-60, No. 180, 1992*

Hispanic Women: Distribution by Income and Age, 1991

The median income of Hispanic women remains below the $20,000 level, even among those in middle-age. Among Hispanic women aged 35 to 44 who work full-time, median income peaks at just $18,508.

(Hispanic women aged 15 or older as of 1992, by income and age in 1991; numbers in thousands)

	total women	15 to 24	25 to 34	35 to 44	45 to 54	55 to 64	65 to 74	75 or older
Total	7,806	1,927	2,022	1,574	952	654	422	255
Without income	1,722	785	354	231	172	131	37	1
With income	6,084	1,141	1,668	1,343	779	522	386	244
Under $2,500	1,101	348	272	184	136	103	38	20
$2,500 to $4,999	899	214	187	148	88	73	115	74
$5,000 to $7,499	896	153	210	172	81	94	105	81
$7,500 to $9,999	713	127	209	152	70	61	56	39
$10,000 to $12,499	589	98	185	133	89	49	28	8
$12,500 to $14,999	329	51	95	83	57	25	12	7
$15,000 to $17,499	361	71	116	89	48	24	11	3
$17,500 to $19,999	218	20	90	51	24	23	3	6
$20,000 to $22,499	232	28	77	51	49	23	3	-
$22,500 to $24,999	141	6	62	42	19	8	4	-
$25,000 to $29,999	239	14	74	91	39	18	2	3
$30,000 to $34,999	133	9	40	53	22	5	2	1
$35,000 to $39,999	81	1	24	31	21	5	-	-
$40,000 to $44,999	53	-	6	27	12	6	2	1
$45,000 to $49,999	31	1	7	12	8	2	1	-
$50,000 to $54,999	19	1	4	2	7	3	2	-
$55,000 to $64,999	22	-	3	11	7	1	-	-
$65,000 to $74,999	7	-	1	5	-	-	1	-
$75,000 to $84,999	7	-	2	3	1	-	1	-
$85,000 to $99,999	6	-	2	3	-	-	1	-
$100,000 or over	4	-	2	-	1	-	1	-
Median income	$8,013	$5,147	$9,478	$10,305	$10,411	$7,253	$5,953	$5,853
Full-time, year-round workers								
Number	2,121	298	680	626	354	147	16	-
Median income	$16,553	$13,229	$17,138	$18,508	$16,826	$16,065	-	-

Note: Hispanics may be of any race.
Source: Bureau of the Census, Current Population Reports, Money Income of Households, Families, and Persons in the United States: 1991, Series P-60, No. 180, 1992

All Men Aged 25 or Older: Distribution by Earnings and Education, 1991

Men with professional degrees who work full-time, year-round had median earnings of just over $70,000 in 1991. Those who went no further than high school had median earnings of just $26,218.

(men aged 25 or older as of 1992, by earnings and education in 1991; numbers in thousands)

	total men	less than 9th grade	9th-12th grade, no diploma	high school graduate	some college, no degree	associate degree	college — bachelor's degree or more total	bachelor's degree	master's degree	profes- sional degree	doctoral degree
Total	76,579	7,462	8,085	25,774	12,521	4,110	18,628	11,753	4,382	1,562	930
Without earnings	16,532	4,119	2,778	5,203	1,892	448	2,092	1,337	483	167	104
With earnings	60,048	3,343	5,307	20,571	10,629	3,662	16,536	10,416	3,899	1,394	827
Under $2,500	2,676	385	421	882	490	111	387	233	101	29	24
$2,500 to $4,999	2,050	275	373	664	304	93	341	246	85	8	3
$5,000 to $7,499	2,687	357	433	1,010	405	98	384	247	86	27	23
$7,500 to $9,999	2,394	360	396	853	368	82	334	248	68	13	5
$10,000 to $12,499	3,523	425	547	1,366	511	172	502	358	109	20	15
$12,500 to $14,999	2,375	223	287	1,034	379	108	345	246	70	19	9
$15,000 to $17,499	3,488	289	482	1,461	573	190	493	356	100	30	8
$17,500 to $19,999	2,727	182	321	1,277	472	140	336	261	54	10	11
$20,000 to $22,499	4,106	257	438	1,752	794	242	624	432	131	33	27
$22,500 to $24,999	2,385	89	218	1,000	461	171	446	360	56	20	10
$25,000 to $29,999	6,133	187	437	2,529	1,216	478	1,287	939	232	73	43
$30,000 to $34,999	5,594	125	318	2,141	1,140	406	1,464	1,012	330	68	54
$35,000 to $39,999	4,629	75	224	1,619	959	344	1,408	978	334	47	50
$40,000 to $44,999	3,717	38	143	1,104	754	288	1,390	905	357	75	53
$45,000 to $49,999	2,467	26	86	615	481	224	1,035	668	260	51	56
$50,000 to $54,999	2,483	20	87	509	469	175	1,222	758	314	78	73
$55,000 to $64,999	2,239	12	62	337	368	160	1,301	719	382	113	87
$65,000 to $74,999	1,282	-	5	145	169	78	885	462	252	115	56
$75,000 to $84,999	1,085	6	9	116	123	42	789	366	213	144	66
$85,000 to $99,999	585	1	4	46	74	17	443	199	109	82	53
$100,000 or over	1,424	13	17	112	119	44	1,119	422	255	340	102
Median earnings	$25,986	$11,733	$16,021	$22,482	$26,818	$29,220	$39,562	$36,009	$41,803	$61,986	$50,930
Full-time, year-round workers											
Number	44,195	1,807	3,083	15,022	8,034	2,899	13,349	8,455	3,073	1,147	674
Median earnings	$30,874	$16,880	$20,944	$26,218	$31,034	$32,221	$42,367	$39,894	$47,002	$70,284	$54,626

Source: Bureau of the Census, Current Population Reports, Money Income of Households, Families, and Persons in the United States: 1991, *Series P-60, No. 180, 1992*

All Men Aged 25 to 34: Distribution by Earnings and Education, 1991

PERSONS

Even among men aged 25 to 34, earnings rise with educational attainment. Full-time workers with bachelor's degrees had median earnings of $32,430 in 1991, versus a median of just $22,477 for high school graduates.

(men aged 25 to 34 as of 1992, by earnings and education in 1991; numbers in thousands)

	total men	less than 9th grade	9th-12th grade, no diploma	high school graduate	some college, no degree	associate degree	college — bachelor's degree or more				
							total	bachelor's degree	master's degree	professional degree	doctoral degree
Total	21,124	913	2,058	8,113	3,855	1,260	4,927	3,680	876	296	74
Without earnings	1,378	162	290	501	202	28	196	135	41	18	3
With earnings	19,746	751	1,768	7,612	3,653	1,232	4,731	3,545	836	279	71
Under $2,500	721	73	148	249	137	38	75	57	16	1	-
$2,500 to $4,999	738	66	119	267	125	32	129	107	22	-	-
$5,000 to $7,499	1,002	93	192	391	164	40	123	83	29	8	3
$7,500 to $9,999	997	113	160	403	155	29	138	107	28	3	-
$10,000 to $12,499	1,522	122	234	680	200	86	199	162	35	1	1
$12,500 to $14,999	1,103	55	134	532	158	47	176	128	34	12	2
$15,000 to $17,499	1,524	77	161	698	290	93	205	163	30	12	-
$17,500 to $19,999	1,226	35	133	576	257	70	155	135	14	4	3
$20,000 to $22,499	1,609	35	141	674	358	122	278	210	50	12	5
$22,500 to $24,999	994	16	56	427	199	71	226	189	21	13	2
$25,000 to $29,999	2,283	34	132	961	466	167	522	439	48	29	6
$30,000 to $34,999	1,926	10	69	779	367	142	559	446	76	29	8
$35,000 to $39,999	1,246	4	35	405	264	93	445	326	96	11	12
$40,000 to $44,999	915	8	19	249	195	68	377	284	70	19	5
$45,000 to $49,999	590	2	9	119	113	75	271	194	65	8	4
$50,000 to $54,999	457	1	14	80	100	20	243	165	61	10	7
$55,000 to $64,999	357	3	5	67	63	22	196	135	41	18	2
$65,000 to $74,999	183	-	-	31	18	5	129	64	31	29	6
$75,000 to $84,999	159	3	4	6	9	3	133	98	19	13	2
$85,000 to $99,999	63	-	-	7	8	5	44	20	12	12	-
$100,000 or over	132	-	1	12	6	5	108	34	36	36	2
Median earnings	$21,616	$10,607	$13,080	$20,040	$22,376	$24,585	$30,890	$29,857	$35,649	$40,622	-
Full-time, year-round workers											
Number	14,087	394	916	5,548	2,665	933	3,631	2,739	608	226	58
Median earnings	$25,894	$14,023	$18,057	$22,477	$26,244	$27,395	$35,331	$32,430	$41,321	$50,825	-

Source: Bureau of the Census, Current Population Reports, Money Income of Households, Families, and Persons in the United States: 1991, *Series P-60, No. 180, 1992*

THE OFFICIAL GUIDE TO AMERICAN INCOMES **171**

All Men Aged 35 to 44: Distribution by Earnings and Education, 1991

Men aged 35 to 44 with bachelor's degrees had median earnings of $40,093 in 1991. In contrast, those who went no further than high school had median earnings of just $24,844.

(men aged 35 to 44 as of 1992, by earnings and education in 1991; numbers in thousands)

	total men	less than 9th grade	9th-12th grade, no diploma	high school graduate	some college, no degree	associate degree	college — bachelor's degree or more			
							total	bachelor's degree	master's degree	profes-sional degree	doctoral degree
Total	19,506	860	1,480	6,373	3,722	1,484	5,586	3,495	1,346	497	249
Without earnings	1,251	202	206	470	207	49	117	84	26	7	1
With earnings	18,255	658	1,274	5,903	3,516	1,435	5,469	3,411	1,320	490	248
Under $2,500	551	48	75	205	136	16	71	54	10	3	4
$2,500 to $4,999	402	48	77	126	67	21	63	44	19	-	-
$5,000 to $7,499	662	71	85	255	112	44	95	66	19	5	5
$7,500 to $9,999	519	63	98	194	86	24	54	33	17	4	-
$10,000 to $12,499	902	93	147	317	172	50	123	96	22	3	3
$12,500 to $14,999	601	57	63	265	113	35	68	53	12	3	-
$15,000 to $17,499	966	78	111	403	174	67	133	94	24	10	5
$17,500 to $19,999	793	42	92	381	128	43	106	76	21	5	3
$20,000 to $22,499	1,198	51	104	546	236	67	193	132	43	9	9
$22,500 to $24,999	675	16	59	276	139	60	124	102	18	2	2
$25,000 to $29,999	1,947	36	116	789	444	192	370	271	67	14	17
$30,000 to $34,999	1,909	31	100	638	470	174	496	325	139	13	19
$35,000 to $39,999	1,635	10	61	545	346	166	506	349	120	26	11
$40,000 to $44,999	1,337	-	33	371	264	120	548	368	136	27	17
$45,000 to $49,999	848	5	16	185	168	91	384	248	91	21	24
$50,000 to $54,999	920	3	14	161	188	92	462	323	93	22	25
$55,000 to $64,999	816	-	13	122	116	79	486	268	146	49	23
$65,000 to $74,999	499	-	2	57	72	41	327	168	110	39	11
$75,000 to $84,999	397	-	2	37	34	21	303	105	98	77	23
$85,000 to $99,999	183	1	-	6	21	9	145	76	31	30	8
$100,000 or over	497	4	8	23	30	22	411	161	84	129	37
Median earnings	$29,684	$12,780	$17,115	$24,844	$29,301	$31,923	$42,082	$40,093	$44,517	$71,174	$50,374
Full-time, year-round workers											
Number	14,451	386	818	4,475	2,786	1,213	4,775	2,971	1,141	443	219
Median earnings	$32,662	$16,442	$21,198	$27,045	$32,026	$35,265	$45,107	$41,369	$47,319	$75,016	$51,488

Source: Bureau of the Census, Current Population Reports, Money Income of Households, Families, and Persons in the United States: 1991, *Series P-60, No. 180, 1992*

All Men aged 45 to 54: Distribution by Earnings and Education, 1991

Men aged 45 to 54 who work full-time and who have professional degrees are the highest earners in the country. In 1991, their median earnings amounted to more than $75,000.

(men aged 45 to 54 as of 1992, by earnings and education in 1991; numbers in thousands)

| | | | | | | | college | | | | |
| | | | | | | | | bachelor's degree or more | | | |
	total men	less than 9th grade	9th-12th grade no diploma	high school graduate	some college, no degree	associate degree	total	bachelor's degree	master's degree	profes- sional degree	doctoral degree
Total	13,114	981	1,270	4,297	2,145	616	3,804	2,083	1,147	314	259
Without earnings	1,144	276	269	345	103	36	114	69	34	8	3
With earnings	11,970	706	1,001	3,952	2,042	580	3,689	2,015	1,112	307	256
Under $2,500	382	38	52	140	62	20	69	37	26	1	5
$2,500 to $4,999	273	48	57	100	27	12	30	25	1	3	2
$5,000 to $7,499	316	61	37	127	48	6	37	27	9	-	1
$7,500 to $9,999	309	76	44	90	42	16	40	34	6	-	-
$10,000 to $12,499	531	88	77	190	78	20	77	51	17	7	2
$12,500 to $14,999	345	59	52	134	43	9	48	28	15	-	4
$15,000 to $17,499	553	63	124	210	57	15	84	52	29	1	2
$17,500 to $19,999	412	54	42	219	50	13	34	25	9	-	-
$20,000 to $22,499	738	62	107	322	122	32	93	58	24	7	5
$22,500 to $24,999	395	19	50	168	74	27	57	40	15	-	2
$25,000 to $29,999	1,154	54	94	477	218	72	240	158	54	15	13
$30,000 to $34,999	1,079	24	81	451	205	54	264	157	76	14	16
$35,000 to $39,999	1,080	21	54	410	244	47	304	195	86	6	16
$40,000 to $44,999	969	22	46	337	181	70	313	170	104	18	21
$45,000 to $49,999	656	5	35	181	138	39	259	153	75	10	22
$50,000 to $54,999	688	7	17	174	133	39	319	165	111	16	26
$55,000 to $64,999	677	-	25	87	138	33	393	192	150	24	27
$65,000 to $74,999	382	-	2	34	51	23	272	130	87	32	22
$75,000 to $84,999	327	-	2	50	41	16	218	102	66	33	15
$85,000 to $99,999	222	-	-	20	30	2	169	73	54	18	24
$100,000 or over	481	4	2	30	59	16	369	141	97	100	31
Median earnings	$31,970	$14,259	$20,341	$27,062	$34,813	$34,324	$47,231	$42,099	$50,272	$72,338	$52,350
Full-time, year-round workers											
Number	9,602	426	678	3,087	1,708	466	3,238	1,778	944	283	233
Median earnings	$36,146	$18,108	$22,176	$30,777	$36,800	$40,010	$49,820	$44,996	$51,556	$75,191	$53,102

Source: Bureau of the Census, Current Population Reports, Money Income of Households, Families, and Persons in the United States: 1991, *Series P-60, No. 180, 1992*

All Men Aged 55 to 64: Distribution by Earnings and Education, 1991

The median earnings of men aged 55 to 64 exceeds $40,000 for those with at least a bachelor's degree. Among those who went no further than high school, median earnings were under $26,000 in 1991.

(men aged 55 to 64 as of 1992, by earnings and education in 1991; numbers in thousands)

	total men	less than 9th grade	9th-12th grade, no diploma	high school graduate	some college, no degree	associate degree	college bachelor's degree or more total	bachelor's degree	master's degree	profes- sional degree	doctoral degree
Total	10,036	1,394	1,403	3,244	1,328	404	2,262	1,269	587	225	183
Without earnings	2,740	589	486	913	275	92	385	253	88	27	16
With earnings	7,296	805	917	2,331	1,053	312	1,877	1,015	498	198	166
Under $2,500	374	76	48	106	71	18	53	19	21	5	9
$2,500 to $4,999	307	57	58	72	45	19	56	33	23	-	1
$5,000 to $7,499	351	56	72	126	45	8	44	24	14	-	6
$7,500 to $9,999	321	68	58	100	56	-	39	30	6	1	1
$10,000 to $12,499	373	80	62	122	37	9	63	29	26	1	7
$12,500 to $14,999	253	40	29	79	57	14	33	29	-	4	-
$15,000 to $17,499	372	62	76	126	41	13	54	32	17	5	-
$17,500 to $19,999	250	48	47	85	26	14	31	18	10	-	2
$20,000 to $22,499	479	102	72	176	61	18	52	29	14	6	3
$22,500 to $24,999	276	25	47	122	37	14	32	29	1	2	-
$25,000 to $29,999	649	61	88	276	74	37	113	45	54	8	5
$30,000 to $34,999	623	57	60	250	95	30	131	76	35	12	7
$35,000 to $39,999	596	37	69	234	94	38	124	81	30	3	10
$40,000 to $44,999	434	9	41	130	103	21	130	71	43	8	7
$45,000 to $49,999	310	9	23	108	49	14	106	70	28	7	2
$50,000 to $54,999	352	8	40	74	44	23	164	93	45	20	6
$55,000 to $64,999	328	6	17	54	39	18	195	111	37	15	31
$65,000 to $74,999	163	-	-	21	25	3	114	67	22	12	13
$75,000 to $84,999	145	-	1	17	23	-	105	39	27	20	18
$85,000 to $99,999	86	-	4	13	11	1	57	20	12	12	13
$100,000 or over	252	5	6	38	22	-	181	70	33	55	23
Median earnings	$26,593	$16,016	$20,278	$25,678	$27,429	$27,775	$43,172	$41,455	$39,482	$65,756	$57,714
Full-time, year-round workers											
Number	5,084	482	571	1,654	742	245	1,389	770	347	148	124
Median earnings	$32,108	$20,800	$25,359	$30,206	$32,764	$31,625	$50,611	$48,271	$45,819	$72,366	$71,302

Source: Bureau of the Census, Current Population Reports, Money Income of Households, Families, and Persons in the United States: 1991, *Series P-60, No. 180, 1992*

All Men Aged 65 or Older: Distribution by Earnings and Education, 1991

Median earnings are low for men aged 65 or older because few work full-time. Among those who do work full-time, median earnings topped $25,000 in 1991 and rose above $50,000 for those with a college degree.

(men aged 65 or older as of 1992, by earnings and education in 1991; numbers in thousands)

| | total men | less than 9th grade | 9th-12th grade, no diploma | high school graduate | some college, no degree | associate degree | college bachelor's degree or more | | | | |
							total	bachelor's degree	master's degree	profes-sional degree	doctoral degree
Total	12,800	3,315	1,874	3,746	1,471	346	2,048	1,227	427	229	166
Without earnings	10,019	2,891	1,527	2,973	1,106	243	1,279	797	294	108	80
With earnings	2,780	424	347	772	365	103	769	430	133	121	86
Under $2,500	648	150	98	181	84	19	118	66	27	19	6
$2,500 to $4,999	330	56	63	99	40	10	63	37	21	5	-
$5,000 to $7,499	356	76	47	111	36	2	84	47	15	15	8
$7,500 to $9,999	247	39	36	66	31	13	63	44	11	4	4
$10,000 to $12,499	195	42	27	57	23	6	40	20	9	8	3
$12,500 to $14,999	73	11	8	23	7	4	20	8	9	-	3
$15,000 to $17,499	73	9	10	25	11	2	18	15	-	1	1
$17,500 to $19,999	45	3	6	15	11	-	10	6	-	1	3
$20,000 to $22,499	83	7	14	34	17	2	8	3	-	-	5
$22,500 to $24,999	45	12	7	7	12	-	7	-	1	2	3
$25,000 to $29,999	100	3	7	25	13	10	41	25	8	7	2
$30,000 to $34,999	56	3	7	22	3	5	15	9	3	-	3
$35,000 to $39,999	72	3	5	24	11	-	29	27	2	-	1
$40,000 to $44,999	63	-	4	17	11	10	22	12	4	4	2
$45,000 to $49,999	63	5	3	23	12	4	15	4	1	6	4
$50,000 to $54,999	65	1	3	19	6	1	35	13	5	9	8
$55,000 to $64,999	62	3	1	8	12	7	31	13	8	7	3
$65,000 to $74,999	54	-	1	2	4	5	43	33	2	4	3
$75,000 to $84,999	57	2	-	6	16	2	30	22	2	-	7
$85,000 to $99,999	31	-	-	-	3	-	28	10	-	10	8
$100,000 or over	61	-	-	8	2	1	50	17	5	20	8
Median earnings	$8,065	$5,197	$5,675	$7,408	$9,334	$14,425	$14,712	$13,063	$8,285	$29,559	$42,491
Full-time, year-round workers											
Number	970	119	100	260	133	42	316	197	33	46	40
Median earnings	$25,470	$11,774	$14,560	$21,798	$24,498	-	$51,654	$41,123	-	-	-

Source: Bureau of the Census, Current Population Reports, Money Income of Households, Families, and Persons in the United States: 1991, *Series P-60, No. 180, 1992*

All Women Aged 25 or Older: Distribution by Earnings and Education, 1991

Among women, median earnings were just $15,439 in 1991. But among women who work full-time and who have a professional degree, median earnings were greater than $42,000.

(women aged 25 or older as of 1992, by earnings and education in 1991; numbers in thousands)

	total women	less than 9th grade	9th-12th grade, no diploma	high school graduate	some college, no degree	associate degree	college — bachelor's degree or more				
							total	bachelor's degree	master's degree	profes-sional degree	doctoral degree
Total	84,248	7,976	9,587	32,086	13,520	5,369	15,709	11,010	3,793	564	342
Without earnings	33,474	6,248	5,744	12,815	4,139	1,269	3,258	2,474	652	92	41
With earnings	50,774	1,728	3,844	19,271	9,380	4,100	12,451	8,537	3,141	472	301
Under $2,500	5,308	303	692	2,246	858	313	896	690	163	18	24
$2,500 to $4,999	3,498	285	454	1,449	626	183	501	385	107	6	4
$5,000 to $7,499	4,195	286	497	1,853	760	234	565	436	114	12	2
$7,500 to $9,999	3,594	250	478	1,691	533	204	439	341	75	16	6
$10,000 to $12,499	4,884	226	544	2,286	844	382	602	466	100	30	6
$12,500 to $14,999	3,196	121	274	1,475	721	209	397	337	47	12	1
$15,000 to $17,499	4,053	114	282	1,850	808	357	642	522	99	10	11
$17,500 to $19,999	2,935	32	136	1,283	668	245	571	452	94	14	11
$20,000 to $22,499	3,830	57	162	1,530	837	402	841	644	158	25	14
$22,500 to $24,999	2,242	13	63	847	438	215	666	490	150	2	23
$25,000 to $29,999	4,321	22	133	1,284	936	443	1,503	1,037	413	37	16
$30,000 to $34,999	3,072	11	62	668	567	356	1,409	894	445	47	23
$35,000 to $39,999	2,102	1	26	394	356	235	1,090	661	367	30	32
$40,000 to $44,999	1,198	1	18	193	162	137	686	346	267	46	28
$45,000 to $49,999	766	2	7	74	93	76	514	306	178	15	16
$50,000 to $54,999	499	1	10	31	66	33	358	184	121	24	29
$55,000 to $64,999	465	-	2	37	64	37	325	167	111	30	17
$65,000 to $74,999	223	2	-	23	20	13	165	74	60	13	19
$75,000 to $84,999	132	-	-	20	5	9	98	52	27	11	8
$85,000 to $99,999	85	-	4	10	9	7	54	18	9	23	5
$100,000 or over	175	-	-	30	9	8	128	36	34	50	8
Median earnings	$15,439	$7,409	$8,958	$12,690	$16,078	$19,202	$25,289	$22,482	$30,377	$35,506	$36,284
Full-time, year-round workers											
Number	29,423	733	1,819	10,936	5,621	2,523	7,790	5,251	2,022	311	206
Median earnings	$21,272	$11,637	$13,538	$18,042	$21,328	$23,862	$30,393	$27,654	$33,122	$42,604	$40,172

Source: Bureau of the Census, Current Population Reports, Money Income of Households, Families, and Persons in the United States: 1991, Series P-60, No. 180, 1992

All Women Aged 25 to 34: Distribution by Earnings and Education, 1991

Among women aged 25 to 34, those with a bachelor's degree who worked full-time had median earnings of $26,281 in 1991. Those who stopped with a high school diploma had median earnings of just $17,319.

(women aged 25 to 34 as of 1992, by earnings and education in 1991; numbers in thousands)

	total women	less than 9th grade	9th-12th grade, no diploma	high school graduate	some college, no degree	associate degree	college — bachelor's degree or more				
							total	bachelor's degree	master's degree	profes-sional degree	doctoral degree
Total	21,369	771	2,013	7,908	4,048	1,696	4,933	3,917	750	203	62
Without earnings	4,656	430	897	1,867	748	201	513	411	82	19	1
With earnings	16,712	341	1,115	6,041	3,300	1,495	4,420	3,506	669	184	61
Under $2,500	1,788	57	247	816	301	99	268	226	25	8	9
$2,500 to $4,999	1,109	52	149	441	226	62	179	145	30	3	1
$5,000 to $7,499	1,366	51	163	581	287	95	188	153	28	7	-
$7,500 to $9,999	1,230	51	175	564	190	89	161	140	10	8	3
$10,000 to $12,499	1,701	64	157	771	315	149	244	190	30	20	4
$12,500 to $14,999	1,096	18	57	463	311	97	150	126	16	8	-
$15,000 to $17,499	1,398	27	53	590	296	143	289	262	18	2	7
$17,500 to $19,999	1,169	8	27	470	279	113	273	228	36	5	3
$20,000 to $22,499	1,370	7	35	470	308	147	403	338	57	6	3
$22,500 to $24,999	842	-	8	263	176	92	303	248	46	1	9
$25,000 to $29,999	1,359	4	32	310	283	158	572	456	103	10	3
$30,000 to $34,999	906	-	4	137	166	120	479	381	79	15	5
$35,000 to $39,999	580	-	-	87	90	62	341	247	76	17	2
$40,000 to $44,999	303	-	4	34	31	37	198	123	39	30	5
$45,000 to $49,999	159	-	2	6	9	13	129	95	28	3	3
$50,000 to $54,999	123	-	-	10	12	12	89	60	17	11	1
$55,000 to $64,999	89	-	-	3	14	8	64	45	5	13	-
$65,000 to $74,999	64	2	-	3	1	-	57	33	19	4	2
$75,000 to $84,999	21	-	-	8	2	-	11	6	3	3	-
$85,000 to $99,999	18	-	3	3	2	-	10	3	-	7	-
$100,000 or over	20	-	-	8	-	-	11	2	5	4	-
Median earnings	$15,118	$8,017	$7,473	$12,002	$15,164	$17,793	$22,953	$22,096	$26,442	$34,519	-
Full-time, year-round workers											
Number	9,538	143	408	3,287	1,891	934	2,876	2,296	430	111	39
Median earnings	$20,592	$11,238	$12,028	$17,319	$20,101	$21,967	$27,146	$26,281	$30,622	$41,187	-

Source: Bureau of the Census, Current Population Reports, Money Income of Households, Families, and Persons in the United States: 1991, *Series P-60, No. 180, 1992*

All Women Aged 35 to 44: Distribution by Earnings and Education, 1991

Among women aged 35 to 44, only those with a professional degree who worked full-time had median earnings above $40,000 in 1991.

(women aged 35 to 44 as of 1992, by earnings and education in 1991; numbers in thousands)

| | | | | | | | college | | | | |
| | | | | | | | | bachelor's degree or more | | | |
	total women	less than 9th grade	9th-12th grade, no diploma	high school graduate	some college, no degree	associate degree	total	bachelor's degree	master's degree	profes- sional degree	doctoral degree
Total	20,065	790	1,554	7,149	3,829	1,710	5,033	3,384	1,357	183	109
Without earnings	4,087	395	585	1,476	677	252	703	555	126	13	9
With earnings	15,978	394	969	5,673	3,152	1,459	4,330	2,829	1,231	170	99
Under $2,500	1,394	48	155	510	282	104	295	235	52	5	3
$2,500 to $4,999	984	78	112	388	189	65	152	117	34	1	-
$5,000 to $7,499	1,239	65	133	526	231	82	203	159	41	4	-
$7,500 to $9,999	1,060	66	126	479	168	80	140	106	33	1	-
$10,000 to $12,499	1,500	51	142	670	296	120	222	172	44	4	1
$12,500 to $14,999	979	35	68	479	218	51	129	114	11	4	-
$15,000 to $17,499	1,205	22	74	565	256	122	167	125	33	5	4
$17,500 to $19,999	824	6	31	334	208	77	168	126	32	5	6
$20,000 to $22,499	1,244	9	47	484	288	140	276	194	63	12	7
$22,500 to $24,999	710	4	21	258	141	73	213	149	58	2	4
$25,000 to $29,999	1,478	6	29	422	307	167	548	336	182	20	9
$30,000 to $34,999	1,113	5	18	242	221	126	501	292	184	19	6
$35,000 to $39,999	806	-	4	170	144	88	400	232	146	9	13
$40,000 to $44,999	457	-	3	70	81	64	239	122	106	11	1
$45,000 to $49,999	320	-	4	29	35	39	212	126	73	5	7
$50,000 to $54,999	196	-	4	9	35	14	135	78	32	7	18
$55,000 to $64,999	215	-	-	20	30	21	143	74	51	8	9
$65,000 to $74,999	77	-	-	6	8	7	57	23	22	7	5
$75,000 to $84,999	63	-	-	5	3	8	48	23	18	4	3
$85,000 to $99,999	37	-	-	4	5	7	21	7	2	11	2
$100,000 or over	77	-	-	3	9	4	61	18	17	25	1
Median earnings	$16,729	$7,750	$9,187	$13,878	$16,890	$20,522	$26,525	$23,609	$30,616	$35,909	$37,428
Full-time, year-round workers											
Number	9,703	173	495	3,460	1,987	904	2,684	1,687	808	118	72
Median earnings	$22,336	$11,266	$13,342	$18,554	$21,906	$25,351	$31,500	$30,018	$32,539	$44,954	-

Source: Bureau of the Census, Current Population Reports, Money Income of Households, Families, and Persons in the United States: 1991, Series P-60, No. 180, 1992

All Women Aged 45 to 54: Distribution by Earnings and Education, 1991

Among women aged 45 to 54, those with at least a bachelor's degree had median earnings of over $25,000 in 1991. Those who stopped with a high school diploma earned a median of just $14,553.

(women aged 45 to 54 as of 1992, by earnings and education in 1991; numbers in thousands)

	total women	less than 9th grade	9th-12th grade, no diploma	high school graduate	some college, no degree	associate degree	college — bachelor's degree or more				
							total	bachelor's degree	master's degree	profes-sional degree	doctoral degree
Total	13,910	876	1,541	5,621	2,252	897	2,722	1,662	883	90	86
Without earnings	3,487	496	678	1,441	450	101	321	243	62	14	3
With earnings	10,422	380	863	4,180	1,802	796	2,400	1,420	821	77	83
Under $2,500	843	48	112	368	117	65	132	97	29	3	3
$2,500 to $4,999	553	42	69	247	85	30	80	63	16	-	-
$5,000 to $7,499	743	67	79	354	128	33	82	57	23	-	2
$7,500 to $9,999	689	72	90	341	93	19	75	60	8	4	3
$10,000 to $12,499	997	55	129	500	148	81	85	66	15	4	-
$12,500 to $14,999	698	26	85	341	117	42	86	68	16	-	1
$15,000 to $17,499	908	32	89	422	186	70	110	91	19	-	-
$17,500 to $19,999	567	4	49	289	115	35	76	56	14	4	2
$20,000 to $22,499	814	17	50	368	170	97	112	72	30	5	4
$22,500 to $24,999	483	3	24	207	101	36	112	72	35	-	6
$25,000 to $29,999	994	9	42	324	244	85	289	184	96	5	4
$30,000 to $34,999	741	3	18	185	125	85	325	176	135	8	7
$35,000 to $39,999	485	-	9	92	81	60	242	126	105	4	7
$40,000 to $44,999	296	1	11	60	29	32	162	64	80	5	14
$45,000 to $49,999	193	2	-	28	37	13	114	50	57	3	4
$50,000 to $54,999	133	1	4	4	14	5	104	31	62	6	5
$55,000 to $64,999	109	-	2	12	3	6	86	35	44	5	2
$65,000 to $74,999	59	-	-	14	7	1	37	13	15	2	7
$75,000 to $84,999	36	-	-	3	-	1	31	20	4	4	2
$85,000 to $99,999	29	-	2	3	2	-	22	8	7	4	3
$100,000 or over	55	-	-	16	-	-	38	11	9	12	7
Median earnings	$16,899	$8,682	$11,575	$14,553	$18,087	$20,623	$29,205	$25,193	$33,409	$42,290	$40,701
Full-time, year-round workers											
Number	6,655	214	535	2,657	1,185	495	1,569	892	561	61	55
Median earnings	$21,778	$11,243	$14,970	$18,827	$22,671	$25,539	$31,976	$29,738	$35,874	-	-

Source: Bureau of the Census, Current Population Reports, Money Income of Households, Families, and Persons in the United States: 1991, Series P-60, No. 180, 1992

All Women Aged 55 to 64: Distribution by Earnings and Education, 1991

Among women aged 55 to 64, those with a bachelor's degree who worked full-time had median earnings of $26,596, much higher than the $12,882 in earnings for all women in this age group.

(women aged 55 to 64 as of 1992, by earnings and education in 1991; numbers in thousands)

	total women	less than 9th grade	9th-12th grade, no diploma	high school graduate	some college, no degree	associate degree	college — bachelor's degree or more total	bachelor's degree	master's degree	profes-sional degree	doctoral degree
Total	11,114	1,271	1,609	4,786	1,492	477	1,479	946	442	38	53
Without earnings	5,404	925	968	2,201	638	209	465	345	108	6	6
With earnings	5,710	346	641	2,586	854	268	1,014	601	334	32	46
Under $2,500	723	64	98	335	77	25	125	85	34	-	5
$2,500 to $4,999	519	51	85	233	75	17	58	33	25	-	-
$5,000 to $7,499	586	54	86	278	78	17	73	54	18	1	-
$7,500 to $9,999	431	44	66	215	52	11	42	22	17	3	-
$10,000 to $12,499	540	46	89	278	74	21	32	29	3	-	-
$12,500 to $14,999	369	30	59	174	61	19	26	23	3	-	-
$15,000 to $17,499	442	27	54	244	59	18	41	28	9	4	-
$17,500 to $19,999	334	9	18	172	61	19	54	42	12	-	-
$20,000 to $22,499	332	12	23	173	66	15	43	33	8	2	-
$22,500 to $24,999	159	5	6	98	14	14	23	18	2	-	3
$25,000 to $29,999	452	3	25	207	92	32	92	58	33	1	-
$30,000 to $34,999	275	1	20	91	51	22	91	34	47	4	6
$35,000 to $39,999	189	1	8	40	37	13	90	43	38	-	9
$40,000 to $44,999	130	-	-	27	21	4	78	29	41	-	8
$45,000 to $49,999	86	-	2	11	11	10	52	31	18	3	-
$50,000 to $54,999	44	-	2	6	5	3	28	15	9	-	4
$55,000 to $64,999	51	-	-	1	17	2	30	11	10	3	5
$65,000 to $74,999	19	-	-	-	2	3	14	5	5	-	5
$75,000 to $84,999	9	-	-	3	-	-	5	3	-	-	2
$85,000 to $99,999	1	-	-	1	-	-	1	-	-	1	-
$100,000 or over	21	-	-	-	-	4	17	5	2	9	-
Median earnings	$12,882	$7,725	$9,463	$12,093	$15,400	$18,334	$23,948	$19,072	$30,236	-	-
Full-time, year-round workers											
Number	3,026	150	305	1,351	500	160	561	319	190	18	34
Median earnings	$19,642	$12,657	$13,612	$17,929	$21,866	$25,017	$32,187	$26,596	$34,722	-	-

Source: Bureau of the Census, Current Population Reports, Money Income of Households, Families, and Persons in the United States: 1991, Series P-60, No. 180, 1992

All Women Aged 65 or Older: Distribution by Earnings and Education, 1991

Median earnings are low for women aged 65 or older no matter what their educational level because few work full-time. In 1991, women in this age group had median earnings of just $5,776.

(women aged 65 or older as of 1992, by earnings and education in 1991; numbers in thousands)

	total women	less than 9th grade	9th-12th grade, no diploma	high school graduate	some college, no degree	associate degree	college — bachelor's degree or more — total	bachelor's degree	master's degree	profes-sional degree	doctoral degree
Total	17,790	4,268	2,870	6,622	1,899	588	1,543	1,100	360	50	32
Without earnings	15,839	4,003	2,616	5,831	1,627	506	1,256	920	274	41	21
With earnings	1,951	266	254	791	272	82	287	180	86	9	12
Under $2,500	560	85	80	216	82	21	76	46	23	3	5
$2,500 to $4,999	334	63	39	140	50	9	33	27	2	2	2
$5,000 to $7,499	261	49	37	114	36	7	19	14	5	-	-
$7,500 to $9,999	185	17	21	92	30	5	20	14	7	-	-
$10,000 to $12,499	145	10	26	67	11	11	20	9	8	3	-
$12,500 to $14,999	55	12	6	18	13	-	6	5	1	-	-
$15,000 to $17,499	100	6	13	29	12	5	35	15	20	-	-
$17,500 to $19,999	40	5	11	18	5	2	-	-	-	-	-
$20,000 to $22,499	71	13	6	35	6	3	8	7	-	-	-
$22,500 to $24,999	48	2	5	21	7	-	14	3	10	-	1
$25,000 to $29,999	39	-	5	21	9	1	2	2	-	-	-
$30,000 to $34,999	37	2	3	12	4	3	13	12	-	1	-
$35,000 to $39,999	42	-	5	4	3	12	17	14	3	-	-
$40,000 to $44,999	11	-	-	2	-	-	9	7	2	-	-
$45,000 to $49,999	8	-	-	-	-	1	7	4	1	-	2
$50,000 to $54,999	3	-	-	1	-	-	2	-	1	-	1
$55,000 to $64,999	2	-	-	-	-	-	2	1	-	1	-
$65,000 to $74,999	4	-	-	-	2	2	-	-	-	-	-
$75,000 to $84,999	3	-	-	-	-	-	3	-	2	-	2
$85,000 to $99,999	-	-	-	-	-	-	-	-	-	-	-
$100,000 or over	3	-	-	2	-	-	1	-	1	-	-
Median earnings	$5,776	$4,376	$5,604	$5,853	$5,313	$9,456	$9,428	$8,130	$12,008	-	-
Full-time, year-round workers											
Number	500	53	77	182	59	30	100	57	33	4	6
Median earnings	$16,626	-	$12,866	$17,781	-	-	$16,709	-	-	-	-

Source: Bureau of the Census, Current Population Reports, Money Income of Households, Families, and Persons in the United States: 1991, *Series P-60, No. 180, 1992*

White Men Aged 25 or Older: Distribution by Earnings and Education, 1991

Among white men who work full-time, median earnings were $31,447 in 1991. But among those with a bachelor's degree, median earnings were over $40,000.

(white men aged 25 or older as of 1992, by earnings and education in 1991; numbers in thousands)

	total men	less than 9th grade	9th-12th grade, no diploma	high school graduate	some college, no degree	associate degree	college — bachelor's degree or more: total	bachelor's degree	master's degree	professional degree	doctoral degree
Total	66,063	6,051	6,446	22,261	11,005	3,648	16,651	10,483	3,892	1,432	844
Without earnings	13,894	3,225	2,250	4,469	1,659	403	1,889	1,219	418	155	97
With earnings	52,169	2,826	4,196	17,792	9,346	3,246	14,762	9,265	3,474	1,277	747
Under $2,500	2,190	314	292	745	414	103	322	198	79	25	21
$2,500 to $4,999	1,565	217	258	504	243	71	271	191	74	4	3
$5,000 to $7,499	2,198	296	341	805	334	89	334	214	77	27	16
$7,500 to $9,999	1,985	313	303	694	306	70	299	220	62	13	5
$10,000 to $12,499	2,843	353	425	1,063	429	136	437	311	96	18	12
$12,500 to $14,999	1,941	204	196	840	331	89	282	201	59	13	9
$15,000 to $17,499	2,900	247	379	1,200	495	150	429	315	77	30	8
$17,500 to $19,999	2,314	153	266	1,085	379	129	302	234	48	10	11
$20,000 to $22,499	3,522	216	366	1,525	673	210	533	364	118	23	27
$22,500 to $24,999	2,081	74	186	897	403	145	376	299	51	17	9
$25,000 to $29,999	5,456	172	375	2,257	1,092	427	1,133	814	211	67	41
$30,000 to $34,999	4,999	105	275	1,943	1,007	365	1,303	878	311	62	52
$35,000 to $39,999	4,090	62	182	1,441	869	309	1,227	858	277	43	48
$40,000 to $44,999	3,343	28	118	1,026	690	252	1,229	782	327	74	46
$45,000 to $49,999	2,220	21	71	566	427	211	924	608	232	41	43
$50,000 to $54,999	2,308	18	86	487	437	165	1,116	694	282	73	67
$55,000 to $64,999	2,112	12	50	323	351	155	1,221	697	334	108	83
$65,000 to $74,999	1,180	-	3	131	163	72	812	439	223	103	47
$75,000 to $84,999	1,021	6	9	107	120	42	738	354	191	138	56
$85,000 to $99,999	549	1	1	46	66	14	420	188	98	82	53
$100,000 or over	1,351	13	16	107	118	44	1,053	406	247	307	93
Median earnings	$26,750	$11,936	$16,868	$23,710	$27,440	$30,039	$40,357	$36,680	$42,042	$62,336	$51,077
Full-time, year-round workers											
Number	38,819	1,557	2,490	13,118	7,097	2,594	11,962	7,537	2,763	1,055	607
Median earnings	$31,447	$16,829	$21,489	$26,790	$31,525	$32,849	$43,689	$40,624	$46,978	$70,301	$54,774

Source: Bureau of the Census, Current Population Reports, Money Income of Households, Families, and Persons in the United States: 1991, Series P-60, No. 180, 1992

White Men Aged 25 to 34: Distribution by Earnings and Education, 1991

Among white men aged 25 to 34 who work full-time, median earnings were $26,461 in 1991. But among those with a bachelor's degree, median earnings were more than $33,000.

(white men aged 25 to 34 as of 1992; by earnings and education in 1991; numbers in thousands)

	total men	less than 9th grade	9th-12th grade, no diploma	high school graduate	some college, no degree	associate degree	college				
								bachelor's degree or more			
							total	bachelor's degree	master's degree	profes- sional degree	doctoral degree
Total	17,736	797	1,631	6,726	3,219	1,097	4,266	3,223	717	262	63
Without earnings	911	124	188	314	135	24	127	95	19	10	1
With earnings	16,825	674	1,444	6,412	3,083	1,073	4,140	3,128	698	252	62
Under $2,500	546	61	92	191	105	35	61	49	12	1	-
$2,500 to $4,999	544	64	88	178	94	27	94	75	19	-	-
$5,000 to $7,499	814	79	159	315	129	34	96	65	21	8	3
$7,500 to $9,999	811	109	127	324	110	23	118	90	25	3	-
$10,000 to $12,499	1,191	108	185	505	162	65	167	132	33	1	1
$12,500 to $14,999	893	53	96	433	125	38	149	111	26	10	2
$15,000 to $17,499	1,257	67	135	568	246	70	171	143	16	12	-
$17,500 to $19,999	1,041	32	126	485	196	65	137	119	12	4	3
$20,000 to $22,499	1,376	30	121	585	302	107	232	177	41	9	5
$22,500 to $24,999	864	13	51	386	167	58	189	156	19	11	2
$25,000 to $29,999	2,043	32	118	857	421	156	459	384	40	29	6
$30,000 to $34,999	1,738	10	67	697	332	131	501	395	72	27	6
$35,000 to $39,999	1,099	3	30	358	233	84	391	298	73	9	12
$40,000 to $44,999	827	3	18	230	166	60	348	265	60	19	5
$45,000 to $49,999	535	2	8	114	104	68	240	174	60	6	1
$50,000 to $54,999	420	1	14	75	89	18	223	154	52	10	7
$55,000 to $64,999	343	3	5	61	62	22	190	134	37	17	2
$65,000 to $74,999	161	-	-	27	16	3	114	61	21	27	5
$75,000 to $84,999	151	3	4	6	9	2	126	97	16	13	-
$85,000 to $99,999	57	-	-	7	8	2	40	18	11	11	-
$100,000 or over	115	-	-	10	6	5	94	32	34	26	2
Median earnings	$22,389	$10,529	$14,341	$20,887	$23,568	$25,363	$31,414	$30,561	$35,836	$40,358	-
Full-time, year-round workers											
Number	12,192	347	775	4,731	2,281	825	3,232	2,445	533	203	51
Median earnings	$26,461	$14,044	$19,055	$23,551	$26,791	$27,712	$35,829	$33,635	$41,364	$50,300	-

Source: Bureau of the Census, Current Population Reports, Money Income of Households, Families, and Persons in the United States: 1991, *Series P-60, No. 180, 1992*

White Men Aged 35 to 44: Distribution by Earnings and Education, 1991

Among white men aged 35 to 44 who work full-time, median earnings were $33,594 in 1991. But among those with a bachelor's degree, median earnings were nearly $42,000.

(white men aged 35 to 44 as of 1992, by earnings and education in 1991; numbers in thousands)

	total men	less than 9th grade	9th-12th grade, no diploma	high school graduate	some college, no degree	associate degree	college bachelor's degree or more total	bachelor's degree	master's degree	profes- sional degree	doctoral degree
Total	16,738	729	1,118	5,386	3,269	1,326	4,909	3,069	1,170	453	217
Without earnings	854	138	147	300	151	36	82	62	16	4	-
With earnings	15,884	591	971	5,086	3,118	1,290	4,827	3,008	1,154	449	217
Under $2,500	434	42	47	164	108	16	57	45	8	-	4
$2,500 to $4,999	304	39	49	101	56	14	45	33	12	-	-
$5,000 to $7,499	509	64	56	173	92	43	80	56	19	5	-
$7,500 to $9,999	424	55	71	153	80	18	46	28	14	4	-
$10,000 to $12,499	733	84	112	241	149	43	103	87	16	1	-
$12,500 to $14,999	502	53	47	208	104	33	59	44	12	3	-
$15,000 to $17,499	812	72	85	328	150	53	123	87	21	10	5
$17,500 to $19,999	668	32	63	335	110	37	91	65	17	5	3
$20,000 to $22,499	1,042	48	80	485	207	62	160	107	40	4	9
$22,500 to $24,999	586	16	45	246	123	54	104	84	15	2	2
$25,000 to $29,999	1,729	36	99	697	389	173	334	240	64	12	17
$30,000 to $34,999	1,701	30	94	582	407	150	438	278	128	13	19
$35,000 to $39,999	1,437	10	49	482	310	152	434	300	98	26	10
$40,000 to $44,999	1,189	-	31	344	244	106	464	299	122	27	16
$45,000 to $49,999	739	3	12	163	146	87	328	224	76	12	16
$50,000 to $54,999	849	3	13	153	181	83	415	295	78	21	22
$55,000 to $64,999	748	-	7	118	109	78	436	253	117	48	19
$65,000 to $74,999	451	-	2	51	71	37	290	152	96	33	9
$75,000 to $84,999	378	-	2	32	34	21	288	105	90	70	23
$85,000 to $99,999	169	1	-	6	16	9	137	69	30	30	8
$100,000 or over	481	4	8	22	30	22	396	158	81	122	35
Median earnings	$30,442	$13,057	$18,237	$25,589	$29,847	$32,340	$42,613	$40,560	$44,455	$72,218	$50,851
Full-time, year-round workers											
Number	12,681	348	640	3,889	2,482	1,100	4,221	2,620	998	410	193
Median earnings	$33,594	$16,601	$22,137	$27,646	$32,360	$35,639	$45,763	$41,921	$47,213	$75,236	$51,824

Source: Bureau of the Census, Current Population Reports, Money Income of Households, Families, and Persons in the United States: 1991, *Series P-60, No. 180, 1992*

White Men Aged 45 to 54: Distribution by Earnings and Education, 1991

Among white men aged 45 to 54 who work full-time, median earnings were $36,838 in 1991. Among those with a bachelor's degree, median earnings were over $46,000.

(white men aged 45 to 54 as of 1992, by earnings and education in 1991; numbers in thousands)

	total men	less than 9th grade	9th-12th grade, no diploma	high school graduate	some college, no degree	associate degree	college — bachelor's degree or more — total	bachelor's degree	master's degree	profes-sional degree	doctoral degree
Total	11,427	811	951	3,744	1,926	540	3,455	1,867	1,056	286	245
Without earnings	876	229	173	257	84	30	103	65	27	8	3
With earnings	10,551	581	778	3,487	1,842	510	3,352	1,803	1,029	278	242
Under $2,500	310	29	30	121	57	17	56	30	19	1	5
$2,500 to $4,999	196	39	31	75	20	8	24	19	1	2	2
$5,000 to $7,499	261	48	31	108	35	5	34	24	8	-	1
$7,500 to $9,999	261	56	38	74	41	16	37	30	6	-	-
$10,000 to $12,499	441	68	56	168	62	16	72	49	16	7	1
$12,500 to $14,999	276	53	25	113	40	7	38	22	12	-	4
$15,000 to $17,499	448	49	93	170	54	13	68	40	26	1	2
$17,500 to $19,999	346	47	38	177	37	13	34	25	9	-	-
$20,000 to $22,499	622	56	91	266	107	22	81	49	22	5	5
$22,500 to $24,999	345	17	47	147	68	19	47	31	15	-	1
$25,000 to $29,999	1,016	43	88	421	199	61	203	128	50	13	13
$30,000 to $34,999	964	24	57	415	178	48	242	139	76	11	16
$35,000 to $39,999	967	17	47	376	226	44	258	158	79	6	15
$40,000 to $44,999	879	18	32	309	170	57	292	154	102	18	19
$45,000 to $49,999	612	5	31	167	124	38	249	146	72	10	20
$50,000 to $54,999	631	5	17	167	117	39	285	145	103	14	24
$55,000 to $64,999	645	-	23	84	134	31	372	186	135	24	27
$65,000 to $74,999	359	-	-	34	46	23	256	126	82	27	20
$75,000 to $84,999	302	-	2	45	40	16	199	95	56	33	15
$85,000 to $99,999	211	-	-	20	28	2	161	71	48	18	24
$100,000 or over	456	4	2	30	59	16	344	135	94	88	27
Median earnings	$33,352	$14,826	$21,328	$28,180	$35,401	$35,722	$48,171	$45,030	$50,104	$75,087	$52,247
Full-time, year-round workers											
Number	8,554	372	538	2,756	1,544	411	2,932	1,585	874	255	219
Median earnings	$36,838	$18,005	$23,160	$31,363	$37,150	$40,862	$50,349	$46,230	$51,322	$75,477	$52,955

Source: Bureau of the Census, Current Population Reports, Money Income of Households, Families, and Persons in the United States: 1991, *Series P-60, No. 180, 1992*

White Men Aged 55 to 64: Distribution by Earnings and Education, 1991

Among white men aged 55 to 64 who work full-time, median earnings were $32,673 in 1991. Among those with a bachelor's degree, median earnings approached $50,000.

(white men aged 55 to 64 as of 1992, by earnings and education in 1991; numbers in thousands)

	total men	less than 9th grade	9th-12th grade, no diploma	high school graduate	some college, no degree	associate degree	college — bachelor's degree or more				
							total	bachelor's degree	master's degree	profes-sional degree	doctoral degree
Total	8,731	1,115	1,061	2,889	1,224	364	2,078	1,153	555	210	159
Without earnings	2,314	465	371	792	245	87	354	231	86	26	12
With earnings	6,417	650	690	2,097	979	277	1,723	923	469	184	147
Under $2,500	320	65	35	95	61	18	46	17	19	4	6
$2,500 to $4,999	238	40	30	60	42	17	49	27	21	-	1
$5,000 to $7,499	299	44	53	114	41	6	41	23	14	-	3
$7,500 to $9,999	259	55	34	84	48	-	37	29	6	1	1
$10,000 to $12,499	309	62	46	98	37	9	57	25	24	1	7
$12,500 to $14,999	212	35	22	71	55	8	21	21	-	-	-
$15,000 to $17,499	318	50	57	112	37	11	50	30	15	5	-
$17,500 to $19,999	216	40	34	73	24	14	31	18	10	-	2
$20,000 to $22,499	411	78	61	158	47	16	52	29	14	6	3
$22,500 to $24,999	248	19	38	113	35	14	30	27	1	2	-
$25,000 to $29,999	581	59	62	256	71	26	106	41	53	8	4
$30,000 to $34,999	544	39	54	227	87	30	107	57	32	11	7
$35,000 to $39,999	523	31	54	204	90	29	116	78	26	2	10
$40,000 to $44,999	386	7	34	126	98	19	103	52	40	8	4
$45,000 to $49,999	277	9	17	99	45	14	92	60	23	7	2
$50,000 to $54,999	343	8	39	71	44	23	158	88	45	20	5
$55,000 to $64,999	320	6	13	51	37	18	195	111	37	15	31
$65,000 to $74,999	157	-	-	17	25	3	111	67	20	12	12
$75,000 to $84,999	138	-	1	17	22	-	98	36	27	20	14
$85,000 to $99,999	81	-	1	13	11	1	55	20	10	12	13
$100,000 or over	238	5	6	37	22	-	169	64	33	51	21
Median earnings	$27,285	$16,187	$21,388	$26,019	$28,823	$29,584	$45,842	$42,143	$39,909	$70,419	$58,104
Full-time, year-round workers											
Number	4,532	395	450	1,499	684	218	1,286	708	326	142	110
Median earnings	$32,673	$20,712	$25,570	$30,406	$34,686	$31,955	$51,250	$49,772	$47,537	$72,109	$70,825

Source: Bureau of the Census, Current Population Reports, Money Income of Households, Families, and Persons in the United States: 1991, Series P-60, No. 180, 1992

White Men Aged 65 or Older: Distribution by Earnings and Education, 1991

White men aged 65 or older earned a median of just $8,251 in 1991 because few worked full-time. Among those who did, median earnings were $26,686 and rose with education.

(white men aged 65 or older as of 1992, by earnings and education in 1991; numbers in thousands)

	total men	less than 9th grade	9th-12th grade, no diploma	high school graduate	some college, no degree	associate degree	college bachelor's degree or more total	bachelor's degree	master's degree	professional degree	doctoral degree
Total	11,431	2,599	1,685	3,516	1,367	321	1,943	1,170	393	221	159
Without earnings	8,939	2,269	1,371	2,806	1,043	226	1,223	766	269	107	80
With earnings	2,492	330	314	710	324	95	719	403	124	114	79
Under $2,500	579	116	88	174	82	17	102	57	21	19	6
$2,500 to $4,999	282	34	61	91	31	6	60	37	21	2	-
$5,000 to $7,499	316	60	41	94	36	2	82	45	15	15	8
$7,500 to $9,999	230	38	33	59	26	13	61	43	11	4	4
$10,000 to $12,499	170	32	27	51	20	3	37	18	8	8	3
$12,500 to $14,999	57	10	6	16	7	4	15	3	9	-	3
$15,000 to $17,499	65	9	10	22	7	2	16	14	-	1	1
$17,500 to $19,999	44	3	5	15	11	-	10	6	-	1	3
$20,000 to $22,499	70	4	14	32	11	2	8	2	-	-	5
$22,500 to $24,999	38	9	7	5	10	-	7	-	1	2	3
$25,000 to $29,999	88	3	7	24	12	10	32	22	5	5	-
$30,000 to $34,999	52	3	3	22	3	5	15	9	3	-	3
$35,000 to $39,999	64	2	2	22	11	-	28	25	2	-	1
$40,000 to $44,999	62	-	3	17	11	10	22	12	4	4	2
$45,000 to $49,999	57	3	3	23	9	4	15	4	1	6	4
$50,000 to $54,999	65	1	3	19	6	1	35	13	5	9	8
$55,000 to $64,999	56	3	1	8	9	7	29	13	8	5	3
$65,000 to $74,999	52	-	1	2	4	5	41	33	2	4	1
$75,000 to $84,999	51	2	-	6	15	2	27	22	2	-	3
$85,000 to $99,999	31	-	-	-	3	-	28	10	-	10	8
$100,000 or over	61	-	-	8	2	1	50	17	5	20	8
Median earnings	$8,251	$5,635	$5,470	$7,408	$8,752	$21,259	$15,248	$14,776	$8,613	$40,076	$38,248
Full-time, year-round workers											
Number	860	95	85	243	107	39	291	179	33	45	35
Median earnings	$26,686	$11,924	$12,681	$22,506	$26,531	-	$53,001	$47,213	-	-	-

Source: Bureau of the Census, Current Population Reports, Money Income of Households, Families, and Persons in the United States: 1991, *Series P-60, No. 180, 1992*

White Women Aged 25 or Older: Distribution by Earnings and Education, 1991

Among all white women, median earnings were just $15,540 in 1991. But among those with a bachelor's degree who worked full-time, median earnings were almost $28,000.

(white women aged 25 or older as of 1992, by earnings and education in 1991; numbers in thousands)

| | | | | | | | college | | | | |
| | | | | | | | | bachelor's degree or more | | | |
	total women	less than 9th grade	9th-12th grade, no diploma	high school graduate	some college, no degree	associate degree	total	bachelor's degree	master's degree	profes-sional degree	doctoral degree
Total	71,583	6,375	7,465	27,784	11,533	4,726	13,701	9,560	3,329	522	290
Without earnings	28,551	5,006	4,557	11,343	3,644	1,149	2,851	2,178	554	86	34
With earnings	43,033	1,368	2,908	16,441	7,888	3,577	10,851	7,383	2,775	436	257
Under $2,500	4,571	237	528	1,960	737	283	826	644	148	18	16
$2,500 to $4,999	2,939	219	324	1,264	527	159	446	347	92	5	2
$5,000 to $7,499	3,577	224	405	1,556	669	212	512	390	109	11	2
$7,500 to $9,999	2,947	210	343	1,400	436	179	379	287	75	13	3
$10,000 to $12,499	4,050	182	426	1,913	682	310	537	412	91	28	6
$12,500 to $14,999	2,702	101	210	1,248	628	166	349	292	46	11	1
$15,000 to $17,499	3,379	90	207	1,561	678	313	530	426	85	10	10
$17,500 to $19,999	2,457	27	111	1,097	518	212	492	390	77	14	11
$20,000 to $22,499	3,263	38	118	1,309	718	347	733	557	138	23	14
$22,500 to $24,999	1,876	10	36	742	344	190	553	415	113	2	23
$25,000 to $29,999	3,682	18	97	1,098	784	389	1,297	886	360	35	15
$30,000 to $34,999	2,699	7	49	598	496	312	1,238	783	392	42	21
$35,000 to $39,999	1,781	1	19	322	296	212	930	553	325	28	25
$40,000 to $44,999	1,049	1	18	172	148	119	590	281	241	44	25
$45,000 to $49,999	686	-	7	72	74	73	460	267	165	15	13
$50,000 to $54,999	437	1	6	29	62	30	309	155	109	24	21
$55,000 to $64,999	408	-	2	33	53	34	286	146	96	27	17
$65,000 to $74,999	204	-	-	23	19	13	148	67	53	13	15
$75,000 to $84,999	112	-	-	20	3	9	80	37	25	11	7
$85,000 to $99,999	68	-	2	6	7	6	48	17	9	18	4
$100,000 or over	143	-	-	20	9	8	106	31	27	43	6
Median earnings	$15,540	$7,543	$8,938	$12,758	$15,979	$19,456	$25,214	$22,258	$30,490	$35,505	$35,981
Full-time, year-round workers											
Number	24,611	568	1,327	9,241	4,666	2,149	6,660	4,425	1,768	285	183
Median earnings	$21,547	$11,615	$13,656	$18,252	$21,506	$24,519	$30,526	$27,840	$33,604	$42,620	$39,050

Source: Bureau of the Census, Current Population Reports, Money Income of Households, Families, and Persons in the United States: 1991, *Series P-60, No. 180, 1992*

White Women Aged 25 to 34: Distribution by Earnings and Education, 1991

Among white women aged 25 to 34, median earnings were $15,444 in 1991. But among those with a bachelor's degree who work full-time, median earnings were over $26,000.

(white women aged 25 to 34 as of 1992, by earnings and education in 1991; numbers in thousands)

	total women	less than 9th grade	9th-12th grade, no diploma	high school graduate	some college, no degree	associate degree	college — bachelor's degree or more				
							total	bachelor's degree	master's degree	profes- sional degree	doctoral degree
Total	17,581	664	1,479	6,442	3,274	1,446	4,276	3,398	643	188	47
Without earnings	3,638	363	641	1,437	624	168	404	328	59	16	1
With earnings	13,943	301	839	5,005	2,649	1,278	3,871	3,070	584	172	46
Under $2,500	1,465	46	167	691	241	88	233	206	19	8	-
$2,500 to $4,999	924	46	112	373	187	47	159	133	24	2	-
$5,000 to $7,499	1,127	42	142	447	246	82	169	135	28	7	-
$7,500 to $9,999	950	49	115	430	140	77	138	123	10	5	-
$10,000 to $12,499	1,371	60	130	636	234	107	205	157	24	20	4
$12,500 to $14,999	927	17	50	395	257	80	128	105	16	6	-
$15,000 to $17,499	1,163	25	42	488	235	128	245	218	18	2	7
$17,500 to $19,999	947	8	21	381	213	92	232	200	23	5	3
$20,000 to $22,499	1,145	7	20	389	253	124	351	296	47	6	3
$22,500 to $24,999	715	-	8	234	131	79	263	224	30	1	9
$25,000 to $29,999	1,179	2	23	267	235	143	509	399	98	9	3
$30,000 to $34,999	806	-	4	125	136	112	430	334	78	14	5
$35,000 to $39,999	510	-	-	79	75	55	300	211	72	15	2
$40,000 to $44,999	282	-	4	32	30	36	179	108	37	30	5
$45,000 to $49,999	146	-	2	6	9	13	117	88	25	3	1
$50,000 to $54,999	102	-	-	8	9	8	77	49	15	11	1
$55,000 to $64,999	80	-	-	2	13	7	59	43	4	12	-
$65,000 to $74,999	56	-	-	3	1	-	52	32	14	4	2
$75,000 to $84,999	21	-	-	8	2	-	11	6	3	3	-
$85,000 to $99,999	14	-	-	1	2	-	10	3	-	7	-
$100,000 or over	12	-	-	8	-	-	4	2	-	2	-
Median earnings	$15,444	$8,331	$7,493	$12,209	$15,216	$18,326	$23,212	$22,181	$27,034	$35,412	-
Full-time, year-round workers											
Number	7,927	123	293	2,724	1,503	781	2,503	1,988	376	102	37
Median earnings	$21,032	$11,283	$12,260	$17,565	$20,402	$22,603	$27,337	$26,396	$31,002	$41,534	-

Source: Bureau of the Census, Current Population Reports, Money Income of Households, Families, and Persons in the United States: 1991, *Series P-60, No. 180, 1992*

White Women Aged 35 to 44: Distribution by Earnings and Education, 1991

Among white women aged 35 to 44, median earnings were $16,674 in 1991. But among those with a bachelor's degree who work full-time, median earnings were over $30,000.

(white women aged 35 to 44 as of 1992, by earnings and education in 1991; numbers in thousands)

	total women	less than 9th grade	9th-12th grade, no diploma	high school graduate	some college, no degree	associate degree	college — bachelor's degree or more				
							total	bachelor's degree	master's degree	professional degree	doctoral degree
Total	16,757	659	1,112	5,972	3,177	1,516	4,320	2,871	1,178	175	97
Without earnings	3,254	314	403	1,178	547	216	597	473	103	13	8
With earnings	13,503	345	709	4,794	2,630	1,300	3,723	2,398	1,074	162	89
Under $2,500	1,234	45	125	439	245	98	282	224	50	5	3
$2,500 to $4,999	824	63	79	344	156	59	124	96	27	1	-
$5,000 to $7,499	1,062	61	95	450	205	74	179	138	38	2	-
$7,500 to $9,999	890	61	83	409	137	73	126	92	33	1	-
$10,000 to $12,499	1,250	44	106	550	242	103	204	157	42	4	1
$12,500 to $14,999	834	29	55	398	198	36	118	103	11	4	-
$15,000 to $17,499	980	17	50	464	203	111	135	105	23	5	2
$17,500 to $19,999	701	5	22	298	165	69	140	100	30	5	6
$20,000 to $22,499	1,045	9	37	404	241	116	238	162	60	10	7
$22,500 to $24,999	561	2	11	214	104	65	165	112	46	2	4
$25,000 to $29,999	1,242	6	22	359	244	149	463	282	151	20	9
$30,000 to $34,999	960	4	12	206	196	109	434	252	159	16	6
$35,000 to $39,999	658	-	4	131	114	82	328	185	123	9	11
$40,000 to $44,999	388	-	3	55	71	62	198	95	91	11	1
$45,000 to $49,999	276	-	4	29	26	37	180	102	66	5	7
$50,000 to $54,999	171	-	2	9	34	14	113	70	22	7	14
$55,000 to $64,999	198	-	-	18	30	19	131	63	50	8	9
$65,000 to $74,999	72	-	-	6	7	7	52	19	20	7	5
$75,000 to $84,999	53	-	-	5	1	8	39	18	16	4	2
$85,000 to $99,999	29	-	-	4	2	6	17	6	2	9	1
$100,000 or over	73	-	-	3	9	4	56	16	14	25	1
Median earnings	$16,674	$7,645	$9,169	$13,790	$16,625	$20,594	$26,358	$22,996	$30,537	$36,612	$37,074
Full-time, year-round workers											
Number	8,039	150	358	2,884	1,618	792	2,237	1,369	693	113	63
Median earnings	$22,473	$11,046	$13,537	$18,637	$21,990	$25,856	$31,624	$30,207	$32,906	$47,066	-

Source: Bureau of the Census, Current Population Reports, Money Income of Households, Families, and Persons in the United States: 1991, *Series P-60, No. 180, 1992*

White Women Aged 45 to 54: Distribution by Earnings and Education, 1991

Among white women aged 45 to 54, median earnings were close to $17,000 in 1991. But among those with a bachelor's degree who work full time, median earnings were over $30,000.

(white women aged 45 to 54 as of 1992, by earnings and education in 1991; numbers in thousands)

	total women	less than 9th grade	9th-12th grade, no diploma	high school graduate	some college, no degree	associate degree	college — bachelor's degree or more				
							total	bachelor's degree	master's degree	profes-sional degree	doctoral degree
Total	11,830	693	1,125	4,922	1,969	765	2,357	1,423	785	78	72
Without earnings	2,922	410	479	1,288	365	97	282	217	53	12	-
With earnings	8,908	283	645	3,633	1,604	668	2,075	1,205	732	66	72
Under $2,500	732	39	89	320	108	59	118	87	25	3	3
$2,500 to $4,999	490	38	53	223	74	27	76	62	14	-	-
$5,000 to $7,499	640	44	61	313	111	33	78	54	23	-	2
$7,500 to $9,999	558	52	66	291	82	15	52	37	8	4	3
$10,000 to $12,499	858	44	101	432	128	69	84	65	15	4	-
$12,500 to $14,999	578	20	55	286	107	33	77	61	15	-	1
$15,000 to $17,499	766	21	67	367	174	55	82	62	19	-	-
$17,500 to $19,999	483	1	41	245	95	31	69	51	12	4	2
$20,000 to $22,499	714	10	36	327	157	88	97	63	24	5	4
$22,500 to $24,999	417	3	8	187	91	32	96	60	30	-	6
$25,000 to $29,999	831	7	31	271	217	64	240	153	78	5	4
$30,000 to $34,999	651	1	14	175	111	69	281	159	109	8	5
$35,000 to $39,999	407	-	6	73	70	50	209	106	93	4	6
$40,000 to $44,999	252	1	11	56	26	18	139	48	77	3	11
$45,000 to $49,999	175	-	-	26	27	13	109	45	57	3	4
$50,000 to $54,999	128	1	2	4	14	5	101	28	62	6	5
$55,000 to $64,999	89	-	2	12	3	6	66	28	34	3	2
$65,000 to $74,999	52	-	-	14	6	1	31	11	14	2	3
$75,000 to $84,999	26	-	-	3	-	1	21	10	4	4	2
$85,000 to $99,999	25	-	2	1	2	-	20	8	7	1	3
$100,000 or over	36	-	-	7	-	-	29	8	9	8	5
Median earnings	$16,951	$8,458	$11,341	$14,579	$17,958	$20,361	$29,237	$25,051	$34,524	-	-
Full-time, year-round workers											
Number	5,595	154	389	2,277	1,052	401	1,322	733	490	50	48
Median earnings	$21,957	$11,136	$14,954	$19,011	$22,668	$25,065	$32,270	$30,114	$36,418	-	-

Source: Bureau of the Census, Current Population Reports, Money Income of Households, Families, and Persons in the United States: 1991, *Series P-60, No. 180, 1992*

White Women Aged 55 to 64: Distribution by Earnings and Education, 1991

Among white women aged 55 to 64, median earnings were $13,104 in 1991. But among those with a bachelor's degree who work full-time, median earnings were over $25,000.

(white women aged 55 to 64 as of 1992, by earnings and education in 1991; numbers in thousands)

	total women	less than 9th grade	9th-12th grade, no diploma	high school graduate	some college, no degree	associate degree	college — bachelor's degree or more				
							total	bachelor's degree	master's degree	profes-sional degree	doctoral degree
Total	9,549	976	1,234	4,244	1,321	449	1,327	843	407	33	44
Without earnings	4,585	717	738	1,954	574	193	409	305	95	4	4
With earnings	4,964	259	496	2,289	747	255	918	538	311	29	39
Under $2,500	637	47	73	310	65	21	121	81	34	-	5
$2,500 to $4,999	434	38	60	200	64	17	55	31	25	-	-
$5,000 to $7,499	518	40	71	249	75	17	67	50	16	1	-
$7,500 to $9,999	373	33	57	186	45	10	42	22	17	3	-
$10,000 to $12,499	444	28	65	233	66	21	29	26	3	-	-
$12,500 to $14,999	316	25	45	153	57	17	20	17	3	-	-
$15,000 to $17,499	388	23	42	217	53	16	38	28	6	4	-
$17,500 to $19,999	289	9	15	157	40	17	51	39	12	-	-
$20,000 to $22,499	298	7	20	156	62	15	38	29	8	2	-
$22,500 to $24,999	140	4	4	86	11	14	21	16	2	-	3
$25,000 to $29,999	392	3	16	180	79	32	82	50	32	1	-
$30,000 to $34,999	249	1	19	80	49	19	81	27	46	3	6
$35,000 to $39,999	165	1	5	35	34	13	76	36	34	-	6
$40,000 to $44,999	119	-	-	27	21	4	67	25	34	-	8
$45,000 to $49,999	81	-	2	11	11	10	48	28	16	3	-
$50,000 to $54,999	33	-	2	6	5	3	17	9	8	-	-
$55,000 to $64,999	39	-	-	1	7	2	28	11	9	3	5
$65,000 to $74,999	19	-	-	-	2	3	14	5	5	-	5
$75,000 to $84,999	9	-	-	3	-	-	5	3	-	-	2
$85,000 to $99,999	1	-	-	-	-	-	1	-	-	1	-
$100,000 or over	19	-	-	-	-	4	15	5	2	8	-
Median earnings	$13,104	$7,843	$9,427	$12,154	$15,082	$18,702	$22,325	$18,402	$29,760	-	-
Full-time, year-round workers											
Number	2,606	110	218	1,190	437	148	502	282	176	15	29
Median earnings	$20,063	$13,406	$14,468	$18,079	$21,955	$25,428	$31,771	$25,697	$33,991	-	-

Source: Bureau of the Census, Current Population Reports, Money Income of Households, Families, and Persons in the United States: 1991, *Series P-60, No. 180, 1992*

White Women Aged 65 or Older: Distribution by Earnings and Education, 1991

White women aged 65 or older earned a median of just $5,959 in 1991 because few worked full-time. Those who did earned a median of $16,923.

(white women aged 65 or older as of 1992, by earnings and education in 1991; numbers in thousands)

	total women	less than 9th grade	9th-12th grade, no diploma	high school graduate	some college, no degree	associate degree	college — bachelor's degree or more: total	bachelor's degree	master's degree	professional degree	doctoral degree
Total	15,866	3,382	2,516	6,205	1,791	550	1,422	1,025	317	48	32
Without earnings	14,151	3,202	2,296	5,485	1,533	475	1,159	854	244	41	20
With earnings	1,715	180	219	719	258	75	263	171	73	7	12
Under $2,500	503	60	74	200	79	17	73	46	19	3	5
$2,500 to $4,999	266	33	21	124	47	9	31	25	2	2	2
$5,000 to $7,499	230	38	37	98	33	7	19	14	5	-	-
$7,500 to $9,999	176	15	21	84	30	5	20	14	7	-	-
$10,000 to $12,499	127	6	23	62	11	10	15	8	6	1	-
$12,500 to $14,999	47	10	6	16	10	-	6	5	1	-	-
$15,000 to $17,499	82	4	6	25	12	4	30	12	18	-	-
$17,500 to $19,999	38	4	11	16	5	2	-	-	-	-	-
$20,000 to $22,499	61	6	6	33	6	3	8	7	-	-	-
$22,500 to $24,999	43	2	5	21	7	-	8	3	5	-	1
$25,000 to $29,999	38	-	5	20	9	1	2	2	-	-	-
$30,000 to $34,999	33	2	-	12	4	3	12	11	-	1	-
$35,000 to $39,999	41	-	4	4	3	12	17	14	3	-	-
$40,000 to $44,999	9	-	-	2	-	-	7	5	2	-	-
$45,000 to $49,999	8	-	-	-	-	1	7	4	1	-	2
$50,000 to $54,999	3	-	-	1	-	-	2	-	1	-	1
$55,000 to $64,999	2	-	-	-	-	-	2	1	-	1	-
$65,000 to $74,999	4	-	-	-	2	2	-	-	-	-	-
$75,000 to $84,999	3	-	-	-	-	-	3	-	2	-	2
$85,000 to $99,999	-	-	-	-	-	-	-	-	-	-	-
$100,000 or over	3	-	-	2	-	-	1	-	1	-	-
Median earnings	$5,959	$4,774	$5,976	$5,906	$5,256	$9,800	$8,556	$7,526	-	-	-
Full-time, year-round workers											
Number	444	30	69	166	56	27	96	53	33	4	6
Median earnings	$16,923	-	-	$18,492	-	-	$16,712	-	-	-	-

Source: Bureau of the Census, Current Population Reports, Money Income of Households, Families, and Persons in the United States: 1991, Series P-60, No. 180, 1992

All Black Men: Distribution by Earnings and Education, 1991

Black men who work full-time had median earnings of $23,372 in 1991. Those with a master's degree had median earnings of more than $40,000.

(black men aged 25 or older as of 1992, by earnings and educaion in 1991; numbers in thousands)

	total men	less than 9th grade	9th-12th grade, no diploma	high school graduate	some college, no degree	associate degree	college bachelor's degree or more				
							total	bachelor's degree	master's degree	professional degree	doctoral degree
Total	7,803	1,127	1,446	2,842	1,138	324	926	633	227	47	20
Without earnings	2,104	738	482	588	196	26	75	31	37	3	4
With earnings	5,699	389	964	2,254	942	298	851	602	190	44	16
Under $2,500	406	62	117	119	68	7	32	26	6	-	-
$2,500 to $4,999	377	47	105	133	34	15	43	41	2	-	-
$5,000 to $7,499	364	42	70	167	48	7	29	21	5	-	3
$7,500 to $9,999	305	32	81	125	45	11	11	8	3	-	-
$10,000 to $12,499	525	46	108	257	63	26	26	15	9	2	-
$12,500 to $14,999	349	16	83	166	44	12	28	25	3	-	-
$15,000 to $17,499	462	33	93	204	59	33	39	27	13	-	-
$17,500 to $19,999	308	20	49	150	67	8	15	11	4	-	-
$20,000 to $22,499	417	33	57	169	79	18	61	50	7	4	-
$22,500 to $24,999	230	7	30	87	50	16	39	36	3	-	-
$25,000 to $29,999	508	11	52	223	94	43	85	68	11	6	-
$30,000 to $34,999	429	18	35	169	88	30	88	75	11	2	-
$35,000 to $39,999	380	9	38	145	76	20	91	56	35	-	-
$40,000 to $44,999	239	9	17	54	41	24	95	76	14	-	5
$45,000 to $49,999	163	4	15	40	44	11	48	24	14	10	-
$50,000 to $54,999	80	-	2	16	15	9	39	24	15	-	-
$55,000 to $64,999	60	-	9	11	11	1	28	5	19	4	-
$65,000 to $74,999	45	-	1	12	6	5	21	7	7	6	2
$75,000 to $84,999	24	-	-	5	3	-	16	6	4	1	5
$85,000 to $99,999	17	-	3	-	5	3	7	2	5	-	-
$100,000 or over	12	-	-	2	-	-	10	1	-	8	1
Median earnings	$18,007	$10,610	$12,530	$16,961	$21,329	$24,468	$30,770	$27,240	$37,693	-	-
Full-time, year-round workers											
Number	3,802	172	509	1,547	691	222	662	476	137	35	13
Median earnings	$23,372	$18,325	$17,507	$20,731	$25,470	$27,887	$34,342	$31,032	$40,815	-	-

Note: Income distributions by age and education of black men are not shown because numbers are too small to be reliable.
Source: Bureau of the Census, Current Population Reports, Money Income of Households, Families, and Persons in the United States: 1991, Series P-60, No. 180, 1992

All Black Women: Distribution by Earnings and Education, 1991

PERSONS

Black women who work full-time had median earnings of $19,363 in 1991. Those with a bachelor's degree had median earnings of more than $26,000.

(black women aged 25 or older as of 1992, by earnings and education in 1991; numbers in thousands)

	total women	less than 9th grade	9th-12th grade, no diploma	high school graduate	some college, no degree	associate degree	college — bachelor's degree or more				
							total	bachelor's degree	master's degree	professional degree	doctoral degree
Total	9,641	1,190	1,878	3,379	1,565	475	1,154	823	291	7	33
Without earnings	3,755	977	1,066	1,096	350	85	182	124	55	-	3
With earnings	5,886	214	812	2,283	1,216	390	972	699	236	7	29
Under $2,500	551	46	150	221	92	21	21	11	1	-	9
$2,500 to $4,999	432	43	121	146	74	19	30	28	3	-	-
$5,000 to $7,499	480	34	78	262	67	17	23	23	-	-	-
$7,500 to $9,999	518	25	117	248	79	18	30	30	-	-	-
$10,000 to $12,499	645	22	95	304	136	59	29	28	-	-	-
$12,500 to $14,999	368	11	56	167	76	28	31	30	1	-	-
$15,000 to $17,499	504	14	65	227	96	28	73	60	11	-	2
$17,500 to $19,999	377	1	20	154	132	26	46	38	7	-	-
$20,000 to $22,499	433	10	38	171	103	35	76	60	15	-	-
$22,500 to $24,999	297	-	27	78	83	24	86	58	28	-	-
$25,000 to $29,999	504	4	30	153	123	39	154	105	47	2	-
$30,000 to $34,999	260	2	4	59	62	36	96	53	39	3	2
$35,000 to $39,999	248	-	6	67	53	16	107	74	31	-	2
$40,000 to $44,999	104	-	-	15	10	16	64	43	18	-	3
$45,000 to $49,999	52	-	-	2	19	3	28	18	11	-	-
$50,000 to $54,999	34	-	4	-	-	4	27	12	7	-	8
$55,000 to $64,999	43	-	-	-	10	2	31	15	14	2	-
$65,000 to $74,999	8	2	-	-	1	-	5	-	2	-	3
$75,000 to $84,999	9	-	-	-	-	-	9	7	2	-	-
$85,000 to $99,999	9	-	3	4	-	-	2	-	-	1	1
$100,000 or over	11	-	-	7	-	-	4	4	-	-	-
Median earnings	$14,660	$6,362	$8,715	$12,182	$17,200	$18,055	$26,124	$24,240	$30,294	-	-
Full-time, year-round workers											
Number	3,714	102	423	1,400	797	282	710	508	181	7	15
Median earnings	$19,363	$11,090	$13,189	$16,957	$20,510	$20,913	$28,132	$26,333	$30,988	-	-

Note: Income distributions by age and education of black women are not shown because numbers are too small to be reliable.
Source: Bureau of the Census, Current Population Reports, Money Income of Households, Families, and Persons in the United States: 1991, *Series P-60, No. 180, 1992*

All Hispanic Men: Distribution by Earnings and Education, 1991

Hispanic men who work full-time had median earnings of $21,230 in 1991. Those with at least a bachelor's degree had median earnings of more than $32,000.

(Hispanic men aged 25 or older as of 1992, by earnings and education in 1991; numbers in thousands)

	total men	less than 9th grade	9th-12th grade, no diploma	high school graduate	some college, no degree	associate degree	college — bachelor's degree or more — total	bachelor's degree	master's degree	profes- sional degree	doctoral degree
Total	5,744	1,768	892	1,557	712	232	583	376	131	54	23
Without earnings	961	444	176	212	57	16	55	38	11	5	1
With earnings	4,784	1,324	716	1,345	655	216	528	338	119	49	22
Under $2,500	209	79	38	60	17	6	10	7	1	1	-
$2,500 to $4,999	210	98	33	46	17	4	12	10	2	-	-
$5,000 to $7,499	367	158	71	91	28	6	12	8	2	2	-
$7,500 to $9,999	419	191	70	91	35	8	24	17	5	3	-
$10,000 to $12,499	563	231	104	146	42	14	25	14	10	-	1
$12,500 to $14,999	317	118	44	94	30	14	16	8	7	1	-
$15,000 to $17,499	404	133	81	105	47	10	28	23	5	-	-
$17,500 to $19,999	285	68	67	95	34	12	9	8	-	-	-
$20,000 to $22,499	356	79	54	112	59	18	35	24	6	5	-
$22,500 to $24,999	165	30	21	61	27	7	17	15	-	2	-
$25,000 to $29,999	425	65	65	134	85	30	46	32	11	3	1
$30,000 to $34,999	313	34	22	113	73	21	51	34	11	2	4
$35,000 to $39,999	264	24	24	80	75	14	48	29	15	1	2
$40,000 to $44,999	168	5	11	56	39	14	43	24	15	3	1
$45,000 to $49,999	84	4	3	16	17	15	28	22	5	1	1
$50,000 to $54,999	84	6	6	19	10	10	31	19	8	3	1
$55,000 to $64,999	55	-	-	12	12	5	26	16	5	4	1
$65,000 to $74,999	32	-	1	8	2	2	19	9	5	3	2
$75,000 to $84,999	26	-	-	1	5	4	16	11	2	2	2
$85,000 to $99,999	10	-	1	1	1	-	7	4	1	2	-
$100,000 or over	27	1	-	1	-	2	22	3	3	11	4
Median earnings	$16,902	$11,479	$14,850	$18,523	$24,163	$25,989	$32,322	$30,356	$34,330	-	-
Full-time, year-round workers											
Number	3,226	751	458	935	505	164	414	264	92	$37	21
Median earnings	$21,230	$14,761	$17,135	$21,690	$27,253	$30,026	$36,132	$32,972	$37,832	-	-

Note: Hispanics may be of any race. Income distribution by age and education of Hispanic men are not shown because numbers are too small to be reliable.
Source: Bureau of the Census, Current Population Reports, Money Income of Households, Families, and Persons in the United States: 1991, Series P-60, No. 180, 1992

All Hispanic Women: Distribution by Earnings and Education, 1991

Hispanic women who work full-time had median earnings of $16,693 in 1991. Those with at least a bachelor's degree had median earnings of more than $25,000.

(Hispanic women aged 25 or older as of 1992, by earnings and education in 1991; numbers in thousands)

	total women	less than 9th grade	9th-12th grade, no diploma	high school graduate	some college, no degree	associate degree	college bachelor's degree or more total	bachelor's degree	master's degree	professional degree	doctoral degree
Total	5,878	1,941	909	1,618	654	256	500	356	97	35	12
Without earnings	2,620	1,215	505	563	179	51	107	78	15	9	4
With earnings	3,258	727	404	1,055	474	204	393	278	82	26	8
Under $2,500	344	95	69	99	37	11	32	29	1	1	-
$2,500 to $4,999	303	127	38	85	29	9	15	12	2	1	-
$5,000 to $7,499	375	129	80	91	35	9	31	26	5	1	-
$7,500 to $9,999	344	134	57	110	28	7	8	5	1	2	-
$10,000 to $12,499	414	116	71	130	51	22	23	16	2	6	-
$12,500 to $14,999	225	46	23	92	30	17	17	14	3	-	-
$15,000 to $17,499	252	42	26	102	40	20	22	19	2	1	-
$17,500 to $19,999	160	13	9	72	34	10	21	18	2	1	-
$20,000 to $22,499	209	13	13	84	52	15	32	23	5	3	-
$22,500 to $24,999	109	2	6	47	24	11	19	14	5	-	-
$25,000 to $29,999	209	6	4	81	44	23	51	34	11	5	1
$30,000 to $34,999	118	2	2	28	32	25	29	18	10	-	1
$35,000 to $39,999	73	-	2	21	14	12	25	11	10	-	4
$40,000 to $44,999	42	-	2	5	8	4	24	17	5	1	1
$45,000 to $49,999	29	-	-	2	7	7	13	6	7	-	1
$50,000 to $54,999	15	1	1	2	3	-	7	4	2	1	-
$55,000 to $64,999	20	-	2	2	2	1	12	7	5	-	-
$65,000 to $74,999	3	-	-	-	-	-	3	2	1	-	-
$75,000 to $84,999	7	-	-	1	2	-	4	1	3	1	-
$85,000 to $99,999	6	-	-	-	2	-	3	2	-	1	1
$100,000 or over	1	-	-	-	-	-	1	-	-	1	-
Median earnings	$11,591	$7,730	$8,178	$12,825	$16,697	$18,965	$22,149	$20,130	$30,986	-	-
Full-time, year-round workers											
Number	1,821	324	186	643	290	136	242	167	59	10	6
Median earnings	$16,963	$10,868	$11,532	$17,179	$21,232	$24,213	$27,251	$25,669	-	-	-

Note: Hispanics may be of any race. Income distributions by age and education of Hispanic women are not shown because numbers are too small to be reliable. Source: Bureau of the Census, Current Population Reports, Money Income of Households, Families, and Persons in the United States: 1991, Series P-60, No. 180, 1992

Median Earnings of Men and Women by Occupation, 1991

In 1991, the median earnings of women who worked full-time were 74 percent of those of men who worked full-time. Women police earned 91 percent as much as male police.

(number and median weekly earnings in 1991 of full-time wage and salary workers by occupation and sex; numbers in thousands)

	both sexes		men		women		ratio of female to male median weekly earnings
	number of workers	median weekly earnings	number of workers	median weekly earnings	number of workers	median weekly earnings	
Total, aged 16 or older	83,525	$430	47,910	$497	35,615	$368	74.0%
Managerial and professional specialty	23,109	627	12,254	753	10,854	527	70.0
Executive, administrative, and managerial	11,320	620	6,402	758	4,918	504	66.5
Administrators and officials, public administration	497	659	268	766	230	582	76.0
Financial managers	449	743	249	953	200	559	58.7
Personnel and labor relations managers	113	752	46	-	66	712	-
Managers, marketing, advertising, and public relations	473	784	335	899	137	589	65.5
Administrators, education and related fields	452	759	228	889	223	619	69.6
Managers, medicine and health	186	683	68	758	118	651	85.9
Management-related occupations	3,335	576	1,588	685	1,747	496	72.4
Accountants and auditors	1,215	580	565	699	650	501	71.7
Management analysts	88	717	58	878	30	-	-
Professional specialty	11,789	634	5,853	748	5,936	559	74.7
Engineers	1,739	847	1,598	863	141	740	85.7
Mathematical and computer scientists	842	785	542	823	299	707	85.9
Natural scientists	398	671	292	726	107	571	78.7
Physicians	271	994	198	1,155	72	623	53.9
Registered nurses	1,170	634	78	703	1,092	630	89.6
Pharmacists	121	845	76	863	45	-	-
Teachers, college and university	529	756	353	824	176	659	80.0
Teachers, prekindergarten and kindergarten	297	329	3	-	294	326	-
Teachers, elementary school	1,344	537	205	605	1,139	522	86.3
Teachers, secondary school	1,070	592	514	624	556	543	87.0
Librarians	141	521	25	-	116	512	-
Social scientists and urban planners	270	612	138	704	132	533	75.7
Economists	97	732	50	946	47	-	-
Psychologists	135	536	59	634	76	506	79.8
Social workers	531	466	180	507	351	445	87.8
Clergy	249	459	228	469	21	-	-
Lawyers	370	1,008	279	1,091	91	821	75.3
Writers, artists, entertainers, and athletes	1,064	524	598	594	466	481	81.0

(continued)

(number and median weekly earnings in 1991 of full-time wage and salary workers by occupation and sex; numbers in thousands)

	both sexes		men		women		ratio of female to male median weekly earnings
	number of workers	median weekly earnings	number of workers	median weekly earnings	number of workers	median weekly earnings	
Designers	319	$512	182	$606	137	$418	69.0%
Photographers	53	424	41	-	12	-	-
Editors and reporters	205	593	105	655	100	509	77.7
Technical, sales, and administrative support	25,141	394	9,363	509	15,779	350	68.8
Health technologists and technicians	1,027	423	202	496	825	409	82.5
Licensed practical nurses	325	396	17	-	308	393	-
Science technicians	212	498	156	517	57	427	82.6
Airplane pilots and navigators	71	932	69	933	3	-	-
Computer programmers	509	662	334	687	176	609	88.6
Sales occupations	7,873	418	4,556	518	3,317	308	59.5
Sales representatives, finance and business services	1,505	520	855	610	650	454	74.4
Insurance sales	370	513	232	596	138	440	73.8
Real estate sales	329	517	151	642	178	488	76.0
Securities and financial services sales	247	698	166	823	81	541	65.7
Advertising and related sales	94	488	40	-	54	437	-
Sales workers, retail and personal services	2,733	263	1,168	330	1,565	225	68.2
Sales workers, motor vehicles and boats	222	475	208	485	14	-	-
Sales counter clerks	103	251	27	-	76	230	-
Cashiers	986	218	204	245	783	214	87.3
Administrative support, including clerical	14,097	365	3,088	459	11,009	348	75.8
Computer operators	636	383	225	464	410	353	76.1
Secretaries	2,991	359	30	-	2,961	359	-
Receptionists	553	296	11	-	542	295	-
Bookkeepers, accounting, and auditing clerks	1,233	345	108	398	1,125	341	85.7
Telephone operators	170	362	18	-	152	364	-
Mail carriers, postal service	307	580	239	587	68	547	93.2
Bank tellers	318	281	30	-	288	279	-
Service occupations	8,908	280	4,492	330	4,416	244	73.9
Private household	306	164	14	-	292	163	-
Protective services	1,818	489	1,587	502	232	421	83.9
Firefighting	197	616	194	619	3	-	-
Police and detectives, public service	486	595	433	602	53	547	90.9
Guards and police, except public service	521	308	445	311	76	294	94.5
Service occupations, except private household and protective	6,784	260	2,892	283	3,892	245	86.6
Food preparation and service occupations	2,477	231	1,190	248	1,287	219	88.3
Bartenders	155	249	71	276	84	225	81.5
Waiters and waitresses	518	218	120	281	398	205	73.0
Cooks, except short order	992	240	579	257	413	219	85.2
Dental assistants	109	322	4	-	105	320	-
Nursing aides, orderlies, and attendants	1,056	267	127	298	929	263	88.3

(continued)

(continued from previous page)

(number and median weekly earnings in 1991 of full-time wage and salary workers by occupation and sex; numbers in thousands)

	both sexes		men		women		ratio of female to male median weekly earnings
	number of workers	median weekly earnings	number of workers	median weekly earnings	number of workers	median weekly earnings	
Janitors and cleaners	1,374	$292	1,067	$304	307	$251	82.6%
Hairdressers and cosmetologists	268	263	29	-	238	252	-
Child care workers	181	217	13	-	168	216	-
Precision production, craft, and repair	10,642	483	9,762	494	880	341	69.0
Automobile mechanics	619	385	617	385	2	-	-
Carpenters	787	425	780	427	7	-	-
Electricians	602	538	593	541	9	-	-
Plumbers, pipefitters, steamfitters, and apprentices	350	509	345	509	5	-	-
Machinists	464	476	448	480	17	-	-
Bakers	93	303	57	334	36	-	-
Operators, fabricators, and laborers	14,329	351	10,801	387	3,528	273	70.5
Machine operators, assemblers, and inspectors	7,003	336	4,272	396	2,731	270	68.2
Transportation and material moving occupations	3,943	419	3,703	423	240	339	80.1
Motor vehicle operators	2,796	407	2,604	412	192	328	79.6
Truckdrivers, heavy	1,676	429	1,644	430	32	-	-
Taxicab drivers and chauffeurs	107	339	92	340	15	-	-
Material moving equipment operators	981	422	934	424	46	-	-
Handlers, equipment cleaners, helpers, and laborers	3,383	305	2,826	315	556	261	82.9
Farming, forestry, and fishing	1,397	263	1,238	269	159	224	83.3
Farm managers	58	362	49	-	9	-	-
Farm workers	563	239	492	243	71	216	88.9

Source: Bureau of Labor Statistics, U.S. Department of Labor, Employment and Earnings, *January 1992*

Median Earnings by Union Status and Demographic Characteristics, 1991

Only 16 percent of full-time wage and salary workers are members of unions. Their weekly earnings were $526 in 1991, versus $404 for nonunion workers.

(union representation and median weekly earnings in 1991 of full-time wage and salary workers by age, sex, race, Hispanic origin, and union affiliation; numbers in thousands)

	total workers	members of unions total	members of unions percent	represented by unions total	represented by unions percent	median weekly earnings total	median weekly earnings members of unions	median weekly earnings represented by unions	median weekly earnings non-union
Both sexes									
Total, aged 16 or older	102,786	16,568	16.1%	18,734	18.2%	$430	$526	$522	$404
Aged 16 to 24	17,340	1,142	6.6	1,341	7.7	278	356	347	272
Aged 25 to 34	30,106	4,228	14	4,824	16	417	496	491	403
Aged 35 to 44	27,056	5,339	19.7	6,040	22.3	499	557	555	479
Aged 45 to 54	16,863	3,743	22.2	4,163	24.7	507	581	580	480
Aged 55 to 64	9,116	1,919	21.1	2,138	23.5	469	534	529	427
Aged 65 or older	2,305	198	8.6	228	9.9	381	522	526	348
Men									
Total, aged 16 or older	53,931	10,430	19.3	11,494	21.3	497	568	567	473
Aged 16 to 24	8,951	738	8.2	851	9.5	286	377	368	279
Aged 25 to 34	16,298	2,702	16.6	2,998	18.4	462	520	518	440
Aged 35 to 44	14,025	3,313	23.6	3,619	25.8	578	591	592	567
Aged 45 to 54	8,680	2,334	26.9	2,547	29.3	614	613	615	612
Aged 55 to 64	4,850	1,231	25.4	1,350	27.8	562	579	580	543
Aged 65 or older	1,127	113	10	129	11.5	465	601	607	404
Women									
Total, aged 16 or older	48,856	6,138	12.6	7,240	14.8	368	467	462	348
Aged 16 to 24	8,389	405	4.8	490	5.8	267	321	317	263
Aged 25 to 34	13,808	1,526	11.1	1,826	13.2	372	440	432	360
Aged 35 to 44	13,031	2,026	15.5	2,421	18.6	408	491	490	389
Aged 45 to 54	8,183	1,408	17.2	1,616	19.7	398	499	497	375
Aged 55 to 64	4,266	689	16.1	788	18.5	363	448	445	337
Aged 65 or older	1,179	85	7.2	99	8.4	319	388	392	306
Race and Hispanic origin									
White, aged 16 or older	87,981	13,587	15.4	15,331	17.4	446	544	539	415
Men	46,586	8,754	18.8	9,604	20.6	509	581	581	488
Women	41,395	4,833	11.7	5,726	13.8	374	477	473	355
Black, aged 16 or older	11,318	2,425	21.4	2,759	24.4	348	461	452	314
Men	5,502	1,355	24.6	1,524	27.7	374	489	485	330
Women	5,816	1,070	18.4	1,236	21.2	323	420	414	302
Hispanic, aged 16 or older	8,193	1,275	15.6	1,447	17.7	315	439	438	295
Men	4,860	823	16.9	906	18.6	328	481	482	305
Women	3,333	451	13.5	541	16.2	293	374	376	278

Note: Because Hispanics may be of any race, the number of workers by race and Hispanic origin will not add to total workers. "Members of unions" refers to members of a labor union or an employee association similar to a union. "Represented by unions" refers to members of a labor union or employee association similar to a union plus workers who report no union affiliation but whose jobs are covered by a union or an employee association contract.
Source: Bureau of Labor Statistics, U.S. Department of Labor, Employment and Earnings, January 1992

Median Earnings by Union Status, Occupation, and Industry, 1991

Union membership makes the biggest difference for people who work in protective services. In those occupations, union members make over $200 a week more than nonunion workers.

(union representation and median weekly earnings in 1991 of full-time wage and salary workers by occupation, industry, and union affiliation)

	total earnings	members of unions	represented by unions	non-union	difference between union and non-union weekly median
OCCUPATION					
Managerial and professional specialty	$627	$634	$630	$626	$8
Executive, administrative, and managerial	620	623	636	619	4
Professional specialty	634	637	628	637	0
Technical, sales, and administrative support	394	480	474	382	98
Technicians and related support	508	554	556	501	53
Sales occupations	418	413	414	418	-5
Administrative support, including clerical	365	477	466	347	130
Service occupations	280	448	437	253	195
Protective service	489	614	609	387	227
Service, except protective service	256	351	345	242	109
Precision production, craft and repair	483	598	593	430	168
Operators, fabricators, and laborers	351	480	475	310	170
Machine operators, assemblers, and inspectors	336	446	440	304	142
Transportation and material moving occupations	419	557	547	374	183
Handlers, equipment cleaners, helpers, and laborers	305	450	442	273	177
Farming, forestry, and fishing	263	414	405	256	158
INDUSTRY					
Agricultural wage and salary workers	267	-	-	264	-
Private nonagricultural wage and salary workers	415	510	506	400	110
Mining	596	588	589	598	-10
Construction	468	679	665	412	267
Manufacturing	444	485	484	425	60
Durable goods	478	501	501	464	37
Nondurable goods	401	446	443	389	57
Transportation and public utilities	532	595	589	501	94
Transportation	500	606	599	452	154
Communications and public utilities	586	583	580	591	-8
Wholesale and retail trade	334	416	413	326	90

(continued)

(continued from previous page)

(union representation and median weekly earnings in 1991 of full-time wage and salary workers by occupation, industry, and union affiliation)

	total earnings	members of unions	represented by unions	non-union	difference between union and non-union weekly median
Wholesale trade	$451	$493	$491	$445	48
Retail trade	303	391	388	298	93
Finance, insurance, and real estate	449	463	454	448	15
Services	394	431	436	390	41
Government workers	506	560	554	461	99

Note: "Members of unions" refers to members of a labor union or an employee association similar to a union. "Represented by unions" refers to members of a labor union or employee association similar to a union plus workers who report no union affiliation but whose jobs are covered by a union or an employee association contract.
Source: Bureau of Labor Statistics, U.S. Department of Labor, Employment and Earnings, *January 1992*

Average Income of Persons by Source of Income and Race, 1991

Nearly 125 million Americans receive wage and salary income. On average, those with wage and salary income received $21,599 from this source in 1991.

(persons with income by source, and average income for those with income in 1991; number of persons aged 15 or older as of 1992; numbers in thousands)

	all persons		white		black		Hispanic	
	number with income	average income	number with income	average income	number with income	average income	number with income	average income
Total	181,222	$20,280	155,299	$20,997	19,670	$14,656	13,022	$14,697
Earnings	133,835	21,797	114,954	22,420	14,108	16,545	10,235	15,981
Wages and salary	124,663	21,599	106,563	22,223	13,706	16,478	9,754	15,868
Nonfarm self-employment	12,379	16,812	11,320	17,044	598	12,328	607	13,921
Unemployment compensation	9,200	2,373	7,907	2,404	1,010	2,190	884	2,261
Workers' compensation	2,619	4,499	2,194	4,306	322	5,321	274	4,382
Social Security	35,509	6,245	31,367	6,377	3,412	5,162	1,372	5,375
SSI (Supplemental Social Security)	4,406	3,268	2,896	3,297	1,322	3,119	510	3,616
Public assistance	5,505	3,211	3,325	3,194	1,913	3,154	845	4,066
Veteran's benefits	2,658	4,633	2,298	4,659	293	4,113	77	5,524
Survivors benefits	3,190	7,510	2,921	7,595	214	4,897	81	7,953
Disability benefits	1,828	7,715	1,494	7,649	291	7,812	136	5,896
Pensions	14,694	9,109	13,547	9,199	944	7,847	353	8,891
Company or union	8,960	6,773	8,338	6,830	511	5,768	200	6,455
Federal government	1,344	16,363	1,221	16,926	94	11,328	50	-
Military retirement	1,160	14,931	1,042	15,244	103	12,427	22	-
State or local government	2,585	9,442	2,340	9,425	208	8,749	50	-
Railroad retirement	350	9,919	333	9,989	17	-	15	-
Annuities	8,019	259	8,072	5	-	7	-	
IRA, KEOGH, or 401(k)	424	5,855	402	6,004	13	-	7	-
Interest	107,248	1,467	98,138	1,525	5,629	701	4,255	662
Dividends	23,600	1,842	22,345	1,877	652	908	407	1,172
Rents, royalties, estates, or trusts	12,883	3,253	11,840	3,260	553	3,136	489	3,092
Education	7,822	2,580	6,433	2,412	1,011	2,947	452	2,579
Child support	4,200	3,089	3,552	3,246	559	2,056	255	2,298
Alimony	441	7,102	415	7,199	22	-	13	-

Note: Because Hispanics may be of any race, the number of persons by race and Hispanic origin will not add to total persons.
Source: Bureau of the Census, Current Population Reports, Money Income of Households, Families, and Persons in the United States: 1991, Series P-60, No. 180, 1992

Average Income of Persons Aged 25 to 44 by Source of Income and Race, 1991

Wages and salaries are the single biggest source of income for people aged 25 to 44. On average, people with wage and salary income received $23,631 from this source in 1991. Wages are highest for whites and lowest for Hispanics.

(persons with income by source, and average income for those with income in 1991; number of persons aged 25 to 44 as of 1992; numbers in thousands)

	all persons		white		black		Hispanic	
	number with income	average income	number with income	average income	number with income	average income	number with income	average income
Total	78,379	$23,064	66,089	$23,876	9,191	$17,198	6,703	$16,648
Earnings	70,692	23,796	60,155	24,485	7,863	18,298	5,876	17,476
Wages and salary	66,388	23,631	56,209	24,334	7,686	18,178	5,602	17,474
Nonfarm self-employment	6,419	16,718	5,879	16,867	305	13,652	346	13,043
Unemployment compensation	5,628	2,326	4,851	2,352	610	2,186	578	2,401
Workers' compensation	1,470	3,977	1,241	3,869	171	4,591	170	4,273
Social Security	1,612	5,847	1,251	5,922	310	5,334	143	5,648
SSI (Supplemental Social Security)	1,161	3,832	774	3,915	354	3,716	96	4,209
Public assistance	3,218	3,577	1,998	3,535	1,075	3,524	507	4,540
Veteran's benefits	497	4,617	433	4,740	42	-	23	-
Survivors benefits	315	9,916	289	9,846	19	-	13	-
Disability benefits	606	7,483	496	7,449	91	7,198	60	-
Pensions	624	6,357	527	6,204	85	7,708	25	-
Company or union	345	4,766	293	4,285	46	-	15	-
Federal government	16	-	14	-	2	-	1	-
Military retirement	91	9,659	71	-	19	-	2	-
State or local government	84	7,038	76	7,149	6	-	1	-
Railroad retirement	5	-	3	-	2	-	-	-
Annuities	8	-	8	-	-	-	1	-
IRA, KEOGH, or 401(k)	56	-	47	-	6	-	2	-
Interest	45,587	574	40,894	593	2,870	288	2,254	331
Dividends	8,922	911	8,277	921	361	557	218	640
Rents, royalties, estates, or trusts	4,448	2,343	4,047	2,273	173	2,073	236	2,302
Education	3,452	2,382	2,825	2,135	419	2,779	164	2,078
Child support	3,359	3,234	2,857	3,381	427	2,269	198	2,504
Alimony	189	5,290	178	5,240	10	-	7	-

Note: Because Hispanics may be of any race, the number of persons by race and Hispanic origin will not add to total persons.
Source: Bureau of the Census, Current Population Reports, Money Income of Households, Families, and Persons in the United States: 1991, Series P-60, No. 180, 1992

Average Income of Persons Aged 45 to 64 by Source of Income and Race, 1991

Over 4 million Americans aged 45 to 64 receive income from pensions. Among these recipients, pension income averaged over $12,000 in 1991.

(persons with income by source, and average income for those with income in 1991; number of persons aged 45 to 64 as of 1992; numbers in thousands)

	all persons		white		black		Hispanic	
	number with income	average income	number with income	average income	number with income	average income	number with income	average income
Total	45,886	$26,083	39,744	$27,020	4,589	$18,067	2,693	$17,855
Earnings	35,398	27,743	30,840	28,521	3,335	20,374	2,012	20,040
Wages and salary	31,821	27,883	27,597	28,667	3,157	20,575	1,852	19,875
Nonfarm self-employment	4,460	19,547	4,071	19,895	212	13,172	197	17,655
Unemployment compensation	2,456	2,720	2,109	2,758	260	2,445	201	2,152
Workers' compensation	784	6,041	636	5,607	117	7,045	69	-
Social Security	5,463	5,640	4,648	5,771	658	4,943	290	5,370
SSI (Supplemental Social Security)	1,235	3,656	834	3,718	372	3,444	120	3,908
Public assistance	722	2,709	435	2,729	243	2,624	132	3,761
Veteran's benefits	813	5,331	663	5,331	127	4,783	25	-
Survivors benefits	810	9,463	700	9,862	83	5,954	26	-
Disability benefits	859	8,500	690	8,330	151	9,165	57	-
Pensions	4,039	12,164	3,658	12,327	300	10,198	135	11,491
Company or union	2,119	10,016	1,936	10,217	140	7,499	81	8,794
Federal government	352	18,055	307	18,813	38	-	21	-
Military retirement	720	15,431	643	15,729	64	-	15	-
State or local government	725	11,939	655	11,806	52	-	13	-
Railroad retirement	54	-	52	-	2	-	1	-
Annuities	40	-	38	-	-	-	2	-
IRA, KEOGH, or 401(k)	73	-	63	-	5	-	-	-
Interest	30,780	1,883	28,310	1,943	1,488	951	1,139	929
Dividends	8,554	1,854	8,107	1,865	227	1,466	138	1,257
Rents, royalties, estates, or trusts	5,458	3,534	5,022	3,594	226	3,122	190	3,488
Education	505	1,377	448	1,323	45	-	25	-
Child support	396	3,729	360	3,826	24	-	16	-
Alimony	210	9,284	199	9,421	8	-	4	-

Note: Because Hispanics may be of any race, the number of persons by race and Hispanic origin will not add to total persons.
Source: Bureau of the Census, Current Population Reports, Money Income of Households, Families, and Persons in the United States: 1991, *Series P-60, No. 180, 1992*

Average Income of Persons Aged 65 or Older by Source of Income and Race, 1991

PERSONS

Over 27 million Americans aged 65 or older receive income from Social Security. They received an average of $6,465 in Social Security payments in 1991.

(persons with income by source, and average income for those with income in 1991; number of persons aged 65 or older as of 1992; numbers in thousands)

	all persons		white		black		Hispanic	
	number with income	average income	number with income	average income	number with income	average income	number with income	average income
Total	30,256	$15,130	27,068	$15,738	2,546	$9,572	1,089	$9,991
Earnings	4,732	14,880	4,207	15,470	388	9,893	153	12,462
Wages and salary	3,757	15,192	3,294	15,871	350	10,118	132	12,496
Nonfarm self-employment	923	12,039	861	12,297	38	-	22	-
Unemployment compensation	156	1,915	141	2,010	11	-	12	-
Workers' compensation	88	5,741	68	-	17	-	4	-
Social Security	27,598	6,465	24,830	6,581	2,271	5,319	870	5,473
SSI (Supplemental Social Security)	1,722	2,517	1,090	2,458	520	2,347	257	3,182
Public assistance	153	2,060	100	1,975	46	-	20	-
Veteran's benefits	1,299	4,259	1,163	4,281	114	4,060	28	-
Survivors benefits	1,996	6,346	1,882	6,386	93	5,011	41	-
Disability benefits	327	6,511	276	6,770	48	-	13	-
Pensions	9,994	8,071	9,329	8,164	556	6,640	190	7,464
Company or union	6,476	5,837	6,092	5,893	322	4,722	103	4,930
Federal government	977	15,888	900	16,396	54	-	28	-
Military retirement	345	15,322	324	15,524	20	-	4	-
State or local government	1,765	8,578	1,598	8,605	149	8,014	34	-
Railroad retirement	292	9,686	278	9,820	13	-	14	-
Annuities	219	7,136	213	7,130	5	-	3	-
IRA, KEOGH, or 401(k)	295	6,215	292	6,240	2	-	5	-
Interest	20,712	3,399	19,673	3,452	704	2,104	387	2,433
Dividends	5,297	3,566	5,196	3,593	48	-	35	-
Rents, royalties, estates, or trusts	2,787	4,178	2,595	4,165	148	4,502	56	-
Education	19	-	19	-	-	-	3	-
Child support	10	-	6	-	4	-	2	-
Alimony	32	-	31	-	1	-	1	-

Note: Because Hispanics may be of any race, the number of persons by race and Hispanic origin will not add to total persons.
Source: Bureau of the Census, Current Population Reports, Money Income of Households, Families, and Persons in the United States: 1991, Series P-60, No. 180, 1992

Child Support: Women Awarded and Receiving Child Support, 1989

Among the 5 million women who were supposed to receive child support payments in 1989, 75 percent did receive support payments. The average amount received was just under $3,000.

(women aged 15 or older living with children under age 21, by child support arrangement and support received from absent fathers as of 1990; numbers in thousands)

	total women	supposed to receive child support in 1989				
		total	actually received child support in 1989			
			percent	average child support	average income	child support as percent of total income
Total	9,955	4,953	75.2%	$2,995	$16,171	18.5%
Current marital status						
Married	2,531	1,685	72.1	2,931	14,469	20.3
Divorced	3,056	2,123	77.0	3,322	19,456	17.1
Separated	1,352	527	79.7	3,060	14,891	20.5
Widowed	65	34	-	-	-	-
Never married	2,950	583	73.2	1,888	9,495	19.9
Race and Hispanic origin						
White	6,905	4,048	76.5	3,132	16,632	18.8
Black	2,770	791	69.7	2,263	13,898	16.3
Hispanic	1,112	364	69.8	2,965	14,758	20.1
Age						
Aged 15 to 17	128	23	-	-	-	-
Aged 18 to 29	3,086	1,208	75.6	1,981	9,938	19.9
Aged 30 to 39	4,175	2,413	74.4	3,032	17,006	17.8
Aged 40 or older	2,566	1,309	76.2	3,903	20,668	18.9
Years of school completed						
Less than 12 years	2,372	741	66.7	1,754	8,201	21.4
4 years high school	4,704	2,470	76.4	2,698	13,535	19.9
1 to 3 years college	1,988	1,139	76.6	3,338	18,462	18.1
4 or more years college	891	603	77.9	4,850	30,872	15.7
Number of children from an absent father						
One child	5,721	2,742	75.8	2,425	15,799	15.3
Two children	2,873	1,608	75.6	3,527	17,465	20.2
Three children	1,030	488	70.1	4,509	14,863	30.3
Four children or more	331	115	77.4	3,226	12,217	26.4

Note: Because Hispanics may be of any race, the number of women by race and Hispanic origin will not add to total women.
Source: Bureau of the Census, Current Population Reports, Child Support and Alimony: 1989, Series P-60, No. 173, 1991.

4

Discretionary Income

by Thomas G. Exter

Discretionary Income: Highlights

■ Most American households have discretionary income. Those with discretionary income had an average of $11,287 in extra spending money in 1991.

■ A majority of households with incomes of $10,000 or more have at least some discretionary income. Virtually all households with incomes of $80,000 or more have such spending money.

■ Regardless of age, a majority of households have discretionary income. Those most likely to have spending money are householders aged 45 to 64.

Discretionary income is the money that remains for spending or saving after people pay their taxes and basic expenses. Many businesses depend on discretionary spending for sales and profits. This dependency makes discretionary income statistics important for marketing strategy. Despite this importance, however, discretionary income statistics are hard to find. No government agency is charged with producing these numbers. Because there are no official discretionary income figures, those that exist are published irregularly and infrequently. The last comprehensive esti-

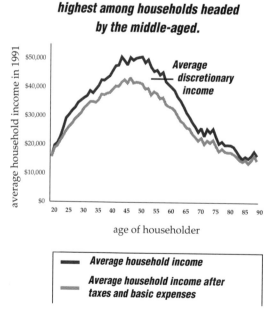

Average discretionary income is highest among households headed by the middle-aged.

average household income in 1991

Average discretionary income

age of householder

—— Average household income

—— Average household income after taxes and basic expenses

mates of discretionary income were done for 1986, the product of a joint effort by the New York City-based Conference Board and the Census Bureau. The American economy was booming in 1986, an era fast receding into the distant past. Up-to-date estimates of discretionary income are long overdue.

In this chapter, we present detailed estimates of discretionary income for 1991. Our calculations may surprise many businesses who find consumers increasingly reluctant to part with their dollars. Americans' hesitancy to spend may have more to do with changing attitudes than shrinking incomes. Despite the fact that 1991 was a year in which Americans were struggling out of recession, 64 percent of households had at least some discretionary spending money. The average household with discretionary income had over $11,000 in "uncommitted dollars." In the aggregate, Americans had $689 billion in discretionary income in 1991.

Estimating Discretionary Income

The estimates of discretionary income presented in this chapter were calculated in three steps. We started with 1991 household income statistics from the Census Bureau's 1992 Current Population Survey. These are the familiar income figures used elsewhere in this book, revealing household income before taxes. We subtracted taxes from these income statistics using the Census Bureau's unpublished estimates of the average taxes paid by households by income level. We subtracted federal and state income taxes, payroll taxes including FICA, and local property taxes. What remains of household income after subtracting tax payments is called "disposable" or after-tax income. Before and after-tax income figures for households are shown in the first table in this chapter.

Next, we estimated basic household expenses for 150 different types of households based on household size, age of householder, and income level. To do this, we used data from the 1991 Consumer Expenditure Survey of the Bureau of Labor Statistics. This annual survey measures household spending by detailed expenditure category. We defined basic expenses to include all food spending, spending on housing (except for spending on "other lodging," which can include spending on hotels and motels on out-of-town trips), spending on apparel and apparel services (except for "other apparel products," which can include jewelry), spending on transportation (except for spending on "public transportation," which can include discretionary spending on airline fares), and spending on health care.

Once we estimated basic expenditures, we subtracted these figures from after-tax income. That is, we calculated the average amount households spend on the basics by household size, age group, and income level.

No definition of basic expenses can be exact. All are likely to include at least some discretionary items, and some nondiscretionary items are likely to be included in discretionary spending as well. The reason for this overlap is that the categories of expenses in the Consumer Expenditure Survey sometimes include both discretionary and nondiscretionary items. Another problem is that what is discretionary to one person may be a necessary expense to another. Often, defining basic expenses is a judgment call. Some of the food spending we include as "basic" is discretionary, for example, such as a birthday dinner at an expensive restaurant. But most food spending is not discretionary, which is why we included all food spending under basic expenses. While some might argue that spending on any restaurant food is discretionary, it's likely that most Americans would strongly disagree. Restaurant meals have become a necessary expense for today's busy households.

The small amount of discretionary spending that is included in such basic items as food spending is likely to be canceled out by some nondiscretionary spending included in items classified as discretionary. We defined spending on personal care products and services, for example, as discretionary. But there are some nondiscretionary items included in this category, such as spending on toothpaste, shaving products, and shampoo.

In the final step, we multiplied by 75 percent any income remaining after subtracting taxes and basic expenses to account for spending above and beyond the basics that some households may consider necessary rather than discretionary. In other words, we were conservative in our estimates of discretionary income, reducing these dollars by 25 percent. The results show that despite recent economic woes, the majority of American households have some money to spend after paying for necessities.

Income Before and After Taxes

Before taxes, American households had an average income of $37,272 in 1991. After taxes, their "disposable" income was significantly less, an average of just $28,854 per household. In other words, taxes reduce Americans' potential spending power by about one-fourth, or one dollar in every four.

It's no surprise that the larger the household income before taxes, the more that remains after taxes. Average after-tax income ranged from just $5,182 among the 14.2 million households with annual before-tax incomes below $10,000 to a high of $82,975 among the 4.2 million households with before-tax incomes of $100,000 or more. The average after-tax income of households at the top of the income scale is 16 times that of households at the bottom of the scale.

On a per capita basis, the gap is narrower, however. Households with incomes of $100,000 plus have an average after-tax income of $26,650 per household member. The poorest households have an average after-tax income of just $2,697 per household member. The per capita income of high-income households is ten times that of the poorest households because high-income households usually include more people than those with lower incomes.

Discretionary Income by Household Income

All of the most affluent households have discretionary income. Households with before-tax incomes of $100,000 or more had average discretionary income of $37,152 in 1991. On a per capita basis, discretionary dollars in these households amounted to $11,932 per household member.

In contrast, just 17.5 percent of the poorest households had any discretionary income in 1991. Among those that did, discretionary dollars averaged $1,117, or $581 per household member.

The poorest households are the only ones in which a majority do not have discretionary income. Most households at all other income levels have such spending money, ranging from $3,656 per household for those with incomes between $10,000 and $19,999 to more than $10,000 per household for those with incomes of $50,000 and above. Discretionary income per household member ranges from about $2,000 for people living in households with incomes between $10,000 and $19,999 to over $5,000 per person for those living in households with incomes of $60,000 and over. Given the likely rise in the proportion of households with incomes of $50,000 or more due to the middle-aging of the population (see Household Income Projections chapter, page 225), discretionary spending should also rise.

Discretionary Income by Age of Householder

Regardless of age, a majority of households have spending money after paying taxes and basic expenses. Those least likely to have discretionary dollars are the youngest and oldest householders. Among householders under age 25, only 54 percent have discretionary dollars. Among those aged 75 or older, 57 percent have such spending money. In contrast, over 70 percent of households headed by people aged 45 to 64 have discretionary income.

On a household basis, discretionary income is greatest for households headed by people aged 45 to 54, at $13,612 in 1991. It is lowest among households headed by people under age 25 or over age 75, at less than $7,000. On a per capita basis, discretionary income is greatest among householders aged 55 to 64, many of whom are empty nesters. Each person living in these households has an average of over $5,000 to spend on his or her whims. Those with the fewest discretionary dollars on a per capita basis are people living in households headed by the youngest householders, with just $2,862 in discretionary income per household member.

The middle-aged clearly control the nation's discretionary spending. In 1991, households headed by people aged 35 to 64 accounted for fully 64 percent of the $689 billion in discretionary dollars in the United States. Households headed by 35 to 54 year olds accounted for nearly half of this discretionary income. As the baby boom fills this age group during the 1990s, the aggregate discretionary income controlled by households headed by 35 to 54 year olds will surpass 50 percent. For the many businesses hoping to capture some fraction of Americans' discretionary spending, the middle-aged market is the target with the greatest potential.

Discretionary Income by Household Type

Most households, regardless of type, have discretionary income. There are some exceptions, however. Among married couples with children and female-headed families, a minority have any discretionary spending money. Only 14 percent of married couples with three or more children, for example, have spending money at their disposal.

Because married couples with children frequently do not have discretionary income, nonfamily households are far more likely to have discretionary income than family households, 78 percent for nonfamily households versus 58 percent for family households. Fully 86 percent of men who live alone have discretionary income, as do 72 percent of women who live alone. Seventy-seven percent of married couples without children at home have spending money, versus only 44 percent of couples with children.

The average amount of discretionary income available to

households is highest for married couples without children at home, at $13,933 in 1991. But the average amount of discretionary income per household member is highest for people who live alone. Men who live alone had an average of over $11,000 in spending money available to them in 1991.

Discretionary Income by Race and Hispanic Origin

A majority of white households (67 percent) have discretionary income. In contrast, a minority of households headed by blacks (44 percent) or Hispanics (38 percent) have such spending money.

On average, white households with discretionary income have $11,471 in spending money. Among the minority of black households with discretionary income, the average amount was $8,519 in 1991. Hispanic households with discretionary income had an average of $8,830. Households headed by people of "other" races, primarily Asian-Americans, had an average discretionary income of $12,276— even higher than that of white households. These households were slightly less likely to have discretionary income than white households, however, and their discretionary income per household member was below that of whites as well.

Discretionary Income by Education

Discretionary income rises steeply with education. Only 39 percent of households headed by householders who did not graduate from high school had any discretionary income in 1991, versus fully 87 percent of households headed by people with graduate-level schooling.

The amount of discretionary income available to the average household also rises with education, from a low of $5,634 for householders who do not have a high school diploma to a high of nearly $20,000 among householders with a master's degree or above. On a per capita basis as well, higher levels of education lead to greater amounts of discretionary income. Householders with graduate-level training have an average of $7,615 in spending money per household member.

Discretionary Income by Household Size

Households of only one or two people are much more likely to have discretionary income than larger households. More than three out of four households with just one or two people had discretionary income, versus 37 percent of households with four people and only 17 percent of households with five or more people.

There are also striking differences in the amount of discretionary income per household member depending on household size. People who live alone had an average of $9,773 in discretionary dollars in 1991. Per capita discretionary income declines with increasing household size to just $1,979 per person for the few households with five or more people that have discretionary income. In the aggregate, households with one or two people control over 70 percent of the nation's discretionary dollars.

Discretionary Income by Region

Households in the Northeast and West are most likely to have discretionary income, and the average amount of extra spending money per household is higher than in the Midwest or South. In both the Northeast and West, households with discretionary income have an average of more than $12,000 in such spending money. In the South and Midwest, the average amount is closer to $10,000.

Discretionary income per household member is also higher in the Northeast and West, at over $4,500 per capita in both regions. In the South, per capita discretionary income is less than $4,000. But because such a large proportion of Americans live in the South, that region controls the largest share of discretionary income, nearly 31 percent in 1991. In contrast, each of the other regions controls less than one-fourth of the nation's discretionary dollars.

Thomas G. Exter is president of TGE Demographics, Inc., of Ithaca, New York, which produced the discretionary income estimates for The Official Guide to American Incomes.

Income Before and After Taxes by Before-Tax Income, 1991

The average American household has an income of $37,000 before taxes and $29,000 after taxes. After-tax income per household member ranges from under $3,000 to over $26,000.

(average income before and after taxes by before-tax income; households as of 1992; numbers in thousands)

	total households	average income before taxes	after-tax income			
			average income	aggregate income (billions)	percent distribution of aggregate	income per household member
All incomes	95,669	$37,272	$28,854	$2,762.6	100.0%	$11,013
Under $10,000	14,237	5,838	5,182	73.8	2.7	2,697
$10,000 to $19,999	17,370	14,790	13,180	228.9	8.3	6,623
$20,000 to $29,999	16,037	24,737	21,011	337.0	12.2	9,499
$30,000 to $39,999	13,101	34,667	28,329	371.1	13.4	12,057
$40,000 to $49,999	10,259	44,527	35,465	363.8	13.2	14,314
$50,000 to $59,999	7,525	54,476	42,220	317.7	11.5	15,970
$60,000 to $69,999	5,283	64,490	48,976	258.7	9.4	17,780
$70,000 to $79,999	3,568	74,581	55,502	198.0	7.2	19,315
$80,000 to $89,999	2,409	84,441	61,785	148.8	5.4	20,633
$90,000 to $99,999	1,636	94,755	68,678	112.4	4.1	22,821
$100,000 or over	4,246	128,231	82,975	352.3	12.8	26,650

Note: For definition of discretionary income, see chapter introduction.
Source: TGE Demographics, Inc., Ithaca, New York

Households with Discretionary Income by Income, 1991

Over 70 percent of all households with incomes of $10,000 or more have discretionary income. Among those with incomes of $80,000 or more, all have discretionary income.

(households with discretionary income by before-tax income; households as of 1992; numbers in thousands)

| | total households | households with discretionary income | percent with discretionary income | discretionary income | | | |
				average amount	aggregate amount (billions)	percent distribution of aggregate	per household member
All incomes	95,669	61,067	63.8%	$11,287	$689.3	100.0%	$4,308
Under $10,000	14,237	2,494	17.5	1,117	2.8	0.4	581
$10,000 to $19,999	17,370	9,179	52.8	3,656	33.6	4.9	1,837
$20,000 to $29,999	16,037	11,337	70.7	6,049	68.6	9.9	2,735
$30,000 to $39,999	13,101	9,645	73.6	8,552	82.5	12.0	3,640
$40,000 to $49,999	10,259	6,483	63.2	9,600	62.2	9.0	3,875
$50,000 to $59,999	7,525	5,605	74.5	11,612	65.1	9.4	4,392
$60,000 to $69,999	5,283	4,637	87.8	14,108	65.4	9.5	5,122
$70,000 to $79,999	3,568	3,396	95.2	17,365	59.0	8.6	6,043
$80,000 to $89,999	2,409	2,409	100.0	20,667	49.8	7.2	6,902
$90,000 to $99,999	1,636	1,636	100.0	26,057	42.6	6.2	8,658
$100,000 or over	4,246	4,246	100.0	37,152	157.7	22.9	11,932

Note: For definition of discretionary income, see chapter introduction.
Source: TGE Demographics, Inc., Ithaca, New York

Households With Discretionary Income by Age of Householder, 1991

Those most likely to have discretionary income are households headed by 45-to-54-year-olds. But those with the most discretionary income per household member are households headed by 55-to-64-year-olds.

(households with discretionary income by age of householder; households as of 1992; numbers in thousands)

People living in households headed by 55-to-64-year-olds have the most discretionary income per household member.

	total households	households with discretionary income	percent with discretionary income	average amount	aggregate amount (billions)	percent distribution of aggregate discretionary income	per household member
All ages	95,669	61,067	63.8%	$11,287	$689.3	100.0%	$4,308
Under age 25	4,859	2,634	54.2	6,810	17.9	2.6	2,862
Aged 25 to 34	20,008	11,948	59.7	10,773	128.7	18.7	3,776
Aged 35 to 44	21,774	13,844	63.6	12,578	174.1	25.3	3,835
Aged 45 to 54	15,549	11,262	72.4	13,612	153.3	22.2	4,599
Aged 55 to 64	12,559	8,962	71.4	12,859	115.2	16.7	5,472
Aged 65 to 74	12,044	7,374	61.2	8,977	66.2	9.6	4,750
Aged 75 or older	8,878	5,043	56.8	6,6890	33.7	4.9	4,298

Note: For definition of discretionary income, see chapter introduction.
Source: TGE Demographics, Inc., Ithaca, New York

Households with Discretionary Income by Type of Household, 1991

The households most likely to have discretionary income are headed by married couples without children at home or by people who live alone. Those least likely to have discretionary income are married couple with three or more children.

(households with discretionary income by type of household; households as of 1992; numbers in thousands)

	total households	households with discretionary income	percent with discretionary income	discretionary income			
				average amount	aggregate amount (billions)	percent distribution of aggregate	per household member
All households	95,669	61,067	63.8%	$11,287	$689.3	100.0%	$4,308
Family households	67,172	38,882	57.9	11,828	459.9	66.7	3,719
Married-couple families	52,451	32,426	61.8	12,587	408.1	59.2	3,885
With no children <18 at home	28,039	21,624	77.1	13,933	301.3	43.7	5,710
With children <18 at home	24,412	10,801	44.2	9,892	106.8	15.5	2,384
With one child at home	9,517	6,636	69.7	9,751	64.7	9.4	-
With two children at home	9,727	3,424	35.2	10,168	34.8	5.0	-
With three or more children at home	5,167	741	14.3	9,879	7.3	1.1	-
Female-headed families, no spouse present	11,695	4,643	39.7	7,200	33.4	4.8	2,400
Male-headed families, no spouse present	3,026	1,813	59.9	10,105	18.3	2.7	3,635
Nonfamily households	28,497	22,185	77.9	10,256	227.5	33.0	8,407
Male householder	12,428	10,527	84.7	11,979	126.1	18.3	9,075
Living alone	9,611	8,248	85.8	11,633	95.9	13.9	11,633
Female householder	16,069	11,658	72.5	8,700	101.4	14.7	7,565
Living alone	14,362	10,320	71.9	8,287	85.5	12.4	8,287

Note: For definition of discretionary income, see chapter introduction.
Source: TGE Demographics, Inc., Ithaca, New York

Households with Discretionary Income by Race and Hispanic Origin, 1991

Among all households, 64 percent have discretionary income. While a majority of white households have discretionary dollars, a minority of black or Hispanic households have such spending money.

(households with discretionary income by race and Hispanic origin; households as of 1992; numbers in thousands)

Discretionary income per household member is highest among households headed by whites and lowest among those headed by Hispanics.

	White	Black	Other races	Hispanic
	$4,446	$3,032	$3,910	$2,559

	total households	households with discretionary income	percent with discretionary income	discretionary income			
				average amount	aggregate amount (billions)	percent distribution of aggregate	per household member
All races	95,669	61,067	63.8%	$11,287	$689.3	100.0%	$4,308
White	81,675	54,485	66.7	11,471	625.0	90.7	4,446
Black	11,083	4,895	44.2	8,519	41.7	6.1	3,032
Other races	2,911	1,687	58.0	12,276	20.7	3.0	3,910
All origins	95,669	61,067	63.8	11,287	689.3	100.0	4,308
Hispanic	6,379	2,389	37.5	8,830	21.1	3.1	2,559
Non-Hispanic	89,290	58,677	65.7	11,356	666.3	96.7	4,402

Note: For definition of discretionary income, see chapter introduction. Source: TGE Demographics, Inc., Ithaca, New York

Households with Discretionary Income by Education of Householder, 1991

Those most likely to have discretionary income are households headed by people with graduate-level degrees.

(households with discretionary income by education of householder; households as of 1992; numbers in thousands)

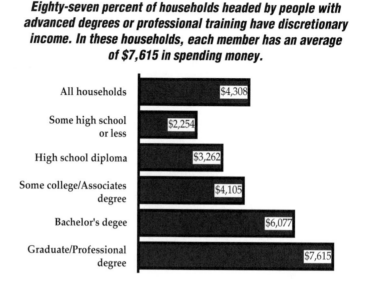

Eighty-seven percent of households headed by people with advanced degrees or professional training have discretionary income. In these households, each member has an average of $7,615 in spending money.

	discretionary income per household member
All households	$4,308
Some high school or less	$2,254
High school diploma	$3,262
Some college/Associates degree	$4,105
Bachelor's degee	$6,077
Graduate/Professional degree	$7,615

	total households	households with discretionary income	percent with discretionary income	discretionary income			
				average amount	aggregate amount (billions)	percent distribution of aggregate	per household member
All households	95,669	61,067	63.8%	$11,287	$689.3	100.0%	$4,308
Less than high school	20,629	8,080	39.2	5,634	45.5	6.6	2,254
High school diploma	31,978	19,628	61.4	8,480	166.4	24.1	3,262
Some college or Associates degree	21,602	15,365	71.1	10,674	164.0	23.8	4,105
Bachelor's degree	13,671	11,203	81.9	15,799	177.0	25.7	6,077
Master's, Professional, or Doctoral degree	7,789	6,789	87.2	19,797	134.4	19.5	7,615

Note: For definition of discretionary income, see chapter introduction.
Source: TGE Demographics, Inc., Ithaca, New York

Households with Discretionary Income by Household Size, 1991

Households with only one or two people are most likely to have discretionary income. These households account for 72 percent of the nation's discretionary dollars.

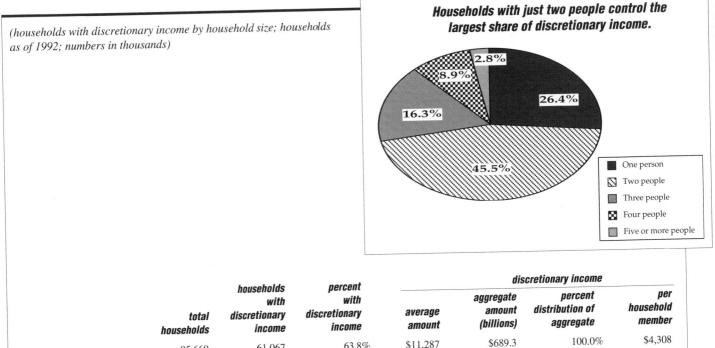

(households with discretionary income by household size; households as of 1992; numbers in thousands)

Households with just two people control the largest share of discretionary income.

2.8%
8.9%
16.3%
26.4%
45.5%

- One person
- Two people
- Three people
- Four people
- Five or more people

	total households	households with discretionary income	percent with discretionary income	discretionary income			
				average amount	aggregate amount (billions)	percent distribution of aggregate	per household member
All sizes	95,669	61,067	63.8%	$11,287	$689.3	100.0%	$4,308
One person	23,974	18,568	77.5	9,773	181.5	26.3	9,773
Two people	30,734	24,191	78.7	12,947	313.2	45.4	6,474
Three people	16,398	11,149	68.0	10,051	112.1	16.3	3,350
Four people	14,710	5,447	37.0	11,324	61.7	8.9	2,831
Five or more people	9,853	1,711	17.4	11,102	19.0	2.8	1,979

Note: For definition of discretionary income, see chapter introduction. Percentages in pie chart are slightly different from those in table due to rounding error.
Source: TGE Demographics, Inc., Ithaca, New York

Households with Discretionary Income by Region, 1991

Households in the Northeast and West have more discretionary income than those in the South and West.

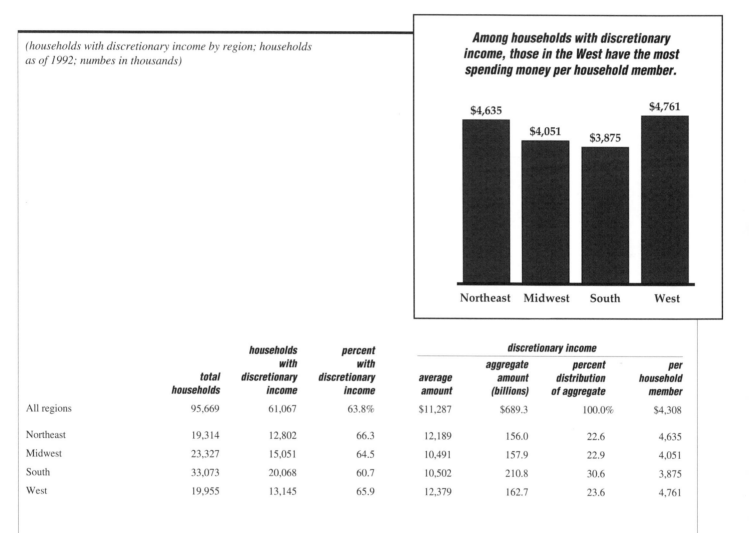

(households with discretionary income by region; households as of 1992; numbes in thousands)

Among households with discretionary income, those in the West have the most spending money per household member.

| | | households with discretionary income | percent with discretionary income | discretionary income | | | |
	total households			average amount	aggregate amount (billions)	percent distribution of aggregate	per household member
All regions	95,669	61,067	63.8%	$11,287	$689.3	100.0%	$4,308
Northeast	19,314	12,802	66.3	12,189	156.0	22.6	4,635
Midwest	23,327	15,051	64.5	10,491	157.9	22.9	4,051
South	33,073	20,068	60.7	10,502	210.8	30.6	3,875
West	19,955	13,145	65.9	12,379	162.7	23.6	4,761

Note: For definition of discretionary income, see chapter introduction.
Source: TGE Demographics, Inc., Ithaca, New York

CHAPTER

5

Household Income Projections

by Thomas G. Exter

Household Income Projections: Highlights

■ Median household income could grow as much as 12 percent between 1991 and 2005, from $30,126 to $33,800, after adjusting for inflation.

■ Because of the middle-aging of the population, the number of affluent households will grow rapidly. Households with incomes of $50,000 or more could grow from 24.7 million in 1991 to as much as 33.8 million in 2005, a 37 percent gain.

■ The number of households headed by 45 to 54 year olds with incomes of $50,000 or more could grow from 6.7 million in 1991 to 11.1 million in 2005, a 66 percent gain. Behind this rapid growth is the middle-aging of the baby-boom generation.

Between 1980 and 1990, median household income grew by $1,894 after adjusting for inflation, to $31,203. This was an average annual gain in real household income of 0.6 percent. If household income growth continues on a similar course during the next ten years and beyond, Americans should see a significant rise in median

Between 1991 and 2005, affluence will increase rapidly among households headed by 45-to-64-year-olds.

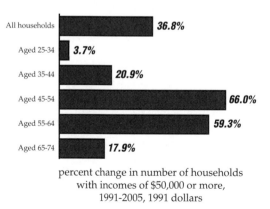

percent change in number of households
with incomes of $50,000 or more,
1991-2005, 1991 dollars

household income and an even more substantial rise in the number of households that achieve affluence. In fact, the U.S. is likely to achieve record levels of affluence between now and 2005.

This chapter presents two scenarios for income growth for U.S. households, showing projected household income distributions for 1995, 2000, and 2005. Scenario number one assumes an annual growth in income of 0.5 percent, after adjusting for inflation. This rate is slightly below the rate of the 1980s and results in a median income of $32,289 in 2005, only 7 percent greater than in 1991. The second projection scenario assumes an annual growth in income of 1.0 percent, after adjusting for inflation. This rate is slightly faster than the rate of the 1980s and results in a median income of $33,844 by 2005, or 12 percent higher than in 1991. It's likely that actual growth in household incomes will fall somewhere between the two scenarios.

Projecting Household Incomes

To project households and income levels over the next ten years, we started with the Census Bureau's new population projections (Current Population Reports, "Population Projections of the United States by Age, Sex, Race, and Hispanic Origin: 1992 to 2050," Series P-25, No. 1092, 1992), the first to use 1990 census benchmarks. From the total population figures in this report, we wanted to estimate the civilian, household (i.e. noninstitutional) population. First, we multiplied the total population figures by the ratio of the institutionalized population to the total population by age for 1992. We applied these same ratios to the total population by age for the years 1993 to 2005 to derive estimates of the household population.

Next, we subtracted estimates of military personnel by age from the household population for each year from 1992 to 2005 to derive projections of the civilian, household population. From these population figures, we wanted to estimate households. We did this by using the household headship rates for the civilian, household population from the Census Bureau's Current Population Survey. We applied these headship rates to the civilian, household population figures through the year 2005.

Our starting income levels were from the March 1992 Current Population Survey, which reports annual household income for 1991. We applied the two income growth scenarios—0.5 percent and 1.0 percent after adjusting for inflation—to the 1991 household income levels. The results show the effects of an aging population under two different conditions of income growth. These projections assume no major shocks to the economy that would cause inflation to exceed the current 4 to 5 percent annual level.

Income Projections: The Results

While growth in median household income is not dramatic in either scenario over the next decade and beyond, there is dramatic change in the number of households with affluent incomes—often defined as incomes of $50,000 or more. Behind this change is the middle-aging of the baby-boom generation into its peak earnings years, typically ages 45 to 54.

Assuming household income grows at a 1.0 percent annual rate after adjusting for inflation, the total number of households with incomes of $50,000 or more should grow from 24.7 million in 1991 to 33.8 million in 2005, a 37 percent increase over 13 years. Among householders aged 45 to 54, the growth in affluence is even more dramatic. The number of these households with incomes of $50,000 or more rises from 6.7 million in 1991 to 11.1 million in 2005, a 66 percent increase.

At the same time, the proportion of households with incomes at the low end of the distribution will shrink. In 1991, 50 percent of households had incomes below $30,000—the national median. By 2005, this proportion would fall to 47.5 under the 0.5 percent growth scenario and to 45.4 percent under the 1.0 percent growth scenario. In part, the decline in the proportion of households with low incomes will be due to demographic change rather than income growth alone. The number of younger householders, those under age 35, will fall during the next decade. This will help to reduce the proportion of households with incomes at the low end of the distribution because young households tend to have low incomes. But a counter-trend will slow the decline in low-income households. At the same time that younger householders are declining, the number of householders aged 75 or older will be rising. These oldest householders also have relatively low incomes. The increase in their numbers will slow the decline in low-income households and cause the low-income population as a whole to age.

And what about the middle-class? There will be little change in the proportion of households in the middle of the income distribution, with incomes between $30,000 and $50,000. From 24.4 percent of all households in 1991, this proportion will remain relatively stable under the 0.5 percent growth scenario, rising marginally to 24.8 percent by 2005. In the 1.0 percent scenario, the proportion could creep up to 25.2 percent. But after a decade when the middle-class seemed to be shrinking before our eyes, this stability could be something to celebrate.

Without doubt, American households took a direct hit in the double-dip recession of the early 1990s. Income growth slowed and white-collar downsizing became the norm. Real median household income declined by 3.5 percent from $31,203 in 1990 to $30,126 in 1991. Even though the underlying demographics look good for a return to growth in the 1990s, analysts can only speculate about how households will recover. These projections provide two hypothetical growth scenarios, one in which incomes grow more slowly than in the 1980s and one in which incomes grow slightly faster. The basic assumption is that American workers will find their way out of the income doldrums.

Three trends are worth monitoring because they will determine the strength of any income rebound. One key trend is the increasing payoff to education and job training. By 1991, households with a B.A. degree or higher had a median income of $45,138 compared with only $26,779 for those with only a high school diploma. As more workers see education and training as crucial to their personal productivity and earnings, they will take advantage of these opportunities.

The second trend worth watching relates to marital status and household composition. More households are dependent on two or more paychecks—45 percent of all households in 1991. An aging baby boom and a stable divorce rate should slow the growth in young, single-parent households with low incomes. If married-couple households respond to economic adversity by keeping marriages together and sending more earners into the workforce, incomes will respond accordingly.

But no rebound is likely to occur without a third trend: increasing entrepreneurship. The economy will undoubtedly continue its "structural adjustment" from one dominated by top-heavy bureaucracies to one in which smaller, more flexible organizations proliferate. Workers in need of a job will do what they have always done—gravitate to opportunities. Smaller companies should provide many of those opportunities. As entrepreneurship takes hold, households will see income growth in the 1990s and beyond.

Baby boomers are entering their peak earning years in times of great economic uncertainty. Their collective generational response will determine not only their own economic future but that of the nation.

Thomas G. Exter is president of TGE Demographics, Inc., of Ithaca, New York, which produced the income projections for The Official Guide to American Incomes.

Household Income Distribution by Age of Householder: 1991

In 1991, nearly 2.5 million households had incomes of $50,000 or more. This number should grow sharply during the 1990s as baby boomers middle age.

(number of households as of 1992; income in 1991 dollars; numbers in thousands)

| | all ages | age of householder | | | | | | |
		15 to 24	25 to 34	35 to 44	45 to 54	55 to 64	65 to 74	75 or older
All incomes	95,669	4,859	20,008	21,774	15,549	12,559	12,044	8,878
Under $10,000	14,237	1,283	2,457	1,803	1,339	1,706	2,619	3,030
$10,000 to $19,999	17,370	1,356	3,317	2,675	1,747	1,941	3,384	2,950
$20,000 to $29,999	16,037	1,108	3,874	3,243	1,943	2,027	2,415	1,427
$30,000 to $39,999	13,101	583	3,460	3,356	2,008	1,709	1,348	637
$40,000 to $49,999	10,259	273	2,629	3,085	1,839	1,395	730	308
$50,000 to $59,999	7,525	112	1,675	2,341	1,750	1,028	453	166
$60,000 to $69,999	5,283	58	923	1,732	1,401	709	351	109
$70,000 to $79,999	3,568	36	630	1,113	989	564	171	65
$80,000 to $89,999	2,409	14	378	783	684	358	144	48
$90,000 to $99,999	1,636	23	213	454	520	278	118	30
$100,000 or over	4,246	13	452	1,189	1,329	844	311	108
Median income	$30,126	$18,313	$30,842	$39,349	$43,751	$33,304	$20,063	$13,933

PERCENT DISTRIBUTION

| | all ages | age of householder | | | | | | |
		15 to 24	25 to 34	35 to 44	45 to 54	55 to 64	65 to 74	75 or older
All incomes	100.0%	100.0%	100.0%	100.0%	100.0%	100.0%	100.0%	100.0%
Under $10,000	14.9	26.4	12.3	8.3	8.6	13.6	21.7	34.1
$10,000 to $19,999	18.2	27.9	16.6	12.3	11.2	15.5	28.1	33.2
$20,000 to $29,999	16.8	22.8	19.4	14.9	12.5	16.1	20.1	16.1
$30,000 to $39,999	13.7	12.0	17.3	15.4	12.9	13.6	11.2	7.2
$40,000 to $49,999	10.7	5.6	13.1	14.2	11.8	11.1	6.1	3.5
$50,000 to $59,999	7.9	2.3	8.4	10.8	11.3	8.2	3.8	1.9
$60,000 to $69,999	5.5	1.2	4.6	8.0	9.0	5.6	2.9	1.2
$70,000 to $79,999	3.7	0.7	3.1	5.1	6.4	4.5	1.4	0.7
$80,000 to $89,999	2.5	0.3	1.9	3.6	4.4	2.9	1.2	0.5
$90,000 to $99,999	1.7	0.5	1.1	2.1	3.3	2.2	1.0	0.3
$100,000 or over	4.4	0.3	2.3	5.5	8.5	6.7	2.6	1.2

Source: TGE Demographics, Inc., Ithaca, New York

Household Income by Age of Householder, 1995 (0.5 percent growth)

Assuming an 0.5 percent annual growth in real income between 1991 and 1995, median household income will grow to $30,763 by 1994. An additional 1.8 million households will have incomes of $50,000-plus.

(projections assume a 0.5 percent annual growth in real income between 1991 and 1995; income in 1991 dollars; numbers in thousands)

		age of householder						
	all ages	**15 to 24**	**25 to 34**	**35 to 44**	**45 to 54**	**55 to 64**	**65 to 74**	**75 or older**
All incomes	99,461	4,827	19,298	23,234	17,636	12,691	12,275	9,501
Under $10,000	14,504	1,256	2,335	1,895	1,496	1,698	2,630	3,194
$10,000 to $19,999	17,717	1,332	3,154	2,811	1,954	1,938	3,402	3,126
$20,000 to $29,999	16,473	1,100	3,700	3,424	2,185	2,034	2,471	1,559
$30,000 to $39,999	13,592	593	3,335	3,562	2,265	1,730	1,402	705
$40,000 to $49,999	10,735	281	2,555	3,291	2,086	1,416	764	341
$50,000 to $59,999	7,974	117	1,647	2,522	1,983	1,050	472	183
$60,000 to $69,999	5,659	60	918	1,871	1,602	728	361	119
$70,000 to $79,999	3,839	37	619	1,214	1,140	575	182	71
$80,000 to $89,999	2,601	15	375	850	790	371	148	52
$90,000 to $99,999	1,772	22	213	500	598	284	121	33
$100,000 or over	4,596	14	446	1,293	1,536	867	323	117
Median income	$30,763	$18,692	$31,379	$39,788	$44,398	$33,907	$20,429	$14,978

PERCENT DISTRIBUTION

		age of householder						
	all ages	**15 to 24**	**25 to 34**	**35 to 44**	**45 to 54**	**55 to 64**	**65 to 74**	**75 or older**
All incomes	100.0%	100.0%	100.0%	100.0%	100.0%	100.0%	100.0%	100.0%
Under $10,000	14.7	26.0	12.1	8.2	8.5	13.4	21.4	33.6
$10,000 to $19,999	17.9	27.6	16.3	12.1	11.1	15.3	27.7	32.9
$20,000 to $29,999	16.7	22.8	19.2	14.7	12.4	16.0	20.1	16.4
$30,000 to $39,999	13.7	12.3	17.3	15.3	12.8	13.6	11.4	7.4
$40,000 to $49,999	10.8	5.8	13.2	14.2	11.8	11.2	6.2	3.6
$50,000 to $59,999	8.0	2.4	8.5	10.9	11.2	8.3	3.8	1.9
$60,000 to $69,999	5.6	1.2	4.8	8.1	9.1	5.7	2.9	1.3
$70,000 to $79,999	3.8	0.8	3.2	5.2	6.5	4.5	1.5	0.8
$80,000 to $89,999	2.6	0.3	1.9	3.7	4.5	2.9	1.2	0.5
$90,000 to $99,999	1.7	0.5	1.1	2.2	3.4	2.2	1.0	0.3
$100,000 or over	4.5	0.3	2.3	5.6	8.7	6.8	2.6	1.2

Note: Real income is adjusted for inflation.
Source: TGE Demographics, Inc., Ithaca, New York

Household Income by Age of Householder, 1995 *(1.0 percent growth)*

Assuming a 1 percent annual growth in real income between 1991 and 1994, median household income will grow to $31,135 by 1994. An additional 2.2 million households will have incomes of $50,000-plus.

(projections assume a 1.0 percent annual growth in real income between 1991 and 1995; income in 1991 dollars; numbers in thousands)

		age of householder						
	all ages	15 to 24	25 to 34	35 to 44	45 to 54	55 to 64	65 to 74	75 or older
All incomes	99,461	4,827	19,298	23,234	17,636	12,691	12,275	9,501
Under $10,000	14,290	1,237	2,300	1,867	1,474	1,673	2,591	3,147
$10,000 to $19,999	17,489	1,317	3,110	2,769	1,928	1,914	3,356	3,095
$20,000 to $29,999	16,406	1,099	3,665	3,389	2,166	2,019	2,480	1,588
$30,000 to $39,999	13,624	606	3,332	3,543	2,254	1,732	1,429	729
$40,000 to $49,999	10,800	291	2,575	3,290	2,085	1,423	784	353
$50,000 to $59,999	8,059	123	1,677	2,545	1,982	1,062	481	189
$60,000 to $69,999	5,741	62	946	1,893	1,614	740	365	121
$70,000 to $79,999	3,910	38	631	1,240	1,158	581	189	73
$80,000 to $89,999	2,653	16	385	865	805	379	149	53
$90,000 to $99,999	1,808	22	220	516	606	288	122	34
$100,000 or over	4,682	15	456	1,317	1,565	880	329	119
Median income	$31,135	$18,930	$31,723	$40,139	$44,780	$34,265	$20,770	$15,180

PERCENT DISTRIBUTION

		age of householder						
	all ages	15 to 24	25 to 34	35 to 44	45 to 54	55 to 64	65 to 74	75 or older
All incomes	100.0%	100.0%	100.0%	100.0%	100.0%	100.0%	100.0%	100.0%
Under $10,000	14.4	25.6	11.9	8.0	8.4	13.2	21.1	33.1
$10,000 to $19,999	17.7	27.3	16.1	11.9	10.9	15.1	27.3	32.6
$20,000 to $29,999	16.6	22.8	19.0	14.6	12.3	15.9	20.2	16.7
$30,000 to $39,999	13.8	12.6	17.3	15.2	12.8	13.6	11.6	7.7
$40,000 to $49,999	10.9	6.0	13.3	14.2	11.8	11.2	6.4	3.7
$50,000 to $59,999	8.0	2.6	8.7	11.0	11.2	8.4	3.9	2.0
$60,000 to $69,999	5.7	1.3	4.9	8.1	9.2	5.8	3.0	1.3
$70,000 to $79,999	3.9	0.8	3.3	5.3	6.6	4.6	1.5	0.8
$80,000 to $89,999	2.6	0.3	2.0	3.7	4.6	3.0	1.2	0.6
$90,000 to $99,999	1.8	0.5	1.1	2.2	3.4	2.3	1.0	0.4
$100,000 or over	4.6	0.3	2.4	5.7	8.9	6.9	2.7	1.2

Note: Real income is adjusted for inflation.
Source: TGE Demographics, Inc., Ithaca, New York

Household Income by Age of Householder, 2000 *(0.5 percent growth)*

Assuming 0.5 percent growth in real income through the 1990s, median household income will climb by about $1,500 dollars. Over 4 million more households will have incomes of $50,000-plus in 2000 than did in 1991.

(projections assume a 0.5 percent growth in real income between 1991 and 2000; income in 1991 dollars; numbers in thousands)

	all ages	age of householder						
		15 to 24	25 to 34	35 to 44	45 to 54	55 to 64	65 to 74	75 or older
All incomes	105,201	5,105	17,617	24,465	21,044	14,385	11,926	10,658
Under $10,000	14,927	1,295	2,079	1,947	1,741	1,878	2,492	3,495
$10,000 to $19,999	18,189	1,383	2,812	2,886	2,279	2,152	3,230	3,448
$20,000 to $29,999	17,090	1,162	3,323	3,542	2,569	2,277	2,413	1,803
$30,000 to $39,999	14,289	650	3,039	3,716	2,679	1,964	1,406	836
$40,000 to $49,999	11,424	315	2,361	3,463	2,487	1,617	775	405
$50,000 to $59,999	8,646	135	1,550	2,695	2,364	1,212	475	216
$60,000 to $69,999	6,236	67	881	2,010	1,935	847	357	138
$70,000 to $79,999	4,280	41	584	1,325	1,396	663	189	84
$80,000 to $89,999	2,913	17	358	923	972	436	146	60
$90,000 to $99,999	2,001	23	206	555	730	330	120	39
$100,000 or over	5,205	17	424	1,405	1,892	1,009	323	135
Median income	$31,676	$19,093	$31,957	$40,409	$45,043	$34,510	$20,998	$15,318

PERCENT DISTRIBUTION

	all ages	age of householder						
		15 to 24	25 to 34	35 to 44	45 to 54	55 to 64	65 to 74	75 or older
All incomes	100.0%	100.0%	100.0%	100.0%	100.0%	100.0%	100.0%	100.0%
Under $10,000	14.3	25.4	11.8	8.0	8.3	13.1	20.9	32.8
$10,000 to $19,999	17.5	27.1	16.0	11.8	10.8	15.0	27.1	32.4
$20,000 to $29,999	16.6	22.8	18.9	14.5	12.2	15.8	20.2	16.9
$30,000 to $39,999	13.8	12.7	17.3	15.2	12.7	13.7	11.8	7.8
$40,000 to $49,999	10.9	6.2	13.4	14.2	11.8	11.2	6.5	3.8
$50,000 to $59,999	8.1	2.6	8.8	11.0	11.2	8.4	4.0	2.0
$60,000 to $69,999	5.7	1.3	5.0	8.2	9.2	5.9	3.0	1.3
$70,000 to $79,999	3.9	0.8	3.3	5.4	6.6	4.6	1.6	0.8
$80,000 to $89,999	2.7	0.3	2.0	3.8	4.6	3.0	1.2	0.6
$90,000 to $99,999	1.8	0.5	1.2	2.3	3.5	2.3	1.0	0.4
$100,000 or over	4.7	0.3	2.4	5.7	9.0	7.0	2.7	1.3

Note: Real income is adjusted for inflation.
Source: TGE Demographics, Inc., Ithaca, New York

Household Income by Age of Householder, 2000 *(1.0 percent growth)*

Assuming a 1 percent annual growth in real income between 1991 and 2000, median household income will grow to $32,645 by 2000. An additional 5.8 million households will have incomes of $50,000-plus.

(projections assume a 1.0 percent annual growth in real income between 1991 and 2000; income in 1991 dollars; numbers in thousands)

	all ages	age of householder						
		15 to 24	25 to 34	35 to 44	45 to 54	55 to 64	65 to 74	75 or older
All incomes	105,201	5,105	17,617	24,465	21,044	14,385	11,926	10,658
Under $10,000	14,346	1,245	1,998	1,871	1,674	1,805	2,395	3,359
$10,000 to $19,999	17,572	1,342	2,708	2,772	2,196	2,083	3,114	3,356
$20,000 to $29,999	16,886	1,157	3,237	3,443	2,509	2,233	2,427	1,880
$30,000 to $39,999	14,353	684	3,027	3,659	2,640	1,966	1,471	906
$40,000 to $49,999	11,590	344	2,403	3,455	2,483	1,635	828	443
$50,000 to $59,999	8,867	153	1,621	2,752	2,360	1,244	503	235
$60,000 to $69,999	6,462	75	949	2,073	1,969	882	369	146
$70,000 to $79,999	4,484	44	616	1,396	1,450	681	207	90
$80,000 to $89,999	3,066	20	384	968	1,019	461	151	63
$90,000 to $99,999	2,108	22	224	598	758	342	123	41
$100,000 or over	5,466	20	451	1,478	1,987	1,052	339	140
Median income	$32,645	$19,745	$32,862	$41,332	$46,056	$35,451	$21,869	$15,869

PERCENT DISTRIBUTION

	all ages	age of householder						
		15 to 24	25 to 34	35 to 44	45 to 54	55 to 64	65 to 74	75 or older
All incomes	100.0%	100.0%	100.0%	100.0%	100.0%	100.0%	100.0%	100.0%
Under $10,000	13.7	24.4	11.3	7.6	8.0	12.5	20.1	31.5
$10,000 to $19,999	16.9	26.3	15.4	11.3	10.4	14.5	26.1	31.5
$20,000 to $29,999	16.4	22.7	18.4	14.1	11.9	15.5	20.3	17.6
$30,000 to $39,999	13.9	13.4	17.2	15.0	12.5	13.7	12.3	8.5
$40,000 to $49,999	11.1	6.7	13.6	14.1	11.8	11.4	6.9	4.2
$50,000 to $59,999	8.3	3.0	9.2	11.2	11.2	8.6	4.2	2.2
$60,000 to $69,999	6.0	1.5	5.4	8.5	9.4	6.1	3.1	1.4
$70,000 to $79,999	4.1	0.9	3.5	5.7	6.9	4.7	1.7	0.8
$80,000 to $89,999	2.8	0.4	2.2	4.0	4.8	3.2	1.3	0.6
$90,000 to $99,999	1.9	0.4	1.3	2.4	3.6	2.4	1.0	0.4
$100,000 or over	4.9	0.4	2.6	6.0	9.4	7.3	2.8	1.3

Note: Real income is adjusted for inflation.
Source: TGE Demographics, Inc., Ithaca, New York

Household Income by Age of Householder, 2005 *(0.5 percent growth)*

Assuming 0.5 percent growth in real income between 1991 and 2005, median household income will climb above $32,000. Nearly 32 million households will have incomes of $50,000-plus.

(projections assume a 0.5 percent growth in real income between 1991 and 2005; income in 1991 dollars; numbers in thousands)

	all ages	age of householder						
		15 to 24	25 to 34	35 to 44	45 to 54	55 to 64	65 to 74	75 or older
All incomes	110,744	5,507	17,132	23,188	23,638	17,776	12,087	11,416
Under $10,000	15,420	1,363	1,972	1,800	1,908	2,263	2,463	3,652
$10,000 to $19,999	18,738	1,464	2,670	2,667	2,501	2,605	3,199	3,631
$20,000 to $29,999	17,786	1,250	3,178	3,298	2,843	2,779	2,454	1,983
$30,000 to $39,999	14,979	724	2,948	3,488	2,981	2,429	1,467	943
$40,000 to $49,999	12,041	360	2,322	3,277	2,790	2,013	819	459
$50,000 to $59,999	9,215	158	1,551	2,589	2,652	1,523	499	244
$60,000 to $69,999	6,714	78	899	1,943	2,198	1,074	369	153
$70,000 to $79,999	4,669	46	588	1,299	1,606	834	203	94
$80,000 to $89,999	3,188	21	364	901	1,125	559	151	66
$90,000 to $99,999	2,211	24	211	552	840	417	123	43
$100,000 or over	5,784	20	429	1,376	2,193	1,281	338	148
Median income	$32,289	$19,501	$32,530	$41,044	$45,685	$35,107	$21,551	$15,663

PERCENT DISTRIBUTION

	all ages	age of householder						
		15 to 24	25 to 34	35 to 44	45 to 54	55 to 64	65 to 74	75 or older
All incomes	100.0%	100.0%	100.0%	100.0%	100.0%	100.0%	100.0%	100.0%
Under $10,000	13.9	24.7	11.5	7.8	8.1	12.7	20.4	32.0
$10,000 to $19,999	17.2	26.6	15.6	11.5	10.6	14.7	26.5	31.8
$20,000 to $29,999	16.4	22.7	18.6	14.2	12.0	15.6	20.3	17.4
$30,000 to $39,999	13.8	13.2	17.2	15.0	12.6	13.7	12.1	8.3
$40,000 to $49,999	11.0	6.5	13.6	14.1	11.8	11.3	6.8	4.0
$50,000 to $59,999	8.2	2.9	9.1	11.2	11.2	8.6	4.1	2.1
$60,000 to $69,999	5.9	1.4	5.2	8.4	9.3	6.0	3.1	1.3
$70,000 to $79,999	4.0	0.8	3.4	5.6	6.8	4.7	1.7	0.8
$80,000 to $89,999	2.7	0.4	2.1	3.9	4.8	3.1	1.3	0.6
$90,000 to $99,999	1.9	0.4	1.2	2.4	3.6	2.3	1.0	0.4
$100,000 or over	4.8	0.4	2.5	5.9	9.3	7.2%	2.8	1.3

Note: Real income is adjusted for inflation.
Source: TGE Demographics, Inc., Ithaca, New York

Household Income by Age of Householder, 2005 *(1.0 percent growth)*

Assuming a 1 percent annual growth in real income between 1991 and 2005, median household income will climb to $33,844 by 2005. An additional 9 million households will have incomes of $50,000-plus.

(projections assume a 1.0 percent annual growth in real income between 1991 and 2005; income in 1991 dollars; numbers in thousands)

	all ages	15 to 24	25 to 34	35 to 44	45 to 54	55 to 64	65 to 74	75 or older
				age of householder				
All incomes	$110,744	$5,507	$17,132	$23,188	$23,638	$17,776	$12,087	$11,416
Under $10,000	14,456	1,278	1,849	1,687	1,789	2,122	2,309	3,424
$10,000 to $19,999	17,716	1,393	2,511	2,498	2,356	2,471	3,015	3,473
$20,000 to $29,999	17,409	1,239	3,042	3,146	2,733	2,688	2,464	2,098
$30,000 to $39,999	15,060	778	2,920	3,397	2,907	2,427	1,567	1,064
$40,000 to $49,999	12,307	410	2,379	3,259	2,777	2,045	907	529
$50,000 to $59,999	9,572	190	1,658	2,667	2,645	1,585	549	279
$60,000 to $69,999	7,090	92	1,005	2,037	2,252	1,143	391	169
$70,000 to $79,999	5,013	52	645	1,407	1,700	874	232	104
$80,000 to $89,999	3,459	25	406	975	1,212	607	162	71
$90,000 to $99,999	2,400	24	242	619	895	445	128	47
$100,000 or over	6,260	25	475	1,497	2,373	1,370	364	157
Median income	33,844	20,665	33,986	42,659	47,328	36,624	22,919	16,578

PERCENT DISTRIBUTION

	all ages	15 to 24	25 to 34	35 to 44	45 to 54	55 to 64	65 to 74	75 or older
				age of householder				
All incomes	100.0%	100.0%	100.0%	100.0%	100.0%	100.0%	100.0%	100.0%
Under $10,000	13.1	23.2	10.8	7.3	7.6	11.9	19.1	30.0
$10,000 to $19,999	16.2	25.3	14.7	10.8	10.0	13.9	24.9	30.4
$20,000 to $29,999	16.1	22.5	17.8	13.6	11.6	15.1	20.4	18.4
$30,000 to $39,999	13.9	14.1	17.0	14.6	12.3	13.7	13.0	9.3
$40,000 to $49,999	11.3	7.4	13.9	14.1	11.7	11.5	7.5	4.6
$50,000 to $59,999	8.6	3.5	9.7	11.5	11.2	8.9	4.5	2.4
$60,000 to $69,999	6.2	1.7	5.9	8.8	9.5	6.4	3.2	1.5
$70,000 to $79,999	4.4	0.9	3.8	6.1	7.2	4.9	1.9	0.9
$80,000 to $89,999	3.0	0.5	2.4	4.2	5.1	3.4	1.3	0.6
$90,000 to $99,999	2.0	0.4	1.4	2.7	3.8	2.5	1.1	0.4
$100,000 or over	5.2	0.5	2.8	6.5	10.0	7.7	3.0	1.4

Note: Real income is adjusted for inflation.
Source: TGE Demographics, Inc., Ithaca, New York

CHAPTER

6

Spending and Wealth

Americans reacted immediately and dramatically to the recession of the early 1990s. Household spending fell as Americans guarded their paychecks and paid off their debts. Later in this decade, budget-conscious consumers are likely to be rewarded for their new-found caution with rising net worth.

Spending and Wealth: Highlights

■ The recession of the early 1990s reduced people's incomes. Consequently, households cut their spending. The average household spent 2 percent less in 1990 than in 1989, after adjusting for inflation.

■ Americans not only reduced their spending, they also reduced their debts. Consumer credit as a percent of disposable personal income fell from a peak of 20.7 percent in the late 1980s to 18.4 percent in 1991.

■ During the 1980s, Americans' median net worth grew from $42,700 to $47,200, a 10.5 percent gain after adjusting for inflation. Though the recession probably reduced net worth in the early 1990s, net worth is likely to resume growth as baby boomers age into their peak earning years.

Between 1990 and 1991, household spending rebounded, while the amount of outstanding consumer credit fell another 2 percent.

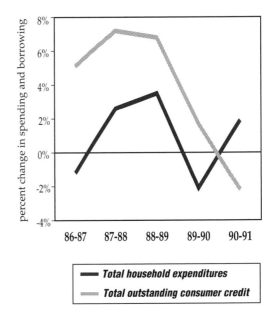

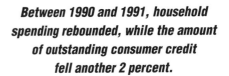

Household Spending Trends, 1986 to 1991

Between 1989 and 1991, household spending fell 2.4 percent. Spending for food at restaurants and carry-outs led the decline.

(average annual expenditures for all households, 1986-91; percent change in expenditures, 1986-89 and 1989-91; in 1991 dollars; number of households in thousands)

	1991	1990	1989	1988	1987	1986	percent change 1989-91	percent change 1986-89
Number of households	97,918	96,968	95,818	94,862	94,150	94,044	2.2%	1.9%
Average income before taxes	$33,901	33,231	34,389	32,859	32,762	31,640	-1.4	8.7
Average number of persons per household	2.6	2.6	2.6	2.6	2.6	2.6	0.0	0.0
Average annual expenditures	$29,827	29,563	30,547	29,810	29,271	29,659	-2.4	3.0
FOOD	**$4,271**	**$4,477**	**$4,560**	**$4,315**	**$4,393**	**$4,285**	**-6.3%**	**6.4%**
Food at home	**2,651**	**2,590**	**2,625**	**2,459**	**2,517**	**2,477**	**1.0**	**6.0**
Cereals and bakery products	405	383	394	360	358	342	2.7	15.2
Cereals and cereal products	145	134	144	125	125	116	1.0	24.3
Bakery products	259	250	250	233	232	227	3.7	10.1
Meats, poultry, fish, and eggs	709	696	671	635	686	698	5.6	-3.9
Beef	228	227	222	209	229	234	2.9	-5.3
Pork	144	138	127	127	139	144	13.4	-11.6
Other meats	102	103	98	95	99	98	4.4	0.0
Poultry	122	113	109	97	104	105	11.3	4.0
Fish and seafood	81	85	78	75	79	79	3.8	-1.3
Eggs	31	31	36	32	33	38	-15.1	-2.8
Dairy products	293	307	333	316	328	312	-12.1	7.0
Fresh milk and cream	129	146	163	154	158	151	-20.6	7.6
Other dairy products	165	162	172	163	170	159	-4.0	7.8
Fruits and vegetables	429	425	448	429	427	398	-4.3	12.6
Fresh fruits	133	132	139	140	135	127	-4.0	9.0
Fresh vegetables	127	123	140	127	132	115	-9.1	21.8
Processed fruits	97	97	98	98	94	90	-1.0	9.3
Processed vegetables	51	73	73	66	66	67	-30.1	9.4
Other food at home	815	777	777	720	679	689	4.8	12.9
Sugar and other sweets	101	98	95	90	89	92	6.5	3.4
Fats and oils	72	71	65	64	61	64	11.4	1.6
Miscellaneous foods	375	350	345	304	297	293	8.7	17.8
Nonalcoholic beverages	224	222	238	229	232	240	-5.7	-0.9
Food prep. by household, out-of-town trips	42	36	36	34	38	39	16.3	-5.4
Food away from home	**1,620**	**1,887**	**1,935**	**1,856**	**1,877**	**1,808**	**-16.3**	**7.0**
ALCOHOLIC BEVERAGES	**$297**	**$305**	**$312**	**$309**	**$347**	**$337**	**-4.7%**	**-7.4%**

(continued)

(average annual expenditures for all households, 1986-91; percent change in expenditures, 1986-89 and 1989-91; in 1991 dollars; number of households in thousands)

	1991	*1990*	*1989*	*1988*	*1987*	*1986*	*percent change*	
							1989-91	*1986-89*
HOUSING	**$9,465**	**$9,260**	**$9,456**	**$9,302**	**$9,074**	**$9,062**	**0.1%**	**4.3%**
Shelter	**5,404**	**5,244**	**5,310**	**5,173**	**4,980**	**4,945**	**1.8**	**7.4**
Owned dwellings	3,280	3,077	3,130	2,957	2,848	2,865	4.8	9.3
Mortgage interest	1,932	1,893	1,912	1,806	1,752	1,778	1.0	7.6
Property taxes	789	622	632	580	556	519	24.9	21.7
Maintenance, repairs, insurance, other	559	563	586	571	539	567	-4.6	3.3
Rented dwellings	1,587	1,598	1,648	1,690	1,612	1,568	-3.7	5.0
Other lodging	536	568	533	525	520	512	0.7	4.1
Utilities, fuels, and public services	**1,990**	**1,970**	**2,015**	**2,011**	**2,004**	**2,045**	**-1.3**	**-1.4**
Natural gas	250	256	271	270	278	308	-7.7	-12.2
Electricity	803	790	811	816	829	838	-1.0	-3.2
Fuel oil and other fuels	102	104	110	113	113	133	-7.7	-17.2
Telephone services	618	617	623	618	598	586	-0.8	6.4
Water and other public services	217	201	200	196	183	180	8.5	11.0
Household operations	**448**	**465**	**505**	**453**	**445**	**440**	**-11.4**	**14.9**
Personal services	211	228	241	197	204	208	-12.3	15.5
Other household expenses	237	237	265	256	241	231	-10.5	14.7
Housekeeping supplies	424	423	432	416	408	393	-2.0	10.1
Laundry and cleaning supplies	116	118	118	117	117	115	-1.5	2.7
Other household products	185	178	181	169	167	156	2.0	16.0
Postage and stationery	123	127	134	130	126	122	-8.5	10.3
Household furnishings and equipment	**1,200**	**1,158**	**1,193**	**1,247**	**1,237**	**1,240**	**0.6**	**-3.8**
Household textiles	100	103	116	108	109	130	-13.5	-11.2
Furniture	294	323	343	375	377	378	-14.2	-9.4
Floor coverings	115	96	77	75	82	69	49.1	12.1
Major appliances	132	153	163	195	192	194	-18.8	-16.1
Small appliances, misc. housewares	81	64	72	69	69	70	12.7	3.0
Miscellaneous household equipment	477	419	424	425	407	400	12.5	6.0
APPAREL AND SERVICES	**$1,735**	**$1,685**	**$1,737**	**$1,714**	**$1,734**	**$1,673**	**-0.1%**	**3.9%**
Men and boys	**429**	**410**	**436**	**447**	**432**	**426**	**-1.5**	**2.2**
Men, aged 16 or older	345	338	356	358	353	346	-3.2	3.0
Boys, aged 2 to 15	84	73	81	89	79	82	3.3	-1.3
Women and girls	**706**	**700**	**721**	**676**	**709**	**676**	**-2.1**	**6.6**
Women, aged 16 or older	607	610	619	567	612	587	-1.9	5.5
Girls, aged 2 to 15	99	91	102	109	97	90	-3.1	14.0
Babies under age 2	**82**	**73**	**79**	**71**	**70**	**70**	**3.5**	**13.4**
Footwear	**242**	**234**	**207**	**226**	**221**	**207**	**16.7**	**0.0**
Other apparel products and services	**277**	**269**	**292**	**296**	**301**	**293**	**-5.1**	**-0.4**
TRANSPORTATION	**$5,151**	**$5,338**	**$5,697**	**$5,864**	**$5,515**	**$6,017**	**-9.6%**	**-5.3%**
Vehicle purchases (net outlay)	**2,111**	**2,219**	**2,517**	**2,718**	**2,424**	**2,905**	**-16.1**	**-13.4**
Cars and trucks, new	1,078	1,208	1,338	1,560	1,370	1,758	-19.4	-23.9
Cars and trucks, used	1,013	988	1,155	1,131	1,031	1,110	-12.3	4.0
Other vehicles	20	23	24	26	22	36	-16.6	-33.3

(continued)

(continued from previous page)

(average annual expenditures for all households, 1986-91; percent change in expenditures, 1986-89 and 1989-91; in 1991 dollars; numbers of households in thousands)

	1991	1990	1989	1988	1987	1986	percent change 1989-91	percent change 1986-89
Gasoline and motor oil	$995	$1,091	$1,082	$1,073	$1,065	$1,137	-8.0%	-4.9%
Other vehicle expenses	1,741	1,713	1,787	1,751	1,699	1,667	-2.6	7.2
Vehicle finance charges	282	313	332	327	336	335	-15.2	-0.6
Maintenance and repairs	614	616	616	637	616	612	-0.3	0.7
Vehicle insurance	614	587	632	585	554	522	-2.8	21.0
Vehicle rental, licenses, other charges	231	198	206	204	192	200	12.0	3.1
Public transportation	304	315	312	321	327	308	-2.4	1.0
HEALTH CARE	$1,554	$1,542	$1,545	$1,494	$1,361	$1,411	0.6%	9.5%
Health insurance	656	605	590	546	470	461	11.2	28.1
Medical services	555	586	595	609	560	624	-6.7	-4.7
Drugs	252	263	264	256	244	239	-4.4	10.5
Medical supplies	92	89	96	81	88	85	-4.0	12.2
ENTERTAINMENT	$1,472	$1,482	$1,564	$1,530	$1,431	$1,428	-5.9%	9.6%
Fees and admissions	378	387	414	406	388	382	-8.6	8.2
Television, radios, sound equipment	468	473	471	479	454	461	-0.6	2.3
Pets, toys, and playground equipment	271	288	273	265	262	251	-0.7	8.7
Other supplies, equipment, and services	356	335	405	380	327	333	-12.2	21.6
PERSONAL CARE PRODUCTS AND SERVICES	$399	$379	$402	$385	$396	$376	-.8%	6.9%
READING	$163	$159	$172	$173	$170	$174	-5.2%	-1.2%
EDUCATION	$447	$423	$403	$394	$404	$390	10.8%	3.5%
TOBACCO PRODUCTS AND SMOKING SUPPLIES	$276	$286	$287	$278	$278	$286	-3.7%	.4%
CASH CONTRIBUTIONS	$950	$850	$989	$798	$889	$927	-3.9%	$6.6%
PERSONAL INSURANCE AND PENSIONS	$2,787	$2,701	$2,716	$2,590	$2,607	$2,643	2.6%	2.8%
Life and other personal insurance	356	360	380	362	352	363	-6.4	4.9
Pensions and Social Security	2,431	2,343	2,334	2,228	2,255	2,279	4.1	2.4
MISCELLANEOUS	$647	$672	$707	$666	$674	$648	-8.4%	9.0%

Note: Households are Bureau of Labor Statistics' consumer units.
Source: New Strategist tabulations of the Bureau of Labor Statistics 1991 Consumer Expenditure Survey

Personal Saving, 1970 to 1991

The personal saving rate bottomed out in the late 1980s, then rose slightly in 1990 and 1991. According to this measure, which does not include the value of home equity, Americans saved just 5 percent of after-tax income in 1991.

(personal income and its disposition, 1970-91; in billions of dollars)

	1991	1990	1989	1988	1985	1980	1970
Personal income	$4,834.4	$4,679.8	$4,380.2	$4,075.9	$3,379.8	$2,265.4	$831.0
minus Social Security and personal taxes	-616.1	-621.0	-591.7	-527.7	-436.8	-312.4	-109.0
Disposable personal income	4,218.4	4,058.8	3,788.6	3,548.2	2,943.0	1,952.9	722.0
Minus personal spending	-3,999.1	-3,853.1	-3,622.4	-3,392.5	-2,753.7	-1,799.1	-664.5
Personal saving	219.3	205.8	166.1	155.7	189.3	153.8	57.5
Personal saving rate personal saving as a percent of disposable personal income	5.2%	5.1%	4.4%	4.4%	6.4%	7.9%	8.0%

Note: Personal income in this table is based on data from the Bureau of Economic Analysis. Personal income is income received by individuals, nonprofit institutions, and private trust funds. Unlike personal income as defined by the Census Bureau, it includes some noncash types of income.
Source: Bureau of the Census, Statistical Abstract of the United States: 1992

Consumer Credit, 1970 to 1991

Consumer credit as a percent of disposable personal income peaked in the mid-1980s at over 20 percent, then fell to 18 percent by 1991.

(amount of outstanding consumer credit at end of year, by type of credit, and consumer credit as a percent of disposable personal income, 1970-91; in billions of dollars)

	total credit	installment credit				noninstallment credit	consumer credit as percent of disposable personal income
		total	automobile	revolving	other		
1991	$777.3	$729.4	$267.9	$234.5	$227.0	$47.9	18.4%
1990	794.4	735.1	284.6	220.1	230.5	59.3	19.6
1989	781.2	718.9	290.7	199.1	229.1	62.3	20.6
1988	731.2	664.0	284.2	174.1	205.7	67.1	20.6
1987	681.9	610.5	265.9	153.1	191.5	71.4	20.7
1986	649.1	573.0	247.4	135.9	189.7	76.1	20.7
1985	592.1	518.3	210.2	121.8	186.2	73.8	20.1
1984	511.3	442.6	173.6	100.3	168.8	68.7	18.5
1983	431.2	369.0	143.6	79.1	146.4	62.2	17.3
1982	383.1	325.8	125.9	66.5	133.4	57.3	16.5
1981	366.9	311.3	119.0	61.1	131.2	55.6	16.9
1980	350.3	298.2	112.0	55.1	131.1	52.1	18.0
1970	131.6	103.9	36.3	4.9	62.6	27.7	18.2

Note: Consumer credit does not include mortgage or home equity credit. Noninstallment credit is single-payment loans.
Source: Bureau of the Census, Statistical Abstract of the United States: 1992

Composition of Household
Assets and Debts, 1983 and 1989

In the 1980s, financial assets were a growing share of Americans' total assets, rising from 26 to 28 percent. Mortgage equity was a declining share of assets, falling from 33 to 32 percent.

(percent distribution of household assets and debts, percentage point change in distribution, and median net worth, 1983-89.)

Assets	1989	1983	percentage point change 1983-89
Total	100.0%	100.0%	0.0
Financial	27.7	25.6	2.1
Nonfinancial	72.3	74.4	-2.1
Vehicles	3.9	3.6	0.3
Principal residence	32.2	33.4	-1.2
Real estate and land investment	15.1	16.0	-0.9
Business investment (excluding real estate)	17.8	20.4	-2.6
Other	3.3	1.0	2.3
Debts			
Total	100.0	100.0	0.0
Home mortgages	53.1	58.1	-5.0
Investment real estate mortgages	25.0	20.5	4.5
Home equity lines of credit	2.6	0.5	2.1
Other lines of credit	1.0	2.8	-1.8
Credit cards	2.2	1.8	0.4
Car loans	8.0	6.1	1.9
Other debts	8.1	10.2	-2.1
Median net worth	$47,200	$42,700	-

Source: Survey of Consumer Finances, Federal Reserve Bulletin, January 1991

Ownership of Financial Assets by Age of Householder, 1983 and 1989

A majority of American households had a savings account in 1983, but this proportion fell to just 44 percent by 1989.

(percent of households owning selected financial assets, by age of householder, 1983 and 1989, and percentage point change in ownership, 1983-89)

1989	total households	under 35	35 to 44	45 to 54	55 to 64	65 to 74	75 or older
Percent owning:							
Any financial assets	87.5%	82.2%	88.4%	90.4%	87.5%	91.5%	90.6%
Checking accounts	75.4	68.4	76.1	78.9	76.7	79.9	79.3
Savings accounts	43.5	45.0	50.0	44.6	38.9	37.7	36.2
Money market accounts	22.2	14.9	20.4	27.0	23.0	28.3	30.5
CDs	19.6	8.5	15.5	21.1	20.9	31.6	39.4
Retirement accounts	33.3	23.0	44.0	45.5	42.6	30.0	6.6
Stocks	19.0	11.4	21.2	23.1	22.0	20.8	21.3
Bonds	4.4	0.8	3.4	3.5	5.9	9.1	9.6
Nontaxable bonds	4.4	0.9	3.5	4.3	7.5	9.4	4.9
Trusts	3.4	2.5	2.8	3.1	3.0	6.4	4.8
Other	47.7	39.5	56.8	52.9	49.6	48.4	35.5
1983							
Percent owning:							
Any financial assets	87.8%	85.0%	90.1%	88.7%	90.1%	88.2%	85.9%
Checking accounts	78.6	71.9	82.9	81.8	81.2	82.5	76.2
Savings accounts	61.7	62.6	68.4	64.9	59.0	55.4	48.9
Money market accounts	15.0	8.5	16.5	14.9	20.0	22.4	15.3
CDs	20.1	8.6	15.5	18.1	20.3	36.9	38.3
Retirement accounts	24.2	17.2	31.0	35.5	36.3	14.8	1.7
Stocks	20.4	12.9	22.8	23.2	25.7	26.1	19.9
Bonds	3.0	1.0	2.5	3.2	4.9	6.7	2.2
Nontaxable bonds	2.1	0.2	1.7	2.1	3.0	6.1	2.2
Trusts	4.0	4.0	3.6	6.0	3.8	3.1	2.9
Other	44.0	36.0	50.2	48.6	47.5	49.2	35.4
Percentage point change, 1983-89:							
Ownership of any financial assets	-0.3	-2.8	-1.7	1.7	-2.6	3.3	4.7
Checking accounts	-3.2	-3.5	-6.8	-2.9	-4.5	-2.6	3.1
Savings accounts	-18.2	-17.6	-18.4	-20.3	-20.1	-17.7	-12.7
Money market accounts	7.2	6.4	3.9	12.1	3.0	5.9	15.2
CDs	-0.5	-0.1	0.0	3.0	0.6	-5.3	1.1
Retirement accounts	9.1	5.8	13.0	10.0	6.3	15.2	4.9
Stocks	-1.4	-1.5	-1.6	-0.1	-3.7	-5.3	1.4
Bonds	1.4	-0.2	0.9	0.3	1.0	2.4	7.4
Nontaxable bonds	2.3	0.7	1.8	2.2	4.5	3.3	2.7
Trusts	-0.6	-1.5	-0.8	-2.9	-0.8	3.3	1.9
Other	3.7	3.5	6.6	4.3	2.1	-0.8	0.1

Source: Survey of Consumer Finances, Federal Reserve Bulletin, January 1992

Value of Financial Assets by Age of Householder, 1983 and 1989

The median net worth of Americans grew by 10.5 percent, after adjusting for inflation, between 1983 and 1989.

(median net worth and median value of selected financial assets of households holding such assets, by age of householder, 1983 and 1989, and percent change in net worth and asset value, 1983-89; in thousands of 1989 dollars)

1989	total households	under 35	35 to 44	45 to 54	55 to 64	65 to 74	75 or older
Median net worth	**$47.2**	**$6.8**	**$52.8**	**$86.7**	**$91.3**	**$77.6**	**$66.1**
Median value of:							
Total financial assets	$10.4	$2.5	$11.2	$14.5	$20.0	$18.2	$21.0
Checking accounts	0.9	0.6	0.9	1.0	1.0	1.0	1.0
Savings accounts	1.5	0.7	1.5	1.5	4.5	2.0	5.0
Money market accounts	5.0	2.6	5.0	2.7	11.0	10.0	8.0
CDs	11.0	5.0	10.0	9.0	12.0	17.0	25.0
Retirement accounts	10.0	4.0	8.0	14.0	22.0	15.0	25.0
Stocks	7.5	2.7	3.0	6.0	18.3	25.0	18.0
Bonds	17.3	0.1	6.2	12.0	20.0	20.0	26.0
Non-taxable bonds	25.0	15.0	11.7	10.0	25.0	32.0	50.0
Trusts	23.0	26.0	10.0	10.0	32.0	48.0	32.0
Other	2.5	1.0	2.5	3.5	5.0	3.0	3.7
1983							
Median net worth	**$42.7**	**$8.5**	**$49.8**	**$69.4**	**$84.4**	**$76.3**	**$49.8**
Median value of:							
Total financial assets	$4.5	$1.5	$4.4	$5.7	$11.7	$17.2	$15.6
Checking accounts	0.6	0.4	0.6	0.7	1.2	1.2	1.1
Savings accounts	1.4	0.6	1.4	1.7	2.0	2.5	3.7
Money market accounts	11.0	5.6	7.5	17.4	12.5	16.3	16.8
CDs	12.5	5.0	10.0	10.6	15.4	23.0	23.0
Retirement accounts	5.0	2.0	5.0	5.6	7.5	12.5	5.0
Stocks	6.2	1.9	5.0	5.0	11.2	16.8	14.9
Bonds	12.5	12.5	8.7	12.5	18.7	31.1	6.2
Nontaxable bonds	52.9	149.4	52.9	54.0	56.3	62.3	18.7
Trusts	12.5	3.7	10.0	12.5	32.4	95.9	12.5
Other	3.0	1.9	2.9	3.9	6.2	2.6	1.9
Percent change, 1983-89							
Median net worth	**10.5%**	**-20.0%**	**6.0%**	**24.9%**	**8.2%**	**1.7%**	**32.7%**
Median value of:							
Total financial assets	131.1%	66.7%	154.5%	154.4%	70.9%	5.8%	34.6%
Checking accounts	50.0	50.0	50.0	42.9	-16.7	-16.7	-9.1
Savings accounts	7.1	16.7	7.1	-11.8	125.0	-20.0	35.1

(continued)

(continued from previous page)

(median net worth and median value of selected financial assets of households holding such assets, by age of householder, 1983 and 1989, and percent change in net worth and asset value, 1983-89; in thousands of 1989 dollars)

	total households	under 35	35 to 44	45 to 54	55 to 64	65 to 74	75 or older
Money market accounts	-54.5%	-53.6%	-33.3%	-84.5%	-12.0%	-38.7%	-52.4%
CDs	-12.0	0.0	0.0	-15.1	-22.1	-26.1	8.7
Retirement accounts	100.0	100.0	60.0	150.0	193.3	20.0	400.0
Stocks	21.0	42.1	-40.0	20.0	63.4	48.8	20.8
Bonds	38.4	-99.2	-28.7	-4.0	7.0	-35.7	319.4
Nontaxable bonds	-52.7	-89.9	-77.9	-81.5	-55.6	-48.6	167.4
Trusts	84.0	602.7	0.0	-20.0	-1.2	-49.9	156.0
Other	-16.7	-47.4	-13.8	-10.3	-19.4	15.4	94.7

Source: Survey of Consumer Finances, Federal Reserve Bulletin, *January 1992*

Ownership of Financial Assets by Income and Housing Status, 1983 and 1989

The most affluent households and homeowners are more likely to own all types of assets than is the average household.

(percent of households owning selected financial assets, by household income and housing status, 1983 and 1989, and percentage point change in ownership, 1983-89)

1989	total households	income					housing status	
		under $10,000	$10,000 to $19,999	$20,000 to $29,999	$30,000 to $49,999	$50,000 or over	own	rent or other
Percent owning:								
Any financial assets	87.5%	59.1%	85.6%	95.2%	98.2%	99.7%	95.6%	72.7%
Checking accounts	75.4	46.2	69.7	80.3	88.8	91.5	84.9	57.8
Savings accounts	43.5	21.9	40.7	47.6	52.9	53.9	49.2	32.9
Money market accounts	22.2	7.8	14.6	21.0	23.2	44.7	27.2	13.1
CDs	19.6	8.6	21.2	20.6	21.0	26.5	24.6	10.4
Retirement accounts	33.3	3.1	14.9	34.4	44.9	69.2	43.6	14.5
Stocks	19.0	2.0	10.9	16.9	20.8	44.6	25.2	7.6
Bonds	4.4	0.8	2.4	3.0	5.0	12.7	6.1	1.2
Non-taxable bonds	4.4	-	-	4.2	4.2	12.6	5.8	2.0
Trusts	3.4	-	3.1	3.0	3.6	7.1	4.6	1.4
Other	47.7	16.6	35.6	49.4	63.5	72.3	58.0	28.7
1983								
Percent owning:								
Any financial assets	87.8%	64.0%	84.5%	93.7%	97.5%	98.8%	93.7%	77.6%
Checking accounts	78.6	49.2	71.7	83.7	92.4	96.0	87.8	62.6
Savings accounts	61.7	36.9	53.4	67.2	76.6	73.8	67.6	51.4
Money market accounts	15.0	2.7	9.0	12.0	17.4	37.1	18.5	8.9
CDs	20.1	8.1	18.4	19.4	22.7	33.1	26.5	9.0
Retirement accounts	24.2	1.9	8.4	19.8	34.5	61.7	30.6	13.0
Stocks	20.4	4.4	10.6	18.0	25.2	48.3	25.7	11.4
Bonds	3.0	-	1.6	1.9	2.4	10.0	3.7	1.9
Non-taxable bonds	2.1	-	-	1.0	1.0	9.3	2.9	0.6
Trusts	4.0	2.6	1.9	2.7	4.4	9.6	4.5	3.2
Other	44.0	22.7	34.5	45.8	54.5	64.6	52.4	29.5
Percentage point change, 1983-89:								
Ownership of any financial assets	-0.3	-4.9	1.1	1.5	0.7	0.9	1.9	-4.9
Checking accounts	-3.2	-3.0	-2.0	-3.4	-3.6	-4.5	-2.9	-4.8
Savings accounts	-18.2	-15.0	-12.7	-19.6	-23.7	-19.9	-18.4	-18.5
Money market accounts	7.2	5.1	5.6	9.0	5.8	7.6	8.7	4.2
CDs	-0.5	0.5	2.8	1.2	-1.7	-6.6	-1.9	1.4
Retirement accounts	9.1	1.2	6.5	14.6	10.4	7.5	13.0	1.5
Stocks	-1.4	-2.4	0.3	-1.1	-4.4	-3.7	-0.5	-3.8
Bonds	1.4	-	0.8	1.1	2.6	2.7	2.4	-0.7
Non-taxable bonds	2.3	-	-	3.2	3.2	3.3	2.9	1.4
Trusts	-0.6	-	1.2	0.3	-0.8	-2.5	0.1	-1.8
Other	3.7	-6.1	1.1	3.6	9.0	7.7	5.6	-0.8

Source: Survey of Consumer Finances, Federal Reserve Bulletin, January 1992

Value of Financial Assets by Income and Housing Status, 1983 and 1989

The median net worth of the most affluent households rose by just 5 percent between 1983 and 1989, far below the increase for all households.

(median net worth and median value of selected financial assets of households holding such assets, by household income and housing status, 1983 and 1989, and percent change in net worth and asset value, 1983-89; in thousands of 1989 dollars)

1989	total households	income under $10,000	$10,000 to $19,999	$20,000 to $29,999	$30,000 to $49,999	$50,000 or over	housing status own	rent or other
Median net worth	**$47.2**	**$2.3**	**$27.1**	**$37.0**	**$69.2**	**$185.6**	**$97.3**	**$2.2**
Median value of:								
Total financial assets	$10.4	$1.3	$4.5	$6.8	$12.2	$41.5	$16.2	$2.3
Checking accounts	0.9	0.4	0.7	0.8	1.0	1.5	1.0	0.6
Savings accounts	1.5	1.0	1.0	1.2	2.0	3.0	2.0	0.9
Money market accounts	5.0	4.0	5.0	3.5	4.0	10.0	6.4	3.0
CDs	11.0	10.0	10.0	10.0	12.0	15.0	13.0	8.0
Retirement accounts	10.0	3.3	4.0	6.0	8.5	21.2	12.4	4.0
Stocks	7.5	30.0	7.0	4.0	5.5	12.0	8.0	5.0
Bonds	17.3	13.0	15.0	6.2	26.0	20.0	16.0	30.0
Non-taxable bonds	25.0	-	-	5.0	25.0	35.0	30.0	6.3
Trusts	23.0	-	20.0	14.0	30.0	32.0	20.0	26.0
Other	2.5	1.0	2.1	2.0	2.8	4.7	3.0	1.5
1983								
Median net worth	**$42.7**	**$3.8**	**$19.3**	**$36.9**	**$67.7**	**$176.1**	**$80.4**	**$3.0**
Median value of:								
Total financial assets	$4.5	$0.9	$2.1	$2.8	$6.0	$31.9	$7.8	$1.5
Checking accounts	0.6	0.4	0.5	0.5	0.6	1.4	0.7	0.5
Savings accounts	1.4	0.6	0.9	1.3	1.7	3.4	1.9	0.7
Money market accounts	11.0	3.2	8.1	6.2	9.7	14.9	12.5	6.2
CDs	12.5	9.1	12.5	14.7	12.5	15.5	13.1	10.0
Retirement accounts	5.0	2.8	2.5	2.5	3.8	8.1	5.6	2.5
Stocks	6.2	2.4	5.1	3.9	3.1	18.7	6.3	3.1
Bonds	12.5	-	12.5	12.5	8.5	24.9	18.7	11.3
Non-taxable bonds	52.9	-	37.4	15.6	12.6	62.3	52.9	49.8
Trusts	12.5	3.9	3.6	3.7	8.3	24.9	13.7	3.8
Other	3.0	1.6	1.9	1.9	3.9	6.2	3.7	1.6
Percent change, 1983-89								
Median net worth	**10.5%**	**-39.5%**	**40.4%**	**0.3%**	**2.2%**	**5.4%**	**21.0%**	**-26.7%**
Median value of:								
Total financial assets	131.1%	44.4%	114.3%	142.9%	103.3%	30.1%	107.7%	53.3%
Checking accounts	50.0	0.0	40.0	60.0	66.7	7.1	42.9	20.0

(continued)

(continued from previous page)

(median net worth and median value of selected financial assets of households holding such assets, by household income and housing status, 1983 and 1989, and percent change in net worth and asset value, 1983-89; in thousands of 1989 dollars)

	total households	income					housing status	
		under $10,000	$10,000 to $19,999	$20,000 to $29,999	$30,000 to $49,999	$50,000 or over	own	rent or other
Savings accounts	7.1%	66.7%	11.1%	-7.7%	17.6%	-11.8%	5.3%	28.6%
Money market accounts	-54.5	25.0	-38.3	-43.5	-58.8	-32.9	-48.8	-51.6
CDs	-12.0	9.9	-20.0	-32.0	-4.0	-3.2	-0.8	-20.0
Retirement accounts	100.0	17.9	60.0	140.0	123.7	161.7	121.4	60.0
Stocks	21.0	1150.0	37.3	2.6	77.4	-35.8	27.0	61.3
Bonds	38.4	-	20.0	-50.4	205.9	-19.7	-14.4	165.5
Non-taxable bonds	-52.7	-	-	-67.9	98.4	-43.8	-43.3	-87.3
Trusts	84.0	-	455.6	278.4	261.4	28.5	46.0	584.2
Other	-16.7	-37.5	10.5	5.3	-28.2	-24.2	-18.9	-6.3

Source: Survey of Consumer Finances, Federal Reserve Bulletin, *January 1992*

Ownership of Financial Assets by Life-Cycle Stage, 1983 and 1989

Retired householders are more likely to own a variety of financial assets, such as CDs and stocks, than the average household.

(percent of households owning selected financial assets, by life-cycle stage of householder, 1983 and 1989, and percentage point change in ownership, 1983-89)

				under age 55		aged 55 or older	
1989	total households	unmarried, no children	married, no children	unmarried, children	married, children	in labor force	retired
Percent owning:							
Any financial assets	87.5%	84.7%	92.8%	68.4%	92.7%	95.6%	93.0%
Checking accounts	75.4	71.9	78.9	54.5	80.8	83.9	81.8
Savings accounts	43.5	40.2	52.6	35.7	52.5	44.4	37.6
Money market accounts	22.2	17.2	31.2	9.5	22.7	25.1	31.3
CDs	19.6	10.7	16.3	9.0	16.4	23.2	35.9
Retirement accounts	33.3	26.7	40.2	21.9	43.1	49.1	25.2
Stocks	19.0	16.8	26.9	8.7	19.9	26.1	23.7
Bonds	4.4	1.8	4.8	1.4	2.5	7.2	10.9
Non-taxable bonds	4.4	3.0	5.8	1.9	2.4	9.8	8.4
Trusts	3.4	2.4	2.2	0.7	3.7	4.6	6.0
Other	47.7	30.3	50.2	30.8	61.5	57.3	45.6
1983							
Percent owning:							
Any financial assets	87.8%	88.9%	90.6%	73.3%	91.7%	93.1%	85.8%
Checking accounts	78.6	74.7	86.1	58.9	84.1	85.1	77.5
Savings accounts	61.7	61.4	67.7	55.2	69.2	64.9	49.9
Money market accounts	15.0	14.6	20.2	7.4	12.4	24.6	17.1
CDs	20.1	8.6	15.0	9.0	15.4	31.2	34.8
Retirement accounts	24.2	19.5	29.1	12.8	31.9	42.0	7.9
Stocks	20.4	18.2	19.3	12.4	20.4	28.9	22.6
Bonds	3.0	2.7	-	2.3	1.8	5.0	4.9
Non-taxable bonds	2.1	1.1	1.3	0.8	1.2	4.7	3.6
Trusts	4.0	4.6	5.8	4.4	4.0	4.3	2.6
Other	44.0	31.6	46.0	32.9	50.3	54.2	41.5
Percentage point change, 1983-89:							
Ownership of any financial assets	-0.3	-4.2	2.2	-4.9	1.0	2.5	7.2
Checking accounts	-3.2	-2.8	-7.2	-4.4	-3.3	-1.2	4.3
Savings accounts	-18.2	-21.2	-15.1	-19.5	-16.7	-20.5	-12.3
Money market accounts	7.2	2.6	11.0	2.1	10.3	0.5	14.2
CDs	-0.5	2.1	1.3	0.0	1.0	-8.0	1.1
Retirement accounts	9.1	7.2	11.1	9.1	11.2	7.1	17.3
Stocks	-1.4	-1.4	7.6	-3.7	-0.5	-2.8	1.1
Bonds	1.4	-0.9	-	-0.9	0.7	2.2	6.0
Non-taxable bonds	2.3	1.9	4.5	1.1	1.2	5.1	4.8
Trusts	-0.6	-2.2	-3.6	-3.7	-0.3	0.3	3.4
Other	3.7	-1.3	4.2	-2.1	11.2	3.1	4.1

Source: Survey of Consumer Finances, Federal Reserve Bulletin, *January 1992*

Value of Financial Assets by Life-Cycle Stage, 1983 and 1989

The net worth of retired householders is twice as high as that of the average household. It climbed 47 percent between 1983 and 1989, over four times as fast as the average.

(median net worth and median value of selected financial assets of households holding such assets, by life-cycle stage of householder, 1983 and 1989, and percent change in net worth and asset value, 1983-89; in thousands of 1989 dollars)

	total households	unmarried, no children	married, no children	under age 55		aged 55 or older	
				unmarried, children	married, children	in labor force	retired
1989							
Median net worth	**$47.2**	**$8.4**	**$27.3**	**$5.7**	**$62.0**	**$104.5**	**$94.1**
Median value of:							
Total financial assets	$10.4	$4.9	$7.1	$3.0	$11.0	$22.2	$22.4
Checking accounts	0.9	0.7	1.0	0.5	0.9	1.0	1.0
Savings accounts	1.5	1.0	1.6	1.0	1.2	3.0	5.0
Money market accounts	5.0	4.5	2.7	1.5	4.0	15.0	10.5
CDs	11.0	10.0	6.2	5.1	7.0	13.0	20.0
Retirement accounts	10.0	5.0	4.9	4.0	10.0	20.0	16.0
Stocks	7.5	3.7	3.6	2.5	3.6	20.0	20.3
Bonds	17.3	30.0	3.0	12.0	6.0	20.0	26.0
Non-taxable bonds	25.0	11.7	7.0	2.0	30.5	50.0	25.0
Trusts	23.0	40.0	8.0	6.0	14.0	32.0	45.0
Other	2.5	1.5	1.0	2.0	2.5	5.0	4.0
1983							
Median net worth	**$42.7**	**$6.0**	**$20.1**	**$10.8**	**$51.3**	**$108.0**	**$63.9**
Median value of:							
Total financial assets	$4.5	$2.0	$3.5	$1.7	$3.5	$15.7	$12.8
Checking accounts	0.6	0.5	0.6	0.5	0.6	1.2	1.2
Savings accounts	1.4	0.6	1.0	0.8	1.4	2.0	3.0
Money market accounts	11.0	6.8	7.5	6.2	9.3	14.1	14.9
CDs	12.5	5.0	6.2	10.6	7.5	16.2	19.0
Retirement accounts	5.0	3.1	3.6	2.5	5.0	10.0	5.6
Stocks	6.2	2.5	3.7	3.7	4.4	11.8	14.7
Bonds	12.5	12.5	-	5.0	12.5	12.5	24.9
Non-taxable bonds	52.9	54.0	124.5	15.6	47.3	56.3	18.7
Trusts	12.5	0.7	5.0	6.2	10.0	62.3	32.4
Other	3.0	1.8	2.8	1.5	3.4	5.1	2.1
Percent change, 1983-89							
Median net worth	**10.5%**	**40.0%**	**35.8%**	**-47.2%**	**20.9%**	**-3.2%**	**47.3%**
Median value of:							
Total financial assets	131.1%	145.0%	102.9%	76.5%	214.3%	41.4%	75.0%
Checking accounts	50.0	40.0	66.7	0.0	50.0	-16.7	-16.7

(continued)

(continued from previous page)

(median net worth and median value of selected financial assets of households holding such assets, by life-cycle stage of householder, 1983 and 1989, and percent change in net worth and asset value, 1983-89; in thousands of 1989 dollars)

	total households	unmarried, no children	married, no children	under age 55		aged 55 or older	
				unmarried, children	married, children	in labor force	retired
Savings accounts	7.1%	66.7%	60.0%	25.0%	-14.3%	50.0%	66.7%
Money market accounts	-54.5	-33.8	-64.0	-75.8	-57.0	6.4	-29.5
CDs	-12.0	100.0	0.0	-51.9	-6.7	-19.8	5.3
Retirement accounts	100.0	61.3	36.1	60.0	100.0	100.0	185.7
Stocks	21.0	48.0	-2.7	-32.4	-18.2	69.5	38.1
Bonds	38.4	140.0	-	140.0	-52.0	60.0	4.4
Non-taxable bonds	-52.7	-78.3	-94.4	-87.2	-35.5	-11.2	33.7
Trusts	84.0	5614.3	60.0	-3.2	40.0	-48.6	38.9
Other	-16.7	-16.7	-64.3	33.3	-26.5	-2.0	90.5

Source: Survey of Consumer Finances, Federal Reserve Bulletin, *January 1992*

Ownership of Nonfinancial Assets by Age, 1983 and 1989

A majority of households own a vehicle and a home. Homeownership peaks among householders aged 55 to 64.

(percent of households owning selected nonfinancial assets, by of age householder, 1983 and 1989, and percentage point change in ownership, 1983-89)

	total households	under 35	35 to 44	45 to 54	55 to 64	65 to 74	75 or older
1989							
Percent owning:							
Any nonfinancial assets	90.2%	84.4%	92.8%	93.3%	92.1%	93.8%	87.3%
Vehicles	84.0	80.7	89.5	90.9	86.9	81.9	66.9
Business	11.5	8.4	17.0	16.2	11.3	7.9	4.7
Investment real estate	20.4	8.1	20.9	28.5	31.3	25.6	16.9
Other assets	22.1	20.5	24.9	25.6	23.9	20.4	13.3
Principal residence	64.7	36.8	65.9	76.6	82.2	80.2	72.8
1983							
Percent owning:							
Any nonfinancial assets	90.3%	87.2%	94.0%	92.7%	93.1%	91.8%	79.6%
Vehicles	84.4	83.3	91.2	90.3	87.7	80.2	57.8
Business	14.2	10.3	18.3	18.2	18.1	12.3	6.4
Investment real estate	20.9	10.4	22.9	24.9	32.6	27.2	16.9
Other assets	7.4	9.1	10.3	6.4	5.9	5.6	1.4
Principal residence	64.4	38.7	68.4	78.0	76.8	78.9	69.5
Percentage point change, 1983-89:							
Ownership of any nonfinancial assets	-0.1	-2.8	-1.2	0.6	-1.0	2.0	7.7
Vehicles	-0.4	-2.6	-1.7	0.6	-0.8	1.7	9.1
Business	-2.7	-1.9	-1.3	-2.0	-6.8	-4.4	-1.7
Investment real estate	-0.5	-2.3	-2.0	3.6	-1.3	-1.6	0.0
Other assets	14.7	11.4	14.6	19.2	18.0	14.8	11.9
Principal residence	0.3	-1.9	-2.5	-1.4	5.4	1.3	3.3

Source: Survey of Consumer Finances, Federal Reserve Bulletin, *January 1992*

Value of Nonfinancial Assets by Age, 1983 and 1989

The most valuable asset owned by most Americans is their home. Home values rose by 8 percent for all households between 1983 and 1989.

(median net worth and median value of selected nonfinancial assets of households holding such assets, by age of householder, 1983 and 1989, and percent change in net worth and asset value, 1983-89; in thousands of 1989 dollars)

	total households	under 35	35 to 44	45 to 54	55 to 64	65 to 74	75 or older
1989							
Median net worth	$47.2	$6.8	$52.8	$86.7	$91.3	$77.6	$66.1
Median value of:							
Total nonfinancial assets	$66.7	$15.5	$81.3	$105.3	$93.9	$63.1	$52.0
Vehicles	6.9	5.7	8.0	9.6	7.1	5.4	3.7
Business	50.0	11.0	50.0	61.6	80.0	53.0	28.5
Investment real estate	39.0	31.5	46.0	50.0	39.0	34.0	35.0
Other assets	5.0	1.6	5.0	8.3	8.0	10.0	10.0
Principal residence	70.0	65.0	80.0	85.0	75.0	58.1	55.0
1983							
Median net worth	$42.7	$8.5	$49.8	$69.4	$84.4	$76.3	$49.8
Median value of:							
Total nonfinancial assets	$59.7	$13.2	$77.4	$88.1	$81.4	$65.5	$49.2
Vehicles	5.1	4.4	5.6	6.6	6.3	3.8	2.3
Business	57.0	24.9	55.2	67.5	93.4	94.7	124.5
Investment real estate	43.6	31.1	47.3	36.1	49.8	49.8	39.8
Other assets	6.2	2.5	6.2	10.7	12.5	12.5	5.8
Principal residence	64.7	56.0	80.9	74.7	74.7	57.3	44.8
Percent change, 1983-89							
Median net worth	10.5%	-20.0%	6.0%	24.9%	8.2%	1.7%	32.7%
Median value of:							
Total nonfinancial assets	11.7%	17.4%	5.0%	19.5%	15.4%	-3.7%	5.7%
Vehicles	35.3	29.5	42.9	45.5	12.7	42.1	60.9
Business	-12.3	-55.8	-9.4	-8.7	-14.3	-44.0	-77.1
Investment real estate	-10.6	1.3	-2.7	38.5	-21.7	-31.7	-12.1
Other assets	-19.4	-36.0	-19.4	-22.4	-36.0	-20.0	72.4
Principal residence	8.2	16.1	-1.1	13.8	0.4	1.4	22.8

Source: Survey of Consumer Finances, Federal Reserve Bulletin, January 1992

Ownership of Nonfinancial Assets by Income and Housing Status, 1983 and 1989

Ownership of all types of nonfinancial assets rises steadily with income. Fully 90 percent of households with incomes of $50,000 or more own a home.

(percent of households owning selected nonfinancial assets, by household income and housing status, 1983 and 1989, and percentage point change in ownership, 1983-89)

	total households	income					housing status	
		under $10,000	$10,000 to $19,999	$20,000 to $29,999	$30,000 to $49,999	$50,000 or over	own	rent or other
1989								
Percent owning:								
Any nonfinancial assets	90.2%	66.9%	90.5%	96.7%	98.0%	99.4%	100.0%	72.3%
Vehicles	84.0	51.6	82.1	94.4	95.5	96.8	92.7	67.9
Business	11.5	2.3	8.0	10.1	12.0	25.4	14.4	6.3
Investment real estate	20.4	5.9	14.4	15.0	27.1	38.7	26.0	10.1
Other assets	22.1	12.1	18.5	23.8	25.4	30.7	23.0	20.3
Principal residence	64.7	36.2	57.0	63.5	76.2	90.0	100.0	na
1983								
Percent owning:								
Any nonfinancial assets	90.3%	67.4%	89.1%	96.1%	98.6%	99.4%	100.0%	73.4%
Vehicles	84.4	50.5	83.2	93.3	97.0	96.4	92.4	70.5
Business	14.2	4.5	6.9	12.0	18.7	31.5	18.8	6.3
Investment real estate	20.9	6.9	14.1	17.9	25.8	42.7	27.1	10.2
Other assets	7.4	3.3	5.5	7.2	8.0	14.3	7.5	7.4
Principal residence	64.4	40.1	52.6	60.3	77.2	88.9	100.0	na
Percentage point change, 1983-89:								
Any nonfinancial assets	-0.1	-0.5	1.4	0.6	-0.6	0.0	0.0	-1.1
Vehicles	-0.4	1.1	-1.1	1.1	-1.5	0.4	0.3	-2.6
Business	-2.7	-2.2	1.1	-1.9	-6.7	-6.1	-4.4	0.0
Investment real estate	-0.5	-1.0	0.3	-2.9	1.3	-4.0	-1.1	-0.1
Other assets	14.7	8.8	13.0	16.6	17.4	16.4	15.5	12.9
Principal residence	0.3	-3.9	4.4	3.2	-1.0	1.1	0.0	na

Source: Survey of Consumer Finances, Federal Reserve Bulletin, *January 1992*

Value of Nonfinancial Assets by Income and Housing Status, 1983 and 1989

Median net worth rises sharply with income. Even among the most affluent households, the home is the most valuable asset.

(median net worth and median value of selected nonfinancial assets of households holding such assets, by household income and housing status, 1983 and 1989, and percent change in net worth and asset value, 1983-89; in thousands of 1989 dollars)

	total households	income					housing status	
		under $10,000	$10,000 to $19,999	$20,000 to $29,999	$30,000 to $49,999	$50,000 or over	own	rent or other
1989								
Median net worth	**$47.2**	**$2.3**	**$27.1**	**$37.0**	**$69.2**	**$185.6**	**$97.3**	**$2.2**
Median value of:								
Total nonfinancial assets	$66.7	$11.4	$39.2	$48.3	$84.9	$190.0	$95.9	$5.5
Vehicles	6.9	2.0	4.1	5.8	8.7	13.4	8.3	8.0
Business	50.0	14.3	5.9	40.0	45.0	93.0	60.0	7.2
Investment real estate	39.0	16.7	18.0	30.0	35.0	80.0	40.0	31.0
Other assets	5.0	1.2	3.0	3.0	5.0	15.0	8.0	2.0
Principal residence	70.0	33.0	50.0	57.0	75.0	130.0	70.0	na
1983								
Median net worth	**$42.7**	**$3.8**	**$19.3**	**$36.9**	**$67.7**	**$176.1**	**$80.4**	**$3.0**
Median value of:								
Total nonfinancial assets	$59.7	$15.5	$31.1	$45.9	$81.5	$163.9	$85.0	$4.2
Vehicles	5.1	1.8	3.2	4.5	6.4	9.8	6.1	3.4
Business	57.0	41.1	31.4	24.9	44.0	121.0	62.3	26.6
Investment real estate	43.6	13.9	27.9	31.1	39.0	89.0	43.6	36.1
Other assets	6.2	2.5	2.9	3.7	6.2	12.5	8.5	3.1
Principal residence	64.7	32.1	49.8	54.2	74.7	112.1	64.7	na
Percent change, 1983-89								
Median net worth	**10.5%**	**-39.5%**	**40.4%**	**0.3%**	**2.2%**	**5.4%**	**21.0%**	**-26.7%**
Median value of:								
Total nonfinancial assets	11.7%	-26.5%	26.0%	5.2%	4.2%	15.9%	12.8%	31.0%
Vehicles	35.3	11.1	28.1	28.9	35.9	36.7	36.1	135.3
Business	-12.3	-65.2	-81.2	60.6	2.3	-23.1	-3.7	-72.9
Investment real estate	-10.6	20.1	-35.5	-3.5	-10.3	-10.1	-8.3	-14.1
Other assets	-19.4	-52.0	3.4	-18.9	-19.4	20.0	-5.9	-35.5
Principal residence	8.2	2.8	0.4	5.2	0.4	16.0	8.2	na

Source: Survey of Consumer Finances, Federal Reserve Bulletin, *January 1992*

Ownership of Nonfinancial Assets by Life-Cycle Stage

People aged 55 or older are most likely to own a home, as are married couples with children. Homeownership increased for these groups between 1983 and 1989.

(percent of households owning selected nonfinancial assets, by life-cycle stage of householder, 1983 and 1989, and percentage point change in ownership, 1983-89)

				under age 55		aged 55 or older	
1989	total households	unmarried, no children	married, no children	unmarried, children	married, children	in labor force	retired
Percent owning:							
Any nonfinancial assets	90.2%	82.1%	97.2%	71.6%	97.7%	94.8%	93.5%
Vehicles	84.0	75.5	95.4	64.7	96.6	91.1	82.6
Business	11.5	10.5	13.0	5.0	17.5	17.6	4.7
Investment real estate	20.4	10.9	19.8	9.2	22.3	34.3	25.0
Other assets	22.1	28.6	26.9	22.2	21.6	28.7	17.4
Principal residence	64.7	23.7	56.9	35.2	74.9	82.0	82.2
1983							
Percent owning:							
Any nonfinancial assets	90.3%	79.1%	97.0%	78.3%	97.8%	95.1%	86.2%
Vehicles	84.4	71.9	96.4	73.1	96.2	89.5	74.4
Business	14.2	9.1	14.3	6.4	19.3	24.1	6.1
Investment real estate	20.9	10.0	14.6	12.0	22.5	36.3	22.1
Other assets	7.4	13.9	13.0	6.2	7.6	7.3	3.4
Principal residence	64.4	23.4	51.8	42.7	73.5	78.1	74.8
Percentage point change, 1983-89:							
Ownership of any nonfinancial assets	-0.1	3.0	0.2	-6.7	-0.1	-0.3	7.3
Vehicles	-0.4	3.6	-1.0	-8.4	0.4	1.6	8.2
Business	-2.7	1.4	-1.3	-1.4	-1.8	-6.5	-1.4
Investment real estate	-0.5	0.9	5.2	-2.8	-0.2	-2.0	2.9
Other assets	14.7	14.7	13.9	16.0	14.0	21.4	14.0
Principal residence	0.3	0.3	5.1	-7.5	1.4	3.9	7.4

Source: Survey of Consumer Finances, Federal Reserve Bulletin, *January 1992*

Value of Nonfinancial Assets by Life-Cycle Stage, 1983 and 1989

Older Americans and married couples with children have the highest net worth. Net worth rose from 1983 to 1989 for all household types except single parents and workers aged 55 or older.

(median net worth and median value of selected nonfinancial assets of households holding such assets, by life-cycle stage of householder, 1983 and 1989, and percent change in net worth and asset value, 1983-89; in thousands of 1989 dollars)

| | total households | unmarried, no children | married, no children | under age 55 | | aged 55 or older | |
				unmarried, children	married, children	in labor force	retired
1989							
Median net worth	**$47.2**	**$8.4**	**$27.3**	**$5.7**	**$62.0**	**$104.5**	**$94.1**
Median value of:							
Total nonfinancial assets	$66.7	$8.8	$66.3	$22.7	$86.4	$98.3	$67.6
Vehicles	6.9	4.3	9.0	4.8	9.3	7.6	5.5
Business	50.0	8.4	45.0	13.4	52.0	80.0	49.2
Investment real estate	39.0	45.0	94.0	46.0	45.0	43.0	35.7
Other assets	5.0	2.0	4.0	3.0	6.0	8.0	11.4
Principal residence	70.0	84.0	84.0	60.0	80.0	80.0	60.0
1983							
Median net worth	**$42.7**	**$6.0**	**$20.1**	**$10.8**	**$51.3**	**$108.0**	**$63.9**
Median value of:							
Total nonfinancial assets	$59.7	$6.2	$39.9	$39.0	$74.3	$91.7	$55.6
Vehicles	5.1	3.6	6.0	3.6	6.3	6.4	3.4
Business	57.0	15.4	49.8	49.0	50.3	93.4	99.6
Investment real estate	43.6	28.0	53.4	37.0	39.0	56.0	43.6
Other assets	6.2	2.8	3.7	11.2	5.1	18.7	8.7
Principal residence	64.7	56.0	62.3	62.3	74.7	74.7	49.8
Percent change, 1983-89							
Median net worth	**10.5%**	**40.0%**	**35.8%**	**-47.2%**	**20.9%**	**-3.2%**	**47.3%**
Median value of:							
Total nonfinancial assets	11.7%	41.9%	66.2%	-41.8%	16.3%	7.2%	21.6%
Vehicles	35.3	19.4	50.0	33.3	47.6	18.8	61.8
Business	-12.3	-45.5	-9.6	-72.7	3.4	-14.3	-50.6
Investment real estate	-10.6	60.7	76.0	24.3	15.4	-23.2	-18.1
Other assets	-19.4	-28.6	8.1	-73.2	17.6	-57.2	31.0
Principal residence	8.2	50.0	34.8	-3.7	7.1	7.1	20.5

Source: Survey of Consumer Finances, Federal Reserve Bulletin, *January 1992*

Households With Debt by Age of Householder, 1983 and 1989

The proportion of American households in debt rose slightly between 1983 and 1989. The greatest increases were for householders aged 45 or older.

(percent of households with selected debts, by age of householder, 1983 and 1989, and percentage point change in households with debt, 1983-89)

1989	total households	under 35	35 to 44	45 to 54	55 to 64	65 to 74	75 or older
Percent with:							
Any debts	72.7%	79.5%	89.6%	85.9%	74.0%	47.9%	23.8%
Home mortgage	38.7	32.8	57.7	56.3	37.5	19.9	8.6
Investment real estate mortgages	7.0	2.6	10.2	12.3	10.7	3.9	1.4
Home equity lines of credit	3.3	1.0	4.3	6.3	6.1	1.0	-
Other lines of credit	3.3	4.5	4.7	4.0	1.9	0.6	-
Credit cards	39.9	44.0	52.4	50.0	34.1	25.4	10.6
Car loans	35.1	37.4	51.5	48.7	29.3	14.0	5.3
Other debt	32.3	45.0	43.0	32.9	24.2	13.4	8.1
1983							
Percent with:							
Any debts	69.6%	79.1%	87.1%	81.0%	67.2%	37.1%	16.8%
Home mortgage	36.9	32.6	58.1	53.5	34.4	15.7	3.7
Investment real estate mortgages	7.6	5.3	11.7	10.4	10.6	3.5	1.2
Home equity lines of credit	0.5	0.4	0.8	0.8	-	-	-
Other lines of credit	11.2	12.6	17.3	13.6	9.6	3.1	-
Credit cards	37.0	38.4	51.5	45.0	37.5	18.2	6.1
Car loans	28.7	36.9	38.4	35.3	21.9	8.4	-
Other debt	29.6	42.3	38.4	31.1	19.0	9.0	6.2
Percentage point change, 1983-89:							
Any debts	3.1	0.4	2.5	4.9	6.8	10.8	7.0
Home mortgage	1.8	0.2	-0.4	2.8	3.1	4.2	4.9
Investment real estate mortgages	-0.6	-2.7	-1.5	1.9	0.1	0.4	0.2
Home equity lines of credit	2.8	0.6	3.5	5.5	-	-	-
Other lines of credit	-7.9	-8.1	-12.6	-9.6	-7.7	-2.5	-
Credit cards	2.9	5.6	0.9	5.0	-3.4	7.2	4.5
Car loans	6.4	0.5	13.1	13.4	7.4	5.6	-
Other debt	2.7	2.7	4.6	1.8	5.2	4.4	1.9

Source: Survey of Consumer Finances, Federal Reserve Bulletin, January 1992

Amount of Household Debt by Age of Householder, 1983 and 1989

Median household debt rose by 13 percent between 1983 and 1989. The biggest increase was for householders aged 75 or older, although their debt levels are small.

(median debt of households having such debts, by age of householder, 1983 and 1989, and percent change in debt level, 1983-89; in thousands of 1989 dollars)	total households	under 35	35 to 44	45 to 54	55 to 64	65 to 74	75 or older
1989							
Median amount of:							
Total debt	$15.2	$11.0	$31.1	$23.7	$10.8	$5.0	$3.0
Home mortgage	32.0	44.0	40.0	26.0	21.0	11.0	4.5
Investment real estate mortgage	30.0	20.0	39.0	21.0	16.3	15.0	18.0
Home equity lines of credit	17.5	18.9	15.0	16.0	30.0	30.0	-
Other lines of credit	2.0	1.7	3.3	1.3	2.0	2.0	-
Credit cards	0.9	1.0	1.2	1.0	0.9	0.5	0.2
Car loans	5.8	5.1	6.6	6.4	5.8	4.0	3.3
Other debt	2.0	2.0	2.0	2.5	1.8	1.1	2.5
1983							
Median amount of:							
Total debt	$13.4	$8.3	$25.4	$16.1	$10.2	$4.9	$1.2
Home mortgage	27.0	34.0	31.9	20.3	15.9	14.1	4.6
Investment real estate mortgage	23.3	23.0	24.2	15.7	29.6	35.6	43.7
Home equity lines of credit	7.5	2.5	30.5	10.0	-	-	-
Other lines of credit	1.2	0.9	1.2	1.4	1.9	0.9	-
Credit cards	0.6	0.6	0.7	0.6	0.6	0.2	0.4
Car loans	3.8	3.2	4.5	4.0	3.7	2.9	-
Other debt	1.6	1.4	2.0	2.3	2.9	0.7	0.4
Percent change, 1983-89							
Median amount of:							
Total debt	13.4%	32.5%	22.4%	47.2%	5.9%	2.0%	150.0%
Home mortgage	18.5	29.4	25.4	28.1	32.1	-22.0	-2.2
Investment real estate mortgage	28.8	-13.0	61.2	33.8	-44.9	-57.9	-58.8
Home equity lines of credit	133.3	656.0	-50.8	60.0	-	-	-
Other lines of credit	66.7	88.9	175.0	-7.1	5.3	122.2	-
Credit cards	50.0	66.7	71.4	66.7	50.0	150.0	-50.0
Car loans	52.6	59.4	46.7	60.0	56.8	37.9	-
Other debt	25.0	42.9	0.0	8.7	-37.9	57.1	525.0

Source: Survey of Consumer Finances, Federal Reserve Bulletin, January 1992

Households With Debt by Income and Housing Status, 1983 and 1989

Affluent households are more likely to have debts than those with smaller incomes. The proportion of affluent households with debts rose between 1983 and 1989.

(percent of households with selected debts, by household income and housing status, 1983 and 1989, and percentage point change in households with debts, 1983-89)

	total households	income					housing status	
		under $10,000	$10,000 to $19,999	$20,000 to $29,999	$30,000 to $49,999	$50,000 or over	own	rent or other
1989								
Percent with:								
Any debt	72.7%	47.2%	58.7%	79.5%	86.5%	91.8%	78.0%	63.1%
Home mortgage	38.7	8.8	21.3	36.8	53.1	72.4	59.8	na
Investment real estate mortgage	7.0	1.0	1.5	4.7	8.8	18.7	9.0	3.4
Home equity lines of credit	3.3	-	1.3	2.4	4.5	7.7	5.0	na
Other lines of credit	3.3	1.5	2.2	1.6	4.1	6.7	2.9	4.0
Credit cards	39.9	15.0	27.3	48.9	55.0	53.1	43.8	32.7
Car loans	35.1	11.1	21.8	39.4	50.9	51.7	39.0	27.9
Other debt	32.3	29.6	31.0	30.0	36.1	34.2	30.7	35.4
1983								
Percent with:								
Any debt	69.6%	41.3%	58.2%	76.6%	85.3%	87.2%	75.1%	60.0%
Home mortgage	36.9	9.9	20.1	34.0	56.4	66.8	58.3	na
Investment real estate mortgage	7.6	1.0	2.6	5.4	9.9	21.3	9.6	4.2
Home equity lines of credit	0.5	-	-	-	0.8	0.7	0.8	na
Other lines of credit	11.2	3.0	7.2	10.7	16.9	18.2	12.0	9.8
Credit cards	37.0	11.9	26.3	45.5	53.0	48.4	41.6	29.1
Car loans	28.7	8.8	21.7	32.9	40.0	40.1	31.0	24.5
Other debt	29.6	24.4	25.1	31.9	34.8	32.1	28.5	31.6
Percentage point change, 1983-89:								
Any debt	3.1	5.9	0.5	2.9	1.2	4.6	2.9	3.1
Home mortgage	1.8	-1.1	1.2	2.8	-3.3	5.6	1.5	na
Investment real estate mortgage	-0.6	0.0	-1.1	-0.7	-1.1	-2.6	-0.6	-0.8
Home equity lines of credit	2.8	-	-	-	3.7	7.0	4.2	na
Other lines of credit	-7.9	-1.5	-5	-9.1	-12.8	-11.5	-9.1	-5.8
Credit cards	2.9	3.1	1.0	3.4	2.0	4.7	2.2	3.6
Car loans	6.4	2.3	0.1	6.5	10.9	11.6	8.0	3.4
Other debt	2.7	5.2	5.9	-1.9	1.3	2.1	2.2	3.8

Source: Survey of Consumer Finances, Federal Reserve Bulletin, January 1992

Amount of Household Debt by Income and Housing Status, 1983 and 1989

The median amount of debt held by Americans increased from 1983 to 1989 in all income categories.

(median debt of households having such debts, by household income and housing status, 1983 and 1989, and percent change in debt level, 1983-89; in thousands of 1989 dollars)

	total households	income					housing status	
		under $10,000	$10,000 to $19,999	$20,000 to $29,999	$30,000 to $49,999	$50,000 or over	own	rent or other
1989								
Median amount of:								
Total debt	$15.2	$1.9	$5.0	$12.5	$26.2	$55.5	$32.0	$3.2
Home mortgage	32.0	7.5	13.0	21.0	33.0	48.0	32.0	na
Investment real estate mortgage	30.0	3.6	24.0	13.5	17.5	47.0	27.0	39.0
Home equity lines of credit	17.5	-	25.0	8.3	16.0	20.0	17.5	na
Other lines of credit	2.0	2.0	0.9	0.5	2.5	3.3	3.0	1.4
Credit cards	0.9	0.3	0.6	0.8	1.0	1.7	1.0	0.8
Car loans	5.8	1.8	3.0	5.5	6.5	7.2	6.6	4.2
Other debt	2.0	1.2	1.3	2.0	2.3	4.0	2.3	1.7
1983								
Median amount of:								
Total debt	$13.4	$1.8	$4.0	$8.5	$21.8	$45.1	$25.5	$2.2
Home mortgage	27.0	13.5	17.6	17.7	28.4	39.1	27.0	na
Investment real estate mortgage	23.3	2.8	10.2	21.4	15.8	40.0	23.3	24.2
Home equity lines of credit	7.5	-	-	-	2.5	24.9	7.5	na
Other lines of credit	1.2	0.5	1.0	0.9	1.2	1.9	1.2	1.0
Credit cards	0.6	0.4	0.5	0.5	0.7	1.0	0.6	0.6
Car loans	3.8	1.6	2.6	3.0	4.0	5.5	4.2	2.8
Other debt	1.6	0.7	0.9	1.4	2.1	5.0	2.2	1.0
Percent change, 1983-89								
Median amount of:								
Total debt	13.4%	5.6%	25.0%	47.1%	20.2%	23.1%	25.5%	45.5%
Home mortgage	18.5	-44.4	-26.1	18.6	16.2	22.8	18.5	na
Investment real estate mortgage	28.8	28.6	135.3	-36.9	10.8	17.5	15.9	61.2
Home equity lines of credit	133.3	-	-	-	540.0	-19.7	133.3	na
Other lines of credit	66.7	300.0	-10.0	-44.4	108.3	73.7	150.0	40.0
Credit cards	50.0	-25.0	20.0	60.0	42.9	70.0	66.7	33.3
Car loans	52.6	12.5	15.4	83.3	62.5	30.9	57.1	50.0
Other debt	25.0	71.4	44.4	42.9	9.5	-20.0	4.5	70.0

Source: Survey of Consumer Finances, Federal Reserve Bulletin, January 1992

Households With Debt by Life-Cycle Stage, 1983 and 1989

Nearly all household segments are likely to have debts, but those most likely to be in debt are married couples with children.

(percent of households with selected debts, by life-cycle stage of householder, 1983 and 1989, and percentage point change in households with debt, 1983-89)

	total households	unmarried, no children	married, no children	under age 55		aged 55 or older	
				unmarried, children	married, children	in labor force	retired
1989							
Percent with:							
Any debt	72.7%	72.8%	89.2%	70.0%	93.6%	79.1%	37.9%
Home mortgage	38.7	18.1	52.0	26.8	63.6	41.2	15.5
Investment real estate mortgage	7.0	5.0	9.8	4.2	9.3	12.0	3.7
Home equity lines of credit	3.3	-	-	1.6	5.4	6.6	1.1
Other lines of credit	3.3	5.6	11.0	2.6	4.0	2.7	0.5
Credit cards	39.9	37.5	57.9	33.4	56.7	43.3	15.2
Car loans	35.1	29.8	50.5	29.9	55.0	32.1	12.5
Other debt	32.3	37.6	49.5	38.4	43.1	21.2	11.5
1983							
Percent with:							
Any debt	69.6%	68.8%	91.1%	70.5%	89.0%	66.7%	33.2%
Home mortgage	36.9	14.8	45.8	31.0	60.0	34.3	13.7
Investment real estate mortgage	7.6	4.3	7.4	5.1	11.2	12.3	2.0
Home equity lines of credit	0.5	-	-	-	0.7	-	-
Other lines of credit	11.2	7.7	17.1	12.8	16.4	10.7	1.8
Credit cards	37.0	33.3	52.8	34.3	49.4	37.3	15.5
Car loans	28.7	21.6	45.0	24.6	45.3	21.7	7.2
Other debt	29.6	35.2	46.0	33.4	40.3	18.6	8.8
Percentage point change, 1983-89:							
Any debt	3.1	4.0	-1.9	-0.5	4.6	12.4	4.7
Home mortgage	1.8	3.3	6.2	-4.2	3.6	6.9	1.8
Investment real estate mortgage	-0.6	0.7	2.4	-0.9	-1.9	-0.3	1.7
Home equity lines of credit	2.8	-	-	-	4.7	-	-
Other lines of credit	-7.9	-2.1	-6.1	-10.2	-12.4	-8.0	-1.3
Credit cards	2.9	4.2	5.1	-0.9	7.3	6.0	-0.3
Car loans	6.4	8.2	5.5	5.3	9.7	10.4	5.3
Other debt	2.7	2.4	3.5	5.0	2.8	2.6	2.7

Source: Survey of Consumer Finances, Federal Reserve Bulletin, *January 1992*

Amount of Household Debt by Life-Cycle Stage, 1983 and 1989

Married couples without children at home carry the most debt, a median of $34,200 in 1989, up from just $15,300 in 1983.

(median debt of households holding such debts, by life-cycle stage of householder, 1983 and 1989, and percent change in debt level, 1983-89; in thousands of 1989 dollars)

				under age 55		aged 55 or older	
	total households	unmarried, no children	married, no children	unmarried, children	married, children	in labor force	retired
1989							
Median amount of:							
Total debt	$15.2	$5.9	$34.2	$7.3	$31.2	$14.0	$5.8
Home mortgage	32.0	50.0	52.5	26.5	38.0	21.0	7.9
Investment real estate mortgage	30.0	53.0	35.0	20.0	31.7	17.0	12.5
Home equity lines of credit	17.5	-	-	16.0	15.0	30.0	4.0
Other lines of credit	2.0	1.4	1.7	3.0	3.0	2.0	1.1
Credit cards	0.9	0.8	0.8	1.0	1.2	0.8	0.5
Car loans	5.8	5.1	7.1	4.3	6.4	4.5	5.8
Other debt	2.0	2.6	4.4	1.5	2.1	2.4	1.8
1983							
Median amount of:							
Total debt	$13.4	$3.6	$15.3	$7.0	$24.0	$12.4	$3.1
Home mortgage	27.0	28.9	38.4	22.5	29.8	17.8	11.8
Investment real estate mortgage	23.3	25.1	43.3	16.4	20.3	32.2	35.6
Home equity lines of credit	7.5	-	-	-	5.0	-	-
Other lines of credit	1.2	1.0	0.9	1.2	1.2	2.4	0.8
Credit cards	0.6	0.5	0.6	0.5	0.7	0.6	0.4
Car loans	3.8	3.3	4.4	2.8	4.0	3.8	3.4
Other debt	1.6	1.6	1.2	1.1	2.0	3.1	0.6
Percent change, 1983-89							
Median amount of:							
Total debt	13.4%	63.9%	123.5%	4.3%	30.0%	12.9%	87.1%
Home mortgage	18.5	73.0	36.7	17.8	27.5	18.0	-33.1
Investment real estate mortgage	28.8	111.2	-19.2	22.0	56.2	-47.2	-64.9
Home equity lines of credit	133.3	-	-	-	200.0	-	-
Other lines of credit	66.7	40.0	88.9	150.0	150.0	-16.7	37.5
Credit cards	50.0	60.0	33.3	100.0	71.4	33.3	25.0
Car loans	52.6	54.5	61.4	53.6	60.0	18.4	70.6
Other debt	25.0	62.5	266.7	36.4	5.0	-22.6	200.0

Source: Survey of Consumer Finances, Federal Reserve Bulletin, *January 1992*

Homeownership Rates by Age of Householder and Household Type, 1973 to 1991

During the past two decades, homeownership rates fell sharply among households headed by people under age 45. Rates rose substantially among householders aged 65 or older.

(percent of households that own a home by age of householder and household type, selected years 1973 to 1991)

	1991	1987	1983	1980	1976	1973	percentage point change 1973-91
All households	**64.0%**	**64.0%**	**64.9%**	**65.6%**	**64.8%**	**64.4%**	**-0.4**
Householder under age 25	15.8	16.1	19.3	21.3	21.0	23.4	-7.6
Single	11.1	11.8	10.9	11.5	7.8	7.7	3.4
Married couple with children	27.0	29.1	32.7	38.8	34.5	38.9	-11.9
Married couple without children	29.1	27.5	30.5	33.6	30.9	26.1	3.0
Single parent	7.8	6.3	7.9	10.1	8.2	13.7	-5.9
Other households	12.1	9.3	11.1	9.9	8.5	7.6	4.5
Householder aged 25 to 34	**42.9**	**45.1**	**47.0**	**52.3**	**52.2**	**51.4**	**-8.5**
Single	24.2	23.2	24.1	24.8	16.0	18.0	6.2
Married couple with children	60.7	62.9	64.7	71.1	69.8	66.8	-6.1
Married couple without children	53.1	54.0	53.5	58.3	49.2	45.4	7.7
Single parent	22.9	22.6	24.5	31.8	28.7	31.7	-8.8
Other households	28.7	27.5	29.1	29.4	25.3	18.0	10.7
Householder aged 35 to 44	**65.6**	**66.9**	**69.6**	**72.3**	**71.4**	**70.7**	**-5.1**
Single	41.0	35.3	37.5	36.8	28.5	28.0	13.0
Married couple with children	80.3	81.2	83.2	85.4	83.0	81.0	-0.7
Married couple without children	75.6	73.9	74.0	75.2	67.3	66.8	8.8
Single parent	44.4	48.6	49.6	50.1	48.0	48.2	-3.8
Other households	47.9	48.5	48.1	53.9	50.8	51.5	-3.6
Householder aged 45 to 64	**77.6**	**78.2**	**78.8**	**78.5**	**77.3**	**75.9**	**1.7**
Single	55.8	54.3	54.2	51.6	48.5	50.7	5.1
Married couple with children	84.6	85.5	86.9	87.7	87.0	85.7	-1.1
Married couple without children	89.8	89.4	89.1	88.4	86.1	83.7	6.1
Single parent	55.9	62.7	57.2	64.5	61.7	61.4	-5.5
Other households	66.1	66.4	68.1	68.0	66.9	66.8	-0.7
Householder aged 65 or older	**76.8**	**75.1**	**74.8**	**72.3**	**70.6**	**69.8**	**7.0**
Single	64.3	61.4	62.0	59.2	56.8	57.8	6.5
Married couple	77.5	88.3	87.3	85.0	83.1	81.5	-4.0
Other households	76.8	77.9	75.9	73.6	73.5	69.3	7.5

Note: Homeownership rates here differ from those in earlier tables in this chapter because they are based on different samples.
Source: Joint Center for Housing Studies of Harvard University, The State of the Nation's Housing: 1992, *Fall 1992.*

Employee Benefits in Small Firms, 1990

In small firms, professional and technical workers are more likely to receive employee benefits than clerical, sales, or production workers.

(percent of full-time employees participating in selected employee benefit programs, private nonfarm industries employing fewer than 100 workers, 1990)

	all employees	professional, technical, and related employees	clerical and sales employees	production and service employees
PAID BENEFITS				
Holidays	84%	95%	91%	75%
Vacations	88	94	93	83
Personal leave	11	17	13	7
Lunch period	8	7	7	8
Rest time	48	42	46	51
Funeral leave	47	57	54	38
Jury duty leave	54	72	62	43
Military leave	21	29	26	15
Sick leave	47	70	61	29
Maternity leave	2	3	3	1
Paternity leave	-	-	-	-
UNPAID BENEFITS				
Maternity leave	17	26	20	12
Paternity leave	8	13	8	5
Sickness and accident insurance	**26**	**25**	**24**	**27**
Wholly employer financed	17	14	15	19
Partly employer financed	9	10	10	9
Long-term disability insurance	**19**	**36**	**25**	**9**
Wholly employer financed	16	30	21	8
Partly employer financed	3	5	4	2
Medical care	**69**	**82**	**75**	**60**
Employee coverage				
Wholly employer financed	40	46	40	37
Partly employer financed	29	36	35	23
Family coverage				
Wholly employer financed	22	23	22	22
Partly employer financed	46	59	53	38
Dental care	**30**	**38**	**35**	**24**
Employee coverage				
Wholly employer financed	17	19	19	15
Partly employer financed	12	18	16	8

(continued)

(continued from previous page)

(percent of full-time employees participating in selected employee benefit programs, private nonfarm industries employing fewer than 100 workers, 1990)

	all employees	professional, technical, and related employees	clerical and sales employees	production and service employees
Family coverage				
Wholly employer financed	11%	11%	12%	11%
Partly employer financed	19	27	23	13
Life insurance	**64**	**79**	**70**	**55**
Wholly employer financed	53	69	60	43
Partly employer financed	11	11	10	11
All retirement	**42**	**49**	**47**	**37**
Defined benefit pension	**20**	**20**	**23**	**18**
Wholly employer financed	19	18	21	18
Partly employer financed	1	2	1	1
Defined contribution*	**31**	**40**	**36**	**24**
Uses of funds				
Retirement	28	36	32	21
Wholly employer financed	16	19	17	15
Partly employer financed	11	17	16	6
Capital accumulation	4	5	4	2
Wholly employer financed	1	2	2	1
Partly employer financed	2	3	3	2
Types of plans				
Savings and thrift	10	16	15	5
Deferred profit sharing	15	17	17	13
Employee stock ownership	1	1	1	-
Money purchase pension	6	9	6	6
Simplified employee pension	1	1	1	-
Stock purchase	-	-	-	-
Cash only profit-sharing	-	-	-	-
Flexible benefits plans	**1**	**3**	**2**	**1**
Reimbursement accounts	**8**	**13**	**9**	**4**
Other benefits				
Free or subsidized parking	86	84	85	88
Nonproduction bonuses	45	42	47	44
Employer assistance for child care	1	2	2	1
Eldercare	2	5	1	1
Wellness programs	6	10	8	4
Employer-subsidized recreation facilities	6	12	6	4
Employee discounts	38	32	46	36
Educational assistance				
Job-related	35	50	41	27
Not job-related	4	8	5	3

The total is less than the sum of the individual items because some employees participated in more than one program.
Source: Bureau of Labor Statistics, Employee Benefits in Small Private Establishments, *1990, Bulletin 2388, September 1991*

Employee Benefits in Medium and Large Firms, 1989

Among employees in medium and large firms, there is little difference in the proportion who receive benefits by occupation. Over 90 percent have employer-provided medical insurance, two-thirds have dental insurance, and over 80 percent have some kind of retirement plan.

(percent of full-time employees participating in selected employee benefit programs, private nonfarm industries employing more than 100 workers, 1989)

	all employees	professional, technical, and related employees	clerical and sales employees	production and service employees
PAID BENEFITS				
Holidays	97%	97%	96%	97%
Vacations	97	98	99	95
Personal leave	22	28	30	14
Lunch period	10	4	4	16
Rest time	71	57	69	80
Funeral leave	84	87	86	80
Jury duty leave	90	95	92	87
Military leave	53	61	57	45
Sick leave	68	93	87	44
Maternity leave	3	4	2	3
Paternity leave	1	2	1	1
UNPAID BENEFITS				
Maternity leave	37	39	37	35
Paternity leave	18	20	17	17
Sickness and accident insurance	**43**	**29**	**29**	**58**
Wholly employer financed	36	22	22	51
Partly employer financed	7	7	7	7
Long-term disability insurance	**45**	**65**	**57**	**27**
Wholly employer financed	35	50	43	23
Partly employer financed	9	15	14	4
Medical care	**92**	**93**	**91**	**93**
Employee coverage				
Wholly employer financed	48	45	41	54
Partly employer financed	44	48	50	39
Family coverage				
Wholly employer financed	31	28	25	37
Partly employer financed	60	64	66	54
Dental care	**66**	**69**	**66**	**65**
Employee coverage				
Wholly employer financed	34	32	31	38
Partly employer financed	32	37	36	27

(continued)

(continued from previous page)

(percent of full-time employees participating in selected employee benefit programs, private nonfarm industries employing more than 100 workers, 1989)

	all employees	professional, technical, and related employees	clerical and sales employees	production and service employees
Family coverage				
Wholly employer financed	25%	23%	21%	28%
Partly employer financed	42	46	46	37
Life insurance	**94**	**95**	**94**	**93**
Wholly employer financed	82	82	81	83
Partly employer financed	12	13	14	11
All retirement	**81**	**85**	**81**	**80**
Defined benefit pension	**63**	**64**	**63**	**63**
Wholly employer financed	60	61	61	60
Partly employer financed	3	3	2	3
Defined contribution*	**48**	**59**	**52**	**40**
Uses of funds				
Retirement	36	43	39	31
Wholly employer financed	14	15	14	12
Partly employer financed	22	28	24	18
Capital accumulation	14	18	14	11
Wholly employer financed	2	1	1	3
Partly employer financed	12	17	13	8
Types of plans				
Savings and thrift	30	41	35	21
Deferred profit sharing	15	13	13	16
Employee stock ownership	3	4	3	3
Money purchase pension	5	8	6	3
Stock purchase	**2**	**3**	**2**	**1**
Cash only profit-sharing	**1**	**1**	**1**	**1**
Flexible benefits plans	**9**	**14**	**15**	**3**
Reimbursement accounts	**23**	**36**	**31**	**11**
Other benefits				
Free or subsidized parking	90	85	86	94
Nonproduction bonuses	27	26	28	28
Employer assistance for child care	5	6	6	3
Eldercare	3	4	3	2
Wellness programs	23	30	25	19
Employer-subsidized recreation facilities	28	36	26	24
Employee discounts	54	53	58	52
Educational assistance				
Job-related	69	81	75	59
Not job-related	19	21	17	19

*The total is less than the sum of the individual items because some employees participated in more than one program.
Source: Bureau of Labor Statistics, Employee Benefits in Medium and Large Firms, 1989, Bulletin 2363, June 1990

Pension Coverage and Participation, 1990

Pension coverage and participation is much higher for employees who work in large firms and for workers in the public sector.

(number and percentage of employees who worked for employers with pension or retirement plans, and who participated in employer/union pension or retirement plan, by selected characteristics in 1990; civilian nonagricultural wage and salary work force; numbers in millions)

	total employed	worked for employer with pension or retirement plan		participated in employer or union-sponsored pension or retirement plan	
		number	*percent*	*number*	*percent*
All workers					
1990	119.3	66.0	55.3%	51.2	42.9%
1989	119.1	64.5	54.2	50.8	42.7
1988	117.7	63.0	53.5	49.0	41.6
Age of employee					
Under age 25	22.6	7.4	33.0	2.8	12.4
25 to 44	63.1	37.8	60.0	30.4	48.2
45 to 64	29.8	19.1	64.0	16.9	56.7
65 or older	3.8	1.6	43.4	1.0	27.9
Sex					
Female	57.2	30.5	53.5	22.1	38.6
Male	62.1	35.5	57.2	29.1	46.9
Annual earnings					
Under $10,000	36.8	10.7	29.1	3.8	10.3
$10,000 to $24,999	43.0	24.5	56.9	19.0	44.2
$25,000 to $49,999	31.2	24.3	78.0	22.2	71.2
$50,000 or over	8.3	6.5	78.3	6.2	74.0
Usual hours worked					
Part-time	25.1	8.1	32.4	3.1	12.5
Full-time	94.2	57.9	61.4	48.1	51.0
Firm size					
Fewer than 25 workers	28.7	5.3	18.6	3.9	13.6
25 to 99	16.5	6.8	41.2	5.2	31.2
100 to 499	18.3	10.9	59.5	8.4	45.6
500 to 999	7.0	5.0	70.9	3.8	54.6
1,000 or more workers	48.7	38.0	78.0	30.0	61.5
Industry					
Private					
Manufacturing	21.2	14.2	66.9	12.0	56.7
Nonmanufacturing	83.3	43.9	52.7	33.3	40.0
Public	5.6	4.9	88.8	4.5	80.7
Other	9.2	3.0	32.2	1.3	14.5

Note: Pension coverage and participation refers to any job held during the year.
Source: Employee Benefit Research Institute, EBRI Databook on Employee Benefits, Second Edition, *Employee Benefit Research Institute, 1992, Washington, D.C.*

7

Poverty Trends

Although poverty among Americans was much higher in the 1960s and earlier decades than it is today, poverty rates in 1991 are far above those of the 1970s—particularly for children. Even when the economic recovery is fully underway, structural changes in the economy may keep poverty rates stubbornly high.

Poverty: Highlights

■ Fourteen percent of Americans had incomes that placed them below the poverty level in 1991, up from an historic low of 11 percent in 1973.

■ There are twice as many poor whites as blacks, but the rate of poverty is three times higher among blacks. In 1991, 33 percent of blacks lived below poverty level, versus 11 percent of whites.

■ By age, those most likely to be poor are children. In 1991, 22 percent of children under the age of 18 were poor, versus 11 percent of people aged 18 to 64 and 12 percent of people aged 65 or older.

Poverty rates for children are rising, while those for people aged 65 or older are falling.

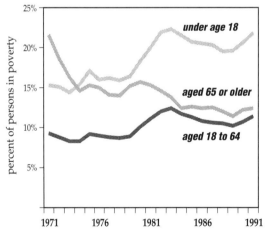

Families Below Poverty Level, 1959 to 1991

The poverty rate among female-headed families is lower today than in the early 1960s. Nevertheless, these families account for over half of all poor families today, up from less than one-fourth in the early 1960s.

(number and percent of families below poverty level by family type, and poverty threshold in current year; families as of the following year; numbers in thousands)

	number of poor families	poverty rate for families	number of poor families with female householder, no spouse present	poverty rate for families with female householder, no spouse present	families with female householder, no spouse present, as a percent of all poor families	poverty threshold for a family of four
1991	7,712	11.5%	4,161	35.6%	53.7%	$13,924
1990	7,098	10.7	3,768	33.4	53.1	13,359
1989	6,784	10.3	3,504	32.2	51.7	12,674
1988	6,874	10.4	3,642	33.4	53.0	12,092
1987	7,005	10.7	3,654	34.2	52.2	11,611
1986	7,023	10.9	3,613	34.6	51.4	11,203
1985	7,223	11.4	3,474	34.0	48.1	10,989
1984	7,277	11.6	3,498	34.5	48.1	10,609
1983	7,647	12.3	3,564	36.0	46.6	10,178
1982	7,512	12.2	3,434	36.3	45.7	9,862
1981	6,851	11.2	3,252	34.6	47.5	9,287
1980	6,217	10.3	2,972	32.7	47.8	8,414
1979	5,461	9.2	2,645	30.4	48.4	7,412
1978	5,280	9.1	2,654	31.4	50.3	6,662
1977	5,311	9.3	2,610	31.7	49.1	6,191
1976	5,311	9.4	2,543	33.0	47.9	5,815
1975	5,450	9.7	2,430	32.5	44.6	5,500
1974	4,922	8.8	2,324	32.1	47.2	5,038
1973	4,828	8.8	2,193	32.2	45.4	4,540
1972	5,075	9.3	2,158	32.7	42.5	4,275
1971	5,303	10.0	2,100	33.9	39.6	4,137
1970	5,260	10.1	1,951	32.5	37.1	3,968
1969	5,008	9.7	1,827	32.7	36.5	3,743
1968	5,047	10.0	1,755	32.3	34.8	3,553
1967	5,667	11.4	1,774	33.3	31.3	3,410
1966	5,784	11.8	1,721	33.1	29.8	3,317
1965	6,721	13.9	1,916	38.4	28.5	3,223
1964	7,160	15.0	1,822	36.4	25.4	3,169
1963	7,554	15.9	1,972	40.4	26.1	3,128
1962	8,077	17.2	2,034	42.9	25.2	3,089
1961	8,391	18.1	1,954	42.1	23.3	3,054
1960	8,243	18.1	1,955	42.4	23.7	3,022
1959	8,320	18.5	1,916	42.6	23.0	2,973

Bureau of the Census, Current Population Reports, Poverty in the United States: 1991, *Series P-60, No. 181, 1992*

All Families Below Poverty Level by Household Type, 1975 to 1991

Poverty rates for male-headed families have increased the most since the 1970s, particularly among those with children. Poverty rates for married couples and for female-headed families have increased more slowly.

(number and percent of families below poverty level by household type and presence of children under age 18; families as of the following year; numbers in thousands)

	all families		married-couple families		female householder, no spouse present		male householder, no spouse present	
	number in poverty	*percent in poverty*	*number in poverty*	*percent in poverty*	*number in poverty*	*percent in poverty*	*number in poverty*	*percent in poverty*
With and without children under age 18								
1991	7,712	11.5%	3,158	6.0%	4,161	35.6%	393	13.0%
1990	7,098	10.7	2,981	5.7	3,768	33.4	349	12.0
1989	6,784	10.3	2,931	5.6	3,504	32.2	348	12.1
1988	6,874	10.4	2,897	5.6	3,642	33.4	336	11.8
1987	7,005	10.7	3,011	5.8	3,654	34.2	340	12.0
1986	7,023	10.9	3,123	6.1	3,613	34.6	287	11.4
1985	7,223	11.4	3,438	6.7	3,474	34.0	311	12.9
1984	7,277	11.6	3,488	6.9	3,498	34.5	292	13.1
1983	7,647	12.3	3,815	7.6	3,564	36.0	268	13.2
1982	7,512	12.2	3,789	7.6	3,434	36.3	290	14.4
1981	6,851	11.2	3,394	6.8	3,252	34.6	205	10.3
1980	6,217	10.3	3,032	6.2	2,972	32.7	213	11.0
1979	5,461	9.2	2,640	5.4	2,645	30.4	176	10.2
1978	5,280	9.1	2,474	5.2	2,654	31.4	152	9.2
1977	5,311	9.3	2,524	5.3	2,610	31.7	177	11.1
1976	5,311	9.4	2,606	5.5	2,543	33.0	162	10.8
1975	5,450	9.7	2,904	6.1	2,430	32.5	116	8.0
With children under age 18								
1991	6,170	17.7%	2,106	8.3%	3,767	47.1%	297	19.6%
1990	5,676	16.4	1,990	7.8	3,426	44.5	260	18.8
1989	5,308	15.5	1,872	7.3	3,190	42.8	246	18.1
1988	5,373	15.7	1,847	7.2	3,294	44.7	232	18.0
1987	5,465	16.1	1,963	7.7	3,281	45.5	221	16.8
1986	5,516	16.3	2,050	8.0	3,264	46.0	202	17.8
1985	5,586	16.7	2,258	8.9	3,131	45.4	197	17.1
1984	5,662	17.2	2,344	9.4	3,124	45.7	194	18.1
1983	5,871	17.9	2,557	10.1	3,122	47.1	192	20.2
1982	5,712	17.5	2,470	9.8	3,059	47.8	184	20.6
1981	5,191	15.9	2,199	8.7	2,877	44.3	115	14.0
1980	4,822	14.7	1,974	7.7	2,703	42.9	144	18.0
1979	4,081	12.6	1,573	6.1	2,392	39.6	116	15.5
1978	4,060	12.8	1,495	5.9	2,462	42.2	103	14.7
1977	4,081	12.9	1,602	6.3	2,384	41.8	95	14.8
1976	4,060	12.9	1,623	6.4	2,343	44.1	94	15.4
1975	4,172	13.3	1,855	7.2	2,252	44.0	65	11.7

Source: Bureau of the Census, Current Population Reports, Poverty in the United States: 1991, *Series P-60, No. 181, 1992*

White Families Below Poverty Level by Household Type, 1975 to 1991

Poverty rates for white families with children have increased slightly since the mid-1970s. The biggest rise has been among male-headed families.

(number and percent of white families below poverty level by household type and presence of children under age 18; families as of the following year; numbers in thousands)

With and without children under age 18	all families		married-couple families		female householder, no spouse present		male householder, no spouse present	
	number in poverty	percent in poverty	number in poverty	percent in poverty	number in poverty	percent in poverty	number in poverty	percent in poverty
1991	5,022	8.8%	2,573	5.5%	2,192	28.4%	257	10.8%
1990	4,622	8.1	2,386	5.1	2,010	26.8	226	9.9
1989	4,409	7.8	2,329	5.0	1,858	25.4	223	9.7
1988	4,471	7.9	2,294	4.9	1,945	26.5	231	10.2
1987	4,567	8.1	2,382	5.1	1,961	26.9	224	9.8
1986	4,811	8.6	2,591	5.6	2,041	28.2	179	8.8
1985	4,983	9.1	2,815	6.1	1,950	27.4	218	11.2
1984	4,925	9.1	2,858	6.3	1,878	27.1	189	10.4
1983	5,220	9.7	3,125	6.9	1,926	28.3	168	10.4
1982	5,118	9.6	3,104	6.9	1,813	27.9	201	12.2
1981	4,670	8.8	2,712	6.0	1,814	27.4	145	8.8
1980	4,195	8.0	2,437	5.4	1,609	25.7	149	9.4
1979	3,581	6.9	2,099	4.7	1,350	22.3	132	9.2
1978	3,523	6.9	2,033	4.7	1,319	23.5	99	7.3
1977	3,540	7.0	2,028	4.7	1,400	24.0	112	8.8
1976	3,560	7.1	2,071	4.8	1,379	25.2	110	9.0
1975	3,838	7.7	2,363	5.5	1394	25.9	81	6.9
With children under age 18								
1991	3,880	13.7%	1,715	7.7%	1,969	39.6%	196	16.5%
1990	3,553	12.6	1,572	7.1	1,814	37.9	167	16.0
1989	3,290	11.8	1,457	6.5	1,671	36.1	162	15.0
1988	3,321	11.9	1,434	6.4	1,740	38.2	147	14.5
1987	3,433	12.3	1,538	6.9	1,742	38.3	153	14.6
1986	3,637	13.0	1,692	7.5	1,812	39.8	132	14.5
1985	3,695	13.3	1,827	8.2	1,730	38.7	138	14.9
1984	3,679	13.4	1,879	8.5	1,682	38.8	117	13.6
1983	3,859	14.1	2,060	9.2	1,676	39.8	123	16.8
1982	3,709	13.7	2,005	9.0	1,584	39.3	120	17.4
1981	3,362	12.4	1,723	7.7	1,564	36.9	75	11.6
1980	3,078	11.2	1,544	6.8	1,433	35.9	100	16.0
1979	2,619	9.2	1,216	5.3	1,211	31.3	82	14.1
1978	2,513	9.3	1,185	5.2	1,268	33.5	60	11.4
1977	2,572	9.6	1,256	5.5	1,261	33.8	55	11.3
1976	2,566	9.6	1,242	5.4	1,260	36.4	64	13.2
1975	2,776	10.3	1,456	6.3	1,272	37.3	48	11.0

Source: Bureau of the Census, Current Population Reports, Poverty in the United States: 1991, Series P-60, No. 181, 1992

Black Families Below Poverty Level by Household Type, 1975 to 1991

POVERTY

Black married couples with children are less likely to be poor today than in the mid-1970s. Black male-headed families with children are more likely to be poor, however, while poverty rates have remained stable among black female-headed families with children.

(number and percent of black families below poverty level by household type and presence of children under age 18; families as of the following year; numbers in thousands)

	all families		married-couple families		female householder, no spouse present		male householder, no spouse present	
	number in poverty	percent in poverty	number in poverty	percent in poverty	number in poverty	percent in poverty	number in poverty	percent in poverty
With and without children under age 18								
1991	2,343	30.4%	399	11.0%	1,834	51.2%	110	21.9%
1990	2,193	29.3	448	12.6	1,648	48.1	97	20.6
1989	2,077	27.8	443	11.8	1,524	46.5	110	24.7
1988	2,089	28.2	421	11.3	1,579	49.0	88	18.9
1987	2,117	29.4	439	11.9	1,577	51.1	101	23.4
1986	1,987	28.0	403	10.8	1,488	50.1	96	24.9
1985	1,983	28.7	447	12.2	1,452	50.5	84	22.9
1984	2,094	30.9	479	13.8	1,533	51.7	82	23.8
1983	2,161	32.3	535	15.5	1,541	53.7	85	24.0
1982	2,158	33.0	543	15.6	1,535	56.2	79	25.6
1981	1,972	30.8	543	15.4	1,377	52.9	52	19.1
1980	1,826	28.9	474	14.0	1,301	49.4	52	17.7
1979	1,722	27.8	453	13.2	1,234	49.4	35	13.7
1978	1,622	27.5	366	11.3	1,208	50.6	48	17.6
1977	1,637	28.2	429	13.1	1,162	51.0	46	17.1
1976	1,617	27.9	450	13.2	1,122	52.2	45	18.2
1975	1,513	27.1	479	14.3	1,004	50.1	30	13.0
With children under age 18								
1991	2,016	39.2%	263	12.4%	1,676	60.5%	77	31.7%
1990	1,887	37.2	301	14.3	1,513	56.1	73	27.3
1989	1,783	35.4	291	13.3	1,415	53.9	77	33.8
1988	1,802	36.0	272	12.5	1,452	56.2	78	31.7
1987	1,788	36.6	290	13.2	1,437	58.6	61	27.5
1986	1,699	35.4	257	11.5	1,384	58.0	58	31.5
1985	1,670	36.0	281	12.9	1,336	58.9	53	29.0
1984	1,758	39.0	331	16.6	1,364	58.4	62	35.5
1983	1,789	39.9	369	18.0	1,362	60.7	58	31.1
1982	1,819	40.7	360	17.2	1,401	63.7	58	32.7
1981	1,652	37.1	357	16.2	1,261	59.5	34	25.0
1980	1,583	35.5	333	15.5	1,217	56.0	34	24.0
1979	1,441	33.5	286	13.7	1,129	54.7	26	18.4
1978	1,431	34.4	247	12.0	1,144	58.4	40	25.5
1977	1,406	34.2	295	14.1	1,081	57.5	30	21.3
1976	1,382	34.2	311	14.5	1,043	58.6	28	23.3
1975	1,314	33.9	349	16.5	949	57.5	16	14.8

Source: Bureau of the Census, Current Population Reports, Poverty in the United States: 1991, *Series P-60, No. 181, 1992*

Hispanic Families Below Poverty Level by Household Type, 1975 to 1991

Hispanic married couples and male-headed families are more likely to be poor today than in the mid-1970s. Hispanic female-headed families are less likely to be poor.

(number and percent of Hispanic families below poverty level by household type and presence of children under age 18; families as of the following year; numbers in thousands)

	all families		married-couple families		female householder, no spouse present		male householder, no spouse present	
	number in poverty	percent in poverty	number in poverty	percent in poverty	number in poverty	percent in poverty	number in poverty	percent in poverty
With and without children under age 18								
1991	1,372	26.5%	674	19.1%	627	49.7%	71	18.5%
1990	1,244	25.0	605	17.5	573	48.3	66	19.4
1989	1,133	23.4	549	16.2	530	47.5	54	16.3
1988	1,141	23.7	547	16.1	546	49.1	48	15.2
1987	1,168	25.5	556	17.4	565	52.2	47	15.8
1986	1,085	24.7	518	16.6	528	51.2	39	15.5
1985	1,074	25.5	505	17.0	521	53.1	48	18.4
1984	991	25.2	469	16.6	483	53.4	39	18.4
1983	981	25.9	437	17.7	454	52.8	40	22.6
1982	916	27.2	465	19.0	425	55.4	26	17.0
1981	792	24.0	366	15.1	399	53.2	27	19.2
1980	751	23.2	363	15.3	362	51.3	26	16.0
1979	614	20.3	298	13.1	300	49.2	16	11.8
1978	559	20.4	248	11.9	288	53.1	23	20.9
1977	591	21.4	280	13.3	301	53.6	10	10.1
1976	598	23.1	312	15.8	275	53.1	11	12.5
1975	627	25.1	335	17.7	279	53.6	13	16.0

Note: Hispanics may be of any race. Numbers for families with children under age 18 not shown because data are not available.
Source: Bureau of the Census, Current Population Reports, Poverty in the United States: 1991, Series P-60, No. 181, 1992

Persons Below Poverty Level, by Selected Characteristics, 1990 and 1991

Poverty rates rose for people of all ages, family types, and races between 1990 and 1991 as the recession took its toll.

(number in poverty and poverty rate of persons by age, family status, sex, race, and Hispanic origin; numbers in thousands; persons as of the following year)

	1991			1990			1990-91 difference	
	total persons	number below poverty level	percent below poverty level	total	number below poverty level	percent below poverty level	number below poverty level	percent below poverty level
Total	251,179	35,708	14.2%	248,644	33,585	13.5%	2,123	0.7%
Age								
Under age 15	55,936	12,514	22.4	55,124	11,802	21.4	712	1.0
Aged 15 to 24	34,416	5,947	17.3	34,825	5,594	16.1	354	1.2
Aged 25 to 44	82,064	9,160	11.2	81,570	8,469	10.4	691	0.8
Aged 45 to 54	27,023	2,167	8.0	25,686	2,002	7.8	165	0.2
Aged 55 to 59	10,620	1,019	9.6	10,692	963	9.0	56	0.6
Aged 60 to 64	10,530	1,120	10.6	10,654	1,098	10.3	22	0.3
Aged 65 or older	30,590	3,781	12.4	30,093	3,658	12.2	123	0.2
Family status								
In families	212,716	27,143	12.8	210,967	25,232	12.0	1,911	0.8
Related children under age 18	64,800	13,658	21.1	63,908	12,715	19.9	943	1.2
Related children under age 6	22,853	5,483	24.0	22,629	5,198	23.0	285	1.0
Unrelated individuals	36,839	7,773	21.1	36,056	7,446	20.7	328	0.5
Men	17,395	3,012	17.3	16,912	2,857	16.9	155	0.4
Women	19,445	4,762	24.5	19,144	4,589	24.0	173	0.5
Race and Hispanic origin								
White	210,121	23,747	11.3	208,611	22,326	10.7	1,421	0.6
Related children under age 18	51,631	8,321	16.1	51,028	7,696	15.1	624	1.0
Black	31,312	10,242	32.7	30,806	9,837	31.9	405	0.8
Related children under age 18	10,178	4,637	45.6	9,980	4,412	44.2	225	1.4
Hispanic	22,068	6,339	28.7	21,405	6,006	28.1	333	0.7
Related children under age 18	7,473	2,977	39.8	7,300	2,750	37.7	227	2.2

Note: Because Hispanics may be of any race, the number of persons by race and Hispanic origin will not add to total persons. Unrelated individuals are people aged 15 or older who are not living with any relatives, even if they are living in a household with other people. The poverty status of unrelated individuals is determined independently of other household members' incomes.
Source: Bureau of the Census, Current Population Reports, Poverty in the United States: 1991, Series P-60, No. 181, 1992

Persons Below Poverty Level by Race and Hispanic Origin, 1959 to 1991

Poverty rates among all Americans fell from 22 percent in 1960 to just 11 percent by the late 1970s. Today, 14 percent of Americans are poor, including one-third of blacks.

(number and percent of persons below poverty level by race and Hispanic origin; persons as of the following year; numbers in thousands)

	total persons		white		black		Hispanic	
	number	percent	number	percent	number	percent	number	percent
1991	35,708	14.2%	23,747	11.3%	10,242	32.7%	6,339	28.7%
1990	33,585	13.5	22,326	10.7	9,837	31.9	6,006	28.1
1989	31,528	12.8	20,785	10.0	9,302	30.7	5,430	26.2
1988	31,745	13.0	20,715	10.1	9,356	31.3	5,357	26.7
1987	32,221	13.4	21,195	10.4	9,520	32.4	5,422	28.0
1986	32,370	13.6	22,183	11.0	8,983	31.1	5,117	27.3
1985	33,064	14.0	22,860	11.4	8,926	31.3	5,236	29.0
1984	33,700	14.4	22,955	11.5	9,490	33.8	4,806	28.4
1983	35,303	15.2	23,984	12.1	9,882	35.7	4,633	28.0
1982	34,398	15.0	23,517	12.0	9,697	35.6	4,301	29.9
1981	31,822	14.0	21,553	11.1	9,173	34.2	3,713	26.5
1980	29,272	13.0	19,699	10.2	8,579	32.5	3,491	25.7
1979	26,072	11.7	17,214	9.0	8,050	31.0	2,921	21.8
1978	24,497	11.4	16,259	8.7	7,625	30.6	2,607	21.6
1977	24,720	11.6	16,416	8.9	7,726	31.3	2,700	22.4
1976	24,975	11.8	16,713	9.1	7,595	31.1	2,783	24.7
1975	25,877	12.3	17,770	9.7	7,545	31.3	2,991	26.9
1974	23,370	11.2	15,736	8.6	7,182	30.3	2,575	23.0
1973	22,973	11.1	15,142	8.4	7,388	31.4	2,366	21.9
1972	24,460	11.9	16,203	9.0	7,710	33.3	-	-
1971	25,559	12.5	17,780	9.9	7,396	32.5	-	-
1970	25,420	12.6	17,484	9.9	7,548	33.5	-	-
1969	24,147	12.1	16,659	9.5	7,095	32.2	-	-
1968	25,389	12.8	17,395	10.0	7,616	34.7	-	-
1967	27,769	14.2	18,983	11.0	8,486	39.3	-	-
1966	28,510	14.7	19,290	11.3	8,867	41.8	-	-
1965	33,185	17.3	22,496	13.3	-	-	-	-
1964	36,055	19.0	24,957	14.9	-	-	-	-
1963	36,436	19.5	25,238	15.3	-	-	-	-
1962	38,625	21.0	26,672	16.4	-	-	-	-
1961	39,628	21.9	27,890	17.4	-	-	-	-
1960	39,851	22.2	28,309	17.8	-	-	-	-
1959	39,490	22.4	28,484	18.1	9,927	55.1	-	-

Note: Because Hispanics may be of any race, the number of persons by race and Hispanic origin will not add to total persons.
Source: Bureau of the Census, Current Population Reports, Poverty in the United States: 1991, Series P-60, No. 181, 1992

All Persons Below Poverty Level by Age, 1959 to 1991

Poverty rates among children have been rising since the early 1970s. Poverty rates among the elderly have fallen since the 1960s.

(number and percent of persons below poverty level by age; persons as of the following year; numbers in thousands)

	under age 18		aged 18 to 64		aged 65 or older	
	number	percent	number	percent	number	percent
1991	14,341	21.8%	17,585	11.4%	3,781	12.4%
1990	13,431	20.6	16,496	10.7	3,658	12.2
1989	12,590	19.6	15,575	10.2	3,363	11.4
1988	12,455	19.5	15,809	10.5	3,481	12.0
1987	12,843	20.3	15,815	10.6	3,563	12.5
1986	12,876	20.5	16,017	10.8	3,477	12.4
1985	13,010	20.7	16,598	11.3	3,456	12.6
1984	13,420	21.5	16,952	11.7	3,330	12.4
1983	13,911	22.3	17,767	12.4	3,625	13.8
1982	13,647	21.9	17,000	12.0	3,751	14.6
1981	12,505	20.0	15,464	11.1	3,853	15.3
1980	11,543	18.3	13,858	10.1	3,871	15.7
1979	10,377	16.4	12,014	8.9	3,682	15.2
1978	9,931	15.9	11,332	8.7	3,233	14.0
1977	10,288	16.2	11,316	8.8	3,177	14.1
1976	10,273	16.0	11,389	9.0	3,313	15.0
1975	11,104	17.1	11,456	9.2	3,317	15.3
1974	10,156	15.4	10,132	8.3	3,085	14.6
1973	9,642	14.4	9,977	8.3	3,354	16.3
1972	10,284	15.1	10,438	8.8	3,738	18.6
1971	10,551	15.3	10,735	9.3	4,273	21.6
1970	10,440	15.1	10,187	9.0	4,793	24.6
1969	9,691	14.0	9,669	8.7	4,787	25.3
1968	10,954	15.6	9,803	9.0	4,632	25.0
1967	11,656	16.6	10,725	10.0	5,388	29.5
1966	12,389	17.6	11,007	10.5	5,114	28.5
1965	14,676	21.0	-	-	-	-
1964	16,051	23.0	-	-	-	-
1963	16,005	23.1	-	-	-	-
1962	16,963	25.0	-	-	-	-
1961	16,909	25.6	-	-	-	-
1960	17,634	26.9	-	-	-	-
1959	17,552	27.3	16,457	17.0	5,481	35.2

Source: Bureau of the Census, Current Population Reports, Poverty in the United States: 1991, *Series P-60, No. 181, 1992*

White Persons Below Poverty Level by Age, 1959 to 1991

Poverty rates among elderly whites are half what they were in the 1960s. Poverty rates among white children are at their highest level since the recession of the early 1980s.

(number and percent of white persons below poverty level by age; persons as of the following year; numbers in thousands)

	under age 18		aged 18 to 64		aged 65 or older	
	number	*percent*	*number*	*percent*	*number*	*percent*
1991	8,848	16.8%	12,098	9.3%	2,802	10.3%
1990	8,232	15.9	11,387	8.8	2,707	10.1
1989	7,599	14.8	10,647	8.3	2,539	9.6
1988	7,435	14.5	10,687	8.3	2,593	10.0
1987	7,788	15.3	10,703	8.4	2,704	10.6
1986	8,209	16.1	11,285	9.0	2,689	10.7
1985	8,253	16.2	11,909	9.5	2,698	11.0
1984	8,472	16.7	11,904	9.6	2,579	10.7
1983	8,862	17.5	12,347	10.0	2,776	11.7
1982	8,678	17.0	11,971	9.8	2,870	12.4
1981	7,785	15.2	10,790	8.9	2,978	13.1
1980	7,181	13.9	9,478	8.0	3,042	13.6
1979	6,193	11.8	8,110	6.9	2,911	13.3
1978	5,831	11.3	7,897	6.9	2,530	12.1
1977	6,097	11.6	7,893	7.0	2,426	11.9
1976	6,189	11.6	7,890	7.1	2,633	13.2
1975	6,927	12.7	8,210	7.5	2,634	13.4
1974	6,223	11.2	7,053	6.6	2,460	12.8
1973	-	-	-	-	2,698	14.4
1972	-	-	-	-	3,072	16.8
1971	-	-	-	-	3,605	19.9
1970	-	-	-	-	4,011	22.6
1969	-	-	-	-	4,052	23.3
1968	-	-	-	-	3,939	23.1
1967	-	-	-	-	4,646	27.7
1966	-	-	-	-	4,357	26.4
1965	-	-	-	-	-	-
1960	-	-	-	-	-	-
1959	-	-	-	-	4,744	33.1

Source: Bureau of the Census, Current Population Reports, Poverty in the United States: 1991, Series P-60, No. 181, 1992

Black Persons Below Poverty Level by Age, 1959 to 1991

Poverty rates among the black elderly are lower today than in the mid-1970s, while rates are higher for blacks under the age of 65.

(number and percent distribution of black persons below poverty level by age; persons as of the following year; numbers in thousands)

	under age 18		aged 18 to 64		aged 65 or older	
	number	*percent*	*number*	*percent*	*number*	*percent*
1991	4,755	45.9%	4,607	25.1%	880	33.8%
1990	4,550	44.8	4,427	24.5	860	33.8
1989	4,375	43.7	4,164	23.3	763	30.7
1988	4,296	43.5	4,275	24.4	785	32.2
1987	4,385	45.1	4,361	25.3	774	32.4
1986	4,148	43.1	4,113	24.3	722	31.0
1985	4,157	43.6	4,052	24.3	717	31.5
1984	4,413	46.6	4,368	26.7	710	31.7
1983	4,398	46.7	4,694	29.2	791	36.0
1982	4,472	47.6	4,415	28.1	811	38.2
1981	4,237	45.2	4,117	26.8	820	39.0
1980	3,961	42.3	3,835	25.6	783	38.1
1979	3,833	41.2	3,478	23.8	740	36.2
1978	3,830	41.5	3,133	22.7	662	33.9
1977	3,888	41.8	3,137	23.3	701	36.3
1976	3,787	40.6	3,163	23.9	644	34.8
1975	3,925	41.7	2,968	23.1	652	36.3
1974	3,755	39.8	3,836	22.6	591	34.3
1973	-	-	-	-	620	37.1
1972	-	-	-	-	640	39.9
1971	-	-	-	-	623	39.3
1970	-	-	-	-	683	48.0
1969	-	-	-	-	689	50.2
1968	-	-	-	-	655	47.7
1967	-	-	-	-	715	53.3
1966	-	-	-	-	722	55.1
1959	-	-	-	-	711	62.5

Source: Bureau of the Census, Current Population Reports, Poverty in the United States: 1991, *Series P-60, No. 181, 1992*

Hispanic Persons Below Poverty Level by Age, 1973 to 1991

Poverty rates are slightly lower for elderly Hispanics today than they were in the 1970s. But poverty rates among Hispanics under age 65 are higher.

(number and percent of Hispanic persons below poverty level by age; persons as of the following year; numbers in thousands)

	under age 18		aged 18 to 64		aged 65 or older	
	number	*percent*	*number*	*percent*	*number*	*percent*
1991	3,094	40.4%	3,009	22.7%	237	20.8%
1990	2,865	38.4	2,896	22.5	245	22.5
1989	2,603	36.2	2,616	20.9	211	20.6
1988	2,631	37.6	2,501	20.7	225	22.4
1987	2,670	39.3	2,509	21.4	243	27.5
1986	2,507	37.7	2,406	21.5	204	22.5
1985	2,606	40.3	2,411	22.6	219	23.9
1984	2,376	39.2	2,254	22.5	176	21.5
1983	2,312	38.1	2,148	22.5	173	22.1
1982	2,181	39.5	1,963	23.8	159	26.6
1981	1,925	35.9	1,642	20.3	146	25.7
1980	1,749	33.2	1,563	20.2	179	30.8
1979	1,535	28.0	1,232	16.8	154	26.8
1978	1,384	27.6	1,098	16.8	125	23.2
1977	1,422	28.3	1,164	17.9	113	21.9
1976	1,443	30.2	1,212	20.1	128	27.7
1975	-	-	-	-	137	32.6
1974	-	-	-	-	117	28.9
1973	-	-	-	-	95	24.9

Note: Hispanics may be of any race.
Source: Bureau of the Census, Current Population Reports, Poverty in the United States: 1991, *Series P-60, No. 181, 1992*

Persons Below Poverty Level by Sex, Age, Race, and Hispanic Origin, 1991

Among whites, blacks, and Hispanics, poverty rates are highest among children and lowest among the middle-aged.

(number and percent of people in poverty by race and Hispanic origin; persons as of 1992; numbers in thousands)

	all persons		white		black		Hispanic	
	number in poverty	percent in poverty	number in poverty	percent in poverty	number in poverty	percent in poverty	number in poverty	percent in poverty
Both sexes								
Total	35,708	14.2%	23,747	11.3%	10,242	32.7%	6,339	28.7%
Under age 18	14,341	21.8	8,848	16.8	4,755	45.9	3,094	40.4
Aged 18 to 24	4,120	16.9	2,791	14.0	1,123	31.9	771	27.6
Aged 25 to 34	5,568	13.1	3,870	11.0	1,428	26.3	1,026	24.1
Aged 35 to 44	3,592	9.1	2,384	7.1	988	22.1	656	20.7
Aged 45 to 54	2,167	8.0	1,541	6.6	544	19.5	328	18.1
Aged 55 to 59	1,019	9.6	716	7.9	246	21.3	113	17.0
Aged 60 to 64	1,120	10.6	796	8.7	278	27.5	115	19.6
Aged 65 or older	3,781	12.4	2,802	10.3	880	33.8	237	20.8
Aged 65 to 74	1,961	10.6	1,345	8.2	547	32.9	137	18.8
Aged 75 or older	1,820	15.0	1,457	13.3	333	35.3	100	24.3
Men								
Total	15,082	12.3%	10,079	9.8%	4,197	28.5%	2,900	26.2%
Under age 18	7,205	21.3	4,456	16.5	2,382	45.2	1,572	40.5
Aged 18 to 24	1,633	13.5	1,132	11.4	395	23.9	331	23.2
Aged 25 to 34	2,049	9.7	1,505	8.5	432	17.2	400	18.0
Aged 35 to 44	1,493	7.7	1,061	6.3	340	16.8	280	17.6
Aged 45 to 54	894	6.8	669	5.9	195	15.8	142	16.5
Aged 55 to 59	387	7.6	271	6.2	87	16.2	60	17.8
Aged 60 to 64	406	8.2	293	6.7	95	21.6	42	16.2
Aged 65 or older	1,015	7.9	693	6.1	271	25.6	72	15.4
Aged 65 to 74	632	7.6	407	5.6	193	26.1	42	13.4
Aged 75 or older	383	8.5	286	7.0	78	24.6	30	19.3
Women								
Total	20,626	16.0%	13,668	12.7%	6,044	36.5%	3,439	31.2%
Under age 18	7,136	22.2	4,392	17.2	2,373	46.7	1,521	40.4
Aged 18 to 24	2,487	20.1	1,659	16.5	728	39.1	440	32.1
Aged 25 to 34	3,519	16.5	2,365	13.5	996	34.1	626	31.0
Aged 35 to 44	2,099	10.5	1,323	7.9	648	26.6	375	23.9
Aged 45 to 54	1,273	9.2	872	7.4	349	22.5	186	19.5
Aged 55 to 59	632	11.5	444	9.4	159	25.8	53	16.2
Aged 60 to 64	714	12.7	503	10.4	183	32.0	73	22.3
Aged 65 or older	2,766	15.5	2,109	13.3	609	39.3	166	24.5
Aged 65 to 74	1,329	13.1	939	10.4	355	38.3	96	22.7
Aged 75 or older	1,436	18.9	1,171	17.0	254	40.8	70	27.4

Note: Because Hispanics may be of any race, the number of persons by race and Hispanic origin will not add to total persons.
Source: Bureau of the Census, Current Population Reports, Poverty in the United States: 1991, *Series P-60, No. 181, 1992*

All Persons Below Poverty Level by Education, 1991

Poverty is rare among people with a college degree. In contrast, one in four high school drop-outs is poor.

(percent of persons aged 25 or older below poverty level by sex, age, and education; persons as of 1992)

	all educational levels	no high school diploma	high school diploma, no college	some college, less than bachelor's degree	bachelor's degree or more
Both sexes					
Total	10.7%	25.2%	9.6%	6.5%	3.1%
Aged 25 to 34	13.1	36.5	13.8	8.3	3.5
Aged 35 to 54	8.6	25.9	8.1	5.9	2.7
Aged 55 to 64	10.1	21.7	7.5	5.6	2.8
Aged 65 or older	12.4	21.0	8.1	5.0	3.8
Aged 65 to 74	10.6	19.6	7.3	4.4	3.0
Aged 75 or older	15.0	22.5	9.6	6.1	5.5
Men					
Total	8.2%	19..0%	7.4%	5.1%	2.9%
Aged 25 to 34	9.7	26.1	9.4	6.5	3.6
Aged 35 to 54	7.3	21.0	7.3	4.9	2.7
Aged 55 to 64	7.9	16.9	6.0	4.4	2.1
Aged 65 or older	7.9	14.3	4.7	2.6	2.5
Aged 65 to 74	7.6	14.7	5.1	2.8	1.9
Aged 75 or older	8.5	13.6	4.0	2.2	4.1
Women					
Total	13.1%	30.7%	11.3%	7.8%	3.4%
Aged 25 to 34	16.5	47.7	18.3	10.0	3.5
Aged 35 to 54	9.9	30.6	8.7	6.8	2.8
Aged 55 to 64	12.1	26.3	8.5	6.6	3.7
Aged 65 or older	15.5	25.9	10.0	6.8	5.6
Aged 65 to 74	13.1	23.9	8.7	5.7	4.8
Aged 75 or older	18.9	27.8	12.4	8.6	6.7

Source: Bureau of the Census, Current Population Reports, Poverty in the United States: 1991, *Series P-60, No. 181, 1992*

White Persons Below Poverty Level by Education, 1991

Fewer than 10 percent of whites who have at least some college experience are poor, regardless of age.

(percent of white persons aged 25 or older below poverty level by sex, age, and education; persons as of 1992)

	all educational levels	no high school diploma	high school diploma, no college	some college, less than bachelor's degree	bachelor's degree or more
Both sexes					
Total	8.8%	21.8%	7.8%	5.5%	2.6%
Aged 25 to 34	11.0	33.4	11.1	7.3	2.7
Aged 35 to 54	6.9	23.0	6.2	4.7	2.3
Aged 55 to 64	8.3	18.1	6.6	4.7	2.5
Aged 65 or older	10.3	17.4	7.3	4.9	3.7
Aged 65 to 74	8.2	14.9	6.3	4.2	3.0
Aged 75 or older	13.3	20.0	9.2	6.1	4.9
Men					
Total	6.8%	16.6%	6.3%	4.4%	2.3%
Aged 25 to 34	8.5	24.3	8.2	5.9	2.5
Aged 35 to 54	6.1	19.7	5.9	4.0	2.3
Aged 55 to 64	6.5	14.0	5.4	3.9	1.9
Aged 65 or older	6.1	10.8	4.1	2.5	2.2
Aged 65 to 74	5.6	10.3	4.2	2.7	2.0
Aged 75 or older	7.0	11.5	3.9	2.1	2.8
Women					
Total	10.6%	26.6%	8.9%	6.4%	3.0%
Aged 25 to 34	13.5	43.6	14.1	8.5	2.9
Aged 35 to 54	7.7	26.2	6.4	5.3	2.4
Aged 55 to 64	9.9	22.2	7.5	5.3	3.3
Aged 65 or older	13.3	22.2	9.1	6.6	5.7
Aged 65 to 74	10.4	19.0	7.5	5.4	4.8
Aged 75 or older	17.0	25.1	11.9	8.6	6.9

Source: Bureau of the Census, Current Population Reports, Poverty in the United States: 1991, *Series P-60, No. 181, 1992*

Black Persons Below Poverty Level by Education, 1991

Poverty rates are dramatically higher among black high school dropouts than among those with college experience. Poverty is rare among black college graduates.

(percent of black persons aged 25 or older below poverty level by sex, age, and education; persons as of 1992)

	all educational levels	no high school diploma	high school diploma, no college	some college, less than bachelor's degree	bachelor's degree or more
Both sexes					
Total	25.0%	40.3%	23.6%	14.6%	5.2%
Aged 25 to 34	26.3	51.3	28.1	15.2	6.0
Aged 35 to 54	21.1	37.7	21.1	14.8	4.8
Aged 55 to 64	24.2	34.0	17.0	15.6	3.3
Aged 65 or older	33.8	40.7	24.5	6.9	7.0
Aged 65 to 74	32.9	41.5	25.1	5.5	3.7
Aged 75 or older	35.3	39.6	22.4	-	-
Men					
Total	18.2%	28.9%	16.2%	10.7%	6.3%
Aged 25 to 34	17.2	34.6	16.2	10.4	9.2
Aged 35 to 54	16.4	25.7	17.1	12.2	5.1
Aged 55 to 64	18.6	26.8	10.8	10.6	1.7
Aged 65 or older	25.6	30.6	18.7	2.0	-
Aged 65 to 74	26.1	32.9	20.9	1.1	-
Aged 75 or older	24.6	26.3	-	-	-
Women					
Total	30.5%	49.9%	29.8%	17.4%	4.3%
Aged 25 to 34	34.1	65.1	39.6	18.7	3.2
Aged 35 to 54	25.0	48.3	24.6	16.6	4.6
Aged 55 to 64	28.7	40.9	21.3	18.9	4.8
Aged 65 or older	39.3	48.1	27.1	11.5	6.0
Aged 65 to 74	38.3	49.0	27.2	-	-
Aged 75 or older	40.8	47.1	26.6	-	-

Source: Bureau of the Census, Current Population Reports, Poverty in the United States: 1991, *Series P-60, No. 181, 1992*

Hispanic Persons Below Poverty Level by Education, 1991

One-third of Hispanics who dropped out of high school are poor. In contrast, just 6 percent of Hispanic college graduates are poor.

(percent of Hispanic persons aged 25 or older below poverty level by sex, age, and education; persons as of 1992)

	all educational levels	no high school diploma	high school diploma, no college	some college, less than bachelor's degree	bachelor's degree or more
Both sexes					
Total	21.3%	32.0%	15.2%	8.8%	6.3%
Aged 25 to 34	24.1	38.2	18.8	10.3	7.4
Aged 35 to 54	19.7	31.5	13.7	8.0	5.8
Aged 55 to 64	18.2	26.1	10.0	6.1	3.5
Aged 65 or older	20.8	25.0	9.3	-	-
Aged 65 to 74	18.8	23.3	8.7	-	-
Aged 75 or older	24.3	27.9	-	-	-
Men					
Total	17.3%	26.2%	13.5%	6.6%	4.7%
Aged 25 to 34	18.0	28.2	14.3	7.1	5.5
Aged 35 to 54	17.2	27.1	13.8	6.0	5.0
Aged 55 to 64	17.1	25.0	10.1	-	-
Aged 65 or older	15.4	18.8	-	-	-
Aged 65 to 74	13.4	16.7	-	-	-
Aged 75 or older	19.3	22.7	-	-	-
Women					
Total	25.2%	37.4%	16.8%	11.2%	8.2%
Aged 25 to 34	31.0	49.2	24.3	13.6	9.2
Aged 35 to 54	22.2	35.7	13.7	10.1	6.9
Aged 55 to 64	19.3	27.0	9.9	-	-
Aged 65 or older	24.5	29.1	9.5	-	-
Aged 65 to 74	22.7	27.9	-	-	-
Aged 75 or older	27.4	30.9	-	-	-

Note: Hispanics may be of any race.
Source: Bureau of the Census, Current Population Reports, Poverty in the United States: 1991, *Series P-60, No. 181, 1992*

Families Below Poverty Level by Type and Work Experience, 1991

Regardless of race, few dual-earner married couples are poor. Even among female-headed families, poverty is uncommon among those with at least one full-time worker.

(number and percent of families below poverty level by family type, work experience, race, and Hispanic origin; families as of 1992; numbers in thousands)

	all families		white		black		Hispanic	
	number below poverty level	percent below poverty level	number below poverty level	percent below poverty level	number below poverty level	percent below poverty level	number below poverty level	percent below poverty level
All families								
Total	7,680	11.6%	5,002	8.8%	2,336	30.8%	1,365	26.6%
With no worker	3,196	31.5	1,910	22.9	1,155	74.6	493	68.5
With one or more workers	4,483	8.0	3,093	6.4	1,181	19.5	872	19.8
One	3,191	17.5	2,084	13.9	957	36.6	588	34.7
Two or more	1,292	3.4	1,009	3.0	224	6.5	284	10.4
With one or more full-time								
year-round workers	1,424	3.2	1,088	2.8	279	6.5	375	11.3
One	1,291	4.6	968	3.9	276	9.9	338	15.5
Two or more	132	0.8	120	0.8	3	0.2	37	3.2
Married-couple families								
Total	3,126	6.0	2,553	5.5	392	11.2	666	19.1
With no worker	965	13.6	742	11.4	158	39.0	126	44.2
With one or more workers	2,162	4.8	1,811	4.5	234	7.5	540	16.9
One	1,245	11.1	1,021	10.1	152	22.1	319	32.1
Two or more	917	2.7	790	2.6	82	3.4	221	10.0
With one or more full-time								
year-round workers	914	2.5	788	2.4	84	3.3	272	10.7
Husband worked full-time, year-round	749	2.4	668	2.4	57	2.8	231	11.2
Wife worked full-time, year-round	117	0.8	101	0.8	12	1.0	20	2.6
Wife did not work full-time, year-round	632	3.7	567	3.6	45	5.7	211	16.3
Female-headed families, no spouse present								
Total	4,161	35.6	2,192	28.4	1,834	51.2	627	49.7
With no worker	2,114	76.0	1,101	67.4	952	89.4	355	87.9
With one or more workers	2,047	23.0	1,091	17.9	883	35.1	272	31.7
One	1,732	31.2	914	24.6	756	45.3	223	41.3
Two or more	315	9.4	176	7.4	126	14.9	49	15.4
With one or more full-time,								
year-round workers	438	7.8	246	6.2	183	12.7	88	16.4
One	424	9.1	234	7.0	181	14.6	78	18.9
Two or more	14	1.6	12	1.8	2	1.0	9	7.7

Note: Because Hispanics may be of any race, the number of families by race and Hispanic origin will not add to total families.
Source: Bureau of the Census, Current Population Reports, Poverty in the United States: 1991, Series P-60, No. 181, 1992

The Working Poor, 1978 to 1991

About 40 percent of the poor work, a proportion that has barely changed in 15 years. Only 9 percent of the poor work full-time, year-round.

(number and percent of people in poverty who work; persons as of the following year; numbers in thousands)

	total poor aged 15 or older	worked		worked full-time, year-round	
		number	percent	number	percent
1991	23,194	9,227	39.8%	2,076	9.0%
1990	21,783	8,770	40.3	2,039	9.4
1989	20,474	8,419	41.1	1,887	9.2
1988	20,857	8,415	40.3	1,929	9.2
1987	21,316	8,440	39.6	1,871	8.8
1986	21,352	8,864	41.5	2,009	9.4
1985	21,954	9,112	41.5	1,972	9.0
1984	22,246	9,104	40.9	2,076	9.3
1983	23,465	9,440	40.2	2,066	8.8
1982	22,812	9,119	40.0	2,000	8.8
1981	21,260	8,631	40.6	1,883	8.9
1980	19,517	7,792	39.9	1,646	8.4
1979	16,907	6,545	38.7	1,365	8.1
1978	16,914	6,599	39.0	1,309	7.7

Source: Bureau of the Census, Current Population Reports, Poverty in the United States: 1991, *Series P-60, No. 181, 1992*

Poverty Rates for Full-Time Workers, 1969, 1979, 1989

Poverty rates for full-time workers fell between 1969 and 1979, then rose between 1979 and 1989, particularly among young workers.

(percent of full-time, year-round workers in poverty by sex and age)

	percent in poverty		
	1989	*1979*	*1969*
Both sexes			
Aged 18 to 64	2.4%	2.1%	3.0%
Aged 18 to 24	3.5	2.4	3.2
Aged 25 to 34	2.6	2.0	2.9
Aged 35 to 54	2.0	2.3	3.1
Aged 55 to 64	2.1	1.8	2.9
Aged 65 or older	2.0	2.8	7.3
Men			
Aged 18 to 64	2.3	2.3	3.0
Aged 18 to 24	3.2	2.8	4.4
Aged 25 to 34	2.5	2.0	2.7
Aged 35 to 54	2.0	2.4	3.1
Aged 55 to 64	2.0	2.0	2.7
Aged 65 or older	2.0	2.5	6.9
Women			
Aged 18 to 64	2.5	1.9	3.0
Aged 18 to 24	3.8	1.9	1.8
Aged 25 to 34	2.7	1.8	3.3
Aged 35 to 54	2.1	2.1	3.1
Aged 55 to 64	2.2	1.6	3.5
Aged 65 or older	2.0	3.5	8.2

Source: Bureau of the Census, Current Population Reports, Workers With Low Earnings: 1964 to 1990, *Series P-60, No. 178, 1992*

Persons Entering or Exiting Poverty by Selected Characteristics, 1987 to 1988

POVERTY

Those most likely to exit poverty are people who marry or who increase their work effort. Half of the poor in 1987 who increased their work effort were no longer poor in 1988.

(number of persons above and below poverty in 1987, and percent entering and exiting poverty in 1988 by selected characteristics; persons as of the following year; numbers in thousands)

Age	number above poverty in 1987	percent entered poverty in 1988	number below poverty in 1987	percent exited poverty in 1988
Under age 18	49,028	3.3%	10,544	22.9%
Aged 18 to 24	22,184	2.7	2,524	34.9
Aged 25 to 44	69,158	2.0	6,289	31.8
Aged 45 to 64	41,442	1.6	3,194	22.8
Aged 65 or older	24,256	1.3	2,371	16.2
Family status				
No change in family status				
Married-couple family	151,562	1.3	9,586	31.0
Other family type	22,986	5.8	9,391	18.6
Family status change				
From married couple to other family type	2,373	15.8	478	33.3
From other family type to married-couple	1,838	2.1	571	59.7
Work experience				
Persons aged 18 or older				
No change in work status				
Worked				
Full-time, year-round	65,298	0.5	881	47.9
Not full-time, year-round	29,733	3.7	3,208	36.8
Did not work	35,182	2.5	7,227	15.6
Change in work status				
Work effort decreased	13,515	4.6	1,043	23.5
Work effort increased	13,312	0.9	2,019	50.3
Number of workers in household				
No change in number of workers				
None	23,212	3.6	11,766	9.6
1 worker	58,870	2.4	7,324	35.3
2 workers or more	81,915	0.5	860	47.0
Change in number of workers				
More workers in 1988	17,321	0.8	3,882	54.6
Less workers in 1988	24,751	7.4	1,089	14.7

Source: Bureau of the Census, Current Population Reports, Poverty in the United States: 1991, *Series P-60, No. 181, 1992*

All Persons by Program Participation Status of Household, 1991

More than one-third of all children under age 18 live in households that receive means-tested assistance from the federal government. Among the poor, 87 percent of children live in households that receive such assistance.

(percent of all persons and percent below poverty level in households receiving selected government benefits, by sex and age; persons as of 1992; numbers in thousands)

ALL INCOME LEVELS	total persons	percent in household that received means-tested assistance	percent in household that received means-tested cash assistance	percent in household that received food stamps	percent in household with one or more persons covered by Medicaid	percent living in public or subsidized housing
Both sexes						
Total	251,179	23.1%	10.8%	10.2%	14.8%	4.3%
Under age 18	65,918	35.5	16.2	18.2	22.6	7.0
Aged 18 to 24	24,434	24.2	11.5	11.6	17.6	4.5
Aged 25 to 34	42,493	21.9	9.7	10.0	13.8	4.1
Aged 35 to 44	39,571	17.3	6.8	6.5	9.4	2.4
Aged 45 to 54	27,023	14.0	7.0	5.3	8.9	1.8
Aged 55 to 59	10,620	15.2	9.4	5.8	10.8	2.1
Aged 60 to 64	10,530	14.9	9.3	5.2	10.4	2.7
Aged 65 or older	30,590	18.0	9.7	4.6	11.9	5.0
Aged 65 to 74	18,441	16.7	9.7	4.4	11.2	4.2
Aged 75 or older	12,149	19.9	9.6	5.0	13.1	6.3
Men						
Total	122,418	21.4	9.6	9.1	13.4	3.4
Under age 18	33,756	35.2	15.8	17.9	22.2	6.9
Aged 18 to 24	12,083	21.3	9.0	9.2	14.4	3.4
Aged 25 to 34	21,124	18.4	7.4	7.3	11.5	2.6
Aged 35 to 44	19,506	15.6	5.8	5.2	8.1	1.6
Aged 45 to 54	13,114	12.1	5.5	4.1	7.3	1.1
Aged 55 to 59	5,108	13.6	8.0	4.7	9.2	1.2
Aged 60 to 64	4,928	12.6	8.1	4.1	8.9	1.3
Aged 65 or older	12,800	14.9	8.1	3.3	9.9	2.8
Aged 65 to 74	8,266	14.7	8.7	3.3	9.9	2.2
Aged 75 or older	4,533	15.1	6.9	3.2	10.0	3.7
Women						
Total	128,761	24.6	12.0	11.3	16.1	5.2
Under age 18	32,162	35.9	16.7	18.6	23.0	7.0
Aged 18 to 24	12,351	27.0	13.9	13.9	20.8	5.6
Aged 25 to 34	21,369	25.2	12.1	12.8	16.2	5.5
Aged 35 to 44	20,065	19.1	7.8	7.8	10.7	3.1
Aged 45 to 54	13,910	15.7	8.3	6.4	10.5	2.5
Aged 55 to 59	5,511	16.7	10.8	6.7	12.4	2.8

(continued)

(percent of all persons and percent below poverty level in households receiving selected government benefits, by sex and age; persons as of 1992; numbers in thousands)

	total persons	percent in household that received means-tested assistance	percent in household that received means-tested cash assistance	percent in household that received food stamps	percent in household with one or more persons covered by Medicaid	percent living in public or subsidized housing
Aged 60 to 64	5,603	17.0%	10.3%	6.1%	11.7%	3.9%
Aged 65 or older	17,790	20.2	10.8	5.6	13.4	6.6
Aged 65 to 74	10,174	18.3	10.5	5.3	12.3	5.7
Aged 75 or older	7,616	22.7	11.3	6.0	15.0	7.9
BELOW POVERTY LEVEL						
Both sexes						
Total	35,708	72.9	43.6	50.2	55.5	20.1
Under age 18	14,341	87.1	54.2	64.7	69.0	24.7
Aged 18 to 24	4,120	62.8	36.1	42.8	50.0	16.9
Aged 25 to 34	5,568	73.0	43.0	50.3	56.1	19.5
Aged 35 to 44	3,592	68.3	35.8	46.0	45.7	14.6
Aged 45 to 54	2,167	63.5	35.5	39.4	42.5	13.5
Aged 55 to 59	1,019	57.7	36.6	37.1	43.9	12.3
Aged 60 to 64	1,120	52.1	32.2	28.3	36.8	16.0
Aged 65 or older	3,781	50.2	29.4	23.3	35.1	19.5
Aged 65 to 74	1,961	53.6	34.2	25.9	39.7	19.9
Aged 75 or older	1,820	46.5	24.3	20.4	30.2	19.0
Men						
Total	15,082	71.6	40.9	48.8	53.2	17.8
Under age 18	7,205	87.1	54.1	64.7	68.4	24.9
Aged 18 to 24	1,633	56.7	28.1	36.4	40.7	13.3
Aged 25 to 34	2,049	63.5	30.4	38.2	45.6	11.6
Aged 35 to 44	1,493	62.0	28.3	38.7	37.0	10.3
Aged 45 to 54	894	55.0	28.1	32.4	34.3	7.9
Aged 55 to 59	387	52.9	28.7	35.1	38.3	8.0
Aged 60 to 64	406	46.4	28.1	24.9	32.1	8.1
Aged 65 or older	1,015	48.1	28.1	21.4	34.5	14.1
Aged 65 to 74	632	49.5	31.7	22.3	36.4	12.1
Aged 75 or older	383	45.9	22.1	19.9	31.3	17.3
Women						
Total	20,626	73.8	45.6	51.2	57.2	21.8
Under age 18	7,136	87.0	54.4	64.6	69.5	24.5
Aged 18 to 24	2,487	66.8	41.4	47.1	56.1	19.2
Aged 25 to 34	3,519	78.6	50.4	57.4	62.2	24.1
Aged 35 to 44	2,099	72.7	41.2	51.2	51.9	17.6
Aged 45 to 54	1,273	69.5	40.7	44.3	48.3	17.5
Aged 55 to 59	632	60.6	41.4	38.4	47.3	15.0
Aged 60 to 64	714	55.3	34.6	30.3	39.5	20.5
Aged 65 or older	2,766	50.9	29.9	23.9	35.4	21.4
Aged 65 to 74	1,329	55.5	35.3	27.6	41.3	23.6
Aged 75 or older	1,436	46.7	24.9	20.5	29.9	19.5

Source: Bureau of the Census, Current Population Reports, Poverty in the United States: 1991, *Series P-60, No. 181, 1992*

White Persons by Program Participation Status of Household, 1991

Two-thirds of poor whites live in households that receive means-tested assistance from the federal government. Half live in households that receive Medicaid.

(percent of all white persons and percent below poverty level in households receiving selected government benefits, by sex and age; persons as of 1992; numbers in thousands)

ALL INCOME LEVELS	total persons	percent in household that received means-tested assistance	percent in household that received means-tested cash assistance	percent in household that received food stamps	percent in household with one or more persons covered by Medicaid	percent living in public or subsidized housing
Both sexes						
Total	210,121	18.6%	8.0%	7.6%	11.5%	2.6%
Under age 18	52,523	28.9	11.7	13.6	17.3	3.7
Aged 18 to 24	19,952	19.7	8.5	8.9	14.3	2.6
Aged 25 to 34	35,318	18.2	7.7	8.2	11.4	2.5
Aged 35 to 44	33,495	14.2	5.1	4.9	7.3	1.5
Aged 45 to 54	23,257	11.3	5.5	4.2	7.1	1.2
Aged 55 to 59	9,083	11.8	7.4	4.1	8.3	1.3
Aged 60 to 64	9,196	11.3	6.8	3.5	7.6	1.8
Aged 65 or older	27,297	14.8	7.5	3.3	9.6	4.2
Aged 65 to 74	16,315	13.6	7.6	3.1	8.8	3.1
Aged 75 or older	10,983	16.7	7.3	3.6	10.7	5.8
Men						
Total	102,907	17.5	7.2	6.9	10.5	2.1
Under age 18	26,937	28.8	11.5	13.5	17.2	3.7
Aged 18 to 24	9,907	17.7	7.0	7.1	12.1	2.2
Aged 25 to 34	17,736	15.9	6.1	6.4	9.7	1.7
Aged 35 to 44	18,738	13.3	4.5	4.3	6.6	1.3
Aged 45 to 54	11,427	10.1	4.4	3.4	6.0	0.9
Aged 55 to 59	4,373	10.7	6.1	3.2	7.2	0.6
Aged 60 to 64	4,357	9.1	5.6	2.9	6.2	1.0
Aged 65 or older	11,431	12.3	6.6	2.3	8.1	2.2
Aged 65 to 74	7,323	12.2	7.4	2.4	8.0	1.5
Aged 75 or older	4,108	12.5	5.4	2.1	8.4	3.3
Women						
Total	107,214	19.7	8.8	8.3	12.4	3.2
Under age 18	25,586	29.0	11.9	13.8	17.4	3.7
Aged 18 to 24	10,045	21.8	10.0	10.7	16.5	3.1
Aged 25 to 34	17,571	20.6	9.2	10.0	13.0	3.2
Aged 35 to 44	16,757	15.0	5.8	5.5	8.0	1.7
Aged 45 to 54	11,830	12.4	6.5	5.1	8.2	1.6
Aged 55 to 59	4,710	12.9	8.5	4.9	9.4	2.0

(percent of all white persons and percent below poverty level in households receiving selected government benefits, by sex and age; persons as of 1992; numbers in thousands)

	total persons	percent in household that received means-tested assistance	percent in household that received means-tested cash assistance	percent in household that received food stamps	percent in household with one or more persons covered by Medicaid	percent living in public or subsidized housing
Aged 60 to 64	4,839	13.3%	7.7%	4.1%	8.9%	2.6%
Aged 65 or older	15,866	16.6	8.1	4.0	10.6	5.7
Aged 65 to 74	8,992	14.7	7.8	3.7	9.4	4.4
Aged 75 or older	6,874	19.2	8.4	4.4	12.0	7.3
BELOW POVERTY LEVEL						
Both sexes						
Total	23,747	66.9	36.6	44.0	49.0	13.7
Under age 18	8,848	83.0	46.5	58.7	62.7	15.5
Aged 18 to 24	2,791	55.5	27.7	36.0	42.5	10.9
Aged 25 to 34	3,870	69.0	38.3	47.2	51.9	13.1
Aged 35 to 44	2,384	63.0	30.7	39.6	40.3	10.5
Aged 45 to 54	1,541	58.1	30.1	36.2	36.7	9.9
Aged 55 to 59	716	50.3	32.0	32.0	37.1	8.5
Aged 60 to 64	796	44.8	26.8	24.1	29.4	13.1
Aged 65 or older	2,802	43.5	24.0	18.2	30.5	17.7
Aged 65 to 74	1,345	47.1	29.2	21.1	35.4	17.0
Aged 75 or older	1,457	40.1	19.3	15.6	25.9	18.3
Men						
Total	10,079	66.4	34.6	43.6	47.7	11.9
Under age 18	4,456	83.6	47.0	59.5	63.4	15.8
Aged 18 to 24	1,132	50.1	21.3	30.5	34.8	10.4
Aged 25 to 34	1,505	60.9	28.3	37.9	43.2	7.9
Aged 35 to 44	1,061	59.0	24.9	34.8	34.4	9.3
Aged 45 to 54	669	50.6	22.4	29.2	28.9	6.6
Aged 55 to 59	271	44.5	22.8	28.0	31.6	4.1
Aged 60 to 64	293	40.6	25.1	23.6	24.7	8.1
Aged 65 or older	693	41.2	25.9	17.8	32.1	12.2
Aged 65 to 74	407	42.6	30.1	20.2	33.9	8.4
Aged 75 or older	286	39.3	19.9	14.5	29.7	17.6
Women						
Total	13,668	67.3	38.0	44.4	49.9	14.9
Under age 18	4,392	82.3	46.0	58.0	62.0	15.1
Aged 18 to 24	1,659	59.2	32.1	39.7	47.6	11.2
Aged 25 to 34	2,365	74.2	44.7	53.1	57.5	16.4
Aged 35 to 44	1,323	66.3	35.4	43.5	45.0	11.5
Aged 45 to 54	872	63.9	36.1	41.6	42.7	12.5
Aged 55 to 59	444	53.9	37.6	34.5	40.5	11.2
Aged 60 to 64	503	47.2	27.9	24.4	32.1	16.0
Aged 65 or older	2,109	44.2	23.4	18.4	29.9	19.5
Aged 65 to 74	939	49.1	28.8	21.5	36.0	20.8
Aged 75 or older	1,171	40.4	19.1	15.8	25.0	18.4

Source: Bureau of the Census, Current Population Reports, Poverty in the United States: 1991, *Series P-60, No. 181, 1992*

Black Persons by Program Participation Status of Household, 1991

Half of all blacks live in households that receive means-tested assistance from the federal government. Among those who are poor, fully 87 percent live in households that receive such help.

(percent of all black persons and percent below poverty level in households receiving selected government benefits, by sex and age; persons as of 1992; numbers in thousands)

	total persons	percent in household that received means-tested assistance	percent in household that received means-tested cash assistance	percent in household that received food stamps	percent in household with one or more persons covered by Medicaid	percent living in public or subsidized housing
ALL INCOME LEVELS						
Both sexes						
Total	31,312	50.8%	28.1%	27.4%	35.1%	14.9%
Under age 18	10,350	67.3	38.3	41.3	47.9	22.6
Aged 18 to 24	3,517	48.5	27.6	27.3	35.6	14.8
Aged 25 to 34	5,423	44.7	21.7	22.4	28.7	13.8
Aged 35 to 44	4,462	38.8	18.5	18.6	23.7	8.3
Aged 45 to 54	2,787	34.5	18.2	14.9	22.6	6.9
Aged 55 to 59	1,155	38.3	22.8	17.2	27.5	6.3
Aged 60 to 64	1,011	46.6	32.3	20.0	34.9	10.0
Aged 65 or older	2,606	46.3	29.6	19.1	33.0	12.6
Aged 65 to 74	1,665	42.3	26.7	17.3	30.3	12.9
Aged 75 or older	941	53.3	34.7	22.2	37.8	12.1
Men						
Total	14,731	46.4	24.5	23.8	31.0	12.2
Under age 18	5,275	65.9	37.1	39.9	46.0	22.4
Aged 18 to 24	1,654	42.2	20.2	22.3	27.1	10.7
Aged 25 to 34	2,505	35.2	14.6	13.7	22.2	7.9
Aged 35 to 44	2,027	32.3	14.8	12.1	18.4	4.2
Aged 45 to 54	1,235	28.9	15.0	11.5	18.0	3.2
Aged 55 to 59	538	32.7	19.0	15.2	21.4	3.9
Aged 60 to 64	439	45.9	32.4	15.7	35.7	3.9
Aged 65 or older	1,058	37.5	21.7	13.7	24.8	7.7
Aged 65 to 74	739	35.4	21.1	11.8	24.9	7.6
Aged 75 or older	319	42.6	23.0	18.2	24.4	8.0
Women						
Total	16,581	54.7	31.3	30.7	38.7	17.4
Under age 18	5,076	68.7	39.5	42.7	49.8	22.8
Aged 18 to 24	1,864	54.2	34.1	31.6	43.1	18.5
Aged 25 to 34	2,918	52.9	27.9	29.9	34.3	18.9
Aged 35 to 44	2,435	44.2	21.5	24.0	28.1	11.7
Aged 45 to 54	1,552	38.9	20.7	17.7	26.3	9.9
Aged 55 to 59	616	43.2	26.1	19.0	32.9	8.5

(continued)

(continued from previous page)

(percent of all black persons and percent below poverty level in households receiving selected government benefits, by sex and age; persons as of 1992; numbers in thousands)

	total persons	percent in household that received means-tested assistance	percent in household that received means-tested cash assistance	percent in household that received food stamps	percent in household with one or more persons covered by Medicaid	percent living in public or subsidized housing
Aged 60 to 64	572	47.2%	32.3%	23.3%	34.2%	14.8%
Aged 65 or older	1,549	52.2	35.0	22.8	38.6	15.9
Aged 65 to 74	926	47.8	31.2	21.7	34.6	17.1
Aged 75 or older	623	58.8	40.7	24.3	44.7	14.2
BELOW POVERTY LEVEL						
Both sexes						
Total	10,242	86.9	59.6	65.0	70.5	34.5
Under age 18	4,755	94.7	68.3	75.8	80.2	41.2
Aged 18 to 24	1,123	81.9	57.3	61.5	68.9	32.1
Aged 25 to 34	1,428	86.7	56.5	60.9	69.0	36.7
Aged 35 to 44	988	80.5	47.8	62.9	58.5	24.1
Aged 45 to 54	544	80.6	50.3	50.7	58.9	24.3
Aged 55 to 59	246	76.3	46.3	48.0	60.6	17.1
Aged 60 to 64	278	73.7	49.5	42.9	59.4	24.5
Aged 65 or older	880	69.8	46.2	40.3	49.6	24.0
Aged 65 to 74	547	67.2	45.3	38.6	49.6	25.5
Aged 75 or older	333	74.1	47.6	43.0	49.5	21.4
Men						
Total	4,197	84.3	55.4	62.1	65.5	31.2
Under age 18	2,382	94.0	67.5	74.8	77.7	41.5
Aged 18 to 24	395	76.6	46.9	55.3	55.9	23.4
Aged 25 to 34	432	75.9	37.8	41.7	54.5	22.2
Aged 35 to 44	340	70.1	35.3	51.7	42.2	12.7
Aged 45 to 54	195	69.2	45.8	45.1	50.1	13.3
Aged 55 to 59	87	72.6	38.7	50.3	51.1	8.6
Aged 60 to 64	95	67.1	38.3	31.8	56.5	9.6
Aged 65 or older	271	62.1	33.5	32.0	38.8	16.9
Aged 65 to 74	193	59.5	34.5	27.8	39.6	17.5
Aged 75 or older	78	68.5	31.1	42.2	37.0	15.6
Women						
Total	6,044	88.7	62.5	67.0	74.0	36.9
Under age 18	2,373	95.4	69.1	76.8	82.8	40.9
Aged 18 to 24	728	84.8	63.0	64.9	76.0	36.8
Aged 25 to 34	996	91.5	64.6	69.2	75.3	43.0
Aged 35 to 44	648	86.0	54.4	68.8	67.1	30.1
Aged 45 to 54	349	86.9	52.9	53.8	63.9	30.5
Aged 55 to 59	159	78.2	50.5	46.8	65.8	21.7
Aged 60 to 64	183	77.1	55.3	48.7	60.8	32.2
Aged 65 or older	609	73.2	51.9	44.0	54.3	27.1
Aged 65 to 74	355	71.3	51.3	44.5	55.0	29.9
Aged 75 or older	254	75.8	52.7	43.2	53.4	23.2

Source: Bureau of the Census, Current Population Reports, Poverty in the United States: 1991, *Series P-60, No. 181, 1992*

Hispanic Persons by Program Participation Status of Household, 1991

Eight-two percent of poor Hispanics live in households that receive means-tested assistance from the federal government. Half live in households receiving Medicaid.

(percent of all Hispanic persons and percent below poverty level in households receiving selected government benefits, by sex and age; persons as of 1992; numbers in thousands)

	total persons	percent in household that received means-tested assistance	percent in household that received means-tested cash assistance	percent in household that received food stamps	percent in household with one or more persons covered by Medicaid	percent living in public or subsidized housing
ALL INCOME LEVELS						
Both sexes						
Total	22,068	48.5%	18.7%	19.8%	30.0%	6.9%
Under age 18	7,648	64.0	24.8	29.5	39.1	9.4
Aged 18 to 24	2,798	42.8	14.8	16.4	29.3	6.0
Aged 25 to 34	4,249	41.0	14.1	16.4	25.0	5.3
Aged 35 to 44	3,168	41.1	12.4	13.1	20.9	4.8
Aged 45 to 54	1,812	34.9	13.4	12.0	19.0	4.5
Aged 55 to 59	662	28.6	15.5	11.3	20.5	4.7
Aged 60 to 64	589	37.1	21.3	12.6	26.8	7.7
Aged 65 or older	1,143	46.0	30.1	15.1	39.3	9.3
Aged 65 to 74	732	42.8	26.8	13.1	35.7	7.1
Aged 75 or older	411	51.8	36.0	18.6	45.7	13.2
Men						
Total	11,051	45.9	16.0	17.7	27.3	5.9
Under age 18	3,880	64.1	24.1	28.9	38.3	9.5
Aged 18 to 24	1,427	40.4	13.1	13.8	27.1	5.2
Aged 25 to 34	2,227	34.7	8.9	11.8	20.0	3.2
Aged 35 to 44	1,594	38.8	10.5	11.6	18.8	3.9
Aged 45 to 54	860	33.3	10.9	9.6	16.3	3.3
Aged 55 to 59	334	26.5	11.8	9.6	16.7	2.6
Aged 60 to 64	263	27.5	16.1	7.9	20.6	4.3
Aged 65 or older	466	38.0	22.5	12.0	31.6	6.6
Aged 65 to 74	310	36.7	21.4	10.9	29.7	5.6
Aged 75 or older	157	40.6	24.5	14.3	35.5	8.5
Women						
Total	11,017	51.0	21.3	21.9	32.7	7.9
Under age 18	3,768	63.8	25.5	30.1	39.8	9.4
Aged 18 to 24	1,371	45.4	16.6	19.2	31.7	6.7
Aged 25 to 34	2,022	48.0	19.8	21.4	30.6	7.6
Aged 35 to 44	1,574	43.4	14.3	14.6	23.0	5.8
Aged 45 to 54	952	36.3	15.6	14.1	21.4	5.5
Aged 55 to 59	327	30.7	19.3	13.1	24.3	6.8

(continued)

(continued from previous page)

(percent of all Hispanic persons and percent below poverty level in households receiving selected government benefits, by sex and age; persons as of 1992; numbers in thousands)

	total persons	percent in household that received means-tested assistance	percent in household that received means-tested cash assistance	percent in household that received food stamps	percent in household with one or more persons covered by Medicaid	percent living in public or subsidized housing
Aged 60 to 64	326	44.8%	25.5%	16.4%	31.9%	10.5%
Aged 65 or older	677	51.5	35.4	17.2	44.6	11.2
Aged 65 to 74	422	47.2	30.7	14.8	40.2	8.3
Aged 75 or older	255	58.7	43.1	21.3	51.9	16.0
BELOW POVERTY LEVEL						
Both sexes						
Total	6,339	82.1	67.1	39.6	50.3	59.1
Under age 18	3,094	89.7	73.5	46.0	58.9	66.6
Aged 18 to 24	771	71.7	60.9	27.2	38.9	51.0
Aged 25 to 34	1,026	77.4	61.6	34.9	45.0	56.1
Aged 35 to 44	656	79.0	60.2	30.8	42.1	48.8
Aged 45 to 54	328	72.8	53.6	31.8	40.9	40.5
Aged 55 to 59	113	68.9	60.8	40.6	48.0	47.2
Aged 60 to 64	115	69.2	64.6	43.5	37.7	47.3
Aged 65 or older	237	72.0	68.9	48.9	41.6	65.4
Aged 65 to 74	137	72.1	68.1	48.7	40.3	64.2
Aged 75 or older	100	71.9	70.0	49.1	43.4	67.1
Men						
Total	2,900	80.3	64.6	35.5	47.5	56.3
Under age 18	1,572	89.7	73.4	45.4	58.3	66.4
Aged 18 to 24	331	70.3	60.1	24.8	36.4	48.5
Aged 25 to 34	400	68.6	50.8	19.4	31.6	45.7
Aged 35 to 44	280	73.7	54.4	20.7	36.4	40.8
Aged 45 to 54	142	67.0	46.4	24.6	31.1	34.4
Aged 55 to 59	60	-	-	-	-	-
Aged 60 to 64	42	-	-	-	-	-
Aged 65 or older	72	-	-	-	-	-
Aged 65 to 74	42	-	-	-	-	-
Aged 75 or older	30	-	-	-	-	-
Women						
Total	3,439	83.7	69.2	43.0	52.7	61.4
Under age 18	1,521	89.8	73.5	46.7	59.5	66.8
Aged 18 to 24	440	72.8	61.5	29.0	40.8	52.9
Aged 25 to 34	626	83.0	68.5	44.8	53.5	62.7
Aged 35 to 44	375	82.8	64.6	38.4	46.4	54.8
Aged 45 to 54	186	77.2	59.2	37.4	48.4	45.2
Aged 55 to 59	53	-	-	-	-	-
Aged 60 to 64	73	-	-	-	-	-
Aged 65 or older	166	72.3	68.4	50.5	41.3	64.9
Aged 65 to 74	96	71.8	67.0	46.1	35.9	64.0
Aged 75 or older	70	-	-	-	-	-

Note: Hispanics may be of any race.
Source: Bureau of the Census, Current Population Reports, Poverty in the United States: 1991, *Series P-60, No. 181, 1992*

8

Income and Geography Trends

The bicoastal economy, a term coined to describe the booming economies of the Northeast and West during the 1980s, turned into a bicoastal recession during the early 1990s. Incomes fell sharply in those regions over the past three years. In contrast, the income drop was more subdued in the Midwest and South, narrowing the regional income gap.

Income and Geography: Highlights

■ The recession of the early 1990s hit the Northeast and West the hardest, but household and family incomes in those regions remain above those in the Midwest and South.

■ Median household income exceeded $40,000 in three states in 1991 (Alaska, Connecticut, and New Jersey), down from six states in 1990.

■ The most affluent households in the nation are found in the suburbs of the nation's metropolitan areas with populations of 1 million or more. Household incomes are lowest in nonmetropolitan areas.

No region of the country was immune from the 1990 recession, but the Northeast and West were hardest hit.

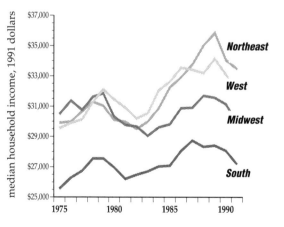

Median Income of Households by Region, 1975 to 1991

Household median income fell in every region between 1989 and 1991, after adjusting for inflation. The largest drop occurred in the Northeast.

(median income of households by region, 1975-91; income in 1991 dollars)

	Northeast	*Midwest*	*South*	*West*
1991	$33,467	$29,927	$27,178	$32,253
1990	34,051	31,155	28,076	33,098
1989	35,855	31,579	28,415	34,144
1988	35,029	31,707	28,330	33,199
1987	33,767	30,915	28,736	33,415
1986	32,924	30,882	28,058	33,554
1985	32,259	29,811	27,084	32,635
1984	30,871	29,607	27,034	32,060
1983	29,982	29,048	26,708	30,542
1982	29,501	29,662	26,486	30,192
1981	29,969	29,766	26,214	30,904
1980	30,106	30,307	26,972	31,458
1979	31,039	31,854	27,549	32,110
1978	31,294	31,625	27,553	31,298
1977	30,671	30,753	26,738	30,128
1976	29,978	31,374	26,279	29,895
1975	29,903	30,473	25,541	29,540

Percent change in median income

	Northeast	Midwest	South	West
1989-91	-6.7%	-5.2%	-4.4%	-5.5%
1980-89	19.1	4.2	5.4	8.5
1975-80	0.7	-0.5	5.6	6.5

Sources: Bureau of the Census, Current Population Reports, Trends in Income, by Selected Characteristics: 1947 to 1988, *Series P-60, No. 167, 1990; and* Money Income of Households, Families, and Persons in the United States: 1991, *Series P-60, No. 180, 1992*

Median Income of Families by Region, 1967 to 1991

Families in the Northeast have the highest incomes, but their incomes fell by more than 7 percent between 1989 and 1991, after adjusting for inflation.

(median income of families by region, 1967-91; income in 1991 dollars)

	Northeast	Midwest	South	West
1991	$40,265	$36,759	$31,940	$37,171
1990	41,154	37,711	33,062	38,231
1989	43,369	38,018	33,500	39,210
1988	41,970	37,863	33,332	38,088
1987	41,088	37,274	34,038	38,391
1986	39,965	36,764	33,190	38,480
1985	38,663	35,354	31,742	37,693
1984	37,343	35,070	31,584	36,805
1983	36,533	33,972	30,880	35,104
1982	35,500	34,504	30,631	35,081
1981	35,835	34,946	31,113	36,088
1980	36,170	35,971	31,678	36,873
1979	37,956	37,862	32,301	38,079
1978	36,703	37,529	32,171	37,147
1977	36,214	36,302	31,393	35,584
1976	35,323	36,554	30,769	35,504
1975	35,095	35,240	29,654	34,695
1974	36,609	36,037	29,712	34,732
1973	37,080	37,025	30,665	35,983
1972	36,633	35,964	29,657	35,332
1971	34,824	34,082	28,378	33,822
1970	35,273	34,057	28,203	33,879
1969	34,631	34,638	28,018	34,696
1968	32,836	32,887	26,676	33,844
1967	34,103	34,155	27,705	35,149
Percent change in median income				
1989-91	-7.2%	-3.3%	-4.7%	-5.2%
1980-89	19.9	5.7	5.7	6.3
1973-80	-2.5	-2.8	3.3	2.5
1967-73	8.7	8.4	10.7	2.4

Sources: Bureau of the Census, Current Population Reports, Trends in Income, by Selected Characteristics: 1947 to 1988, *Series P-60, No. 167, 1990; and* Money Income of Households, Families, and Persons in the United States: 1991, *Series P-60, No. 180, 1992*

Median Income of Men by Region, 1967 to 1991

The median income of men rose in every region but the West during the 1980s, then fell in all regions between 1989 and 1991, after adjusting for inflation.

(median income of men aged 15 or older, 1967-91; income in 1991 dollars)

	Northeast	Midwest	South	West
1991	$22,349	$20,571	$18,474	$21,572
1990	22,829	21,543	19,205	21,872
1989	24,355	21,928	19,608	22,453
1988	24,804	20,626	19,311	22,371
1987	23,759	20,907	19,596	22,124
1986	23,523	21,670	19,220	22,744
1985	22,254	19,859	18,905	22,012
1984	21,847	19,641	18,626	22,173
1983	21,238	19,951	18,301	21,182
1982	20,721	20,219	18,264	20,827
1981	21,107	20,165	18,451	22,070
1980	21,782	20,928	18,899	22,701
1979	22,377	21,643	19,670	22,734
1978	22,522	21,828	19,901	23,600
1977	22,783	22,036	19,284	22,714
1976	22,746	21,792	19,141	22,530
1975	23,050	22,160	18,811	22,589
1974	24,112	22,999	19,218	22,941
1973	24,790	23,091	19,599	24,790
1972	24,522	22,547	19,491	24,470
1971	23,511	22,519	18,392	23,224
1970	23,194	23,194	18,471	23,494
1969	23,828	22,414	17,969	24,440
1968	22,818	21,633	17,399	24,162
1967	23,698	22,467	18,070	25,094
Percent change in median income				
1989-91	-8.2%	-6.2%	-5.8%	-3.9%
1980-89	11.8	4.8	3.8	-1.1
1973-80	-12.1	-9.7	-3.6	-8.4
1967-73	4.6	2.8	8.5	-1.2

Sources: Bureau of the Census, Current Population Reports, Trends in Income, by Selected Characteristics: 1947 to 1988, *Series P-60, No. 167, 1990; and* Money Income of Households, Families, and Persons in the United States: 1991, *Series P-60, No. 180, 1992*

Median Income of Women by Region, 1967 to 1991

Women's median incomes rose by more than 25 percent in every region during the 1980s, then fell in the Northeast and West between 1989 and 1991, after adjusting for inflation.

(median income of women aged 15 or older, 1967-91; income in 1991 dollars)

	Northeast	Midwest	South	West
1991	$11,047	$10,119	$10,053	$10,976
1990	11,184	9,528	9,813	10,907
1989	11,580	9,116	9,939	11,321
1988	11,065	9,010	9,699	11,167
1987	10,482	8,710	9,571	10,719
1986	9,966	9,028	9,054	10,165
1985	9,548	8,262	8,601	10,272
1984	9,180	7,922	8,775	9,922
1983	8,868	7,674	12,648	9,615
1982	8,512	7,497	8,089	9,410
1981	8,316	7,238	7,886	9,031
1980	8,175	7,023	7,866	8,920
1979	8,319	7,368	7,395	8,682
1978	8,882	7,887	7,512	8,680
1977	9,071	7,750	7,775	9,000
1976	8,722	7,764	7,654	8,461
1975	8,851	7,409	7,556	8,475
1974	8,823	7,309	7,345	8,427
1973	8,772	7,549	7,275	8,504
1972	8,810	7,338	7,246	8,126
1971	8,959	6,845	6,674	7,720
1970	8,653	6,569	6,536	7,516
1969	8,542	6,648	6,616	7,671
1968	8,262	6,203	6,467	7,919
1967	8,581	6,442	6,716	8,225
Percent change in median income				
1989-91	-4.6%	11.0%	1.1%	-3.0%
1980-89	41.7	29.8	26.4	26.9
1973-80	-6.8	-7.0	8.1	4.9
1967-73	2.3	17.2	8.3	3.4

Sources: Bureau of the Census, Current Population Reports, Trends in Income, by Selected Characteristics: 1947 to 1988, *Series P-60, No. 167, 1990; and* Money Income of Households, Families, and Persons in the United States: 1991, *Series P-60, No. 180, 1992*

Northeast and Midwest: Distribution of Households by Income, 1991

Households in New England have the highest median incomes, at just over $35,000 in 1991.

(households by selected regions and income in 1991; households as of 1992; numbers in thousands)

| | total U.S. households | Northeast | | | Midwest | | |
		total	New England	Middle Atlantic	total	East North Central	West North Central
Total	95,669	19,314	5,036	14,278	23,327	16,274	7,053
Less than $5,000	4,576	816	150	665	1,073	780	293
$5,000 to $9,999	9,660	2,006	470	1,536	2,356	1,589	767
$10,000 to $14,999	8,992	1,616	384	1,231	2,165	1,404	761
$15,000 to $19,999	8,376	1,449	388	1,061	1,984	1,381	603
$20,000 to $24,999	8,255	1,528	418	1,110	2,092	1,426	665
$25,000 to $29,999	7,780	1,319	320	999	2,020	1,417	603
$30,000 to $34,999	6,773	1,263	328	935	1,671	1,115	555
$35,000 to $39,999	6,327	1,273	338	935	1,705	1,159	546
$40,000 to $44,999	5,620	1,159	308	851	1,493	1,043	450
$45,000 to $49,999	4,640	1,000	288	712	1,170	861	310
$50,000 to $54,999	4,173	912	254	658	1,018	686	332
$55,000 to $59,999	3,353	729	211	518	822	601	221
$60,000 to $64,999	2,944	687	213	474	690	517	173
$65,000 to $69,999	2,340	550	168	383	529	399	130
$70,000 to $74,999	1,899	448	119	330	434	311	123
$75,000 to $79,999	1,668	396	119	277	389	297	91
$80,000 to $84,999	1,341	348	98	249	290	218	72
$85,000 to $89,999	1,069	280	76	204	238	178	61
$90,000 to $94,999	875	216	55	161	178	141	37
$95,000 to $99,999	762	201	48	152	172	124	48
$100,000 or over	4,246	1,119	284	835	839	627	212
Median income	$30,126	$33,467	$35,786	$32,549	$29,927	$30,570	$28,572

Source: Bureau of the Census, Current Population Reports, Money Income of Households, Families, and Persons in the United States: 1991, *Series P-60, No. 180, 1992*

South and West: Distribution of Households by Income, 1991

Households in the East South Central states of Alabama, Kentucky, Mississippi, and Tennessee have the lowest median incomes.

(households by selected regions and income in 1991; households as of 1992; numbers in thousands)

	total U.S. households	South total	South Atlantic	East South Central	West South Central	West total	Mountain	Pacific
Total	95,669	33,073	17,085	5,943	10,045	19,955	5,219	14,736
Less than $5,000	4,576	2,003	921	479	604	684	234	450
$5,000 to $9,999	9,660	3,592	1,649	799	1,144	1,706	478	1,228
$10,000 to $14,999	8,992	3,430	1,626	709	1,095	1,782	503	1,279
$15,000 to $19,999	8,376	3,192	1,637	592	963	1,750	487	1,263
$20,000 to $24,999	8,255	2,970	1,485	560	926	1,666	514	1,152
$25,000 to $29,999	7,780	2,840	1,518	479	843	1,601	425	1,176
$30,000 to $34,999	6,773	2,322	1,195	388	738	1,518	412	1,106
$35,000 to $39,999	6,327	2,074	1,083	375	616	1,275	366	910
$40,000 to $44,999	5,620	1,769	997	268	504	1,200	314	886
$45,000 to $49,999	4,640	1,521	791	304	426	948	241	707
$50,000 to $54,999	4,173	1,375	741	207	427	869	190	679
$55,000 to $59,999	3,353	1,080	638	160	283	722	211	510
$60,000 to $64,999	2,944	920	483	151	286	648	149	499
$65,000 to $69,999	2,340	642	384	71	187	618	132	486
$70,000 to $74,999	1,899	561	322	87	151	456	109	347
$75,000 to $79,999	1,668	470	287	47	137	414	86	328
$80,000 to $84,999	1,341	377	223	37	117	326	71	255
$85,000 to $89,999	1,069	296	165	54	77	254	57	197
$90,000 to $94,999	875	254	160	26	68	228	38	189
$95,000 to $99,999	762	201	121	22	58	188	26	162
$100,000 or over	4,246	1,183	658	129	396	1,105	179	926
Median Income	$30,126	$27,178	$28,985	$23,383	$26,517	$32,253	$29,616	$33,450

Source: Bureau of the Census, Current Population Reports, Money Income of Households, Families, and Persons in the United States: 1991, *Series P-60, No. 180, 1992*

Median Household Income by Place of Residence, 1989 to 1991

Between 1990 and 1991, median household income fell the most in the suburbs of the nation's smaller metropolitan areas.

(median income for households by region and residence, 1989-91; income in 1991 dollars; households as of 1992; numbers in thousands)

	1991		median income		percent change	
	number	median income	1990	1989	1990-91	1989-91
Total households	95,669	$30,126	$31,203	$31,750	-3.5%	-5.1%
Region						
Northeast	19,314	33,467	34,051	35,855	-1.7	-6.7
Midwest	23,327	29,927	31,155	31,579	-3.9	-5.2
South	33,073	27,178	28,076	28,415	-3.2	-4.4
West	19,955	32,253	33,098	34,144	-2.6	-5.5
Residence						
Inside metropolitan areas	74,535	31,975	33,162	34,186	-3.6	-6.5
1 million or more	47,675	34,472	35,249	36,426	-2.2	-5.4
Inside central cities	18,851	26,891	27,857	28,612	-3.5	-6.0
Outside central cities	28,824	39,998	40,465	42,299	-1.2	-5.4
Under 1 million	26,859	28,551	29,782	30,565	-4.1	-6.6
Inside central cities	11,461	24,959	25,948	27,460	-3.8	-9.1
Outside central cities	15,399	31,255	32,716	33,437	-4.5	-6.5
Outside metropolitan areas	21,134	24,691	24,707	24,623	-0.1	0.3

Source: Bureau of the Census, Current Population Reports, Money Income of Households, Families, and Persons in the United States: 1991, Series P-60, No. 180, 1992

Relative Income of Persons by Place of Residence, 1969 to 1989

One in five suburban residents has an income that is more than twice the median. Twenty-eight percent of central city residents have incomes less than half the median.

(percent of population with income less than half and greater than twice the median, by place of residence and region, 1969-89)

	percent with relative income less than .50					percent with relative income greater than 2.00				
	1989	*1984*	*1979*	*1974*	*1969*	*1989*	*1984*	*1979*	*1974*	*1969*
Place of residence										
Metropolitan areas	20.2%	-	18.2%	16.2%	14.4%	16.9%	-	13.9%	13.0%	13.0%
In central cities	28.3	-	25.1	22.1	18.7	12.8	-	10.6	10.4	11.3
Outside central cities	14.9	-	13.3	11.8	10.7	19.5	-	16.2	15.0	14.5
Nonmetropolitan areas	28.8	-	24.0	24.0	25.8	6.9	-	7.7	6.7	6.1
Region										
Northeast	17.5	19.9	18.3	15.5	13.7	19.6	15.8	12.4	12.6	12.4
Midwest	20.1	21.0	17.0	15.1	14.7	13.0	12.6	12.3	11.3	11.0
South	26.5	24.8	24.3	24.6	25.5	12.1	13.2	9.9	8.9	8.3
West	21.6	19.8	18.8	17.9	15.4	15.8	15.9	14.4	12.3	13.4

*Note: Relative income is calculated in the following way: 1. An income is assigned to each person equal to the income of the person's family. Persons who live alone or with nonrelatives are assigned their personal incomes. 2. These incomes are then adjusted for differences in family size using equivalence factors which reduce the incomes assigned to members of large families compared to members of small families because living costs increase as family size increases. 3. The median level of equivalence-adjusted income is determined using the entire universe of persons. 4. Each person is assigned a relative income equal to the ratio of his or her equivalence-adjusted income to the median equivalence-adjusted income. Low relative income is equivalence-adjusted income that is less than one-half of the median equivalence-adjusted income. High relative income is equivalence-adjusted income at least twice that of the median equivalence-adjusted income. Median relative income for the entire universe of persons is by definition equal to 1.00. Population subgroups may have median relative incomes below or above 1.00 depending on the distribution of relative income within the population subgroups.
Source: Bureau of the Census, Current Population Reports,* Trends in Relative Income: 1964 to 1989, *Series P-60, No. 177, 1991*

All Households: Distribution by Income and Metropolitan Residence, 1991

Households in the suburbs of the nation's largest metropolitan areas have a median income of nearly $40,000.

(households by metropolitan residence and income in 1991; households as of 1992; numbers in thousands)

	total households	inside metropolitan areas							outside metro areas
		total	inside central cities			outside central cities			
			total	metro areas of 1 million+	metro areas < 1 million	total	metro areas of 1 million+	metro areas < 1 million	
Total	95,669	74,535	30,312	18,851	11,461	44,223	28,824	15,399	21,134
Less than $5,000	4,576	3,407	1,978	1,268	710	1,428	798	630	1,169
$5,000 to $9,999	9,660	6,957	3,813	2,344	1,469	3,143	1,876	1,267	2,704
$10,000 to $14,999	8,992	6,436	3,215	1,891	1,323	3,222	1,901	1,321	2,556
$15,000 to $19,999	8,376	6,217	2,827	1,653	1,174	3,390	1,960	1,430	2,158
$20,000 to $24,999	8,255	6,156	2,727	1,666	1,061	3,429	2,075	1,353	2,100
$25,000 to $29,999	7,780	5,737	2,379	1,451	928	3,359	1,988	1,370	2,043
$30,000 to $34,999	6,773	5,209	2,114	1,318	795	3,095	1,937	1,157	1,564
$35,000 to $39,999	6,327	4,950	1,898	1,218	680	3,052	1,877	1,176	1,377
$40,000 to $44,999	5,620	4,491	1,618	966	652	2,873	1,911	963	1,129
$45,000 to $49,999	4,640	3,708	1,247	757	490	2,461	1,584	876	932
$50,000 to $54,999	4,173	3,395	1,053	643	410	2,342	1,659	683	778
$55,000 to $59,999	3,353	2,721	850	525	326	1,870	1,315	556	632
$60,000 to $64,999	2,944	2,487	796	497	299	1,691	1,190	501	457
$65,000 to $69,999	2,340	2,013	595	389	206	1,418	1,048	371	327
$70,000 to $74,999	1,899	1,641	473	326	147	1,168	836	332	259
$75,000 to $79,999	1,668	1,447	448	303	145	999	782	217	221
$80,000 to $84,999	1,341	1,206	309	227	82	897	689	208	134
$85,000 to $89,999	1,069	962	280	189	91	681	486	195	107
$90,000 to $94,999	875	789	264	193	71	525	381	145	86
$95,000 to $99,999	762	695	209	125	84	485	402	83	68
$100,000 or over	4,246	3,912	1,219	903	316	2,693	2,129	564	334
Median income	$30,126	$31,975	$26,150	$26,891	$24,959	$36,590	$39,998	$31,255	$24,691

Source: Bureau of the Census, Current Population Reports, Money Income of Households, Families, and Persons in the United States: 1991, *Series P-60, No. 180, 1992*

White Households: Distribution by Income and Metropolitan Residence, 1991

White households in the suburbs of the nation's largest metropolitan areas have a median income of over $40,000.

(white households by metropolitan residence and income in 1991; households as of 1992; numbers in thousands)

| | total households | inside metropolitan areas | | | | | | | outside metro areas |
| | | total | inside central cities | | | outside central cities | | | |
			total	metro areas of 1 million+	metro areas < 1 million	total	metro areas of 1 million+	metro areas < 1 million	
Total	81,675	62,635	22,688	13,396	9,292	39,947	25,777	14,170	19,040
Less than $5,000	3,014	2,148	1,029	602	427	1,119	624	495	866
$5,000 to $9,999	7,406	5,182	2,492	1,411	1,080	2,690	1,592	1,098	2,224
$10,000 to $14,999	7,445	5,192	2,321	1,305	1,016	2,872	1,682	1,189	2,252
$15,000 to $19,999	7,061	5,127	2,085	1,128	957	3,042	1,734	1,308	1,934
$20,000 to $24,999	7,070	5,162	2,050	1,202	847	3,113	1,849	1,264	1,908
$25,000 to $29,999	6,743	4,848	1,820	1,043	778	3,028	1,754	1,274	1,895
$30,000 to $34,999	5,866	4,421	1,636	971	665	2,785	1,710	1,075	1,445
$35,000 to $39,999	5,585	4,274	1,460	888	572	2,814	1,703	1,112	1,311
$40,000 to $44,999	4,932	3,872	1,290	735	555	2,581	1,700	881	1,060
$45,000 to $49,999	4,129	3,243	984	552	432	2,259	1,424	835	886
$50,000 to $54,999	3,758	3,011	857	497	361	2,154	1,496	657	747
$55,000 to $59,999	3,016	2,407	715	420	295	1,692	1,168	524	609
$60,000 to $64,999	2,657	2,224	681	416	265	1,543	1,077	466	433
$65,000 to $69,999	2,123	1,811	479	290	189	1,332	981	351	312
$70,000 to $74,999	1,730	1,486	399	268	131	1,086	774	313	244
$75,000 to $79,999	1,507	1,295	384	252	132	911	716	195	212
$80,000 to $84,999	1,262	1,131	270	190	80	861	661	200	131
$85,000 to $89,999	976	874	240	153	86	634	449	185	102
$90,000 to $94,999	780	698	232	166	65	466	335	131	82
$95,000 to $99,999	692	628	171	103	68	457	378	80	64
$100,000 or over	3,922	3,601	1,092	802	290	2,509	1,971	539	321
Median income	$31,569	$33,988	$28,664	$30,027	$26,885	$37,196	$40,652	$31,871	$25,804

Source: Bureau of the Census, Current Population Reports, Money Income of Households, Families, and Persons in the United States: 1991, *Series P-60, No. 180, 1992*

Black Households: Distribution by Income and Metropolitan Residence, 1991

Black households in the suburbs of the nation's largest metropolitan areas have a median income of nearly $30,000.

(black households by metropolitan residence and income in 1991; households as of 1992; numbers in thousands)

	total households	inside metropolitan areas							outside metro areas
			inside central cities			outside central cities			
		total	total	metro areas of 1 million+	metro areas < 1 million	total	metro areas of 1 million+	metro areas < 1 million	
Total	11,083	9,402	6,343	4,514	1,829	3,059	2,081	978	1,680
Less than $5,000	1,394	1,131	874	607	267	257	138	119	263
$5,000 to $9,999	2,018	1,590	1,208	863	346	382	236	146	427
$10,000 to $14,999	1,291	1,041	752	497	255	289	173	116	250
$15,000 to $19,999	1,078	903	636	447	189	267	159	108	175
$20,000 to $24,999	940	789	562	377	185	226	162	65	152
$25,000 to $29,999	843	729	470	337	133	259	181	77	114
$30,000 to $34,999	690	602	383	273	110	219	161	58	88
$35,000 to $39,999	574	526	359	272	87	167	115	52	48
$40,000 to $44,999	536	481	260	181	79	222	156	66	55
$45,000 to $49,999	373	342	210	159	51	132	97	35	31
$50,000 to $54,999	271	251	143	112	31	108	95	14	20
$55,000 to $59,999	230	217	91	71	20	126	103	23	13
$60,000 to $64,999	170	159	69	46	22	91	60	30	11
$65,000 to $69,999	149	139	87	76	10	52	38	15	10
$70,000 to $74,999	112	104	57	45	12	47	36	11	8
$75,000 to $79,999	82	79	33	26	7	46	33	13	4
$80,000 to $84,999	56	56	33	32	2	22	19	4	
$85,000 to $89,999	52	48	22	20	3	26	19	6	4
$90,000 to $94,999	53	50	14	14	-	36	26	11	3
$95,000 to $99,999	37	37	23	15	8	13	10	3	-
$100,000 or over	135	130	58	44	13	72	64	8	5
Median income	$18,807	$20,211	$17,437	$18,243	$15,963	$27,033	$29,776	$20,066	$13,120

Source: Bureau of the Census, Current Population Reports, Money Income of Households, Families, and Persons in the United States: 1991, *Series P-60, No. 180, 1992*

Hispanic Households: Distribution by Income and Metropolitan Residence, 1991

The median income of Hispanic households varies by less than $10,000—from $29,000 in large suburbs to $19,000 in nonmetropolitan areas.

(Hispanic households by metropolitan residence and income in 1991; households as of 1992; numbers in thousands)

	total households	inside metropolitan areas							outside metro areas
		total	inside central cities			outside central cities			
			total	metro areas of 1 million+	metro areas < 1 million	total	metro areas of 1 million+	metro areas < 1 million	
Total	6,379	5,928	3,408	2,581	828	2,520	1,973	546	451
Less than $5,000	435	400	293	215	77	107	70	38	35
$5,000 to $9,999	884	813	559	426	133	255	182	72	71
$10,000 to $14,999	771	698	447	324	122	251	180	72	73
$15,000 to $19,999	715	664	378	281	97	286	206	80	51
$20,000 to $24,999	662	597	328	243	84	269	205	65	65
$25,000 to $29,999	542	514	284	226	59	229	174	55	28
$30,000 to $34,999	465	436	232	180	53	204	170	34	28
$35,000 to $39,999	393	361	192	145	47	169	140	29	32
$40,000 to $44,999	313	295	150	119	31	145	115	29	18
$45,000 to $49,999	239	223	115	86	29	107	89	18	17
$50,000 to $54,999	197	189	92	64	28	98	78	19	7
$55,000 to $59,999	140	136	71	55	15	66	59	6	4
$60,000 to $64,999	137	130	59	46	13	72	66	6	7
$65,000 to $69,999	98	97	45	35	11	51	49	2	1
$70,000 to $74,999	69	69	34	30	4	35	32	3	-
$75,000 to $79,999	60	56	28	22	6	28	27	2	4
$80,000 to $84,999	42	39	16	11	5	23	21	2	2
$85,000 to $89,999	35	34	15	13	2	20	18	2	1
$90,000 to $94,999	24	24	9	8	1	14	11	3	-
$95,000 to $99,999	25	24	11	9	2	13	13	-	1
$100,000 or over	134	129	51	43	8	78	70	-	5
Median income	$22,691	$23,052	$20,387	$20,776	$19,076	$26,811	$29,079	$20,651	$19,354

Note: Hispanics may be of any race.
Source: Bureau of the Census, Current Population Reports, Money Income of Households, Families, and Persons in the United States: 1991, Series P-60, No. 180, 1992

Distribution of Households by Place of Residence and Income, 1991

Households in the suburbs of the nation's largest metropolitan areas have the highest incomes. Those in nonmetropolitan areas have the lowest incomes.

(households by place of residence and income in 1991; households as of 1992; numbers in thousands)

	total households	under $5,000	$5,000 to $9,999	$10,000 to $14,999	$15,000 to $24,999	$25,000 to $34,999	$35,000 to $49,999	$50,000 to $74,999	$75,000 to $99,999	$100,000 or over	median income
Total	95,669	4,576	9,660	8,992	16,631	14,553	16,586	14,709	5,715	4,246	$30,126
Place of residence											
Inside metropolitan areas	74,535	3,407	6,957	6,436	12,373	10,946	13,149	12,257	5,098	3,912	31,975
Inside central cities	30,312	1,978	3,813	3,215	5,554	4,492	4,763	3,767	1,510	1,219	26,150
Metro of 1 million+	18,851	1,268	2,344	1,891	3,319	2,769	2,941	2,379	1,037	903	26,891
Metro of < 1 million	11,461	710	1,469	1,323	2,235	1,723	1,822	1,388	473	316	24,959
Outside central cities	44,223	1,428	3,143	3,222	6,819	6,453	8,386	8,489	3,588	2,693	36,590
Metro of 1 million+	28,824	798	1,876	1,901	4,035	3,926	5,372	6,047	2,740	2,129	39,998
Metro of < 1 million	15,399	630	1,267	1,321	2,784	2,528	3,014	2,442	849	564	31,255
Outside metropolitan areas	21,134	1,169	2,704	2,556	4,258	3,607	3,437	2,453	616	334	24,691
Region											
Northeast	19,314	816	2,006	1,616	2,977	2,582	3,432	3,326	1,440	1,119	33,467
Midwest	23,327	1,073	2,356	2,165	4,076	3,691	4,368	3,493	1,267	839	29,927
South	33,073	2,003	3,592	3,430	6,162	5,162	5,364	4,578	1,598	1,183	27,178
West	19,955	684	1,706	1,782	3,416	3,119	3,423	3,312	1,410	1,105	32,253

Source: Bureau of the Census, Current Population Reports, Money Income of Households, Families, and Persons in the United States: 1991, Series P-60, No. 180, 1992

Distribution of Families by Place of Residence and Income, 1991

Families living in the suburbs of the nation's largest metropolitan areas have the highest incomes. Those living in nonmetropolitan areas have the lowest incomes.

(families by place of residence and income in 1991; families as of 1992; numbers in thousands)

	total families	under $5,000	$5,000 to $9,999	$10,000 to $14,999	$15,000 to $24,999	$25,000 to $34,999	$35,000 to $49,999	$50,000 to $74,999	$75,000 to $99,999	$100,000 or over	median income
Total	67,176	2,442	4,079	4,844	10,745	10,502	13,116	12,661	5,029	3,755	$35,939
Place of residence											
Inside metropolitan areas	51,677	1,852	2,951	3,280	7,638	7,566	10,097	10,394	4,449	3,450	38,370
Inside central cities	19,034	1,087	1,677	1,580	3,204	2,936	3,354	2,937	1,275	982	31,379
Metro of 1 million+	11,706	701	1,083	907	1,913	1,771	2,030	1,738	862	700	31,655
Metro of < 1 million	7,328	386	594	674	1,291	1,165	1,324	1,199	413	282	30,918
Outside central cities	32,643	765	1,274	1,700	4,434	4,630	6,743	7,457	3,174	2,468	42,283
Metro of 1 million+	21,147	432	741	957	2,506	2,705	4,186	5,255	2,424	1,943	46,061
Metro of < 1 million	11,496	333	533	743	1,928	1,925	2,557	2,202	750	525	36,381
Outside metropolitan areas	15,496	591	1,128	1,564	3,107	2,936	3,019	2,266	580	305	29,127
Region											
Northeast	13,428	402	769	778	1,858	1,862	2,686	2,790	1,272	1,010	40,265
Midwest	16,170	544	901	1,041	2,490	2,636	3,562	3,093	1,136	767	36,759
South	23,679	1,077	1,622	2,048	4,225	3,851	4,310	4,048	1,455	1,042	31,940
West	13,897	419	787	977	2,173	2,153	2,558	2,730	1,165	936	37,171

Source: Bureau of the Census, Current Population Reports, Money Income of Households, Families, and Persons in the United States: 1991, *Series P-60, No. 180, 1992*

Distribution of Men by Place of Residence, Work Experience, and Income, 1991

Among men who work year-round, full-time, those who live in the suburbs of the nation's largest metropolitan areas have the highest incomes. Those who live in nonmetropolitan areas have the lowest incomes.

(men by place of residence, work status, and income in 1991; persons aged 15 or older as of 1992; numbers in thousands)

	total men	under $5,000	$5,000 to $9,999	$10,000 to $14,999	$15,000 to $24,999	$25,000 to $34,999	$35,000 to $49,999	$50,000 to $74,999	$75,000 to $99,999	$100,000 or over	median income
Total	93,760	88,653	10,727	11,499	11,154	18,709	13,832	12,172	6,746	3,812	$20,469
Place of residence											
Inside metropolitan areas	73,047	69,005	7,968	8,399	8,266	13,937	10,891	10,136	5,945	3,463	21,569
Inside central cities	27,823	25,970	3,364	3,762	3,610	5,457	3,856	3,159	1,712	1,051	18,790
Metro of 1 million+	17,614	16,268	2,093	2,303	2,207	3,378	2,437	1,983	1,100	766	19,258
Metro of < 1 million	10,210	9,702	1,271	1,459	1,403	2,078	1,419	1,176	612	285	18,048
Outside central cities	45,224	43,034	4,604	4,637	4,656	8,480	7,035	6,977	4,233	2,412	23,622
Metro of 1 million+	29,756	28,268	2,933	2,787	2,885	5,168	4,523	4,920	3,154	1,898	25,600
Metro of < 1 million	15,467	14,766	1,671	1,850	1,772	3,312	2,511	2,057	1,079	514	20,923
Outside metropolitan areas	20,713	19,648	2,759	3,100	2,888	4,772	2,941	2,036	801	350	16,876
Region											
Northeast	19,071	17,976	2,034	2,065	2,085	3,601	2,918	2,710	1,640	923	22,349
Midwest	22,401	21,483	2,721	2,510	2,693	4,732	3,443	3,145	1,449	789	20,571
South	31,969	30,010	3,867	4,466	4,058	6,552	4,375	3,611	1,939	1,142	18,474
West	20,320	19,184	2,105	2,458	2,318	3,825	3,096	2,706	1,718	958	21,572
Full-time, year-round workers											
Place of residence											
Inside metropolitan areas	38,114	38,112	370	1,346	3,259	8,105	8,303	8,555	5,181	2,993	31,592
Inside central cities	13,601	13,600	136	646	1,582	3,257	3,004	2,661	1,429	887	28,238
Metro of 1 million+	8,555	8,555	82	398	957	1,995	1,887	1,683	906	645	28,949
Metro of < 1 million	5,046	5,046	54	248	625	1,261	1,117	977	522	241	27,207
Outside central cities	24,513	24,512	234	700	1,677	4,849	5,299	5,894	3,752	2,106	33,595
Metro of 1 million+	16,390	16,389	133	394	1,035	2,872	3,353	4,120	2,793	1,689	36,097
Metro of < 1 million	8,123	8,123	101	307	642	1,976	1,946	1,774	959	418	29,940
Outside metropolitan areas	9,783	9,780	254	514	1,209	2,887	2,268	1,694	674	279	25,085
Region											
Northeast	9,665	9,663	97	253	687	1,909	2,235	2,227	1,434	821	32,596
Midwest	11,795	11,795	163	374	1,045	2,809	2,701	2,714	1,297	694	30,275
South	16,101	16,101	225	795	1,801	4,100	3,428	3,094	1,691	967	27,358
West	10,336	10,333	139	439	935	2,175	2,207	2,215	1,433	790	31,193

Source: Bureau of the Census, Current Population Reports, Money Income of Households, Families, and Persons in the United States: 1991, *Series P-60, No. 180, 1992*

Distribution of Women by Place of Residence, Work Experience, and Income, 1991

Among women who work year-round, full-time, those who live in the suburbs of the nation's largest metropolitan areas have the highest incomes. Those who live in nonmetropolitan areas have the lowest incomes.

(women by place of residence, work status, and income in 1991; persons aged 15 or older as of 1992; numbers in thousands)

	total women	under $5,000	$5,000 to $9,999	$10,000 to $14,999	$15,000 to $24,999	$25,000 to $34,999	$35,000 to $49,999	$50,000 to $74,999	$75,000 to $99,999	$100,000 or over	median income
Total	101,483	92,569	24,601	20,122	13,804	17,821	8,882	4,999	1,671	669	$10,476
Place of residence											
Inside metropolitan areas	79,346	72,410	18,311	15,060	10,552	14,316	7,529	4,479	1,539	625	11,133
Inside central cities	31,246	28,140	6,939	6,422	4,177	5,663	2,646	1,484	579	229	10,709
Metro of 1 million+	19,583	17,421	4,135	3,953	2,485	3,536	1,652	1,026	457	177	10,995
Metro of < 1 million	11,663	10,718	2,803	2,469	1,692	2,128	994	459	122	52	10,232
Outside central cities	48,100	44,271	11,373	8,637	6,375	8,653	4,882	2,994	960	396	11,415
Metro of 1 million+	31,698	29,189	7,193	5,458	3,955	5,743	3,509	2,262	752	317	12,097
Metro of < 1 million	16,402	15,082	4,180	3,180	2,420	2,910	1,374	732	209	79	10,317
Outside metropolitan areas	22,137	20,159	6,290	5,062	3,252	3,505	1,353	521	132	44	8,461
Region											
Northeast	21,158	19,422	4,816	4,216	2,762	3,720	2,005	1,257	489	158	11,047
Midwest	24,361	22,862	6,252	5,014	3,495	4,487	2,090	1,098	290	136	10,199
South	35,050	31,473	8,841	6,835	4,830	5,967	2,848	1,508	465	179	10,053
West	20,914	18,812	4,692	4,057	2,717	3,647	1,939	1,137	427	195	10,976
Full-time, year-round workers											
Place of residence											
Inside metropolitan areas	26,259	26,250	436	1,523	4,141	9,254	5,749	3,526	1,180	441	22,143
Inside central cities	10,114	10,114	175	734	1,709	3,698	2,055	1,158	420	164	21,135
Metro of 1 million+	6,365	6,365	113	457	980	2,278	1,278	809	327	124	21,612
Metro of < 1 million	3,749	3,749	63	277	729	1,420	778	349	93	40	20,242
Outside central cities	16,145	16,135	261	789	2,432	5,556	3,693	2,368	760	277	22,897
Metro of 1 million+	10,857	10,852	157	435	1,342	3,639	2,663	1,785	604	228	24,549
Metro of < 1 million	5,287	5,284	104	354	1,090	1,917	1,030	583	156	49	20,205
Outside metropolitan areas	6,232	6,226	247	699	1,587	2,216	1,003	377	73	24	16,897
Region											
Northeast	6,581	6,578	109	304	947	2,273	1,481	972	377	116	23,132
Midwest	7,936	7,932	214	511	1,447	2,937	1,635	885	207	95	20,668
South	11,655	11,646	252	997	2,377	4,167	2,189	1,190	351	124	19,778
West	6,319	6,319	109	410	956	2,094	1,447	857	318	129	22,668

Source: Bureau of the Census, Current Population Reports, Money Income of Households, Families, and Persons in the United States: 1991, *Series P-60, No. 180, 1992*

Distribution of Households Within Income Fifth by Place of Residence, 1991

Fully 92 percent of households with the highest incomes are found in the nation's metropolitan areas. Only 8 percent are in nonmetropolitan areas.

(percent distribution of households within income quintile by place of residence and region; households as of 1992; numbers in thousands)

	total households	bottom fifth	second fifth	middle fifth	fourth fifth	top fifth	top 5 percent
Total	95,669	19,134	19,134	19,134	19,134	19,134	4,784
Income lower limit	-	-	$12,588	$24,000	$37,070	$56,760	$96,400
Place of residence							
Total	100.0%	100.0%	100.0%	100.0%	100.0%	100.0%	100.0%
Inside metropolitan areas	77.9	72.7	73.4	75.9	79.9	87.6	92.0
Inside central cities	31.7	39.6	33.7	31.3	27.3	26.5	28.2
Metro of 1 million+	19.7	24.4	20.1	19.4	16.6	18.1	20.4
Metro of < 1 million	12.0	15.2	13.6	11.8	10.7	8.4	7.8
Outside central cities	46.2	33.1	39.7	44.6	52.6	61.1	63.9
Metro of 1 million+	30.1	19.3	23.5	27.1	35.0	45.7	50.7
Metro of < 1 million	16.1	13.8	16.2	17.5	17.6	15.4	13.2
Outside metropolitan areas	22.1	27.3	26.6	24.1	20.1	12.4	8.0
Region							
Total	100.0	100.0	100.0	100.0	100.0	100.0	100.0
Northeast	20.2	19.4	17.8	18.3	20.9	24.5	26.3
Midwest	24.4	24.0	24.3	25.4	25.9	22.2	19.9
South	34.6	38.9	37.5	35.0	32.6	28.8	28.0
West	20.9	17.7	20.4	21.3	20.5	24.4	25.7

Source: Bureau of the Census, Current Population Reports, Money Income of Households, Families, and Persons in the United States: 1991, *Series P-60, No. 180, 1992*

Distribution of Households by Income Fifth and Place of Residence, 1991

Thirty percent of households in the suburbs of the nation's largest metropolitan areas have incomes that place them in the top income fifth.

(percent distribution of households by income quintile, place of residence, and region; households as of 1992)

	total households	bottom fifth	second fifth	middle fifth	fourth fifth	top fifth	top 5 percent
Total	100.0%	20.0%	20.0%	20.0%	20.0%	20.0%	5.0%
Place of residence							
Inside metropolitan areas	100.0	18.7	18.8	19.5	20.5	22.5	5.9
Inside central cities	100.0	25.0	21.3	19.7	17.3	16.7	4.4
Metro of 1 million+	100.0	24.7	20.4	19.7	16.9	18.3	5.2
Metro of < 1 million	100.0	25.5	22.8	19.8	17.9	14.1	3.2
Outside central cities	100.0	14.3	17.2	19.3	22.7	26.4	6.9
Metro of 1 million+	100.0	12.8	15.6	18.0	23.2	30.3	8.4
Metro of < 1 million	100.0	17.1	20.1	21.7	21.8	19.2	4.1
Outside metropolitan areas	100.0	24.7	24.1	21.8	18.2	11.2	1.8
Region							
Northeast	100.0	19.2	17.7	18.1	20.8	24.3	6.5
Midwest	100.0	19.7	20.0	20.9	21.2	18.2	4.1
South	100.0	22.5	21.7	20.3	18.9	16.7	4.1
West	100.0	17.0	19.5	20.4	19.7	23.4	6.2

Source: Bureau of the Census, Current Population Reports, Money Income of Households, Families, and Persons in the United States: 1991, *Series P-60, No. 180, 1992*

Families Below Poverty Level by Place of Residence, 1991

Black families in the central cities of Midwestern metropolitan areas are most likely to be poor. White families in the suburbs of the Northeast are least likely to be poor.

(number and percent of families below poverty level by place of residence, race, and Hispanic origin; families as of 1992; numbers in thousands)

	all families		white		black		Hispanic	
	number in poverty	percent in poverty	number in poverty	percent in poverty	number in poverty	percent in poverty	number in poverty	percent in poverty
Total U.S.	7,712	11.5%	5,022	8.8%	2,343	30.4%	1,372	26.5%
Metropolitan	5,750	11.1	3,565	8.2	1,903	29.3	1,262	26.3
Central city	3,270	17.2	1,710	12.3	1,397	32.9	829	31.0
Not central city	2,480	7.6	1,854	6.3	506	22.5	433	20.3
Not metropolitan	1,961	12.7	1,457	10.4	440	35.8	110	29.6
Northeast	1,328	9.9	947	8.0	326	25.3	295	34.4
Metropolitan	1,166	10.0	792	7.8	322	25.2	292	34.6
Central city	755	18.9	454	15.8	268	28.8	254	39.7
Not central city	411	5.3	337	4.7	54	15.4	38	18.6
Not metropolitan	162	9.4	155	9.2	4	-	3	-
Midwest	1,714	10.6	1,100	7.7	557	35.8	76	21.3
Metropolitan	1,258	11.0	665	6.9	552	36.3	66	20.0
Central city	856	20.2	330	11.4	496	40.5	51	23.4
Not central city	402	5.6	335	5.0	56	18.8	15	13.3
Not metropolitan	455	9.6	435	9.3	6	-	10	-
South	3,054	12.9	1,690	8.9	1,315	30.9	396	24.0
Metropolitan	1,973	11.7	1,049	7.8	893	28.8	345	23.2
Central city	1,010	16.4	448	10.6	543	30.5	234	27.3
Not central city	962	9.0	601	6.5	350	26.6	110	17.5
Not metropolitan	1,081	15.8	641	11.5	423	36.5	52	31.8
West	1,616	11.6	1,285	10.6	145	23.4	605	26.2
Metropolitan	1,353	11.6	1,059	10.5	137	23.1	560	26.1
Central city	648	13.9	478	12.5	90	29.1	290	30.3
Not central city	705	10.0	581	9.3	46	16.5	270	22.8
Not metropolitan	263	12.0	226	11.2	8	-	45	26.7
Division								
New England	286	8.2	236	7.2	41	27.8	43	37.4
Middle Atlantic	1,043	10.5	711	8.4	285	24.9	252	34.0
East North Central	1,255	11.0	757	7.6	467	35.6	63	20.9
West North Central	459	9.7	343	7.8	90	37.3	13	-
South Atlantic	1,356	11.2	693	7.3	641	25.9	99	17.0
East South Central	666	15.4	346	9.8	318	39.7	1	-
West South Central	1,032	14.3	651	10.7	356	36.5	297	28.1
Mountain	392	10.7	326	9.5	27	32.5	110	25.6
Pacific	1,224	12.0	959	11.1	117	22.0	495	26.3

Note: Because Hispanics may be of any race, the number of families by race and Hispanic origin does not add to total families.
Source: Bureau of the Census, Current Population Reports, Poverty in the United States: 1991, Series P-60, No. 181, 1992

Married-Couple Families Below Poverty Level by Place of Residence, 1991

As a rule, poverty rates among married couples are low, but fully one-fourth of Hispanic couples in the nation's nonmetropolitan areas are poor.

(number of percent of married couple families below poverty level by place of residence, race, and Hispanic origin; families as of 1992; numbers in thousands)

	all families		white		black		Hispanic	
	number in poverty	percent in poverty	number in poverty	percent in poverty	number in poverty	percent in poverty	number in poverty	percent in poverty
Total U.S.	3,158	6.0%	2,573	5.5%	399	11.0%	674	19.1%
Metropolitan	2,133	5.4	1,705	4.8	277	9.2	599	18.5
Central city	1,027	7.9	748	7.1	195	11.1	361	21.7
Not central city	1,106	4.1	957	3.9	82	6.6	238	15.1
Not metropolitan	1,026	8.0	868	7.3	122	19.4	75	25.9
Northeast	467	4.5	393	4.1	49	8.2	64	14.0
Metropolitan	379	4.2	308	3.8	47	8.0	62	13.8
Central city	200	7.7	145	7.1	37	9.7	47	15.9
Not central city	178	2.8	163	2.7	9	4.6	15	9.8
Not metropolitan	89	6.3	85	6.1	2	-	2	-
Midwest	628	4.9	526	4.4	71	11.5	37	14.4
Metropolitan	394	4.5	298	3.8	71	11.9	31	12.7
Central city	212	7.8	130	5.9	66	14.6	24	15.3
Not central city	182	3.1	168	2.9	5	3.5	7	8.0
Not metropolitan	234	5.8	228	5.7	-	-	7	-
South	1,279	7.0	988	6.2	259	12.4	247	20.6
Metropolitan	725	5.6	566	5.1	140	9.3	212	19.8
Central city	321	7.6	229	6.9	79	10.1	138	23.8
Not central city	404	4.7	337	4.3	62	8.4	74	15.1
Not metropolitan	554	10.1	422	8.8	119	20.4	35	27.0
West	784	7.1	665	6.8	20	6.2	327	20.1
Metropolitan	635	6.9	533	6.6	19	6.2	295	19.8
Central city	294	8.6	244	8.3	13	8.9	152	24.0
Not central city	341	6.0	289	5.7	6	3.6	143	16.7
Not metropolitan	148	8.1	132	7.7	1	-	31	23.6
Division								
New England	89	3.3	83	3.2	2	-	4	-
Middle Atlantic	378	4.9	310	4.5	47	8.8	59	14.9
East North Central	446	5.0	380	4.6	47	9.3	31	14.6
West North Central	182	4.7	146	4.0	24	21.6	6	-
South Atlantic	552	5.9	429	5.4	106	8.4	62	14.4
East South Central	237	7.2	167	5.7	70	20.4	-	-
West South Central	490	8.6	393	7.8	84	17.1	184	24.5
Mountain	212	7.0	183	6.3	8	-	63	20.1
Pacific	572	7.2	483	7.0	12	4.4	264	20.1

Note: Because Hispanics may be of any race, the number of families by race and Hispanic origin does not add to total families.
Source: Bureau of the Census, Current Population Reports, Poverty in the United States: 1991, Series P-60, No. 181, 1992

Married-Couple Families with Children Below Poverty Level by Place of Residence, 1991

Regardless of race, poverty among married couples with children is least common in the suburbs of the Northeast and most common in the nonmetropolitan areas of the South.

(number and percent of married couple families with children under age 18 below poverty level by place of residence, race, and Hispanic origin; families as of 1992; numbers in thousands)

	all families		white		black		Hispanic	
	number in poverty	percent in poverty	number in poverty	percent in poverty	number in poverty	percent in poverty	number in poverty	percent in poverty
Total U.S.	2,106	8.3%	1,715	7.7%	263	12.4%	575	23.5%
Metropolitan	1,460	7.5	1,176	7.0	177	10.1	519	23.0
Central city	694	11.3	521	10.7	119	12.8	301	26.1
Not central city	766	5.8	655	5.5	58	7.1	218	19.7
Not metropolitan	646	10.9	539	10.0	86	22.7	56	29.8
Northeast	312	6.4	253	5.8	36	10.4	54	18.4
Metropolitan	252	5.9	196	5.3	33	9.9	53	18.4
Central city	137	11.3	94	10.3	28	13.1	41	21.3
Not central city	114	3.8	102	3.6	6	4.6	12	12.6
Not metropolitan	60	9.5	57	9.2	2	-	1	-
Midwest	383	6.3	312	5.6	50	14.6	32	16.8
Metropolitan	237	5.7	171	4.6	50	15.2	25	14.5
Central city	124	9.8	72	7.3	45	19.6	19	16.5
Not central city	113	3.9	99	3.6	5	5.1	7	-
Not metropolitan	146	7.7	140	7.5	-	-	7	-
South	830	9.5	654	8.9	162	13.0	196	24.5
Metropolitan	489	7.9	401	7.7	79	8.8	171	23.9
Central city	207	10.9	164	11.3	37	9.0	106	27.7
Not central city	283	6.6	237	6.3	42	8.6	65	19.6
Not metropolitan	341	13.3	253	11.7	83	23.6	24	29.8
West	581	10.3	497	10.1	16	8.2	293	25.2
Metropolitan	481	10.0	408	9.8	15	8.0	269	24.9
Central city	226	12.7	191	12.6	10	12.0	135	29.2
Not central city	255	8.4	217	8.2	5	4.9	134	21.7
Not metropolitan	100	11.8	89	11.6	1	-	24	28.3
Division								
New England	57	4.6	52	4.5	1	-	4	-
Middle Atlantic	254	7.0	200	6.3	35	11.3	50	20.2
East North Central	277	6.5	234	6.1	32	11.5	26	16.4
West North Central	107	5.8	77	4.5	18	-	6	-
South Atlantic	347	8.0	267	7.7	72	9.2	43	17.3
East South Central	134	9.0	100	7.7	34	19.0	-	-
West South Central	349	11.8	286	11.1	56	19.5	153	27.9
Mountain	139	9.3	119	8.5	8	-	50	25.2
Pacific	442	10.6	377	10.7	8	5.2	243	25.2

Note: Because Hispanics may be of any race, the number of families by race and Hispanic origin does not add to total families.
Source: Bureau of the Census, Current Population Reports, Poverty in the United States: 1991, Series P-60, No. 181, 1992

Female-Headed Families Below Poverty Level by Place of Residence, 1991

Over half of all black and Hispanic female-headed families in the nation's central cities are poor. Among whites, one-third are poor.

(number and percent of female-headed families with no spouse present below poverty level by place of residence, race, and Hispanic origin; families as of 1992; numbers in thousands)

	all families		white		black		Hispanic	
	number in poverty	percent in poverty	number in poverty	percent in poverty	number in poverty	percent in poverty	number in poverty	percent in poverty
Total U.S.	4,161	35.6%	2,192	28.4%	1,834	51.2%	627	49.7%
Metropolitan	3,331	34.8	1,683	27.1	1,539	50.4	599	49.4
Central city	2,079	41.9	880	33.9	1,140	52.3	432	53.3
Not central city	1,252	27.1	802	22.3	399	45.8	166	41.6
Not metropolitan	830	39.2	510	33.3	296	55.7	28	-
Northeast	810	33.4	509	29.1	273	44.3	221	63.2
Metropolitan	740	33.8	443	29.0	271	44.1	220	63.1
Central city	528	45.2	288	44.1	226	46.4	199	65.3
Not central city	212	20.7	155	17.7	45	35.1	21	-
Not metropolitan	70	30.2	66	29.4	2	-	1	-
Midwest	1,012	36.9	514	27.7	474	57.0	35	-
Metropolitan	829	37.3	345	25.2	468	57.0	33	-
Central city	621	49.3	190	34.9	418	60.4	26	-
Not central city	207	21.5	155	18.8	50	39.0	7	-
Not metropolitan	183	35.6	170	34.8	6	-	2	-
South	1,611	37.1	623	26.0	973	51.6	131	37.4
Metropolitan	1,135	35.0	432	23.8	691	50.2	119	36.0
Central city	621	38.6	190	26.2	425	49.3	87	38.4
Not central city	514	31.5	242	22.2	266	51.6	31	30.5
Not metropolitan	476	43.2	191	32.8	282	55.4	13	-
West	729	33.3	546	31.7	115	46.3	239	48.4
Metropolitan	628	32.8	462	31.1	109	45.6	226	48.2
Central city	309	33.6	212	31.4	71	51.0	119	51.1
Not central city	319	31.9	250	30.8	38	38.0	107	45.4
Not metropolitan	102	37.2	83	35.4	7	-	13	-
Division								
New England	184	30.9	140	27.6	40	48.0	36	-
Middle Atlantic	626	34.3	370	29.7	233	43.7	185	61.9
East North Central	757	36.9	338	26.0	409	57.1	29	-
West North Central	255	37.0	177	31.9	65	56.6	6	-
South Atlantic	741	33.2	240	20.8	498	47.2	33	29.6
East South Central	402	44.0	162	33.2	237	56.2	1	-
West South Central	468	39.0	222	29.4	237	58.0	97	40.7
Mountain	166	32.6	132	30.1	19	-	40	45.5
Pacific	563	33.5	414	32.2	96	43.9	199	49.1

Note: Because Hispanics may be of any race, the number of families by race and Hispanic origin does not add to total families.
Source: Bureau of the Census, Current Population Reports, *Poverty in the United States: 1991, Series P-60, No. 181, 1992*

Female-Headed Families with Children Below Poverty Level by Place of Residence, 1991

Among single-parent families headed by Hispanic women, nearly three out of four in the central cities of the Northeast are poor.

(number and percent of female-headed families with no spouse present and with children under age 18 at home below poverty level by place of residence, race, and Hispanic origin; families as of 1992; numbers in thousands)

	all families		white		black		Hispanic	
	number in poverty	percent in poverty	number in poverty	percent in poverty	number in poverty	percent in poverty	number in poverty	percent in poverty
Total U.S.	3,767	47.1%	1,969	39.6%	1,676	60.5%	584	60.1%
Metropolitan	3,034	46.5	1,528	38.7	1,408	59.5	558	59.9
Central city	1,891	53.7	799	46.7	1,037	61.0	400	63.9
Not central city	1,143	38.0	729	32.6	371	55.6	158	51.6
Not metropolitan	733	50.1	441	43.3	269	66.2	27	-
Northeast	732	46.7	450	43.5	256	51.5	207	72.5
Metropolitan	669	47.2	390	43.9	255	51.4	206	72.4
Central city	482	57.8	255	60.0	212	54.4	186	73.2
Not central city	188	32.1	135	29.1	43	40.5	20	-
Not metropolitan	63	41.9	60	41.1	1	-	1	-
Midwest	916	47.3	468	37.9	426	64.3	32	-
Metropolitan	758	48.0	323	36.0	420	64.3	30	-
Central city	567	60.3	180	48.8	375	68.0	23	-
Not central city	191	29.9	143	27.0	46	44.7	7	-
Not metropolitan	157	44.3	145	42.9	6	-	2	-
South	1,439	49.1	534	36.8	892	62.0	116	48.6
Metropolitan	1,023	46.8	377	34.3	637	60.4	104	46.9
Central city	560	50.1	168	38.0	388	58.3	78	50.1
Not central city	463	43.5	209	31.8	249	64.0	26	-
Not metropolitan	415	55.8	157	44.6	255	66.3	13	-
West	680	43.6	517	41.5	102	59.2	229	57.9
Metropolitan	583	43.3	438	41.2	95	58.9	218	57.7
Central city	282	45.0	196	41.3	62	67.2	113	61.9
Not central city	301	41.9	242	41.1	33	-	104	53.9
Not metropolitan	97	45.5	79	43.6	7	-	11	-
Division								
New England	170	43.6	128	41.1	37	-	35	-
Middle Atlantic	562	47.7	322	44.6	219	51.5	172	71.7
East North Central	684	47.5	308	36.5	366	63.8	27	-
West North Central	232	46.8	160	40.8	60	67.9	5	-
South Atlantic	667	46.0	199	31.2	465	57.8	27	-
East South Central	354	57.6	137	47.8	215	65.9	-	-
West South Central	418	48.4	198	37.5	212	68.7	89	53.8
Mountain	153	42.7	123	40.0	19	-	36	-
Pacific	527	43.9	394	42.0	83	57.2	193	58.3

Note: Because Hispanics may be of any race, the number of families by race and Hispanic origin does not add to total families.
Source: Bureau of the Census, Current Population Reports, Poverty in the United States: 1991, Series P-60, No. 181, 1992

Persons Below Poverty Level by Place of Residence, 1991

Hispanics living in nonmetropolitan areas of the Midwest are most likely to be poor. Whites living in the suburbs of the Northeast are least likely to be poor.

(number and percent of persons below poverty level by place of residence, race, and Hispanic origin; persons as of 1992; numbers in thousands)

	all persons		white		black		Hispanic	
	number in poverty	percent in poverty	number in poverty	percent in poverty	number in poverty	percent in poverty	number in poverty	percent in poverty
Total U.S.	35,708	14.2%	23,747	11.3%	10,242	32.7%	6,339	28.7%
Metropolitan	26,827	13.7	17,076	10.6	8,380	31.6	5,833	28.3
Central city	15,314	20.2	8,378	15.4	6,163	35.3	3,780	32.9
Not central city	11,513	9.6	8,698	8.2	2,217	24.4	2,053	22.6
Not metropolitan	8,881	16.1	6,672	13.6	1,861	38.9	506	33.9
Northeast	6,177	12.2	4,389	10.0	1,546	28.1	1,217	36.3
Metropolitan	5,422	12.1	3,661	9.7	1,524	28.0	1,194	36.2
Central city	3,400	21.3	2,022	18.0	1,233	31.3	1,030	40.8
Not central city	2,022	7.0	1,639	6.2	292	19.4	164	21.2
Not metropolitan	755	12.3	728	12.1	22	-	22	-
Midwest	7,989	13.2	5,242	9.9	2,380	37.7	346	23.5
Metropolitan	5,846	13.5	3,231	9.0	2,355	38.2	293	21.6
Central city	3,917	23.1	1,625	14.1	2,126	42.8	221	24.5
Not central city	1,928	7.4	1,606	6.6	229	19.2	72	15.9
Not metropolitan	2,143	12.4	2,011	12.0	25	16.7	53	44.6
South	13,783	16.0	7,837	11.7	5,716	33.6	1,765	26.1
Metropolitan	9,044	14.6	4,944	10.3	3,927	31.4	1,540	25.1
Central city	4,788	20.0	2,236	13.8	2,457	33.6	1,019	28.8
Not central city	4,256	11.2	2,708	8.5	1,469	28.2	521	20.0
Not metropolitan	4,738	19.8	2,892	15.2	1,789	39.9	225	35.9
West	7,759	14.3	6,279	13.5	600	24.0	3,012	28.8
Metropolitan	6,514	14.1	5,239	13.4	574	23.9	2,806	28.7
Central city	3,208	16.9	2,494	16.0	347	28.4	1,510	33.4
Not central city	3,307	12.2	2,745	11.7	227	19.2	1,296	24.6
Not metropolitan	1,245	15.6	1,040	14.4	26	25.5	206	29.7
Division								
New England	1,347	10.4	1,097	9.1	195	31.0	181	38.0
Middle Atlantic	4,830	12.8	3,292	10.4	1,351	27.8	1,035	36.0
East North Central	5,752	13.5	3,584	9.8	1,980	37.4	289	23.1
West North Central	2,237	12.6	1,658	10.2	400	39.1	57	25.2
South Atlantic	6,210	14.2	3,262	9.9	2,852	28.6	455	19.6
East South Central	2,848	18.6	1,510	12.5	1,308	41.4	6	-
West South Central	4,724	17.6	3,064	13.9	1,555	40.1	1,304	29.6
Mountain	1,907	13.9	1,599	12.5	107	31.1	522	29.2
Pacific	5,852	14.5	4,681	13.9	493	22.8	2,490	28.7

Note: Because Hispanics may be of any race, the number of persons by race and Hispanic origin does not add to total persons.
Source: Bureau of the Census, Current Population Reports, Poverty in the United States: 1991, Series P-60, No. 181, 1992

Persons Below Poverty Level in Metropolitan Areas by Sex, Age, Race, and Hispanic Origin, 1991

Between one-fourth and one-third of blacks and Hispanics living in the nation's metropolitan areas are poor.

(number and percent of persons below poverty level in metropolitan areas by sex, age, race, and Hispanic origin; persons as of 1992; numbers in thousands)

	all persons		white		black		Hispanic	
	number in poverty	percent in poverty	number in poverty	percent in poverty	number in poverty	percent in poverty	number in poverty	percent in poverty
Both sexes								
Total	26,827	13.7%	17,076	10.6%	8,380	31.6%	5,833	28.3%
Under age 18	10,992	21.5	6,449	16.2	3,960	45.4	2,847	40.1
Aged 18 to 24	3,236	16.6	2,118	13.6	953	31.6	714	27.2
Aged 25 to 34	4,324	12.5	2,901	10.3	1,204	25.3	955	23.8
Aged 35 to 44	2,656	8.5	1,679	6.4	787	20.8	610	20.6
Aged 45 to 54	1,571	7.4	1,047	5.9	463	19.1	299	17.9
Aged 55 to 59	685	8.6	449	6.8	188	20.0	105	16.6
Aged 60 to 64	760	9.6	524	7.7	206	24.2	99	18.2
Aged 65 or older	2,601	11.5	1,909	9.5	620	30.3	204	19.5
Aged 65 to 74	1,356	9.9	906	7.5	399	30.2	115	17.2
Aged 75 or older	1,246	13.9	1,004	12.5	221	30.4	90	23.5
Men								
Total	11,255	11.8	7,188	9.1	3,428	27.4	2,653	25.8
Under age 18	5,518	21.1	3,230	15.8	1,995	44.7	1,448	40.2
Aged 18 to 24	1,270	13.2	850	11.0	342	24.0	304	22.9
Aged 25 to 34	1,582	9.2	1,143	8.1	350	16.0	367	17.5
Aged 35 to 44	1,058	6.9	714	5.5	263	15.4	257	17.3
Aged 45 to 54	639	6.2	438	5.0	174	16.1	127	16.1
Aged 55 to 59	270	6.9	178	5.5	67	14.8	55	17.3
Aged 60 to 64	264	7.1	194	6.0	60	15.8	39	15.8
Aged 65 or older	654	7.0	442	5.4	178	21.7	57	13.5
Aged 65 to 74	397	6.6	249	4.7	124	21.6	32	11.6
Aged 75 or older	257	7.9	193	6.6	54	21.7	24	17.5
Women								
Total	15,571	15.5	9,888	12.0	4,952	35.3	3,180	30.9
Under age 18	5,475	22.0	3,219	16.6	1,965	46.1	1,399	40.1
Aged 18 to 24	1,966	19.9	1,268	16.1	611	38.4	410	31.8
Aged 25 to 34	2,742	15.8	1,758	12.6	854	33.2	589	30.7
Aged 35 to 44	1,599	10.0	965	7.4	524	25.3	352	24.0
Aged 45 to 54	932	8.5	609	6.7	289	21.5	173	19.5
Aged 55 to 59	415	10.3	270	8.0	121	24.8	50	16.0
Aged 60 to 64	496	11.8	330	9.3	146	30.8	60	20.3
Aged 65 or older	1,947	14.5	1,468	12.4	442	36.0	148	23.5
Aged 65 to 74	959	12.4	657	9.8	275	36.7	82	21.3
Aged 75 or older	988	17.4	811	15.8	167	34.9	65	27.0

Note: Because Hispanics may be of any race, the number of persons by race and Hispanic origin does not add to total persons.
Source: Bureau of the Census, Current Population Reports, Poverty in the United States: 1991, Series P-60, No. 181, 1992

Persons Below Poverty Level in Central Cities by Sex, Age, Race, and Hispanic Origin, 1991

GEOGRAPHY

Fully one-third of children living in the nation's central cities are poor. Among blacks, the proportion is 50 percent.

(number and percent of persons below poverty level in central cities by sex, age, race, and Hispanic origin; persons as of 1992; numbers in thousands)

	all persons		white		black		Hispanic	
	number in poverty	percent in poverty	number in poverty	percent in poverty	number in poverty	percent in poverty	number in poverty	percent in poverty
Both sexes								
Total	15,314	20.2%	8,378	15.4%	6,163	35.3%	3,780	32.9%
Under age 18	6,369	32.5	3,177	24.7	2,860	50.4	1,839	46.4
Aged 18 to 24	1,939	23.6	1,133	19.4	697	36.5	469	30.9
Aged 25 to 34	2,451	17.4	1,446	14.1	874	28.6	592	26.9
Aged 35 to 44	1,491	13.0	800	9.6	601	24.7	385	24.2
Aged 45 to 54	920	12.3	527	9.5	362	23.1	213	22.6
Aged 55 to 59	374	12.9	203	9.6	146	23.2	69	19.1
Aged 60 to 64	356	11.9	195	8.8	151	23.5	59	20.2
Aged 65 or older	1,414	15.4	895	12.3	472	30.5	154	25.3
Aged 65 to 74	806	14.9	495	11.8	278	28.5	88	22.8
Aged 75 or older	608	16.1	400	12.9	194	34.0	66	29.7
Men								
Total	6,359	17.5	3,497	13.3	2,506	30.9	1,665	29.5
Under age 18	3,214	32.4	1,613	24.7	1,444	50.2	912	45.9
Aged 18 to 24	729	18.4	439	15.6	234	26.2	198	26.1
Aged 25 to 34	851	12.2	554	10.6	247	18.0	219	19.1
Aged 35 to 44	576	10.3	329	7.8	210	18.9	148	18.9
Aged 45 to 54	373	10.5	221	8.3	137	19.7	89	20.5
Aged 55 to 59	134	9.6	66	6.3	52	19.1	31	17.8
Aged 60 to 64	122	8.9	68	6.6	51	17.5	23	17.7
Aged 65 or older	359	10.1	207	7.4	132	21.7	44	19.3
Aged 65 to 74	225	10.0	126	7.3	88	20.7	26	17.4
Aged 75 or older	134	10.4	81	7.6	44	24.0	18	22.8
Women								
Total	8,955	22.6	4,880	17.3	3,657	39.2	2,115	36.2
Under age 18	3,155	32.6	1,565	24.7	1,416	50.7	927	46.9
Aged 18 to 24	1,210	28.5	694	22.8	464	45.5	271	35.7
Aged 25 to 34	1,600	22.5	891	17.7	627	37.3	373	35.2
Aged 35 to 44	915	15.7	471	11.3	391	29.6	237	29.3
Aged 45 to 54	547	13.8	306	10.6	225	25.8	124	24.4
Aged 55 to 59	239	15.9	137	12.8	94	26.3	37	20.4
Aged 60 to 64	233	14.5	128	10.8	100	28.6	37	22.2
Aged 65 or older	1,055	18.7	688	15.3	341	36.3	110	29.0
Aged 65 to 74	581	18.5	369	14.9	190	34.6	62	26.3
Aged 75 or older	474	19.1	319	15.6	150	38.7	48	33.5

Note: Because Hispanics may be of any race, the number of persons by race and Hispanic origin does not add to total persons.
Source: Bureau of the Census, Current Population Reports, Poverty in the United States: 1991, Series P-60, No. 181, 1992

Persons Below Poverty Level in Metropolitan Areas Outside of Central Cities by Sex, Age, Race, and Hispanic Origin, 1991

Fewer than 10 percent of whites living in the suburbs are poor. Among blacks and Hispanics, the proportion is about one in four.

(number and percent of persons below poverty level in metropolitan areas outside of central cities by sex, age, race, and Hispanic origin; persons as of 1992; numbers in thousands)

	all persons		white		black		Hispanic	
	number in poverty	percent in poverty	number in poverty	percent in poverty	number in poverty	percent in poverty	number in poverty	percent in poverty
Both sexes								
Total	11,513	9.6%	8,698	8.2%	2,217	24.4%	9,092	22.6%
Under age 18	4,623	14.7	3,271	12.1	1,101	36.09	3,130	32.2
Aged 18 to 24	1,297	11.5	985	10.1	255	23.1	1,103	22.2
Aged 25 to 34	1,873	9.2	1,455	8.1	330	19.4	1,806	20.1
Aged 35 to 44	1,165	5.9	879	5.0	186	13.8	1,360	16.5
Aged 45 to 54	651	4.8	520	4.2	101	11.7	731	11.8
Aged 55 to 59	311	6.2	245	5.4	42	13.6	270	13.4
Aged 60 to 64	405	8.2	329	7.1	55	26.1	252	15.9
Aged 65 or older	1,187	8.8	1,014	7.9	147	29.5	440	11.4
Aged 65 to 74	550	6.6	411	5.3	121	34.9	281	9.5
Aged 75 or older	638	12.3	603	12.2	27	17.2	159	14.8
Men								
Total	4,896	8.3	3,691	7.0	922	21.0	4,636	21.3
Under age 18	2,304	14.2	1,617	11.6	551	34.7	1,615	33.2
Aged 18 to 24	541	9.6	411	8.4	109	20.3	571	18.5
Aged 25 to 34	731	7.2	588	6.6	103	12.7	948	15.5
Aged 35 to 44	482	5.0	385	4.4	53	8.9	701	15.6
Aged 45 to 54	266	4.0	217	3.6	37	9.5	351	10.7
Aged 55 to 59	135	5.5	113	5.1	15	8.3	140	16.7
Aged 60 to 64	142	6.0	126	5.7	9	10.3	120	13.7
Aged 65 or older	295	5.1	235	4.3	46	21.7	190	6.6
Aged 65 to 74	172	4.6	123	3.5	36	24.5	130	4.8
Aged 75 or older	123	6.2	112	5.9	10	-	60	-
Women								
Total	6,617	4.0	5,007	9.3	1,295	27.6	4,455	23.9
Under age 18	2,319	15.3	1,655	12.7	550	37.4	1,515	31.2
Aged 18 to 24	756	13.5	574	11.8	147	25.7	532	26.2
Aged 25 to 34	1,142	11.2	867	9.7	228	25.5	858	25.1
Aged 35 to 44	683	6.8	494	5.5	132	17.7	659	17.4
Aged 45 to 54	385	5.5	303	4.8	64	13.6	380	12.9
Aged 55 to 59	176	6.9	133	5.7	27	20.7	130	9.8
Aged 60 to 64	263	10.2	203	8.5	46	37.1	131	17.9
Aged 65 or older	892	11.5	779	10.6	101	35.2	250	15.1
Aged 65 to 74	378	8.3	288	6.8	85	42.6	151	13.5
Aged 75 or older	515	16.0	492	16.0	16	18.5	99	17.5

Note: Because Hispanics may be of any race, the number of persons by race and Hispanic origin does not add to total persons.
Source: Bureau of the Census, Current Population Reports, Poverty in the United States: 1991, *Series P-60, No. 181, 1992*

Persons Below Poverty Level in Nonmetropolitan Areas by Sex, Age, Race, and Hispanic Origin, 1991

In nonmetropolitan areas, children are more likely to be poor than adults, regardless of race. The only exception is black women aged 75 or older, 60 percent of whom are poor.

(number and percent of persons below poverty level in nonmetropolitan areas by sex, age, race, and Hispanic origin; persons as of 1992; numbers in thousands)

	all persons		white		black		Hispanic	
	number in poverty	percent in poverty	number in poverty	percent in poverty	number in poverty	percent in poverty	number in poverty	percent in poverty
Both sexes								
Total	8,881	16.1%	6,672	13.6%	1,861	38.9%	506	33.9%
Under age 18	3,349	22.5	2,399	18.9	794	48.9	247	44.6
Aged 18 to 24	884	17.7	673	15.4	170	33.9	57	32.1
Aged 25 to 34	1,244	15.5	970	13.6	224	33.4	71	29.8
Aged 35 to 44	936	11.2	705	9.5	202	29.3	46	21.6
Aged 45 to 54	596	10.2	494	9.2	81	22.4	28	20.3
Aged 55 to 59	335	12.4	267	10.9	58	26.9	8	-
Aged 60 to 64	360	13.9	271	11.4	72	45.0	16	-
Aged 65 or older	1,180	14.9	893	12.3	261	46.6	33	34.7
Aged 65 to 74	606	12.8	440	10.2	148	43.2	23	-
Aged 75 or older	574	18.0	453	15.5	112	51.8	10	-
Men								
Total	3,827	14.1	2,891	12.0	769	34.5	247	32.0
Under age 18	1,687	22.3	1,226	19.0	387	47.5	125	44.9
Aged 18 to 24	363	14.5	282	12.8	52	22.9	27	27.9
Aged 25 to 34	467	11.7	362	10.2	82	25.3	34	25.2
Aged 35 to 44	435	10.4	346	9.2	77	24.1	23	20.9
Aged 45 to 54	255	8.8	231	8.6	21	13.9	15	-
Aged 55 to 59	118	9.6	93	8.2	21	23.3	5	-
Aged 60 to 64	141	12.0	99	9.0	35	-	3	-
Aged 65 or older	361	10.3	251	7.8	93	39.2	15	-
Aged 65 to 74	235	10.5	158	7.7	69	41.1	9	-
Aged 75 or older	126	10.0	93	8.0	24	-	6	-
Women								
Total	5,054	17.9	3,780	15.1	1,092	42.8	259	35.9
Under age 18	1,661	22.8	1,173	18.9	408	50.2	122	44.3
Aged 18 to 24	521	20.9	391	18.1	118	43.0	30	37.1
Aged 25 to 34	777	19.3	607	17.0	142	41.0	37	35.7
Aged 35 to 44	501	12.0	358	9.7	124	33.8	23	22.3
Aged 45 to 54	341	11.4	263	9.7	60	28.6	13	-
Aged 55 to 59	217	14.7	174	13.2	38	29.4	3	-
Aged 60 to 64	218	15.5	173	13.5	36	37.5	13	-
Aged 65 or older	819	18.6	642	16.0	167	52.0	18	-
Aged 65 to 74	371	15.0	282	12.5	79	45.3	14	-
Aged 75 or older	448	23.3	360	20.5	88	60.1	5	-

Note: Because Hispanics may be of any race, the number of persons by race and Hispanic origin does not add to total persons.
Source: Bureau of the Census, Current Population Reports, Poverty in the United States: 1991, Series P-60, No. 181, 1992

Median Income of Households by State, 1984 to 1991

After adjusting for inflation, median household income by state has changed little since the mid-1980s.

(median household income by state, 1984-91; income in 1991 dollars)									percent change 1984-91
	1991	*1990*	*1989*	*1988*	*1987*	*1986*	*1985*	*1984*	
Alabama	$23,346	$24,340	$23,378	$22,966	$23,660	$23,775	$23,206	$22,691	2.9%
Alaska	40,612	40,952	39,549	38,112	39,844	38,966	44,027	42,415	-4.3
Arizona	30,737	30,454	31,361	30,435	32,071	31,689	30,223	28,085	9.4
Arkansas	23,435	23,745	23,542	23,224	22,572	23,276	22,089	20,547	14.1
California	33,664	34,691	36,257	34,870	36,143	36,051	34,153	33,148	1.6
Colorado	31,499	32,026	29,443	30,180	31,743	33,791	35,673	33,822	-6.9
Connecticut	42,154	40,506	46,485	41,692	39,400	40,662	39,354	39,262	7.4
Delaware	32,585	32,100	35,223	35,121	35,062	31,845	29,088	33,845	-3.7
District of Columbia	29,885	28,545	29,384	30,787	32,917	30,225	26,678	26,752	11.7
Florida	27,252	27,808	28,651	29,250	29,361	28,394	27,016	25,936	5.1
Georgia	27,212	28,721	30,252	30,586	32,029	30,285	26,644	26,197	3.9
Hawaii	37,246	40,559	38,482	38,021	41,989	36,042	36,659	37,854	-1.6
Idaho	26,116	26,370	27,080	26,998	24,884	25,785	26,279	27,649	-5.5
Illinois	31,884	33,911	34,380	33,991	32,472	32,945	31,480	31,136	2.4
Indiana	27,089	28,061	28,446	30,271	26,999	28,244	28,702	29,849	-9.2
Iowa	28,553	28,436	28,849	27,983	26,605	27,910	26,489	26,038	9.7
Kansas	29,295	31,176	29,505	29,434	30,673	29,733	28,845	32,286	-9.3
Kentucky	23,764	25,823	25,574	22,919	24,786	24,697	21,976	23,176	2.5
Louisiana	25,299	23,348	25,110	23,598	25,596	25,960	26,808	24,840	1.8
Maine	27,868	28,620	30,998	30,397	28,295	29,109	25,973	27,067	3.0
Maryland	36,952	40,492	39,560	42,083	41,927	38,032	38,146	38,943	-5.1
Massachusetts	35,714	37,772	39,636	38,238	38,655	37,702	35,704	35,340	1.1
Michigan	32,117	31,197	33,803	33,931	33,213	33,062	30,685	30,104	6.7
Minnesota	29,479	32,789	33,155	33,488	33,669	32,861	30,197	32,033	-8.0
Mississippi	19,475	21,027	21,877	20,915	22,196	20,521	20,776	20,227	-3.7
Missouri	27,926	28,482	29,104	26,990	28,439	27,246	27,770	27,233	2.5
Montana	24,827	24,359	26,023	25,595	24,547	25,262	25,615	25,609	-3.1
Nebraska	29,549	28,638	28,908	28,966	27,897	27,056	27,593	28,049	5.3
Nevada	32,937	33,371	32,227	32,217	32,225	32,580	29,460	33,789	-2.5
New Hampshire	36,032	42,522	41,225	39,864	38,771	37,962	33,421	33,970	6.1
New Jersey	40,049	40,364	42,969	41,778	41,053	39,412	39,214	36,411	10.0
New Mexico	26,540	26,093	24,826	22,216	24,888	24,661	25,851	27,043	-1.9
New York	31,794	32,920	34,595	33,290	31,633	31,099	29,922	28,875	10.1
North Carolina	26,853	27,437	29,004	28,109	27,288	27,167	27,153	26,963	-0.4
North Dakota	25,892	26,327	27,711	27,737	27,067	26,728	26,841	27,228	-4.9

(continued)

(continued from previous page)

(median household income by state, 1984-91; income in 1991 dollars)

	1991	1990	1989	1988	1987	1986	1985	1984	percent change 1984-91
Ohio	$29,790	$31,276	$31,876	$31,937	$30,900	$31,210	$31,865	$30,311	-1.7%
Oklahoma	25,462	25,410	25,996	27,248	26,006	26,032	26,841	27,722	-8.2
Oregon	30,190	30,513	31,336	31,947	30,019	30,785	27,713	28,051	7.6
Pennsylvania	30,367	30,226	31,513	30,788	30,482	29,585	28,958	26,671	13.9
Rhode Island	30,836	33,313	33,088	34,357	33,920	32,981	31,170	28,331	8.8
South Carolina	27,463	29,944	26,139	29,396	30,032	27,300	25,362	26,623	3.2
South Dakota	24,639	25,605	26,480	25,667	25,359	24,727	22,964	25,443	-3.2
Tennessee	24,453	23,543	24,836	24,012	25,392	22,687	22,503	21,999	11.2
Texas	27,733	29,416	27,433	28,740	29,639	30,026	30,054	30,182	-8.1
Utah	28,016	31,410	33,739	30,294	31,807	32,659	31,946	30,225	-7.3
Vermont	29,155	32,407	34,374	33,374	30,471	30,569	32,911	29,597	-1.5
Virginia	36,137	36,549	37,475	37,588	35,963	36,927	35,985	34,771	3.9
Washington	33,970	33,463	35,106	37,218	32,754	33,405	30,379	32,794	3.6
West Virginia	23,147	23,069	23,810	22,281	20,630	20,460	20,231	22,079	4.8
Wisconsin	31,133	32,003	31,988	34,050	31,615	32,845	29,425	27,191	14.5
Wyoming	29,050	30,700	32,425	30,416	33,079	29,277	27,950	31,220	-7.0

Source: Bureau of the Census, Current Population Reports, Money Income of Households, Families, and Persons in the United States: 1991, *Series P-60, No. 180, 1992*

Persons Below Poverty Level by State, 1989 to 1991

Eight states had poverty rates below 10 percent in 1991. Two had poverty rates above 20 percent. Poverty rates were highest in Mississippi and lowest in New Hampshire in 1991.

(percent of persons below poverty level by state, 1989-91)	1991	1990	1989	three-year average 1989-91
Alabama	18.8%	19.2%	18.9%	19.0%
Alaska	11.8	11.4	10.5	11.2
Arizona	14.8	13.7	14.1	14.2
Arkansas	17.3	19.6	18.3	18.4
California	15.7	13.9	12.9	14.2
Colorado	10.4	13.7	12.1	12.1
Connecticut	8.6	6.0	2.9	5.8
Delaware	7.5	6.9	10.0	8.1
District of Columbia	18.6	21.1	18.0	19.2
Florida	15.4	14.4	12.5	14.1
Georgia	17.2	15.8	15.0	16.0
Hawaii	7.7	11.0	11.3	10.0
Idaho	13.9	14.9	12.4	13.7
Illinois	13.5	13.7	12.7	13.3
Indiana	15.7	13.0	13.7	14.1
Iowa	9.6	10.4	10.3	10.1
Kansas	12.3	10.3	10.8	11.1
Kentucky	18.8	17.3	16.1	17.4
Louisiana	19.0	23.6	23.3	22.0
Maine	14.1	13.1	10.4	12.5
Maryland	9.1	9.9	9.0	9.3
Massachusetts	11.0	10.7	8.8	10.2
Michigan	14.1	14.3	13.2	13.9
Minnesota	12.9	12.0	11.2	12.0
Mississippi	23.7	25.7	22.0	23.8
Missouri	14.8	13.4	12.6	13.6
Montana	15.4	16.3	15.6	15.8
Nebraska	9.5	10.3	12.8	10.9
Nevada	11.4	9.8	10.8	10.7
New Hampshire	7.3	6.3	7.7	7.1
New Jersey	9.7	9.2	8.2	9.0
New Mexico	22.4	20.9	19.5	20.9
New York	15.3	14.3	12.6	14.1
North Carolina	14.5	13.0	12.2	13.2
North Dakota	14.5	13.7	12.2	13.5

(continued)

(percent of persons below poverty level by state, 1989-91)

	1991	*1990*	*1989*	*three-year average 1989-91*
Ohio	13.4%	11.5%	10.6%	11.8%
Oklahoma	17.0	15.6	14.7	15.8
Oregon	13.5	9.2	11.2	11.3
Pennsylvania	11.0	11.0	10.4	10.8
Rhode Island	10.4	7.5	6.7	8.2
South Carolina	16.4	16.2	17.0	16.5
South Dakota	14.0	13.3	13.2	13.5
Tennessee	15.5	16.9	18.4	16.9
Texas	17.5	15.9	17.1	16.8
Utah	12.9	8.2	8.2	9.8
Vermont	12.6	10.9	8.0	10.5
Virginia	9.9	11.1	10.9	10.6
Washington	9.5	8.9	9.6	9.3
West Virginia	17.9	18.1	15.7	17.2
Wisconsin	9.9	9.3	8.4	9.2
Wyoming	9.9	11.0	10.9	10.6

Source: Bureau of the Census, Current Population Reports, Money Income of Households, Families, and Persons in the United States: 1991, *Series P-60, No. 180, 1992*

Glossary

adjusted for inflation Income or a change in income that has been adjusted for the rise in the cost of living, or the consumer price index (CPI-U-XI). In most of the tables in this book, income figures for years prior to 1991 are adjusted using the CPI-U-XI and expressed in 1991 dollars. The CPI-U-XI adjustment factors are as follows:

year	index	year	index
1991	136.2	1968	37.7
1990	130.7	1967	36.3
1989	124.0	1966	35.2
1988	118.3	1965	34.2
1987	113.6	1964	33.7
1986	109.6	1963	33.3
1985	107.6	1962	32.8
1984	103.9	1961	32.5
1983	99.6	1960	32.2
1982	95.6	1959	31.6
1981	90.1	1958	31.4
1980	82.3	1957	30.5
1979	74.0	1956	29.6
1978	67.5	1955	29.1
1977	63.2	1954	29.2
1976	59.4	1953	29.0
1975	56.2	1952	28.8
1974	51.9	1951	28.3
1973	47.2	1950	26.2
1972	44.4	1949	25.9
1971	43.1	1948	26.2
1970	41.3	1947	24.2
1969	39.4		

To figure the inflation rate between two years, divide the index in the later year by the index in the earlier year. Multiply the result by the income of the earlier year. For example, to adjust 1989 income for inflation through 1991, divide 136.2 by 124.0 to arrive at the ratio 1.09839. Multiply that figure by income in 1989 to arrive at 1989 income expressed in 1991 dollars.

average income Average income is the total income of a group divided by the number of units in the group. Average income for households or families is based on all households or families. Average income for persons is based on all persons aged 15 or older with income.

baby boom Americans born between 1946 and 1964. There are 78 million baby boomers in 1993.

central cities The largest city in a metropolitan area is called the central city. The balance of the metropolitan area outside the central city is regarded as the "suburbs."

consumer unit (on spending tables in Wealth and Spending chapter only) For convenience, consumer units are called households in this book although consumer units are somewhat different from the Census Bureau's households. Consumer units are all related members of a household, or financially independent members of a household. A household may include more than one consumer unit.

dual-earner couple A married couple in which both the householder and the householder's spouse are in the labor force.

educational attainment Beginning in January 1992, the Census Bureau changed the way its Current Population Survey (CPS) collects data on educational attainment. Consequently, data on educational attainment from the 1992 CPS are not directly comparable to CPS data for earlier years. Prior to 1992, CPS interviewers asked respondents for the highest grade of school they had attended or the number of years they spent in college, regardless of whether they finished the grade or earned a degree. Beginning in 1992, CPS interviewers ask respondents for the highest grade or degree completed.

employed All civilians who did any work as a paid employee or farmer/self-employed worker, or who worked 15 hours or more as an unpaid farm worker or in a family-owned business, during the reference period. All those who have jobs but who are temporarily absent from their jobs due to illness, bad weather, vacation, labor management dispute, or personal reasons are considered employed.

expenditure The transaction cost including excise and sales taxes of goods and services acquired during the survey period. The full cost of each purchase is recorded even though full payment may not have been made at the date of purchase. Expenditure estimates include money spent on gifts for others.

family A group of two or more people (one of whom is the householder) related by birth, marriage, or adoption and living together in the same household.

family household A household maintained by a householder who lives with one or more people related to him or her by blood, marriage, or adoption.

female/male householder A male or female who maintains a household without a spouse present. May head family or nonfamily households.

full-time, year-round Indicates 50 or more weeks of full-time employment during the previous calendar year.

geographic regions The four major regions and nine census divisions of the United States are the state groupings as shown below:

Northeast:
—New England: Connecticut, Maine, Massachusetts, New Hampshire, Rhode Island, and Vermont
—Middle Atlantic: New Jersey, New York, and Pennsylvania
Midwest
—East North Central: Illinois, Indiana, Michigan, Ohio, and Wisconsin
—West North Central: Iowa, Kansas, Minnesota, Missouri, Nebraska, North Dakota, and South Dakota
South:
—South Atlantic: Delaware, District of Columbia, Florida, Georgia, Maryland, North Carolina, South Carolina, Virginia, and West Virginia
—East South Central: Alabama, Kentucky, Mississippi, and Tennessee
—West South Central: Arkansas, Louisiana, Oklahoma, and Texas

West:
—Mountain: Arizona, Colorado, Idaho, Montana, Nevada, New Mexico, Utah, and Wyoming
—Pacific: Alaska, California, Hawaii, Oregon, and Washington

Hispanic Persons or householders who identify their origin as Mexican, Puerto Rican, Central or South American or some other Hispanic origin. Persons of Hispanic origin may be of any race. In other words, there are black Hispanics, white Hispanics, and Asian Hispanics.

household All the persons who occupy a housing unit. A household includes the related family members and all the unrelated persons, if any, such as lodgers, foster children, wards, or employees who share the housing unit. A person living alone is counted as a household. A group of unrelated people who share a housing unit as roommates or unmarried partners is also counted as a household. Households do not include group quarters such as college dormitories, prisons, or nursing homes.

household, race/ethnicity of Households are categorized according to the race or ethnicity of the householder only.

householder The householder is the person (or one of the persons) in whose name the housing unit is owned or rented or, if there is no such person, any adult member. With married couples, the householder may be either the husband or wife. The householder is the reference person for the household.

householder, age of The age of the householder is used to categorize households into age groups such as those used in this book. Married couples, for example, are classified according to the age of either the husband or wife, depending on which one identified him or herself as the householder.

income Money received in the preceding calendar year by each person 15 years old or older from each of the following sources: (1) earnings from longest job (or self-employment); (2) earnings from jobs other than longest job; (3) unemployment compensation; (4) workers' compensation; (5) Social Security; (6) Supplemental Security income; (7) public assistance; (8) veterans' payments; (9) survivor benefits; (10) disability benefits; (11) retirement pensions; (12) interest; (13) dividends; (14) rents and royalties or estates and trusts; (15) educational assistance; (16) alimony; (17) child support; (18) financial assistance from outside the household, and other periodic income. Income is reported in several ways in this book. Household income is the combined income of all household members. Income of persons is all income accruing to a person from all sources. Earnings is the amount of money a person receives from his or her job.

income fifths or quintiles Where the total number of households or persons are divided into fifths based on household or personal income. One-fifth of households or persons falls into the lowest income quintile, one fifth into the second income quintile, and so on. This is a useful way to compare the characteristics of low, middle and high income households.

industry Refers to the industry in which a person worked longest in the preceding calendar year.

labor force All the labor force tables in this book are based on the civilian labor force, which includes all employed and unemployed civilians.

labor force participation rate The percent of the population in the labor force. The labor force participation rates appearing in this book are based on the civilian labor force and civilian population. Labor force participation rates may also be shown for sex–age groups or other special populations such as mothers of children of a given age.

married couples with or without children under age 18 Refers to married couples with or without children under age 18 living in the same household. Couples without children under age 18 may be parents of grown children who live elsewhere or they could be childless couples.

means-tested assistance Government benefits received by persons or households whose incomes fall below a certain threshold. Examples include cash assistance such as Aid to Families with Dependent Children (AFDC), often referred to as welfare. Some means-tested assistance is noncash, such as food stamps, Medicaid, and rent subsidies.

median The median is the amount (income, age, or years of school completed, for example) that divides the population or households into two equal portions; one below and one above the median.

median income Median income is the amount that divides the income distribution into two equal groups, half having incomes above the median, half having incomes below the median. The medians for households or families are based on all households or families. The medians for persons are based on all persons aged 15 or older with income.

metropolitan area An area qualifies for recognition as a metropolitan area if (1) it includes a city of at least 50,000 population, or (2) it includes a Census Bureau-defined urbanized area of at least 50,000 with a total metropolitan population of at least 100,000 (75,000 in New England). In addition to the county containing the main city or urbanized area, a metropolitan area may include other counties having strong commuting ties to the central county.

nonfamily household A household maintained by a householder who lives alone or who lives with people to whom he or she is not related.

nonfamily/nonfamily householder A householder who lives alone or with nonrelatives.

nonmeans-tested assistance Government benefits received regardless of a person's or household's income level. Examples include Social Security and Medicare.

nonmetropolitan area Counties that are not classified as metropolitan areas.

occupation Occupational classification is based on the kind of work a person does at his or her job. If the person changed jobs, the data refer to the occupation of the job held the longest during the previous calendar year.

outside central city The portion of a metropolitan county or counties that falls outside of the central city or cities; generally regarded as the suburbs.

part-time or full-time employment Part-time is less than 35 hours of work per week in a majority of the weeks worked during the year. Full-time indicates 35 or more hours of work per week during a majority of the weeks worked.

per capita income Per capita income is average income computed for every man, woman, and child in a particular group, It is calculated by dividing the total income of a group by the total population of that group.

percent change The change (either positive or negative) in a measure that is expressed as a proportion of the starting measure. When median income changes from $20,000 to $25,000, for example, this is a 25 percent increase.

percentage point change The change (either positive or negative) in a value which is already expressed as a percentage. When a labor force participation rate changes from 70 percent to 75 percent, for example, this is a 5 percentage point increase.

poverty level The official income threshold below which families and persons are classified as living in poverty. The threshold rises each year with inflation and varies depending on family size and age of householder. In 1991, the poverty threshold for one person under age 65 was $6,932. The threshold for a family of four was $13,924.

proportion or share The value of a part expressed as a percentage of the whole. If there are 4 million people aged 25 and 3 million of them are white, then the white proportion is 75 percent.

race Race is self-reported and usually appears in three categories in this book: white, black, and Asian or other. A household is assigned the race of the householder.

rounding Percentages are rounded to the nearest tenth of a percent; therefore, the percentages in a distribution do not always add exactly to 100.0 percent. The totals, however, are always shown as 100.0. Moreover, individual figures are rounded to the nearest thousand without being adjusted to group totals, which are independently rounded; percentages are based on the unrounded numbers.

suburbs *See* outside central city.

symbols A dash (-) represents data not available, not applicable, or sample too small to provide reliable data.

tenure A housing unit is "owner occupied" if the owner lives in the unit, even if it is mortgaged or not fully paid for. A cooperative or condominium unit is "owner occupied" only if the owner lives in it. All other occupied units are classified as "renter occupied."

work experience Work experience is based on work for pay or work without pay on a family-operated farm or business at any time during the previous year, on a part-time or full-time basis.

Index

Metropolitan residence
  households, 310
    black, 312
    Hispanic, 313
    white, 311

Occupation, 202
  men, 198
  women, 198

Pension coverage and participation, 270

Persons, 60
  age, 61, 162-169
    race, 204-207
    source of income, 202-207
  blacks. *See* Blacks
  education, 63
  Hispanics. *See* Hispanics
  men. *See* Men
  poverty, below 277-278, 283
    age, 279
    education, 284
    entering and exiting, 291
    residence, place of, 325
      central cities, 327
      metropolitan areas, 326
      metropolitan areas outside central cities, 328
      nonmetropolitan areas, 329
    state, 332
  residence, place of, 309
  source of income, 204
  whites. *See* Whites
  women. *See* Women
  work experience
    full-time with low earnings, 56

Poverty
  families, 272
    black, 275
    female-headed, 323
      children, presence of, 324
    Hispanic, 276
    married-couple, 321
      children, presence of, 322
      residence, place of, 321
    residence, place of, 320
    type, 273
    white, 274
    work experience, 288

households
  black, 275
  Hispanic, 276
  type of, 273
  white, 274
persons, 277-279, 283, 291, 325
  age, 279
  black, 281
    education, 286
  education, 284
  Hispanic, 282
    education, 287
  residence, place of
    central cities, 327
    metropolitan areas, 326
    metropolitan areas outside central cities, 328
    nonmetropolitan areas, 329
  white, 280
    education, 285
  work experience, 289, 290
state, 330, 332

Projections of income
  age of householder
    1995, 0.5 percent growth, 230
    1995, 1.0 percent growth, 231
    2000, 0.5 percent growth, 232
    2000, 1.0 percent growth, 233
    2005, 0.5 percent growth, 234
    2005, 1.0 percent growth, 235

Race. *See* Blacks and Whites

Regions
  discretionary income, 223
  families, 303
  households, 302
  men, 304
  Midwest, 306
  Northeast, 306
  South, 307
  West, 307
  women, 305

Residence, place of
  central cities, 327
  families, 315
    female-headed
      poverty, below, 323, 324
    married-couple
      poverty, below, 321, 322
    poverty, below, 320

households, 308, 314, 318, 319
men, 316
metropolitan areas outside central cities, 328
nonmetropolitan areas, 329
persons, 309
  poverty, below, 325, 326
women, 317

Saving, personal, 241

Source of income
  families, 135
    black, 137
    Hispanic, 138
    white, 136
  persons
    race, 204-207

Spending, household, 328

States, 330

Taxes, 17
  before-tax, discretionary income 216

Union status, 201, 202

Whites, 36
  benefits, government, receipt of, 294
  discretionary income, 220
  families, 19, 23, 27, 95
    age of householder, 95
    children, presence of, 113
    female-headed
      age of householder, 97
      children, presence of, 115
    male-headed
      age of householder, 98
      children, presence of, 116
    married-couple
      age of householder, 96
      children, presence of, 114
    poverty, below, 274
    source of income, 136
  households, 3, 7, 11, 67, 92
    age of householder, 92
    earners, number of, 106
    metropolitan residence, 311
    type, 76
  men, 39, 51
    age, 163
      education, 182-187
    work experience, 155